Bryn Thomas was born in Southern Rhodesia (now Zimbabwe) where he grew up on a farm. His wanderlust began early with camping holidays by the Indian Ocean in Mozambique and journeys to game parks in other parts of Africa. Since graduating from Durham University with a degree in anthropology, travel on four continents has included a Saharan journey in a home-built kit-car, a solo 2500km Andean cycling trip and 40,000km of Asian rail travel. He worked for five years for the London travel publisher, Roger Lascelles.

The first edition of this book, shortlisted for the Thomas Cook Travel and Guide Book Awards, was the result of several trips on the Trans-Siberian Railway and six months in the Reading Room of the British Library, followed by two further rail journeys for the second edition. Subsequent publications have included *Trekking in the Annapurna Region* and *India - a travel survival kit* (which he co-authored for Lonely Planet).

The third edition of *Trans-Siberian Handbook* was updated by **Dominic Streatfeild-James** who covered almost 20,000km on trains between Beijing, Moscow and Vladivostok. Born in Malta, he has spent a large part of his life on the move, having lived and travelled extensively in Europe, North America and Asia.

After leaving Charterhouse he became a naval officer, serving in the Mediterranean and the Caribbean where he particularly distinguished himself by losing HMS Gloucester's anchor in Portland Harbour. Resigning in 1989 he went up to King's College, London, graduating in 1992. In the following year he researched and wrote *Silk Route by Rail*, the first guide to this new rail route through the Central Asian cities of Bukhara and Samarkand to the ancient Chinese capital of Xi'an.

Trans-Siberian Handbook
First edition August 1988
Third edition April 1994

Publisher: Trailblazer Publications
The Old Manse, Tower Road, Hindhead, Surrey, GU26 6SU, UK
Fax (+44) 0428-607571

British Library Cataloguing in Publication Data
Thomas, Bryn, *1959-*
 Trans-Siberian Handbook. - 3Rev.ed
 1. Title
 914.704854

ISBN 1-873756-04-6

Edited by Patricia Thomas
Maps and index by Jane Thomas

Cover photograph © Ron Ziel (USA)

Other photographs by the author unless otherwise indicated
Engravings from *Siberia and the Exile System* by Kennan, G (London, 1891)

Every effort has been made by the author and publisher to ensure that the information contained herein is as accurate and up-to-date as possible. However, the
author and publisher are unable to accept responsibility for any inconvenience,
loss or injury sustained by anyone as a result of the advice and information given
in this guide.

Distribution: Britain: through Roger Lascelles (47 York Rd, Brentford, Middx,
TW8 0QP, UK. Tel 081-847 0935, fax 081-568 3886); Belgium (Brussels:
Peuples et Continents); Denmark (Copenhagen: Arnold Busck, Boghallen);
Finland (Helsinki: Akateeminen Kirjakauppa); Germany (through major book-
sellers); Ireland (through all booksellers with good travel sections); Italy (Milan:
Libreria dell' Automobile); Netherlands (Weesp: Nilsson & Lamm); Norway
(Oslo: Arne Gimnes, Tanum); Sweden (Stockholm: Esselte, Akademi Bokhan-
del, Fritzes, Hedengrens; Gothenburg: Gumperts, Esselte; Lund: Gleerupska);
Switzerland (Basel: Bider; Berne: Atlas; Geneva/Lausanne: Artou; Zurich:
Travel Bookshop).
 Australia & New Zealand (through Ozzie Wholesale Book Co, tel 02-600
6519); Hong Kong (from major booksellers); India (Delhi: UBS); Japan (Tokyo:
Yohan); Nepal (from major booksellers); Thailand (Bangkok: Asia Books),
South Africa (through Faradawn); USA: through Seven Hills Book Distributors
(tel 513-381 3881).

Set in Times and Univers by Trailblazer Publications, UK
Printed and bound by Kelso Graphics, Kelso, Roxburghshire, TD5 7BH

TRANS-SIBERIAN HANDBOOK

BRYN THOMAS

Third edition researched and updated by
DOMINIC STREATFEILD-JAMES

TRAILBLAZER PUBLICATIONS

Acknowledgements

From Bryn: I am greatly indebted to the numerous people who have helped me with the research and execution of this project since the first publication of this book in 1988. First, I should like to thank Jane Thomas, for her extensive work in drawing the strip-maps and town-plans (without which this guide would be incomplete) and for the index. I'd also like to thank Patricia Thomas for her scrupulously thorough editing of the text and Dominic S-J for taking up the challenge of yet another 20,000kms of rail travel. Thanks also to Brian and Val Colyer, Neil Taylor, Christina Gibbons, André de Smet and Boris Samarianov.

Previous editions have generated a considerable amount of feedback from readers. Thanks to: Christopher Knight (UK), Elizabeth Hehir (Netherlands), Annabel Boyes (UK), Mary Fox (UK), Susan Sexton (UK), Dolf van der Haven (Netherlands), David and Siriporn Brian (Hong Kong), Jacqui Williams (UK), Graham and Sue Small (New Zealand), Felix Patton (Australia), Andre Lvov (Russia), Ian Button (UK), Philip Robinson (UK, for the aside on Siberian post past), James Cherkoff (UK), Matthew Parsons (UK), Jovita da Silva (South Africa), Michael Crick (UK), Maarten Langemeijer (Netherlands), Cmndr RM Williams (Canada), Susan Pares (UK), WD Webber (UK), RC Rider (UK), Colin Baker (UK), Heather and Steve Oxley +? (Portugal), Bob and Hilda Helling (UK), Andrew and Val White, Christopher Turner, Keith Fothergill (Guernsey), Keith Watson (UK), Jeffrey de Forrestier (Canada), Joan Eriksson (Finland), Robert Bray, Joan Nicholls (UK). Thanks also to Bernard Taylor for the photograph opposite page 113, and Ron Ziel for the cover photograph. Quotations used in the Route Guide (Part 5) are from the original *Guide to the Great Siberian Railway 1900*.

From Dominic: I am particularly indebted to Val and Brian Colyer for putting up with a Whingeing Pom for so long and to Neil Magowan for enduring the weekly phonecalls. Special thanks go to the de Smet brothers and Boris Samarianov and Jan Passoff for being so helpful. Thanks also to those who helped along the way, especially Steven Caron (RYH St Petersburg), Helen Nehonova (Ekaterinburg), Ludmilla, Lingard and Maxim (Irkutsk), Svetlana Rabdanova (Ulan Ude) and Huang Rui Li (Beijing). Also to the travellers: Alex Malone and Rupert Dunbar-Rees (UK), Angels Castro and Genis Aymerich (Spain), Anne Lavelle and Pauline Wilson (UK), Nick and Hilma (UK), Sandy Macmillan and John Podgora (USA) and Hal Sharpe (USA). Special recognition goes to the American jokers ('ice cream; that sounds good') who nearly broke me on my first trip and the fabulously famous David Bentley (Australia), who kept me sane on the second. And stole my joke about Stevie Wonder, incidentally.

Back in the UK thanks go to Bryn, Jane and Patricia Thomas for deciphering my maps and unique punctuation constructions, and to my parents and grandmother for making encouraging noises when appropriate. Thanks to the Clapham posse again. And Rollo (you owe me another drink).

A note on prices and a request

Rapid inflation in Russia means that it would be pointless to give prices in roubles. US$ are used throughout but this should not be taken to mean that you should pay in dollars. See p59 for more information. The authors and publisher have tried to ensure that this guide is as accurate and up-to-date as possible but it's difficult to keep up with the pace of change in Russia. If you notice any changes that should be included in the next edition of this book, please write to Bryn Thomas, c/o the publisher (address on page 2). A free copy of the new edition will be sent to persons making a significant contribution.

Front cover: A rare picture, taken in the early 1970s, of the Trans-Siberian being hauled by a steam engine. (Ron Ziel, USA)

CONTENTS

Introduction

PART 1: PLANNING YOUR TRIP

Routes and costs
Route options 9 - Costs 9 - Breaking your journey 13

When to go
Seasons 14

Bookings and visas
Organised tours or individual itineraries? 15
Route planning 17 - Visas 18 - Making a booking in Britain 20
From Continental Europe 24 - From North America 27
From Australasia 28 - From South Africa 29 - From Asia 30

What to take
Clothes 34 - Gifts 36 - Money 37 - Background reading 39

Health precautions and inoculations
Inoculations 41 - Medical services 42 - Drinking water 42

PART 2: RUSSIA

Facts about the country
Geographical background (climate, transport and
communications, flora and fauna) 44 - Historical outline 45
Economy 50 - The People (government, education and social
welfare, religion) 52

Practical information for the visitor
Documents 54 - Crossing the border 54 - Hotels 55
Local transport 57 - Electricity 59 - Time 59 - Money 59
Post and telephones 60 - National holidays 61 - Festivals 61
Food and drink 61 - Restaurants 64 - What to do in the
evening 65 - Shopping 66 - Speculation 69 - Crime 70

PART 3: SIBERIA AND THE RAILWAY

Historical outline
Early history 71 - The nineteenth century 74 - The Exile
System 75 - Early travellers 82 - Building the railway 89 - The
first rail travellers 96 - The twentieth century 101

The Trans-Siberian Railway today
Engines and carriages 103 - Life on the train 108
Steam locomotives in Siberia 110 - BAM line 111 - Yakutia
Railway 112 - Sakhalin Line 112 - Silk Route 113

PART 4: CITY GUIDES AND PLANS
St Petersburg
History 115 - Arrival and departure 117 - Orientation and
services 118 - Where to stay 118 - Transport 120 - Tours 121
The Hermitage Museum 122 - St Isaac's Cathedral 123
Nevsky Prospekt 123 - Peter and Paul Fortress 126 - Where to
eat 127 - Moving on 128

Moscow
History 129 - Arrival and departure 131 - Orientation and
services 133 - Where to stay 134 - Transport 136 - Tours 137
Red Square 137 - St Basil's Cathedral 137 - Lenin's
Mausoleum 138 - GUM 139 - The Kremlin 139 - Other
sights 141 - Where to eat 142 - Nightlife 144 - What to
buy 144 - Moving on 145

Ekaterinburg
History 147 - Orientation and services 149 - Where to
stay 149 - Transport 150 - The Romanov House 150 - Other
sights 150 - Excursions 153 - Where to eat 153

Novosibirsk
History 154 - Orientation and services 155 - Where
to stay 155 - Transport 156 - Tours 157 - What to see 157
Where to eat 158 - What to buy 159 - Akademgorodok 159

Irkutsk
History 161 - Orientation and services 163 - Where to
stay 163 - Transport 164 - Tours 164 - What to see 164
Where to eat 170 - What to buy 170 - Lake Baikal 171
Listvyanka 173 - Bolshoi Koti & Kadilnaya Pad 175
Bratsk 176 - Abakan 177 - Yakutsk 178

Ulan Ude
History 181 - Orientation and services 182 - Where
to stay 182 - Transport 182 - Tours 183 - Ivolginsky
Datsan 183 - Other sights 184 - Where to eat 186
What to buy 186

Khabarovsk

History 187 - Orientation and services 188 - Where to stay 189 - Transport 189 - Tours 189 - Museum of Regional History 190 - Other sights 190 - Where to eat 192 What to buy 193 - Excursions from Khabarovsk 194

Vladivostok

History 195 - Orientation and services 198 - Where to stay 198 - Transport 199 - Tours 199 - Pacific Fleet 199 Other sights 199 - Where to eat 201 - What to buy 201

Ulan Bator

History 203 - Orientation and services 204 - Banks and currency 205 - Where to stay 205 - Transport 206 - Tours 206 Ganden Monastery 207 - Other sights 207 - Where to eat 210 What to buy 211 - Moving on 211 - Excursions 212

Beijing

History 213 - Orientation and services 215 - Where to stay 217 - Transport 218 - Tours 218 - Tiananmen Square and the Forbidden City 219 - Great Wall 219 - Other sights 220 Where to eat 220 - What to buy 221 - Moving on 221

PART 5: ROUTE GUIDE AND MAPS

Trans-Siberian route
Moscow -Irkutsk - Khabarovsk - Vladivostok (Maps 1-18) 222

Trans-Mongolian route
Ulan Ude - Ulan Bator - Beijing (Maps 19-20) 270

Trans-Manchurian route
Chita - Harbin - Beijing (Maps 21-23) 281

PART 6: DESTINATIONS AND DEPARTURES

Japan 289 - Hong Kong 291 - Helsinki 293 - Berlin 294 Budapest 295 - Prague 296

APPENDICES

A. Timetables 297
B. List of Siberian fauna 304
C. Phrase lists: Russian, Mongolian and Chinese 307
D. Bibliography 313

INDEX

INTRODUCTION

There can be few people who have not, at some time in their lives, wondered what it must be like to travel on the Trans-Siberian Railway - to cross Russia and the wild forests and steppes of Siberia on the world's longest railway journey. The distances spanned by this famous line are immense: almost six thousand miles (a seven-day journey) between Moscow and the Pacific port of Vladivostok (for boat connections to Japan) and just under five thousand miles (five days) between Moscow and Beijing.

Ever since a rail service linking Europe with the Far East was established at the turn of the century, foreign travellers and adventurers have been drawn to this great journey. Most of the early travellers crossed Siberia in the comfort of the carriages of the Belgian Wagon Lits company, which were as luxurious as those of the Venice-Simplon Orient Express of today. Things changed somewhat after the Russian Revolution in 1917 and it became increasingly difficult for foreigners to obtain travel permits for Siberia. It was not until the 1960s that the situation improved and Westerners began to use the railway again for getting to Japan, taking the boat from Nakhodka (it now leaves from Vladivostok) for the last part of the journey. In the early 1980s, travel restrictions for foreigners visiting China were eased and since then many people have found the Trans-Siberian a cheap and interesting way to get to or from the Middle Kingdom.

In this jet age, the great advantage of going by rail is that it allows passengers to absorb some of the atmosphere of the country through which they are travelling. On a journey on this train you are guaranteed to meet local people for this is no 'tourist special' but a working service; you may find yourself draining a bottle of vodka with a Russian soldier, discussing politics with a Chinese academic or drinking Russian champagne with a Mongolian trader.

Russia is currently undergoing phenomenal changes after years of stagnation and *glasnost* has brought about the opening up of many hitherto 'closed' areas. While the ending of the Cold War may have removed some of the mystique of travelling in the former USSR, the fact that Russia is now much more accessible means that there are new travel opportunities right across the country. With the opening of budget guest houses in Moscow, St Petersburg and also in Siberia, visiting the country is now cheaper than ever before.

Although travel in Siberia today presents few of the dangers and difficulties that it did earlier this century, a journey on the Trans-Siberian still demands a considerable amount of planning and preparation. The aim of this guide is to help you cut through the red tape when arranging the trip, to give background information on Russia and Siberia and to provide a kilometre-by-kilometre guide to the entire route of the greatest rail adventure - the Trans-Siberian.

PART 1: PLANNING YOUR TRIP

Routes and costs

*Best of all, he would tell me of the great train that ran across half the world ...
He held me enthralled then, and today, a life-time later, the spell still holds. He
told me the train's history, its beginnings ... how a Tzar had said, 'Let the
Railway be built!' And it was ...*

*For me, nothing was ever the same again. I had fallen in love with the Travel-
ler's travels. Gradually, I became possessed by love of a horizon and a train
which would take me there ...* **Lesley Blanch** *Journey into the Mind's Eye*

ROUTE OPTIONS

Travellers crossing Siberia have a choice of three routes. Since the
early 1980s, when China opened its doors to the independent traveller the first two routes (to Beijing via Mongolia or Manchuria) have
rapidly increased in popularity: a Trans-Siberian journey makes an
interesting start or end to a visit to China. Travelling via Mongolia
gives you the chance to stop off in Ulan Bator; independent travel in
Mongolia has become cheaper and easier to organise than it once
was. The third route makes for a rather more expensive journey,
crossing the entire length of Siberia to the Pacific terminus at Vladivostok, from where, between late May and early October, passenger
ships sail to Japan.

COSTS

Overall costs

How much you pay for a trip on the world's longest railway line
depends on the level of comfort you demand, the number of stops
you wish to make along the way and the amount of time you're
prepared to put into getting hold of a budget ticket. Although the
cheapest tickets for rail travel from Moscow to Beijing or vice versa
currently cost £120-160/US$180-240, when purchased in these cities
this price does not reflect what you'll end up paying for your trip.
There are several major costs to add on to this: getting to your departure point and getting back at the end of your journey, accommodation in Moscow and Beijing, food etc. In the light of this, the pack-

age deals offered by travel agents can be better value than they might at first appear. Even more important, it must be emphasised that although you may be able to buy a ticket for as little as the above-mentioned price, a ticket is no use without a reservation on the train. Since certain trains may be fully booked for some time in advance, you may find the services of a travel agent invaluable.

Packages on the Trans-Siberian between Moscow and Beijing, including transfers and a night's accommodation in Moscow, cost from £220/US$325 to £400/US$600 depending on when you want to travel and the country in which you buy your ticket. Flights from London to Moscow cost from £150/US$225 single, £240/US$360 return. Flights between London and Beijing cost from £250/US$375 single, £420/US$630 return.

The cheapest fully inclusive Trans-Siberian holidays cost from around £1000 for a ten day package including flights to and from London. Most packages cost between £1000 and £1500. If a luxurious 26-day guided tour from London to Hong Kong via Siberia on the 'Central Kingdom Express' is more your idea of travelling then be prepared to part with £2800/US$4200.

Travel in Russia - better value, fewer restrictions

Travel in Russia is becoming better value and a little less restricted than it was in the communist era. Unless they have an invitation from a Russian, most foreign visitors are still required to book all their travel and accommodation in advance in order to qualify for a Russian visa. The situation is changing, however, and it's possible to get less restrictive visas (see p16). Entry and exit dates and the towns to be visited are all still listed on the visa but you can now extend a visa once you're in Russia.

In the past it would have been virtually impossible for a foreigner simply to walk into a hotel and get a bed for a night; the hotel proprietor would not only have refused but might even have called the police. With fewer restrictions on tourism, Russians are getting more used to dealing directly with foreigners in smaller hotels and restaurants. Russian prices are often payable in places such as these which means that accommodation can be very cheap; but the more astute hotels charge special foreigners' prices so that non-Russians pay more. Foreigners' prices now also apply to all rail and air tickets.

Hotel costs

For many years, foreign tourists visiting the former Soviet Union were forced to pay very high prices for low quality hotels. The state tourist department, Intourist, had a monopoly on all tourist services but this ended after the collapse of communism. Competition between companies (particularly between joint venture hotels) has raised standards and there are now some excellent hotels of an international class in Russia. Their prices are also of an international class: £100-200/US$150-300 in Moscow or St Petersburg.

Lower down the price range the tradition of charging foreign tourists more for rooms than they're worth lives on, largely because although Intourist's monopoly has been broken they still own most of the hotels. A basic room with attached bathroom will cost £30-70/US$45-105 for a single or £45-70/US$70-105 for a double, booked from abroad. Note that in Russia a single room is only marginally cheaper than a double, so it pays to have a travelling companion. Breakfast is usually included in the price.

There's better news for **budget travellers**: with the recent relaxation of visa regulations and trading laws, independent guesthouses have been set up in Moscow and St Petersburg offering accommodation for as little as £8/US$12 a night. In addition, a number of non-Russian companies organise private homestays, either for individuals or for groups, from about £10/US$15. It would seem likely that with the development of the free market economy these smaller businesses will continue to flourish, offering better value accommodation for travellers.

Train classes and prices
Foreigners are offered three levels of accommodation. See p104 for more information about each. The prices shown in each category below range from the cheapest ticket bought from the railway ticket office in Moscow or Beijing to the most expensive ticket offered by a travel agent in the West. Note that because of the difficulty in getting reservations the price that most travellers pay is nearer the higher figure in each category.

●**First/Deluxe/Soft Class, two berth** On the **Moscow-Japan route** prices are: £280-400/US$420-600 for the rail trip to Vladivostok plus £470/US$700 for a semi-deluxe berth on the ship to Japan. For the **Moscow-Beijing route**, prices are £160-400/US$240-600. Deluxe Class is available only on the Trans-Mongolian train and comprises the most luxurious compartments of any train crossing Siberia, and the only ones containing showers.

●**First/Soft Class, four berth** Available only on the Trans-Mongolian, prices for the **Moscow-Beijing route** are £190-320/US$280-480.

●**Second/Hard Class, four berth** Most people find the cheapest rail accommodation available to foreigners perfectly adequate. Prices for the **Moscow-Japan route** are £145-230/US$216-345 for the Moscow-Vladivostok rail section plus £185-205/US$280-310 for a bunk in a four-berth cabin on the boat. For the **Moscow-Beijing route** prices range from £120-330/US$180-495.

Foreigners will usually find themselves sharing with other foreigners if they've booked through a large agency that deals mainly with non-Russians; and compartments are not single sex. When it comes to sharing compartments, I'm not sure which is worse - the elderly German who complains non-stop about the food or the female tractor driver from Krasnoyarsk who snores like a Massey-Ferguson.

Truly independent travel - costs and possibilities
With the opening up of the Eastern Bloc and the lifting of restrictions on foreign visitors in some of these countries, independent travellers had hoped that very soon they would be able to pick up their visa at the border and then travel round Russia making arrangements as they went, as in most other countries in the world. Even in Tsarist times, however, travel for foreigners in Russia was restricted; and old habits die hard.

You may, however, meet a few hardened travellers who are finding ways around the system and managing to travel across Siberia on local trains, visiting tiny villages, staying in local hotels and paying local prices. As yet they're very much in the minority. This is not something to be recommended for any but the most experienced traveller and certainly not for people worried about bending the law when it comes to visa regulations and local versus foreigner prices. Conditions can be harsh in tiny Siberian villages, you could easily be stranded far from the nearest hospital, and no-one will speak any English. If your visa's not in order, these days the worst that can happen to you is a fine, expulsion from the country and prohibition on ever entering Russia again. In the past, though, they'd have extended your stay in Siberia but with the requirement that you spend it in one of the many gulags here. See p16 for visas.

Cheap rail tickets In the 1980s there was a hot trade in black market tickets, usually brought in from Hungary or other countries in the Communist Bloc. The days when you could travel all the way from Budapest to Beijing for under £40/US$60 are now over: these tickets simply don't exist any more. Within Russia, however, there are certainly some bargains to be had travelling around paying local prices for trains but you should be aware that in doing so you'll be breaking the law. There is now a two-tier pricing system for rail tickets; travel on a Russian-priced ticket is illegal for foreigners.

Although you should be able to get away with paying local prices for short journeys, if you use a local price ticket for a Trans-Siberian trip you not only risk being fined but also being thrown off the train. If you're offered a 'cheap' ticket for the train be sure you know what you're paying for: the chances are that it's a Russian priced ticket.

Cheap accommodation If you can convince the receptionist that it's OK to let you stay, you can check into virtually any hotel in Russia but this isn't always easy. While hotels can be cheap (from less than £4/US$6) they can be very basic: few in Siberia will have hot water.

BREAKING YOUR JOURNEY

Most people will want to break their journey and stop off along the way. This is a good idea not only because it gives you a chance to get off the train, stretch your legs and, most importantly, have a shower, but also because some of the places you pass through are well worth exploring; you won't learn much about life in Siberia by looking through a train window. As in Tsarist times, not all places in Russia are open to foreign tourists. The list of open cities has, however, grown considerably in the 1990s and even 'closed' cities can open if you have the right contacts or are prepared to pay.

If your trip starts in **Moscow** (see p129) it's usually necessary to spend one night there but you'd need several days to see just the main sights. A side-trip to **St Petersburg** (p115) is highly recommended if only for a visit to the Hermitage; if your starting (or ending) point is Helsinki, you could go via this city. At the other end of the rails, it's worth spending several days in **Beijing** (p213).

Along the routes, Irkutsk and Ulan Bator are the most popular places to stop off at. **Irkutsk** (p161) is the eastern capital of Siberia and 64km from Lake Baikal, the world's deepest freshwater lake. It's possible to stay at **Listvyanka** (p173), right by the lake. **Ulan Bator** (p203), the capital of Mongolia, used to be so expensive to visit that few travellers could afford to stop. Cheaper visits are now possible. South of Lake Baikal, **Ulan Ude** (p181) is interesting for the Buddhist monastery nearby. **Khabarovsk** (p187) is a pleasant place and **Ekaterinburg** (p147) opened to tourists recently. There's also **Novosibirsk** (p154), the capital of Western Siberia, and **Vladivostok** (p195), eastern railway terminus and port for ships to Japan.

Other places to visit in Siberia include **Bratsk** (p176), **Abakan** (p177), **Yakutsk** (p178), **Sakhalin Island** (p194), **Magadan** (with air connections to Alaska, see p28 and p194), **Perm** (p229), **Omsk** (p236), **Tomsk** (p241), **Krasnoyarsk** (p243), **Barnaul, Komsomolsk** and **Kamchatka**.

When to go

The mode of life which the long dark nights of winter induce, the contrivances of man in his struggle with the climate, the dormant aspect of nature with its thick coverage of dazzling snow and its ice-bound lakes now bearing horses and the heaviest burdens where ships floated and waves rolled, perhaps only a fortnight ago: - all these scenes and peculiar phases of life render a journey to Russia very interesting in winter. **Murray's Handbook for Travellers in Russia, Poland and Finland (1865)**

For most people the mention of Siberia evokes a picture of snowy scenes from the film *Doctor Zhivago* and if they are not to be disappointed, then winter is probably the best time to go. It is, after all, the most Russian of seasons, a time of fur-coats, sleigh-rides and vodka. In sub-zero temperatures, with the bare birch trees and firs encased in ice, Siberia looks as one imagines it ought to - a bare desolate waste-land. The train, however, is kept well heated. Russian cities, too, look best and feel most 'Russian' under a layer of snow. St Petersburg with its brightly painted Classical architecture is far more attractive in the winter months, when the weather is crisp and skies clear. If you want to visit some of the Siberian cities, you'll probably find it more enjoyable to go in the late spring, summer or autumn, when there is more to do.

In Siberia, the heaviest snowfalls and coldest temperatures (as low as minus 40°C/F in some of the towns the train passes through), occur in late November and December. Between January and early April the weather is generally cold and clear. Spring comes late and then the warmest months are July and August, when it is warm enough for an invigorating dip in Lake Baikal. The birch and aspen provide a beautiful autumnal display in September and October; the weather in summer and autumn is particularly unpredictable. In Moscow the average temperature is 17°C (63°F) in summer, -9°C (+16°F) in winter; there are occasional heavy summer showers.

The tourist season reaches its peak between mid July and early September. In the low season, between October and April, some companies offer discounts on tours; you'll also find it much easier to get a booking for the train at short notice at this time. During the summer it can be difficult to get a place on the popular Moscow - Beijing route without giving notice of several months.

Bookings and visas

ORGANISED TOURS OR INDIVIDUAL ITINERARIES?

To a certain extent all travel within Russia is 'organised' since every night you spend there is still supposed to be accounted for as an hotel booking or a train reservation before you go (unless you can arrange an invitation by some other means, see p19). Most people still visit the country in tour groups, and this is how the Russian authorities would prefer you to travel. Groups are easier to control and tend to spend more money in the country than the itinerant back-packer. The independent visitor to the Soviet Union was often financially discriminated against by being made to pay for certain services that were included in the price of a package tour; and in some cases this remains true.

Although Intourist has lost its monopoly of the hotel and tourist facilities market, most bookings still go through them because they are the company with the most extensive connections across the country. Nevertheless, numerous smaller companies have started dealing with the Russian tourist market and offer very competitive terms.

Group tours

Going with a tour group takes all the hassle out of making a booking and dealing with the tourist infrastructure when you're in Russia. Most tours are accompanied by an English-speaking guide from the moment you arrive in Russia right up until you leave the country. See pp20-33 for tour companies.

Semi independent travel

This is currently the most popular way for foreigners to travel on the Trans-Siberian: using a specialist agency who makes the accommodation and train bookings (with or without stops along the way) that are required in order to get a Russian tourist visa. You are able to choose the number and length of stops and departure dates, in effect you design your own package. Once you're in Russia, you're on your own but some agencies also offer transfer services to or from the railway station in Moscow.

A number of travel agents in the West (see pp20-33) will make arrangements, and you can even deal directly with one of the locally-based organisations (see p25, p26 and p33) that offer packages on the Trans-Siberian with a night's accommodation in Moscow. They will send/fax you **visa support**, (a letter confirming your booking with them) to take to your nearest Russian embassy in order to get a tourist visa.

Fully independent travel

The twin problems that deter fully independent travel on the Trans-Siberian are that visa support is needed for a Russian (and Mongolian) tourist visa and that reservations for tickets on the trains are difficult to get. Truly independent travel that is both cheap and entirely legal (see p12) doesn't really exist yet in Russia.

Attempting to book your own tickets in Moscow or Beijing is not recommended unless you have enormous amounts of time at your disposal. With increasing numbers of traders competing for places on these trains the wait for a reservation is likely to increase. Since visas for independent travel in China are issued without difficulty, travellers wanting to arrange things themselves usually try for tickets in Beijing rather than Moscow. Once a reservation is made, a **transit visa** can be issued, and this usually allows enough time to spend a day or so in Moscow, where a 5-7 day visa extension is currently possible.

Trying to do things from the opposite direction is further complicated by the need for a Russian **tourist visa**, which is almost impossible to get without booking some accommodation for the required visa support. Some companies may be able to get you a **business** visa which is less restricted but this again will need support from a Russian-based organisation.

Not the Trans-Siberian Express!

Writers of travel articles may wax lyrical about trips on the fabled 'Trans-Siberian Express' but in fact no train of that name exists. While we generally refer to our trains by a time ('the 10.35 to Clapham'), the Russians and Chinese identify theirs by a number ('Train No19', from Beijing to Moscow). Just as in the West a few crack services have been singled out and given a name ('The Orient Express') some of the better services in Russia also have names but 'Trans-Siberian Express' is not among them. 'Trans-Siberian', 'Trans-Mongolian' and 'Trans-Manchurian' are, however, convenient terms for the routes across Siberia and between Moscow and Beijing.

The service which runs from Moscow to Vladivostok is train No2, also known as the 'Rossiya'. Running from Vladivostok to Moscow it's train No1. The 'Baikal' is train No9 from Irkutsk to Moscow, train No10 when it runs in the other direction. The services which run between Moscow and Beijing are usually identified only by their numbers.

ROUTE PLANNING

Planning your route across Siberia can be rather more complicated than you might imagine, especially if you wish to make a number of stops. These trains are not tourist specials but working services used by local people and they're very popular. On most routes they run to capacity and, as has been explained above, travel is usually impossible without a reservation.

Trains at a glance

For more information see p297 but note that all timetables are subject to change, nowhere more so than in this part of the world. Local times are given below.

No	Name	Departs	on	at	Arrives	on	at
1	Rossiya	Vladivostok	see p297	01.05	Moscow	Day 7	06.45
2	Rossiya	Moscow	see p297	14.00	Vladivostok	Day 7	09.45
3	-	Beijing	Wed	07.40	Ulan Bator	Thur	13.20
		Ulan Bator	Thur	13.50	Moscow	Mon	19.00
4	-	Moscow	Tue	19.50	Ulan Bator	Sun	09.00
		Ulan Bator	Sun	09.30	Beijing	Mon	15.33
5	-	Ulan Bator	Sat	20.15	Moscow	Wed	11.05
6	-	Moscow	Wed	21.25	Ulan Bator	Mon	08.00
9	Baikal	Irkutsk	see p298	20.10	Moscow	Day 5	05.55
10	Baikal	Moscow	see p298	12.05	Irkutsk	Day 5	06.30
19	-	Beijing	Fri/Sat	20.32	Moscow	Thu/Fri	20.50
20	-	Moscow	Fri/Sat	21.25	Beijing	Fri/Sat	06.32
23	-	Beijing	Sat	07.40	Ulan Bator	Sun	13.20
24	-	Ulan Bator	Thu	09.30	Beijing	Fri	15.33
89	-	Beijing	Tue/Fri	18.53	Ulan Bator	Thu/Sun	10.45
90	-	Ulan Bator	Tue/Fri	12.10	Beijing	Thu/Sun	06.20
263	-	Ulan Bator	daily	21.00	Irkutsk	Day 3	08.50
264	-	Irkutsk	daily	19.10	Ulan Bator	Day 3	06.40

Moscow to Vladivostok and Japan

If you're travelling to or from Japan you must begin by deciding on the date of your sailing into or out of Vladivostok. There are about four sailings a month in both directions and the service runs only between May and October (check departure dates with Intourist). If you are stopping off anywhere on your journey across Russia, the hotel confirmations will have to be received before the intermediate rail journeys can be booked. This complication will be dealt with by the travel agent or Intourist office you are dealing with; but the procedure may take six weeks or more.

Many trains leave Moscow for Siberia each day but the direct service to Vladivostok is train No2 (see table above). If you're making a stop in Irkutsk, try to get on train No9, the 'Baikal', which is one of the best-run services in the country.

Itineraries to and from China

Summer is the most difficult time to get bookings for these two routes so make arrangements several months in advance. There are weekly departures in each direction on the Trans-Mongolian trains (Nos 3 & 4, operated by the Chinese) and the Trans-Manchurian trains (Nos 19 & 20, run by the Russians), with an additional service on the latter route in the summer.

Travellers endlessly debate the pros and cons of each service. The Trans-Manchurian service takes a day longer since it travels around Mongolia; but it saves you the expense of a Mongolian transit visa. The Trans-Mongolian gives you the chance to stop off in Ulan Bator but this train is now extremely popular with traders which means long delays at the borders and a greater incidence of petty theft on the train itself. For more information about the trains see p103 and note that the food isn't necessarily 'better on the Trans-Mongolian'.

Stopping off in Mongolia

If you're taking the Trans-Mongolian route, breaking your journey in Ulan Bator is highly recommended. It's easiest to organise through a specialist agency since visa support is required, as for Russia. This can be done through the state tourist agency, **Zhuulchin**, or one of the private organisations in the country (see p206) that are now providing it with much-needed competition; but dealing direct with them is difficult: Zhuulchin has no office in London, only in Berlin (see p25). Before beginning your dealings with the Mongolians you must have confirmed reservations as far as Ulan Bator (see table on p17 for the most convenient trains).

Side trips

The possibilities for side trips are numerous. As well as the BAM-line (see p111) and the Silk Route (see p113) it's also possible to travel by rail into North Korea from Moscow to Pyongyang (via Ussuriyisk, near Khabarovsk) and on to Beijing. Independent travel in communist North Korea is, however, strictly controlled.

VISAS

Russian visa

A **transit visa** is issued provided you have a booked ticket into Russia and can prove that you are going to leave the country (by producing either a ticket out and the visa, if necessary, for the next destination). It covers a period of time just long enough for you to come in by train and then depart immediately, usually ten days. It's currently possible to extend a transit visa for 5-7 days. A **tourist visa** gives you more time in the country but is more difficult to arrange since you must provide the embassy with visa support: a letter from a Russian agency confirming that they will be responsible for you. These letters used to be issued only by Intourist but the recent increase in the number of private companies in Russia means that now many other agencies can provide them.

If you're going on a group tour or organising things semi-independently through a specialist agency these organisations will procure the necessary visa support. (For a fee they'll also get your visa for you.)

For those booking independently, getting a Russian visa becomes a quest for visa support. A Russian friend can write you a letter of invitation, which is acceptable. Alternatively use an agency or hotel in Russia (see p26) that will provide visa support if you book some accommodation with them. It may also be worth trying travel agents in other countries and at home. Note that on the visa itself, a separate document to your passport, will be printed the names of all cities to which you are allowed access. Thus you must make sure that the person writing your covering letter knows where you want to go. There is no set penalty for those visiting cities not listed on their visa but if you get caught doing this you may face the prospect of 'fines' from the local police or find yourself refused admittance to hotels.

Mongolian visa

Mongolia's visa system operates in much the same way as Russia's did five years ago. Visas granted are likewise **tourist** and **transit**, and for the former you're supposed to book everything in advance. Most travellers opt for one of the stopover packages organised by specialist travel agencies. Feedback from readers suggests that even the Mongolians are unsure of the visa regulations so it's worth checking with the local embassy before you leave. There are embassies in Moscow, Irkutsk and Beijing but it's safer to try to organise your visa before departure, although transit visas are easy to obtain in Beijing. Theoretically it should be possible to get a visa at the border but you're strongly advised not to rely on this being so.

Chinese visa

The process of getting a visa is straightforward at most Chinese embassies; but if you're entering China via Russia or Mongolia, get a Chinese visa before you reach Moscow as current reports suggest that their embassy here is not easy to deal with. Visas are generally given for up to a month but if your application form indicates that you will be in the country for less time than this you'll be given less. Extensions within China are easy to arrange in most cities.

MAKING A BOOKING IN BRITAIN

Note that Russia has no tourist office in Britain and no doubt in response to the numerous questions they receive some of the travel agents below produce very informative brochures. The closest branch of Zhuulchin is in Berlin (see below). For the Chinese section of the journey visit the **China National Tourist Office** (tel 071-935 9427), 4 Glentworth St, London NW1.

● **Regent Holidays** (tel 0272-211711; fax 0272-254866; from Sep 94 replace 0272 code with 01179), 15 John St, Bristol BS1 2HR. Recommended by several readers, they specialise in independent travel to the CIS, China and Mongolia. Moscow-Beijing tickets (Trans-Mongolian or Trans-Manchurian routes) cost from £300; Beijing-Moscow (either route) from £240; all include the first night's hotel accommodation and transfers. They have stopover packages in Irkutsk and Ulan Bator, and good flight deals (UB £265 one way).

● **One Europe Travel** (tel 081-566 9424; fax 081-566 8845) Research House, Fraser Rd, Perivale, Middlesex UB6 7AQ. This company specialises in budget travel in Russia and the CIS, offering tickets from Moscow to Beijing, but not vice versa, from £280. Homestay accommodation starts at £12.50 and they can arrange two-night stopovers in Abakan, Listvyanka (£115 for one person, £147 for three), Ulan Ude (interesting Buryatia trip) and Ulan Bator (£134-170 per person including rail travel to Beijing).

● **Intourist Travel** (tel 071-538 3202), Intourist House, 219 Marsh Wall, Isle of Dogs, London E14 9FJ. **Tours:** Intourist offers two Trans-Siberian tours: 12 nights from £1245 including Moscow, Khabarovsk, Irkutsk and St Petersburg with only two nights on the train; and 17 nights from £1335 visiting Moscow, Irkutsk, Khabarovsk, Vladivostok and St Petersburg with six nights on the train. Their 15-night Trans-Mongolian tour includes stops in Ulan Bator and Irkutsk and costs £1445. All prices are ex London. **Independent travel:** (tel 071-538 5965) Intourist's bookings on the Moscow-Beijing train include one night's accommodation in Moscow, food on the train as far as the Russian border, and transfers. The cheapest tickets are £260/£330 (low/high season). Bookings on the Beijing-Moscow route are available from £242. There's also a range of stopover packages which you can tailor to your own requirements. Boat ticket for the Vladivostok-Niigata trip cost £185-470 depending on class. Intourist hotels are priced from £30 in Moscow, £50 in St Petersburg and £45 in Irkutsk/Listvyanka (all doubles at low season).

● **China Travel and Information Centre** (tel 071-388 8838), 3-5 Charlton St, London NW1 1JD. The friendly and efficient staff here can help with tickets from Beijing to Moscow (in this direction only) as well as tours throughout China. Prices ex Beijing are from £215 for the Trans-Manchurian route, £220 for the Trans-Mongolian, £115-145 to Ulan Bator, £150-200 to Irkutsk. You'll be given a voucher which you exchange for a confirmed ticket in Beijing.

● **Progressive Tours** (tel 071-262 1676), 12 Porchester Place, Marble Arch, London W2 2BS. Specialises in budget and youth travel to Russia and offers tickets on the Moscow-Beijing route from £340 (June-Sept) and £285 (Oct-May). They can arrange homestays in St Petersburg (£23); hotels in Moscow start at £23 for a double.

● **China Travel Service Ltd** (tel 071-836 9911), 24 Cambridge Circus, London WC2H 8HD. CTS will book individual itineraries across China as well as offering a 21-day tour from London to Hong Kong and back (£1400-1600). Individual tickets are sold only for the Trans-Mongolian and Trans-Manchurian trains; cheapest tickets from Moscow to Beijing cost £290 and from Beijing to Moscow £155.

● **Room with the Russians** (tel 081-472 2694), Lynton Cooper Travel, Station Chambers, High St North, London E6 1JE. Offers reasonably priced itineraries to St Petersburg and Moscow but in order to get their discounts you must book a return flight to Russia.

Budget travellers booking from Britain should note that they can also arrange Trans-Siberian rail tickets through agencies based in Hong Kong (see p33) and Russia (p26).

The following companies offer organised tours only

● **Page & Moy** (tel 0533-524433) 136-140 London Road, Leicester LE2 1EN. Recommended by readers, their 12-day trip from Moscow to Khabarovsk, stopping at Irkutsk along the way, is very good value at under £1000. Flights are included at either end of the trip.

● **Iris Mikof Ltd** (see p28) Although they do not yet have agents in the UK, this Australian-Russian joint venture company is worth contacting for their upmarket Trans-Siberian tours and individual itineraries, all using excellent accommodation. Prices £1000-1300.

● **Goodwill Holidays** (tel 0438-716421), Manor Chambers, School Lane, Welwyn, Herts AL6 9EB. Their 19-day Siberian tour (£1335) uses a combination of rail and air travel and includes a two-day visit to Tomsk. They will also organise individual itineraries.

● **Sundowners** (tel 071-370 1482), 267 Old Brompton Rd, London SW5. Trips across Siberia on the Trans-Mongolian and Trans-Siberian routes cost from £1350, a 25-day tour from Japan to St Petersburg is £3400 and a 25-day tour from Hong Kong via Ulan Bator costs £3450. For another £1350 you can start the journey in Kathmandu and visit Tibet on the way to Beijing, too.

● **Explore Worldwide Ltd** (tel 0252-319448) 1 Frederick Street, Aldershot, Hants GU11 1BR. Specialising in adventure holidays for small groups, this company offers a 22-day 'Siberia and the Gobi Desert' trip for £2200; and a two-week Mongolian tour including desert excursions and some trekking, for £2400. You travel from Moscow to Beijing by rail, bus and air.

● **Bales Tours Ltd** (tel 0306-885991), Bales House, Junction Rd, Dorking, Surrey RH4 3HB. Their Trans-Siberian tour lasts for 17 days and follows the Trans-Mongolian route, stopping in Irkutsk and Ulan Bator. It costs around £1950.

● **Cox and Kings Travel Ltd** (tel 071-873 5003), St James Court, Buckingham Gate, London SW1E 6AF. Cox and Kings provide some good upmarket rail tours across Russia using the luxurious 'Bolshoi Express', in carriages built for Khrushchev, and steam locomotives are used for some sectors. A Trans-Siberian leg should start in 1994 and is likely to cost around £150 per person per day.

● **Voyages Jules Verne** (tel 071-723 5066), 21 Dorset Square, London NW1 6QG. The most luxurious Trans-Siberian tour of all, the 'Central Kingdom Express', will take you from Moscow to Hong Kong with stops at Omsk, Novosibirsk, Krasnoyarsk, Irkutsk, Ulan Bator, Datong, Beijing, Xi'an and Guilin. After Beijing the journey continues in the 'Chinese State Train', fitted out for Chairman Mao in 1955. Twenty-seven days for £2800.

● **Exodus** (tel 081-675 5550), 9 Weir Road London SW12 0LT. Although they do not feature Trans-Siberian rail journeys, their Siberian trekking tours could be tagged onto a trip.

Rail enthusiasts'/special interest tours
● **Enthusiasts' Holidays** (tel 081-699 3654), 146 Forest Hill Road, London SE23 3QR.
● **Dorridge Travel Service** (tel 0564-776252), 7 Station Approach, Dorridge, Solihull, B93 8JA.
● **Intourist** Special interest tours department: 071-538 5966.

Getting to Moscow or Beijing from the UK

By air: Flights to Moscow start at around £150 one-way, £240 return; Aeroflot (tel 071-493 2410) usually offer the cheapest seats. Beijing is more expensive: at least £250 one way, £460 return. Air China are usually a good bet for cheap seats and can be booked from CTS (tel 071-388 8838). **By rail:** The completion of the Channel Tunnel means that British rails are at last linked with those of the Far Eastern Railway in Vladivostok. When passenger services commence in summer 1994 it will theoretically be possible to ride the rails all the way from London (tel 081-784 1333 for details). Currently the London-Moscow via Ostende service, departing from Liverpool St on Mon, Wed and Fri is all that's available. Prices are: £179 single, £357 return (£131/255 if you're under 26) second class, or £262/524 first class. In addition, you'll have to pay a sleeper fee of £35-80 (depending on class). There are reductions for OAPs. The train does have a restaurant car but you will be able to pay only in travellers cheques or the currency of the country you're in at the time.

Foreign Embassies in London

● **Russia** (tel 071-229 8027), 5 Kensington Palace Gardens, London W8 4QS. Open weekdays 10.00-12.30, not Wed. The queues here are extremely long so it may be worth paying for the visa services offered by most travel agents who deal in Russia (prices for this service vary considerably). Your passport is not required, only a photocopy of the personal information pages from it, along with three photos. For a tourist or business visa you'll need a letter from an accredited company (see p19). The charges for this service range from £5 within ten days to £60 for the next day.

● **China** (tel 071-636 1835), 31 Portland Place, London W1 3AG. Open 09.00-12.00 (Mon to Fri). This is quite easy to do yourself. One passport photo is required. A visa valid for one month from the date of entry and three months from the date of issue costs £25. Check these dates before leaving the embassy.

● **Mongolia** (tel 071-937 0150), 7 Kensington Court, London W8 5DL. Open 10.00-12.30 (Mon to Fri). Transit visas cost £10, take three days to process (there's an express service for £16) and rail confirmation is not required. If you're staying in Mongolia a tourist visa is required and for this you'll need a letter from Zhuulchin or another accredited travel agent. The tourist visa takes one week to process and costs £17. Mongolia also has embassies in Moscow (p134), Irkutsk (p163) and Beijing (p32), along the route of the Trans-Siberian but it's best to get your visa before you go.

MAKING A BOOKING IN CONTINENTAL EUROPE

From Austria
- **Okista** (tel 0222-40 14 80), Turkenstrasse 4, A 1090 Vienna.
- **Intourist** (tel 533 95 47), Schwedenplatz 3/4, 1010 Vienna.

From Belgium
- **Explore (Ghent)** (tel 091-23 00 69), Divantoura, Bagattenstraat 176, 9000 Ghent; **(Antwerp)** (tel 03-233 1916), St Jacobsmarkt 5, 2000 Antwerp.
- **Intourist** (tel 02-513 8234), Galerie Ravenstein 2, 1000 Brussels.
- **Connections** (tel 02-512 7830) Kolenmarkstraat 13, 1000 Brussels.

From the Czech Republic
- **Cedok** Na Prikope 18, for international train tickets.
- **STA Uniset** 28 Rijna 9. Student travel agency.

See p296 for visitor information for **Prague**.

From Denmark
- **SSTS** (tel 33-21 85 30), Hauchsvej 17, DK-1825, Copenhagen V. This student travel service offers several competitively priced tours and is worth contacting for more information.
- **Intourist** (tel 33-11 25 27) Vester Farimagsgade 6, Copenhagen V.
- **STA** (tel 33-11 00 44), Skindergade 28, DK-1159, Copenhagen K.
- **Explore Inter Travel** (tel 33-15 00 77), Frederiksholms Kanal 2, DK-1220, Copenhagen K.

From Finland
- **Kilroy Travels** (tel 624 101), Mannerheimintie 5C, 00100, Helsinki 10. Student travel centre, formerly Travela Oy.
- **Intourist** (tel 631 875), Mikonkatu 15, 00130 Helsinki.
- **Eurohostel** (tel 90-664 452), Linnankatu 9, Katajanokka, is a good place for information for budget travellers. Has links with the Russian Youth Hostel in St Petersburg (see Russia below).
- **Russian Embassy** (tel 661 449), Vuorimiehenkatu 6. Open 09.30-12.00 Mon-Fri.

See p293 for visitor information for **Helsinki**.

From France
- **Intourist** (tel 47 42 47 40) 7 Boulevard des Capucines, 75002 Paris.
- **Voyages et Decouvertes** (tel 42 61 00 01) 21 rue Cambon, 75001 Paris.
- **Wagon-lits Tourisme** (tel 42 68 25 83) 126 rue de Provence, 75008 Paris.

From Germany

● **Travel Service Asia** (TSA-Reisen) (tel 07371 85 22; fax 07371-12 593) Schulgasse 1, D-88499 Riedlingen. Worth contacting even if you don't live in Germany. Rail prices: Moscow-Beijing, from DM725; rail packages: Moscow to Japan with stops in Irkutsk and Vladivostok, 2nd class on train and boat, from DM2040; Moscow to Beijing with stops in Irkutsk and Ulan Bator from DM1420; six-day Mongolian excursion from Beijing DM1860. Homestay in Boshoi Koti (by Lake Baikal) from DM98 per day.

● **Lernidee Reisen** (tel 030-786 50 56; fax 030-786 55 96) Dudenstrasse 78, 10965 Berlin. Siberian itineraries from this company range from a 2nd class ticket on the Moscow-Beijing train for US$513 to a tour that includes five days gold-washing in northern Siberia (US$2495). They also have a rail trip with a stop-over in Ulan Bator to coincide with the Nadaam Festival.

● **SRS** (tel 030-281 6741), Studenten Reiseservice GmbH, Marienstrasse 25, 1040 Berlin.

● **Intourist Reisen Gmbh** (tel 030-880070), Kurfurstendamm 63, 1000 Berlin 15.

● **Intourist** (tel 229 1704), Friedrichstrasse 153A, 1080 Berlin.

● **Srid Reisen** (tel 069-430191) Bergerstrasse 118, 6000 Frankfurt 1

● **China Tourist Office** (tel 069-520135), Ilkenhanstrasse 6, 6000 Frankfurt.

● **CTS** (tel 069-250515), Dusseldorferstrasse 14, 6000 Frankfurt.

● **Zhuulchin (Mongolia Tourist Dept)** (tel/fax 030-471 8833) 2 Arnold Zweig St, 3R 13189 Berlin. This office will make bookings in Mongolia for non-Germans.

See p294 for visitor information for **Berlin**.

From Hungary

Despite what you may have heard, the under US$50 rail bargain of a lifetime ticket that could be bought here in the 1980s is no longer available. Organising a Trans-Siberian trip from here is not easy.

● **Star Tours**/Intourist (tel 1137 062), Jozsef Krt 45, H-1085.

See p295 for visitor information for **Budapest**.

From the Netherlands

● **Intourist** (tel 020-679 8964), Honthorstsraat 42, 1071 DH, Amsterdam 2.

● **NBBS** (tel 071-25 33 33), Schipholweg 101, PO Box 360, 2300 AJ Leiden. Also in Groningen (tel 050-12 63 33), Amsterdam (tel 020-20 50 71), Utrecht (030-31 45 20), Rotterdam (010-414 9822).

● **China Winkel** Haarlemmerstraat 32, Amsterdam.

● **Perestrojka Reizen**, Prins Hendrikkade 104, 1011 AJ Amsterdam

From Norway
- **STA** (tel 42 10 20), Nedre Slottsgate 23, 0157 Oslo 1.
- **Intourist** (tel 83 83 65), Ruselqkkveien 14, 0251 Oslo.

From Russia
- **Travellers Guest House Moscow** (tel +7-095-971 40 59; fax +7-095-280 7686 - note that you should not omit the '0' of the 095 code when dialling from outside Russia), PO Box 27, 51 Prospekt Mira, 121110 Moscow. If you book some accommodation with this guest house from abroad they will send you visa support for a Russian visa. They will also help with visa extensions but this can be done only for visas originally arranged through them. As well as good clean budget accommodation (see p135) they can organise homestays in Irkutsk and Listvyanka (from US$14), Trans-Siberian tickets for the Moscow to Beijing trip from US$225 to US$499 and a range of packages with stops in Irkutsk, Listvyanka and Ulan Bator.
- **Russian Youth Hostel** (tel +7-812-277 05 69; fax +7-812 277 51 02), Box 57, 193312 St Petersburg. They provide a visa support service similar to that of the Travellers Guest House Moscow but usually pass travel enquiries on to the TGHM. Forms for visa application via the Russian YH can be obtained from the YHA in Covent Garden, London (tel 071-836 1036); from Eurohostel in Helsinki (see above) or from the US (see below).
- **Mikof-Iris (MNTK)** (tel +7-095-483 04 60), Beskudnikovsky Blvd 59A, Suite 266 MNTK, Moscow 127486. See p28 for fax contact and further information about this Russian-Australian joint venture. Their hotels are listed under MNTK in the 'City guides' section (Part 4).
- **Bamtour Co** (tel 30139-52116) Ul Oktyabrya 16, Flat 2, Severobaikalsk 671717. Arranges tours on the BAM line (Bratsk, Severobaikalsk, Tynda, Komsomolsk, Khabarovsk) and fishing/camping excursions around Lake Baikal. Books tickets for the hydrofoil between Irkutsk and Severobaikalsk.

From Sweden
- **STA** (tel 234515), Box 7144, Kungsgatan 4, S103 87, Stockholm.
- **Intourist** (tel 215934), Drottninggatan 25, 1TR, 1151 Stockholm.

From Switzerland
- **Julian Pignat** (fax 22-340 1530) 2 Ch Mouille-Galland, 1214 Vernier. European representative for Bamtour Co (see above).

MAKING A BOOKING IN NORTH AMERICA

From the USA

● **Russian Youth Hostels** (tel 310-379 4316; fax 310-379 8420) 409 Pacific Coast Highway #106, Suite 390, Redondo Beach, CA 90277. RYH organises visa support for foreign visitors who want to travel independently, and they set up the first youth hostel in St Petersburg (see p119). They'll send you a form to fill in and then a letter to take to the consulate when you apply for your visa. Service is fast by fax but it's wise to make arrangements as far in advance as possible.

● **Intourist** (tel 212-757 3884), 630 5th Ave, Suite 868, NY-10111. Worth contacting for their range of Trans-Siberian tours and individual packages from Moscow to Beijing with stopovers in Siberia or Mongolia.

● **General Tours** (tel 800-221 2216), 770 Broadway, New York NY 10003. Recommended by several readers.

● **Russia Tours** (tel 718-816 6828) 27 Occident Ave, Staten Island, NY 10304.

● **Russian Travel Bureau Inc** (tel 800-847 1800) 225 East 44 Street, New York, NY 10017. Features several Trans-Siberian packages and can also organise individual itineraries.

● **Robert T Moore** (tel 202-242 4796; fax 202-898 1659), 1119 12th St, NW Washington DC 20005. USA representative for Bamtour Co (see p26).

● **Adventure Center** (tel 510-654 1879), 1311 63rd St, Suite 200, Emeryville, CA 94608.

● **Baylis International Journeys**, 2392 Telegraph Avenue, Berkeley, California 94704.

● **STA** (tel 415-391 8407), 166 Geary St, 702, San Francisco CA 94108. STA also has branches in Boston (273 Newbury St, Boston, MA 02116, tel 617-266 6014), Santa Monica (120 Broadway, 108, Santa Monica, CA 90401, tel 310-394 5126) and New York (48E 11th St, New York, NY 1000B, tel 212-477 7166).

● **Lees Travel Service Inc** (tel 213-626 1287), 928-934 Meiling Way, Los Angeles, CA 90012.

● **Rahim Tours** (tel 407-585 5305; fax 407-), 12 South Dixie Highway, Lake Worth, Florida 33460. Offers Trans-Siberian tours and will also arrange individual itineraries.

● **Trains Unlimited Tours** (tel 702-329 5590; fax 702-329 6578), 235 West Pueblo St, Reno, Nevada 89509.

Foreign Embassies in the USA There are **Russian Consulates** in Washington (tel 202-332 1483, 1825 Phelps Place NW, DC

20008); San Francisco (tel 415-922 6642, 2790 Green St, CA 94123), also in New York and Seattle. The **Chinese Embassy** (tel 202-797 8909) is at 2300 Connecticut Ave NW Washington DC 20008; and there are consulates in Houston (3417 Montrose Blvd, Houston, TX 77066), New York (520 12th Ave, NY 10036) and San Francisco (1450 Laguna St, CA 94115). The **Mongolian Embassy** (tel 301-983 1962) is at 10201 Iron Gate Rd, Potomac, MD 20854.

Further information Neither Russia nor Mongolia maintains a tourist office in North America. You can get information about China from: **China International Travel Service** (tel 212-867 0271), Lincoln Building, 60E 42nd St, Suite 3126, NY 10165. There's another branch at 333 W Broadway, Suite 201, Glendale, CA 91204 (tel 818-545 7504).

Getting to Russia from the USA Numerous airlines fly from the US to Russia. Aeroflot is among the cheapest with departures from many US cities. There are now also weekly flights on Aeroflot between Magadan (on the north-east Pacific coast of Russia) and Anchorage (tel 248 8400) or Seattle. Magadan is linked by air to main cities in Siberia.

From Canada
● **Intours Corporation** (tel 416-537 2165; fax 416-537 1627), 1013 Bloor St West, Toronto, Ontario M6H 1M1.
● **Travel Cuts** (tel 416-979 2406), 107 College St, Toronto, Ontario M5T 1P7.
● **Westcan Treks/Explore/Adventure Centre** (tel 416-922 7584), 17 Hayden St, Toronto, Ontario M4Y 2P2; branches in Vancouver (1965 West 4th Avenue, Vancouver BC V6J 1M8, tel 604-734 1066), Edmonton (8412 109th St, Edmonton, Alberta T6G 1E2, tel 403-439 9118) and Calgary (336 14th St NW, Calgary, Alberta T2N 1Z7, tel 403-283 6115).
● **Intourist** (tel 514-849 6394), 1801 McGill College Avenue, Suite 630, Montreal, Quebec H3A 2N4.
● **Exotik Tours** (tel 514-284 3324), Suite 905, 1117 Ste-Catherine West, Montreal, Quebec H3B 1H9.

MAKING A BOOKING IN AUSTRALASIA
From Australia
● **Iris Hotels Pty Ltd** (tel +61-2-580 6466; fax +61-2-580 7256), PO Box 60, Hurstville Business Centre, NSW 2220. This Australian-Russian joint venture has offices in both countries but accepts bookings from abroad at this office. The Russian partner is pioneering

eye surgeon Professor SN Fyodorov, whose Mikof Group operates 13 hotels in Russia (listed in Part 4 under MNTK), each attached to an eye micro-surgery clinic. Aimed at the mature independent traveller, their 14-day rail tour from Khabarovsk to St Petersburg costs from US$1480. Homestays and individual itineraries are also available. Staying in hotels beside clinics may sound unusual but you're guaranteed hot water, absolute cleanliness and if you happened to fall ill you couldn't be in better hands.

● **Sundowners Travel Centre** There are branches in Sydney (tel 02 281 4066, 108 Albion Street, Surry Hills 2010); Melbourne (tel 03-690 2499, 151 Dorcas Street, South Melbourne 3205); Perth (tel 09-321 2335, 1167 Hay Street, West Perth 6005. Arrangements for tours are as for their London office (see p22).

● **Adventure World** (tel 956 7766), 73 Walker St, North Sydney, NSW 2060. Also has branches in Melbourne (3rd Floor, 343 Little Collins St, Melbourne, Vic 3000, tel 670 0125), Brisbane (Level 3, 333 Adelaide St, Brisbane, Qld 4000, tel 229 0599) and Adelaide (7th fl, 45 King William St, Adelaide, SA 5000, tel 231 6844).

● **STA** (tel 212 1255), 1st Floor, 732 Harris St, Ultimo, Sydney NSW 2007. There are branches at 235 Rundle St, Adelaide 5000 (tel 223 2426) and at 13-15 Garema Place, Canberra (tel 247 863).

● **Bay Travel** (tel 327 8266), Level 1, 20-26 Cross St, Double Bay, Sydney NSW 2028.

● **Passport Travel** (tel 824 7183), 320 Glenferrie Rd, Malvern, Melbourne, Vic 3144.

● **CTS** (tel 211 2633), G/F, 757-759 George St, Sydney, NSW 2000

● **China Tourist Office** (tel 02-299 4057), Floor 11, 55 Clarence St, Sydney, NSW 2000.

From New Zealand

● **Adventure World** (tel 524 5118), 101 Great South Road, Remuera, PO Box 74008, Auckland.

● **STA** (tel 309 9995), 10, High St, Auckland. STA also has branches at 223 High St, Christchurch (tel 799098) and 207 Cuba St, Wellington (tel 850561).

● **Suntravel** (tel 09-525 3074) PO Box 12-424, 407 Great South Rd, Penrose, Auckland. Specialises in China, Russia and Mongolia.

MAKING A BOOKING IN SOUTH AFRICA

● **Concorde Travel** (tel 486 1850), 3rd fl, Killarney Mall, Riviera Rd, Killarney, Jo'burg 2193. Agents for Iris Hotels (see above).

● **Travelcor Tours** (tel 419 7750; fax 25 3092), 913 Picbel Strand St, Cape Town 8001.

MAKING A BOOKING IN ASIA

From Japan

The friendly and efficient **Japan Russia Travel Bureau** (formerly JSTB, tel 3432 6161, fax 3436 5530), Kamiyacho Building, (3rd Floor), 5-12-12, Toranomon, Minato-ku, Tokyo 105, will handle bookings for rail journeys to Europe. Nearest subway station is Kamiya-cho (Hibiya line). They offer a series of itineraries, combinations of flights and train journeys, and it's possible to fly from Japan (Niigata) to Khabarovsk or to arrange ferry tickets to Vladivostok. Note that the boat does not operate in the winter. They can also organise your journey via Shanghai, Beijing and Ulan Bator. Write for full details and prices.

Alternatively, you could take the boat from Kobe to Shanghai, make your own way to Beijing and organise your ticket there. The journey takes two days and although the boat is Chinese-run, the chef is Japanese, there are *futons* (mattresses) in the cabins and Japanese-style baths. Details of the weekly service and tickets from:

● **Tokyo Tourist Information Center** (tel 3502 1461), 6-6, Yurakucho 1-chome, Chiyoda-ku, Tokyo. (Subway: Ginza/Yurakucho).

● **STA** Tokyo: 4th Floor, Nukariya Bldg, 1-16-20 Minami Ikebukuro, Toshima-Ku, Tokyo 171, (tel 5391 2922). Osaka: Honmachi Meidai Bldg, 2-5-5, Azuchimachi, Chuuo-Ku, (tel 262 7066).

● **Far Eastern Shipping Co** New Aoyama Building, Nishinkan, Floor 21, 1-1-1 Minami Aoyama, Minato-Ku, Tokyo, (tel 03-3475 2841-3, fax 03-3475 2844). Sells boat tickets for the Niigata/Fushiki to Vladivostok trip. Current prices are Y36,600-89,000, (US$340-830) including meals and the port tax at Vladivostok.

● **Russian Embassy** (tel 3584 6617), Roppongi Heights 1-16, 4-chome Roppongi, Minato-ku, Tokyo.

See p289 for further information about **Japan.**

Buying tickets in Beijing

Nineteen days to Christmas and the only response I could get from the booking clerk for trains to Europe was: 'Wo mei yo'. He said there were no places. The last train which would get us home for Christmas was leaving in eight days time. I tried offering a bribe: 'Wo mei yo'. The prospect of spending Christmas in cold, drab Beijing was not a merry one. I asked the clerk to check his reservations list again. We'd been in the office for over an hour by then and the clerk was thoroughly bored with us. He threw down the comic he'd been trying to read and, thrusting a form at me said 'Okay'. Not really believing him I asked 'Number 19 train okay?'. 'Okay, okay,' he replied. We'd got our reservations. For tickets in the summer, however, you'd need to allow much longer but given enough time, determination and patience, almost anything is possible in China.

From China

● **CITS Ticket Office** (tel 512 0510), Beijing International Hotel, 9 Jianguomenwei Avenue, Beijing. Open Mon-Sat, 8.30-11.30 & 13.30-16.30. The rail ticket office is on the south-western corner of the hotel, a 10-minute walk from the railway station, on Chang'an Ave (see map p214). The cheapest Trans-Siberian tickets you are likely to get anywhere are sold here, although a ticket is no good without a reservation and there can be a long wait in the summer. Some travellers have managed to get tickets from another office in the Beijing Plaza Hotel, just to the east of the station. The office is signposted in English but will make bookings (if any places are available) only for departures in the next four weeks. Prices are the same as at the Beijing International: the cheapest ticket to Moscow is Y1464 on train No19 (Hard Class). Other Hard Class prices include Moscow Y1771 (No3), Irkutsk Y923, Novosibirsk Y1124, Ulan Bator Y417 and Pyongyang (train No27) Y396.

● **Monkey Business Infocenter** (tel 301 2244 ext 716, fax ext 444), Room 716, Qiao Yuan Hotel (new building), Dongbinhe Rd, Youanmenwai 100054, Beijing. Conveniently located in the Qiao Yuan Hotel, these people are definitely worth a visit to pick up the latest travel information. Can arrange tickets, stopovers and accommodation in Moscow. See p33 for further information.

● **TSA**, Room 312, Hotel Taiwan, 5 Jinyu Wutong, Wangfujing North, Beijing. Coordinates the individual packages offered by this German company (see p25).

Procedure In the summer trains fill up quickly so if you plan to spend some time travelling around China make Beijing your first stop and get your reservations. It may also be possible to reserve a place on the train in Shanghai (ask at the travel bureau in the Peace Hotel) and there's also a Russian embassy there (opposite Hotel Pujiang at 20 Huangpu Lu).

Once you've made your reservation and paid your deposit, do the rounds of the embassies and collect your visas. You'll need US$ in cash and a stock of passport photos.

You'll have a reserved berth only as far as Moscow. See p145 for where to make reservations for the next stage of your journey.

Embassies in Beijing You'll need to visit the Russian embassy and, for the Trans-Mongolian route, the Mongolian embassy. The policy of one embassy granting you a visa only if you already had a visa for the next country to be visited meant that you had to obtain your visas in strict order of furthest country first. This is now less strictly adhered to but it's probably still a good idea to visit the

Russian embassy before the Mongolian. Note that most European nationalities no longer need visas for Poland; Australians and New Zealanders still do.

If you need visas for the countries you'll be visiting after Moscow it may be better to get all your visas here rather than in Moscow.

● **Russia** (tel 532 2051), 4 Dongzhimen Beizhong Jie. Open 09.00-12.00 weekdays. It's possible to get a transit visa without having to show your ticket out of Russia but queues here can be very long. Transit visas can be extended but not indefinitely. You'll need three photos and a photocopy of the personal pages of your passport; the service costs Y200 (3 day wait) or US$50 (same day). If you want a tourist or a business visa you'll need visa support.

● **Mongolia** (tel 532 1203), 2 Xiushui Beijie, Jianguomenwai. Open 08.30-11.30 weekdays except Wed. Queues are also long here, though some travellers have managed to get to the front by flashing their foreign passports at the guards. You'll need two passport photos and US$20 for a transit visa (three days to process); the express service costs US$25 (same day).

You won't be allowed to stop off in Mongolia on a transit visa. You'll need visa support for a tourist visa (US$25-30) and this will be difficult to get hold of without booking a tour. Expensive tours can be arranged at the embassy itself but it's worth calling in at Monkey Business for information first.

For more information on **Beijing** and other embassies see p213.

From Hong Kong
Hong Kong can be a good place to arrange a ticket or stopover package on the Trans-Siberian. The agencies here offer a range of services and booking with them from abroad is usually no problem. The international dialling code for Hong Kong is +852.

Trans-Siberian tours and individual itineraries Organising a Russian tour in Hong Kong can take several weeks. Although it's easy to get a Chinese visa here, there's no Russian embassy as yet, so your passport will have to be sent to Japan or Thailand.

● **Wallem Travel** (tel 865 1777; fax 865 2652), Hopewell Centre, 46th floor, 183 Queen's Rd East, Central.

● **American Express** (tel 844 8668; fax 810 4757), G/F, New World Tower, 16-18 Queen's Rd, Central.

Trans-Siberian tickets and stopover packages Many of the travel agencies in the Nathan Road area can arrange tickets at short notice (two weeks or under) from less than US$300. Some will sell you a voucher to exchange at their branch in Beijing for a ticket with reservation. Others will sell you an open ticket with a reservation voucher and you must get the ticket endorsed by CITS in Beijing. Getting the reservation is the difficult part so don't accept an open ticket without a reservation voucher. You get your Mongolian and Russian visas in Beijing. Transit visas are sufficient if you're not making any stops along the way. If you want to visit Ulan Bator or Irkutsk you'll need tourist visas and for these you need visa support.

● **Monkey Business/Moonsky Star Ltd** (tel +852-723 1376; fax 723 6653) E-Block, 4th floor, Flat 6, Chungking Mansion, 36-44 Nathan Rd, Kowloon. The Monkeys are two Belgian brothers who've now put more than 10,000 budget travellers on the trains across Siberia. One's based in Hong Kong selling tickets and the other in Beijing at their **infocentre** (see p31) making sure everyone gets on the right train. The advantage of travelling with the Monkeys is that they provide the vital visa support you'll need for stopovers in Russia and Mongolia. They sell tickets for transit travel and a range of individual packages (from US$325) and stopovers including Ulan Bator (from US$530), Irkutsk (from US$530), Listvyanka and Moscow (one night's accommodation included in most packages). In the summer they run two-week Mongolian tours by jeep, plane and helicopter (from US$1355). Trans-Siberian tickets are also available for the journey in the opposite direction, from Moscow to Beijing (from US$375, including Russian visa support).

● **Time Travel Services** (tel 366 6222; fax 739 5413), Block A, 16th floor, Chungking Mansions, 40 Nathan Rd, Kowloon. Conveniently located beside the Travellers' Hostel.

● **Phoenix Services Agency** (tel 722 7378; fax 369 8884), Room B, 6th floor, Milton Mansion, 96 Nathan Rd, Kowloon.

● **Hong Kong Student Travel Bureau** (tel 730 3269) Room 1021, 10th floor, Star House, Salisbury Rd, Kowloon. Agents for Scandinavian Student Travel Service (SSTS), they offer tickets and tours on the Trans-Siberian.

● **China Travel Service (HK) Ltd** (tel 721 1331; fax 721 7757), 1st floor, Alpha House, 27-33 Nathan Road, Kowloon. The Hong Kong branch of this international company can arrange both individual travel and 'tickets only' on the Trans-Siberian. There are other branches at: 2nd floor, China Travel Building, 77 Queen's Road, Central; and 4th floor, CTS House, 78-83 Connaught Road, Central (tel 853 3533).

● **Shoestring Travel** (tel 723 2306; fax 721 2085), Flat A, 4th floor, Alpha House, 27-33 Nathan Rd, Kowloon.

See p291 for further information about **Hong Kong**.

What to take

Woollen underwear is the best safeguard against sudden changes in temperature. High goloshes or 'rubber boots' are desirable, as the unpaved streets of the towns are almost impassable in spring and autumn; in winter felt overshoes or 'arctics' are also necessary. A mosquito-veil is desirable in E. Siberia and Manchuria during the summer. It is desirable to carry a revolver in Manchuria and in trips away from the railway. **Karl Baedeker** *Russia with Teheran, Port Arthur and Pekin, 1914*

The best advice today is to travel as light as possible. Some people recommend that you put out everything you think you'll need and then pack only half of it. Remember that unless you're going on an upmarket tour, you'll be carrying your luggage yourself.

Clothes
For summer in Moscow and Siberia pack as for an English summer: thin clothes, a sweater and a raincoat. Clothes washing facilities in Russia are limited so it's best to take shirts and blouses of a quick-drying cotton/polyester mixture and wash them yourself. Summer in China and Japan is very hot - uncomfortably humid in Tokyo.

Winter in Russia and northern China is extremely cold, although trains and buildings are kept well-heated: inside the train you can be quite warm enough in a thin shirt as you watch Arctic scenes pass by your window. A thick winter overcoat is an absolute necessity, as well as gloves and a warm hat. It's easy to buy good quality overcoats/jackets in Beijing for about £20/US$30. If you're travelling in winter and plan to stop off in Siberian cities along the way you might consider taking thermal underwear. Shoes should be strong, light and comfortable; most travellers take sturdy running shoes. For wearing on the train some people recommend slip-on kung-fu slippers available cheaply from sports shops in the West, Hong Kong or China. Russians wear track-suits or even pyjamas throughout the journey.

Dress casually; jeans are quite acceptable even for a visit to the Bolshoi. If you forget anything, clothes are expensive in Japan, over-priced and shoddy in Russia, cheap and fashionable in Hong Kong, very cheap and curiously dated in China.

Luggage
If you're going on one of the more expensive tours which include baggage handling, take a suitcase. Those on individual itineraries

have the choice of rucksack (comfortable to carry for long distances but bulky) or shoulder-bag (not so good for longer walks but more compact than the rucksack). Unless you are going trekking in Russia or China, a zip-up hold-all with a shoulder-strap or a frameless backpack are probably the best bet. It's also useful to take along a small day-pack for camera, books etc. Since bedding on the train and in hotels is supplied you don't need to take a sleeping-bag even when travelling in winter. However, sheets provided on the train are occasionally still damp from the laundry, so a sheet sleeping-bag might be worth considering.

A lesson in travelling light

On my first Trans-Siberian trip from Beijing we had so much luggage that several taxi-drivers refused to take us to the station. Unfortunately all thirteen bags were necessary as we were moving back from Japan. We'd managed to get some of them stowed away in the compartments above the door and under the seats when we were joined by a German girl travelling home after three years in China. Her equally voluminous baggage included two full-size theatrical lanterns which were very fragile. Then the man from Yaroslavl arrived with three trunks. We solved the storage situation by covering the floor between the bottom bunks with luggage and spreading the bedding over it, making a sort of triple bed on which we all lounged comfortably - eating, drinking, reading, playing cards and sleeping for the next six days. Dragging our bags around Moscow, Berlin and Paris was no fun, however. On subsequent journeys I didn't even take a rucksack, only a light 'sausage' bag with a shoulder strap and a small day-pack. Never travel with an ounce more than you absolutely need.

Medical supplies

Essential items are: aspirin or paracetamol; lipsalve; suntan lotion; insect repellent (if you're travelling in summer); antiseptic cream and some plasters; an anti-AIDS kit containing sterile syringes and swabs for emergency medical treatment. Note that Western brands of tampons and condoms are not easily available in Russia or China.

Take something for an upset stomach ('Arrêt', for example) but use it only in an emergency, as changes in diet often cause slight diarrhoea which stops of its own accord. Avoid rich food, alcohol and strong coffee to give your stomach time to adjust. Paradoxically, a number of travellers have suggested that it's a good idea to take along laxatives. For vaccination requirements see p41.

General items

A moneybelt is essential to safeguard your documents and cash. Wear it underneath your clothing and don't take it off on the train, as compartments are occasionally broken into. A good pair of sunglasses is necessary in summer as well as in winter when the sun on the snow is particularly bright. The following items are also useful: soap; universal bathplug; bike lock for securing your rucksack while you sleep; penknife with corkscrew and can-opener (although there's a bottle opener fixed underneath the tables in each compartment on the train); ball-point pens; adhesive tape; string (to use as a washing-line); a few clothes pegs; washing powder (liquid 'Travel Soap' is good); tissues (including the wet variety) and lavatory paper; sewing-kit; folding umbrella; spare passport photographs for visas; flash-light; games (cards, chess - the Russians are very keen chess players - Scrabble etc); notebook or diary; the addresses of friends and relatives (don't take your address book in case you lose it); camera and adequate supplies of film (see below). You may also want to take your Walkman and some cassettes. Alkaline batteries can be hard to find, so take spares. Don't forget to take a good book (see p39).

Gifts

Not so long ago the sale of a pair of Levis in Moscow could cover your spending money for the entire trip but this is just not the case any more. Although you may have heard stories about how difficult it is to get hold of Western items in Russia it is now very hard for foreigners to trade anything on the black market.

Rather than things to trade, what you should bring in abundance is gifts. The Russians are great present givers and there's nothing more embarrassing than being entertained in a Russian home and then being presented with a truckload of souvenirs when you have nothing to offer in return. Bring any small Western products that you think might be useful: Russian women love Western cosmetics and soaps but generally can't afford them; businessmen may appreciate sello-tape, Tipp-Ex, highlighters and other things taken for granted in Western offices. Children almost invariably collect badges, stickers and coins (everyone will be interested to see foreign coins). It is also worth bringing things to share: instant coffee (another good gift), chocolate biscuits, sweets (but don't bother with Twixes, Mars Bars or Snickers bars, as they are all easily available now) and cigarettes will always go down well.

It's also a good idea to bring things to show people: copies of glossy magazines (as many glamorous pictures of celebrities as possible), postcards of London or the Royal Family, pictures of your family will all be interesting to someone who has never been abroad. The Chinese in particular adore looking at photographs of people.

Provisions

The range of food and drink available on the train is improving and you can now buy numerous things in the dining car that weren't previously available: alcohol, chocolate and sometimes even biscuits. It's still wise to buy some provisions before you take the train, though, especially if you are going the whole way without a break; dining-car food can get mind-numbingly monotonous.

Some travellers bring rucksacks filled with food, though most people bring just some biscuits, tea-bags or instant coffee (with whitener and sugar if required); hot water is always available from the samovar in each carriage. Other popular items include drinking chocolate, beer and vodka (much cheaper on the platform than on the train), dried soups, tinned or fresh fruit, peanut butter, chocolate and pot noodles. If you forget to buy provisions at home there are Western-style supermarkets in both Moscow and Beijing where you can stock up with essentials.

It's always worth seeing what's for sale on the platforms along the way, too: ice creams, fresh bread, milk, sour cream, fried potatoes with vegetables and Snickers bars are usually easy to find at the larger stations.

'The Russians don't seem to comprehend what a vegetarian is. They would just take the meat off a plate or out of a meat-based soup and call it 'vegetarian'. We found a packet of Complan very useful'. **Hilda Helling** (UK)

Money

Unless you are staying in the most upmarket hotels you will have considerable trouble cashing travellers' cheques. In Moscow this means that you may have to take the metro for half an hour to the nearest cashier; in Ekaterinburg or Vladivostok you could be completely stuck. Thus it is best to take as much as possible of the money you will need in Russia in cash (preferably US dollars) and the rest in travellers' cheques. Other currencies may be acceptable (UK£, German DM and, in St Petersburg, Finnish Marks) but everyone in Russia understands the word 'dollar'. The above is also true for Mongolia but in China travellers' cheques are widely accepted. Some places in China now also accept credit cards.

It's important that you bring notes of small denominations like US$1s and US$5s, and certainly not too many US$50 bills because it can be hard to get the correct change. Paying for a coffee in the Mongolian dining car with a US$20 bill will mean either donating the change to the waiter or accepting a suitcase full of tugriks. Make sure your US$ notes are in immaculate condition, as traders and even banks are likely to reject them if they are torn, badly creased or worn.

Photographic equipment

Most travellers will want to bring a camera with them. Bring more film than you think you'll need, as you'll find there's a lot to photograph. Don't forget to bring some faster film for shots from the train (400 ASA). It's wise to carry all your films in a lead-lined pouch (available from camera shops) if you are going to let them go through Russian X-Ray machines at airports.

Major brands of film are available in Russia, though they may be time-expired, so check the 'use by' date. Slide or high/low ASA film will be difficult to find, even in the big tourist hotels. Have film developed when you return home or in Hong Kong. Developing is naturally of a high standard in Japan but, unless you request otherwise, prints will be small. The large Friendship Stores and big hotels in Beijing may be all right but it's probably not a good idea to have film developed in Russia; you certainly shouldn't risk it in Mongolia.

What not to photograph

Taking pictures from the train used to be forbidden but now it's OK, although it would be wise not to get trigger-happy at aerodromes, military installations or other politically sensitive areas.

Please remember that in Russia, as in most other countries, it's considered rude to take pictures of strangers, their children or possessions without asking permission. Often people are keen to have their picture taken but you must always ask. This is particularly the case during political demonstrations or rallies: I got stoned by a group of pensioners outside the White House in September 1993 for trying to get the next cover for *Time* magazine. Beware!

Photography from the train

The problem on the train is to find a window that isn't opaque or that opens. They're usually locked so that air conditioners can work in summer, and in winter so that no warmth escapes. Try opening doors and hanging out although this will upset the carriage attendants if they catch you; if one carriage's doors are locked try the next, and remember that the kitchen car's doors are always open. Probably the best place for undisturbed photography is right at the end of the train: 'No one seemed to mind if we opened the door in the very last carriage. We got some great shots of the tracks extending for miles behind the train'. (Elizabeth Hehir, The Netherlands).

'A squeegie, an instrument used by window-cleaners to remove water, can be easily obtained in a small size for car windows. This tool is an invaluable aid for cleaning the train's windows for photography, or for that matter just for passengers' viewing'. **Robert Bray** (UK)

Background reading

A number of excellent books have been written about the Trans-Siberian, several of which are unfortunately out of print. If they're not in your library they should be available through the inter-library loans system. The following are well worth reading before you go:

● *Journey Into the Mind's Eye* by Lesley Blanch, is a fascinating book: the witty semi-autobiographical story of the author's romantic obsession with Russia and the Trans-Siberian Railway.

● *To the Great Ocean* by Harmon Tupper (Secker and Warburg, 1965 and out of print) gives an entertaining account of Siberia and the building of the railway.

● *Guide to the Great Siberian Railway 1900* by A.I.Dmitriev-Mamanov, a reprint (David and Charles 1971 and also out of print) of the guide originally published by the Tsar's government to publicise their new railway. Highly detailed but interesting to look at.

● *Peking to Paris: A Journey across two Continents* by Luigi Barzini tells the story of the Peking to Paris Rally in 1907. The author accompanied the Italian Prince Borghese and his chauffeur in the winning car, a 40 horse-power Itala. Their route took them across Mongolia and Siberia and for some of the journey they actually drove along the railway tracks.

● *The Big Red Train Ride* by Eric Newby. A perceptive account of the journey, written in Newby's characteristically humorous style.

● *The Trans-Siberian Railway: A Traveller's Anthology*, edited by Deborah Manley, is well worth taking on the trip for a greater insight into the railway and the trip, as seen through the eyes of travellers from Annette Meakin to Bob Geldof.

● *The Princess of Siberia* is Christine Sutherland's biography of Princess Maria Volkonsky, who followed her husband to Siberia after he'd been exiled for his part in the Decembrists' Uprising. Her house in Irkutsk is now a museum.

● *Martin Walker's Russia* is an astute account of Russian life-styles written just before the collapse of the USSR.

● *Stalin's Nose* by Rory Maclean. Maclean explores the former Eastern Bloc in a battered Trabant with his elderly aunt Zita and a pig named Winston. Although he doesn't use the Trans-Siberian, as he recounts the histories of some of his more notorious relatives the book reveals itself to be a darkly humorous commentary on Communism and its demise. Highly recommended.

● *East of the Sun: The Conquest and Settlement of Siberia* by Benson Bobrick. Recently published (1993), this is a clear and readable narrative of the last four centuries of Siberian history.

However well written and accurate, these books are only the impressions of foreign travellers. You will get more of an idea of the Russian mind and soul from their own literature, even from the pre-Revolution classics. If you haven't already read them you might try some of the following:

● Dostoyevsky's *Crime and Punishment* (set in the Haymarket in St Petersburg).

● Tolstoy's *War and Peace*.

● The weird but fascinating *Master and Margarita* by Mikhail Bulgakov.

● *Dr Zhivago* by Boris Pasternak (whose grave you can visit in Moscow).

● *The Gulag Archipelago* by Alexander Solzhenitsyn.

● *Memories from the House of the Dead* is a semi-autobiographical account of Dostoyevsky's life as a convict in Omsk.

● *A Day in the Life of Ivan Denisovitch* by Alexander Solzhenitsyn details twenty-four hours in the life of a Siberian convict.

No **guidebook** can keep up with the changes in Russia so it's unfair to expect one to be totally up-to-date. The basic facts remain the same, though, and the following are recommended:

● *CIS/USSR - a travel survival kit* by John King and John Noble is the best and most comprehensive practical guide available. A new edition should be available soon, entitled either 'Russia' or 'CIS'.

● *Collins Independent Guide - Soviet Union* (Martin Walker is good on Moscow and St Petersburg but not a fan of either Siberia or the Railway).

● *Lascelles City Guides - Moscow & St Petersburg* by Christopher Knowles contains good, detailed coverage of these cities.

● *Holy Russia* by Fitzroy Maclean is probably the best historical summary (with walking tours) for the traveller.

● *Mongolia - a travel survival kit* If you're spending any time in Mongolia, Robert Storey's excellent practical guide is invaluable.

Other areas of interest to Trans-Siberian travellers that are covered by Lonely Planet *travel survival kits* include: North East Asia, China, Tibet, Japan, Hong Kong, Korea, Western Europe, Eastern Europe, the Baltic States, Poland, Hungary and Scandinavia.

Health precautions and inoculations

No inoculations are listed as official requirements for Western tourists visiting Russia, China, Mongolia or Japan. Some may be advisable, however, for certain areas (see below).

Up-to-date health information and on-the-spot vaccination services are available in London at **Trailfinders** (tel 071-938 3999) at 194 Kensington High Street, and at **Thomas Cook** (tel 071-408 4157), at 45 Berkeley St (nearest tube Green Park). **Nomad Travel Pharmacy** (tel 081-889 7014) at 3-4 Turnpike Lane (Wellington Terrace), London N8 0PX offers travel medical advice and supplies.

In the USA, the **Centre for Disease Control and Prevention** (tel 404-332 4559) in Atlanta is the best place to call for information. If you have a fax an automated service is provided on the above number to fax you back the latest health information for the countries you are visiting.

You should have **health insurance**, available from any travel agent, wherever you are travelling but especially if you are visiting Japan and Hong Kong where medical costs are astronomical. A useful reference book is *The Traveller's Health Guide* by Dr A C Turner (Lascelles).

INOCULATIONS

● **Diphtheria** In the light of outbreaks of diphtheria in Russia and the CIS in 1993 you should check with your doctor that you were given the initial vaccine as a child and a booster within the last ten years. The World Health Organisation recommends a combined booster dose of tetanus-diphtheria toxoid. If you have not had the original vaccine in any form you will need two jabs at least one month apart, followed by a booster after six months.

● **Tetanus** A tetanus vaccination is advisable if you haven't had one in the last ten years. If you then cut yourself badly while travelling you won't need to have another.

● **Infectious hepatitis** Those travelling on a tight budget who will be eating in the cheaper restaurants in China run the risk of catching infectious hepatitis, a disease of the liver that drains you of energy and can last from three to eight weeks. It's spread by infected water or food, or by using utensils handled by an infected person. Gamma globulin injections give a certain amount of protection and are effective for six months. A new vaccine, 'Havrix', lasts twice that time but needs to be administered in two shots, two weeks apart.

● **Others** If you plan to go further south than Beijing you may need to take **anti-malarial tablets**. In certain parts of China, the parasite (carried by the *Anopheles* mosquito) that causes malaria is resistant to chloroquine, so you may need to take two kinds of tablet. Start taking the tablets one week before you go and continue for six weeks after you leave the malarial zone. If you are going to be in a malarial area you would be foolish not to take anti-malarials as the disease is dangerous, occasionally fatal and on the increase.

Those travelling on to South East Asia and India will need to have had typhoid and polio vaccinations and should consider having a cholera shot if travelling to or through an epidemic area.

MEDICAL SERVICES

Those travelling with tour groups will be with guides who can sort out medical problems; simple treatment from a doctor will usually be free in these cases. More serious problems can be expensive but you'll get the best treatment possible from doctors used to dealing with foreigners. If you are travelling independently and require medical assistance contact Intourist or an upmarket hotel for help. In Moscow or St Petersburg the best places to go in an emergency are the US Medical Centres. If you are in St Petersburg, Moscow, Ekaterinburg, Novosibirsk, Irkutsk or Khabarovsk, medical assistance is available at the MNTK clinics (see hotels in the individual city guides for addresses and how to get there). Large hotels in China almost invariably have a doctor in residence and in Beijing, Shanghai and Canton there are special hospitals for foreigners. Take supplies of any prescription medicine you may need. Dentists in Russia are not recommended, so visit yours before you leave.

DRINKING WATER

Do not drink tap-water in St Petersburg since it can cause a nasty form of diarrhoea (giardia), especially in summer. Although the water is probably all right in other cities it's best to stick to mineral water. In Irkutsk and Listvyanka you can drink the tap-water, which comes directly from Lake Baikal. Drink only boiled or bottled water in Mongolia and China; boiled water (in a thermos) is provided on trains and in hotels. Tap water is safe in Japan and Hong Kong.

PART 2: RUSSIA

Facts about the country

GEOGRAPHICAL BACKGROUND

The Russian Federation includes over 75% of the former USSR. It is still the largest country in the world, incorporating 17,175,000 square km (over 6.5 million square miles) and stretching from well into the Arctic Circle right down to the northern Caucasus in the south, and from the Black Sea in the west to the Bering Straits in the east, only a few miles from Alaska. Russia is 1½ times bigger than the USA; the UK could fit into this vast country some 69 times.

Climate

Much of the country is situated in far northern latitudes. Moscow is at the same latitude as Edinburgh, St Petersburg is almost as far north as Anchorage in Alaska. Winters are extremely cold, and temperatures as low as -68°C (-90°F) have been recorded in Oymyakon in Siberia. It is not only the extremes of latitude which cause the severe winters: the physical make-up of the country is as much to blame. Most of the land is an open plain stretching up across Siberia to the Arctic. While there is higher ground in the south there are no mountains in the north to shield it from the cold Arctic air which blows down to fill this plain. To the west are the Urals, the low range which divides Europe and Asia. The Himalayan and Pamir ranges beyond the southern borders stop warm tropical air from reaching the Siberian and Russian plains. Thus blocked off, the plains warm rapidly in summer and become very cold in winter. Olekminsk, in north-east Siberia, holds the record for the place with the greatest temperature range in the world: from -60°C (-87°F) in winter to a record summer high of 45°C (113°F). Along the route of the Trans-Siberian, however, summers are rather more mild.

Transport and communications

Railways remain the principal transport system for both passengers and goods, and there are some 87,000km of track in the country. The heaviest traffic on the entire system, and in the world, is on certain stretches of the Trans-Siberian, with trains passing every few minutes. Although Russia's road network is comparatively well-developed (624,000km), few people own cars which means that, as well as the 47% of freight, 31% of all passengers also travel by rail.

The rivers of Russia have always been of vital importance as a communication network across the country. Some of these rivers are huge, navigable by ocean-going ships for considerable distances. Harsh winters preclude year-round navigation and air travel is taking over. In 1991 some 140 million passengers travel 900,000km by air.

Landscape zones: flora and fauna (see also Appendix B)
The main landscape zones of interest to the Trans-Siberian traveller are as follows:

● **European Russia** West of the Urals the flora and fauna is similar to that found in the rest of northern Europe. Trees include oak, elm, hazel, ash, apple, aspen, spruce, lime and maple.

● **North Siberia and the Arctic regions** The *tundra* zone (short grass, mosses and lichens) covers the tree-less area in the far north. Soil is poor and much of it permanently frozen. In fact *permafrost* affects over 40 per cent of Russia and extends down into southern Siberia, where it causes building problems for architects and engineers. In this desolate northern zone the wildlife includes reindeer, arctic fox, wolf, lemming and vole. Birdlife is more numerous: ptarmigan, snow-bunting, Iceland falcon and snow-owl as well as many kinds of migratory water and marsh fowl.

● **The Siberian plain** Much of this area is covered with *taiga* (pronounced 'tiger') - thick forest. To the north the trees are stunted and windblown; in the south they grow into dark impenetrable forests. More than 30 per cent of all the world's trees grow in this taiga zone. These include larch, pine and silver fir, intermingled with birch, aspen and maple. Willow and poplar line the rivers and streams. Much of the taiga forest along the route of the Trans-Siberian has been cleared and replaced with fields of wheat or sunflowers. Parts of this region are affected by permafrost and in places rails and roads sink, and houses, trees and telegraph poles keel over drunkenly. Fauna in this region includes species once common in Europe: bear, badger, wolverine, polecat, ermine, sable, squirrel, weasel, otter, wolf, fox, lynx, beaver, several types of rodent, musk deer, roebuck, reindeer and elk.

● **East Siberia and Trans-Baikalia** Much of the flora and fauna of this region is unique (see p171) including, in Lake Baikal, such rarities as the world's only fresh-water seals. Amongst the ubiquitous larch and pine there grows a type of birch with dark bark, *Betula* *daurica*. Towards the south and into China and Mongolia, the forests give way to open grassy areas known as *steppes*. The black earth (*chernozem*) of the northern steppes is quite fertile and some areas are under cultivation.

● **The Far Eastern territories: the Amur region** Along the Amur River the flora and fauna are similar to that found in northern China and it is here that the rare Amur tiger (see p269) is found. European flora makes a reappearance in the Far Eastern region including such trees as cork, walnut and acacia.

HISTORICAL OUTLINE

The first Russians

Artefacts recently uncovered at the Dering Yuryakh site in Siberia suggest that human history may stretch back very much further than had previously been believed, perhaps between one and two million years. Around the thirteenth millennium BC there were Stone Age nomads living beside Lake Baikal. By the second millennium BC when fairly advanced civilisations had emerged here (see p71), European Russia was inhabited by Ural-Altaic and Indo-European peoples. In the sixth century BC the Scythians (whose magnificent goldwork may be seen in the Hermitage) settled in southern Russia, near the Black Sea. Through the early centuries of the first millennium AD trade routes developed between Scandinavia, Russia and Byzantium, following the Dnieper River. Centres of trade grew up along the route (Novgorod, Kiev, Smolensk, Chernigov) and by the sixth century AD the towns were populated by Slavic tribes known as the Rus (hence 'Russian'). The year 830 saw the first of the Varangian (Viking) invasions and in 862 Novgorod fell to the Varangian chief, Rurik, Russia's first sovereign.

Vladimir and Christian Russia

The great Tsar Vladimir (978-1015) ruled Russia from Kiev and was responsible for the conversion of the country to Christianity. At the time the Slavs worshipped a range of pagan gods and it is said that in his search for a new religion Vladimir invited bids from the Muslims, the Jews and the Christians. Since Islam and the consumption of vodka were not compatible and Judaism did not make for a unified nation, he chose Christianity as the state religion and had himself baptised at Constantinople in 988 AD. At his order the mass conversion of the Russian people began, with whole towns being baptised simultaneously. The eleventh century was marked by continual feuding between his heirs. It was at this time that the northern principalities of Vladimir and Suzdal were founded.

The Mongol invasion and the rise of Muscovy

Between 1220 and 1230 the Golden Horde brought a sudden halt to economic progress in Russia, burning towns and putting the local population to the sword. By 1249 Kiev was under their control and the Russians moved north, establishing a new political centre at Muscovy (Moscow). All Russian principalities were obliged to pay tribute to the Mongol khans but Muscovy was the first to challenge their authority. Over the next three centuries Moscow gained control of the other Russian principalities and shook off the Mongol yoke.

Ivan the Terrible (1530-84)

When Ivan the Terrible came to the throne he declared himself Tsar of All the Russias and by his military campaigns extended the borders of the young country. He was as wild and blood-thirsty as his name suggests and in a fit of anger in 1582 he struck his favourite son with a metal staff, fatally injuring him (a scene used by Ilya Repin as the subject of one of his greatest paintings). Ivan was succeeded by his mentally-retarded son, Fyodor (the last of the descendants of Rurik), with Boris Godunov ruling first as regent and later as Tsar (1598-1605). The early part of the seventeenth century was marked by dynastic feuding which ended with the election of Michael Romanov (1613-45), the first of a long line that lasted until the Revolution in 1917.

Peter the Great and the Westernisation of Russia

Peter (1672-1725) well deserved his soubriquet 'the Great' for it was due to his policy of Westernisation that Russia emerged from centuries of isolation and backwardness into the eighteenth century. He founded St Petersburg in 1703 as a 'window open on the West' and made it his capital in 1712. During his reign there were wars with Sweden and Turkey. Territorial gains included the Baltic provinces and the southern and western shores of the Caspian. The extravagant building programme in St Petersburg continued under Catherine the Great (1762-96). While her generals were taking the Black Sea steppes, the Ukraine and parts of Poland for Russia, Catherine conducted extensive campaigns of a more romantic nature with a series of favourites in her elegant capital.

Alexander I and the Napoleonic Wars

In Russia during the nineteenth century, the political pendulum swung back and forth between conservatism and enlightenment. The mad Tsar Paul I came to the throne in 1796 but was murdered five years later. He was succeeded by his son Alexander I (1801-25) who was said to have had a hand in the sudden demise of his father. In the course of his reign he abolished the secret police, lifted the laws of censorship and would have freed the serfs had the aristocracy not objected so strongly to the idea. In 1812 Napoleon invaded Russia and Moscow was burnt to the ground (by the inhabitants, not by the French) before he was pushed back over the border.

Growing unrest among the peasants

Nicholas I's reign began with the first Russian Revolution, the Decembrists' uprising (see p116), and ended, after he had reversed most of his older brother's enlightened policies, with the Crimean War against the English and the French in 1853-6. Alexander II (1855-81) was known as the Tsar Liberator, for he it was who freed the serfs. His reward was his assassination by a student in St Petersburg in 1881. He was succeeded by the strong Tsar Alexander III, during whose reign work began on the Trans-Siberian Railway.

Nicholas II: last of the Tsars

The dice were heavily loaded against this unfortunate Tsar. Nicholas inherited a vast empire and a restless population that was beginning to discover its own power. In 1905 his army and navy suffered a most humiliating defeat at the hands of the Japanese. Just when his country needed him most, as strikes and riots swept through the cities in the first few years of this century, Nicholas's attention was drawn into his own family crisis. It was discovered that the heir to the throne, Alexis, was suffering from haemophilia. The Siberian monk, Rasputin, ingratiated himself into the court circle through his ability to exert a calming influence over the Tsarevich. His influence over other members of the royal family, including the Tsar, was not so beneficial.

October 1917: the Russian Revolution

After the riots in 1905, Nicholas had agreed to allow the formation of a national parliament (Duma) but its elected members had no real power. Reforms came too slowly for the people and morale fell further when, during the First World War, Russia suffered heavy losses. By March 1917 the Tsar had lost all control and was forced to abdicate in favour of a provisional government led by Alexander Kerensky. The Revolution that abruptly changed the course of Russian history took place in October 1917, when the reins of government were seized by Lenin and his Bolshevik Party. Nicholas and his family were taken to Siberia where they were murdered (see p147). Civil war raged across the country and it was not until 1920 that the Bolsheviks brought the lands of Russia under their control, forming the Union of Soviet Socialist Republics.

The Stalin era

After the death of Lenin in 1924, control of the country passed to
Stalin and it was under his leadership that the USSR was transformed
from a backward agricultural country into an industrial world power.
The cost to the people was tremendous and most of those who were
unwilling to swim with the current were jailed for their 'political'
crimes. During the Great Terror in the 1930s, millions were sentenced to work-camps, which provided much of the labour for
ambitious building projects. During the Second World War the
USSR played a vital part in the defeat of the Nazis and extended its
influence to the East European countries that took on Communist
governments after the war.

Khrushchev, Brezhnev, Andropov and Chernenko

After Stalin's death in 1953, Khrushchev became Party Secretary and
attempted to ease the strict regulations which now governed Soviet
society. In 1962 his installation of missiles in Cuba almost led to war
with the USA. Khrushchev was forced to resign in 1964, blamed for
the failure of the country's economy and for his clumsy foreign
policy. He was replaced by Brezhnev who continued the USSR's
policy of adopting friendly 'buffer' states along the Iron Curtain by
ordering the invasion of Afghanistan in 1979 'at the invitation of the
leaders of the country'. When Brezhnev died in 1982, he was replaced by the former head of the KGB, Yuri Andropov. He died in
1984 and was succeeded by the elderly Chernenko, who managed a
mere thirteen months in office before becoming the chief participant
in yet another state funeral.

Gorbachev and the end of the Cold War

Mikhail Gorbachev, the youngest Soviet premier since Stalin, was
elected in 1985 and quickly initiated a process of change categorised
under the terms *glasnost* (openness) and *perestroika* (restructuring).
The West credits him with bringing about the end of the Cold War
(he received the Nobel Prize in 1990) but it would be misguided to
think that he was the sole architect behind the changes that took place
in the USSR: it was widely acknowledged before he came to power
that things had gone seriously wrong.

Gorbachev launched a series of bold reforms: Soviet troops were
pulled out of Afghanistan, Eastern Europe and Mongolia, political
dissidents were freed, laws on religion relaxed and press censorship
lifted. These changes displeased many of the Soviet 'old guard',

(Opposite) Russian Orthodox priests outside St Basil's Cathedral, Moscow.

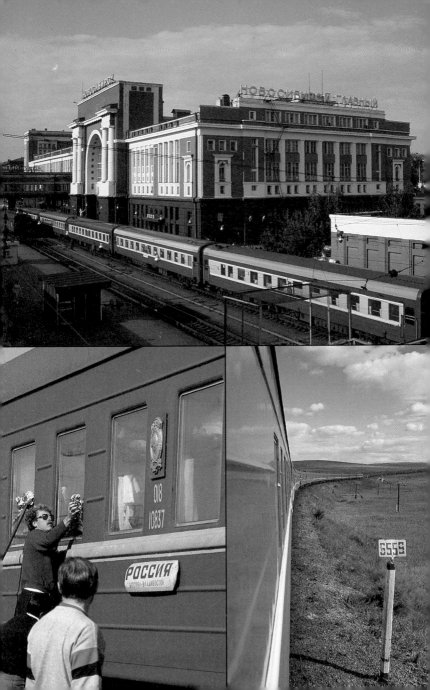

and on 19 August 1991 a group of senior military and political figures staged a coup. Gorbachev was isolated at his Crimean villa and
Vice President Yanaev took over, declaring a state of emergency.
Other politicians, including the President of the Russian Republic,
Boris Yeltsin, denounced it and rallied popular support. There were
general strikes and, after a very limited skirmish in Moscow (three
casualties), the coup committee was put to flight.

The collapse of the USSR

Because most levels of the Communist Party had been compromised
in the failed coup attempt, it was seen as corrupt and ineffectual.
Gorbachev resigned his position as Chairman in late August and the
Party was abolished five days later. The Communist Party's collapse
heralded the demise of the republic it had created, and Gorbachev
commenced a desperate struggle to stop this happening. His reforms,
however, had already sparked nationalist uprisings in the Baltic
republics, Armenia and Azerbaijan. Despite his suggestions for loose
'federations' of Russian states, by the end of 1991 the USSR had
split into 15 independent republics. Having lost almost all his support, Gorbachev resigned and was relieved by Yeltsin.

Yeltsin vs the Congress of Deputies

Yeltsin's plans for economic reforms were thwarted at every turn by
the Congress of People's Deputies (parliament). Members of Congress, elected before the collapse of Communism, were well aware
that by voting for reforms they were, in effect, removing themselves
from office. In the Western press this struggle was described as the
fight between the reformists (Yeltsin and his followers) and the hard-
liners (Vice President Alexander Rutskoi, Congress's speaker Ruslan
Khasbulatov, and the rest of Congress). Yeltsin's hard-won referendum in April 1993 gave him a majority of 58% but this did not give
him a mandate to overrule parliament.

On 22 September 1993, Yeltsin suddenly dissolved parliament and
declared presidential rule. (Some have suggested that this swift
action was to avert another coup attempt). The Congress denounced
his action, stripped him of all powers and swore in Rutskoi as President. The Constitutional Court ruled that, having thus acted illegally,
Yeltsin could now be impeached. Khasbulatov accused him of effect-
ing a 'state coup' and appealed for a national strike. The deciding
factor in the confrontation between parliament and president was the

(Opposite) Top: In Russia, the Trans-Siberian is known as the *Rossiya*, pictured
here at Novosibirsk station. **Bottom left:** Passengers cleaning train windows.
Bottom right: The entire route is marked with kilometre posts (see p222).

question of whom the military would support. Rutskoi, an Afghan war veteran with a keen military following, ordered troops to march on Moscow. They never did but some 5000 supporters surrounded the White House. Inside, the Congress voted to impeach Yeltsin, who retaliated by severing their telephone lines. The White House vigil turned into a siege; electricity lines were cut and the building surrounded by troops faithful to Yeltsin.

On 3 October a crowd of 10,000 communist supporters converged on the White House where Rutskoi exhorted the people to seize the Kremlin and other strategic locations around the city. All through the night there were confrontations as rioters attacked the mayor's office, the Tass building and the main TV station. At dawn on 4 October Yeltsin's troops stormed the White House. Fighting went on for most of the day but by the evening the building, charred and battered, was taken. By the end of the week when order had been restored 171 people had been killed.

The future
The state elections, held in December 1993, supported Yeltsin's draft constitution, which outlined Russia's new democratic architecture. Although the immediate threat was seen to have been the constitution's rejection (Yeltsin warned that this might lead to civil war), the election revealed a new problem in the form of the Liberal Democrat Party. Its leader, Vladimir Zhirinovsky, espouses some extremely sinister policies. Particularly worrying are his comments about reuniting the former USSR, his racist jibes and his aim to re-establish a Russian empire reaching 'from Murmansk to Madras'. Zhirinovsky scooped the public vote, leading to fears that he might win the 1996 presidential election, picking up the powers recently granted to Yeltsin. Whether this happens or not will probably depend on how fast living conditions improve in the former USSR.

ECONOMY

Russia has vast amounts of natural resources and in this sense it is an extremely rich country. It has the world's largest reserves of natural gas as well as deposits of oil, coal, iron ore, manganese, asbestos, lead, gold, silver and copper that will continue to be extracted long after most other countries have exhausted their supplies. The forested areas in Russia cover an area almost four times the size of the Amazon basin.

Yet, owing to gross economic mismanagement under communism, the country is experiencing severe financial hardship and has been receiving Western aid since 1990. A series of reforms first under Gorbachev and now Yeltsin means that change is on the way: privation on the route to Yeltsin's 'healthy mixed economy with a powerful private sector' is generally characterised as a bitter medicine for the Russian economy. Many don't see it this way, however, protesting for a return to the communist days when there was, at least, enough food for everyone.

Privatisation

Mass privatisation is taking place. In place of large collective farms and industries, the government is encouraging smaller, independent ones. In October 1992 vouchers worth R10,000 were distributed in an attempt to kick start the stock market. These could be sold for cash or exchanged for shares in the growing number of private companies. Although the idea of buying and selling stocks is catching on, there is more than a little confusion over how exactly the market works. Western economic advisers are often asked such questions as 'If I own part of the company, why can't I take the computer home?'.

Industry

Russian industry has traditionally been centred on heavy industry. This is now all collapsing; 1993 saw industrial output down a further 20%. Spares for the factories are difficult to find, raw materials are too expensive, and the final products are often too shoddy to sell on the open market. Industries once supported by state subsidies are finding that they just can't afford to stay operational.

Small private businesses, however, are flourishing, a sure sign that things are improving. In 1992 some 30,000 enterprises were auctioned off, selling, on average, for four times predicted prices.

Hyperinflation

When the markets for most commodities, previously artificially regulated, were freed on 2 January 1992 prices immediately soared by 300-400%. Inflation was already being fuelled by a law passed in 1990, allowing possession of hard currency, which led to a rush for dollars. Another factor adding to inflation was that in some instances the debts of former Communist Bloc countries to Russia were payable in roubles. These countries reserved their right to print Russian banknotes and simply set their presses running, releasing their own debts but fuelling the Russian problem. In an effort to limit the amount of Russian currency on the streets, a new law in August 1993 withdrew all old rouble notes, replacing them with new ones. By late 1993, however, inflation was still running at around 25% per month.

THE PEOPLE

Russia is the sixth most populous nation in the world, with just under 150 million people (about half the population of the former USSR). Of these, a high proportion (82%) are actually Russian. The rest belong to any one of nearly 100 ethnic minorities, most commonly Tartar (4%) and Ukrainian (3%). In the former USSR it was always unwise to refer to people as 'Russian' because of the vast number of other republics they might have come from. With the establishment of independence for many of these states you must be even more careful: Kazakhs or Ukrainians, for example, will not appreciate being called Russians.

Russia is divided up into *oblasts* (the basic administrative unit), *krays* (smaller territories) and *autonomous republics* (containing ethnic minority groups such as the Buryats in Siberia). Siberia forms part of the Russian Federation and exists only as a geographical, not a political, unit.

Government

Russia moved briskly down the political path from autocracy to 'socialist state', with a period of a few months in 1917 when it was a republic. From November 1917 until August 1991 the country was in the hands of the Communist Party and until September 1993 it was run by the Congress of People's Deputies. This 1068-seat forum was elected from throughout the USSR. At its head sat the Supreme Soviet, the legislative body, elected from Congress. Since only Party members could stand for election in Congress, only Party members could ever run the country.

The confirmation of the new Russian Constitution in December 1993 means that the country is now to be governed by a European-style two-tier parliament very similar to that of France. At the head of the state remains the Russian president, currently Boris Yeltsin.

Education and social welfare

Education and health care are provided free for the entire population but standards of both are now falling. School is compulsory between the ages of seven and seventeen with the result that Russia has a literacy rate of almost 100%. Although funding for research is currently at an all-time low, until a few years ago the country used to plough 5% of its national income directly into scientific research in its 900 universities and institutes. Russia's present inability to maintain its scientists has led to serious fears of a brain drain; certain states in the Middle East are very keen for Russian scientists to help them with their nuclear programmes.

The national health care programme is likewise suffering through lack of funds. Russia has produced some of the world's leading surgeons yet recent outbreaks of diseases extinct in first world countries has demonstrated that health services here were never comprehensive. The most publicised epidemic in the last year has been diphtheria: hundreds of Russians who should have been inoculated at birth have died.

Religion

Russia was a pagan nation until 988 when Vladimir ordered the mass conversion of the country to Christianity. The state religion adopted was that of the Greek Orthodox Eastern Church (Russian Orthodox) rather than Roman Catholicism. After the Revolution religion was suppressed until the late 1930s when Stalin, recognising the importance of the Church's patriotism in time of war, restored Orthodoxy to respectability. This policy was reversed shortly after the war and many of the country's churches, synagogues and mosques were closed down. Labour camps were filled with religious dissidents, particularly under Khrushchev.

Gorbachev's attitude towards religion was more relaxed and the Freedom of Conscience law passed in 1990 took religion off the blacklist. Numerous churches are now being restored to cater for the country's 35-40 million Orthodox believers. In 1991 Yeltsin even legalised Christmas. Russian Christmas Day, celebrated on 7 January, is now an official public holiday again.

Numbers of Christian sects are growing. Sects as diverse as the so-called 'Old Believers' (who split from the Orthodox church in the 17th century), Scientology and Jehovah's Witnesses are attempting to find converts here. This has worried some, and on 14 June 1993 the Supreme Soviet passed an amendment to the 1990 Freedom of Conscience law banning foreign organisations from recruiting by 'independent' religious activities, without permission.

Russian Jews, historically subject to the most cruel discrimination, have been less trusting of the greater religious freedoms. In 1990 more than 200,000 moved to Israel, pouring in at a rate of up to 3000 per day; fewer are emigrating now and there are still large Jewish communities in Moscow and St Petersburg.

In Buryatia, the centre of Russian Buddhism, many of the monasteries have reopened. Since all were a long way off the tourist beat they were not kept in good repair as museums (unlike churches in European Russia).

With the independence of the Central Asian Republics there are now few Moslems in the country.

Practical information for the visitor

DOCUMENTS, TICKETS AND VOUCHERS

(Also see Part 1: Planning Your Trip.) I read somewhere of one Englishman who left his passport and tickets behind in London and yet still managed to travel across Siberia carrying no other document than a six-monthly ticket to the Reading Room at the British Library. Entry requirements are somewhat stricter these days. The essential documents are your passport, Russian visa (supplied as a separate document) and a visa for the first country that you'll be entering after Russia. If you are travelling with Intourist, don't forget the rail and hotel vouchers, and if you've arranged a Beijing-Moscow ticket from abroad don't forget your voucher to exchange for a ticket at CITS in Beijing. It's worth bringing some additional document of identification (eg driving licence) as your passport will be confiscated by the hotel when you check in. It is now possible to rent self-drive cars in Moscow and St Petersburg for which you'll need an international driving licence (available from the AA).

International student cards were never much use in the USSR but now that prices are tiered, it's worth bringing one. Part of the IS card is written in Russian, too, which might impress someone. Note that if you're arriving from Africa or South America you may be required to show a yellow fever vaccination certificate. Travellers arriving from countries where there have been recent outbreaks of cholera may be asked to show proof of vaccination.

CROSSING THE BORDER

Baedeker gave the following warning to travellers in his 1914 guide-book (*Russia with Teheran, Port Arthur and Pekin*): 'Whether at the railway frontier station or at a sea-port the customs examination of passengers' luggage is generally thorough.' Things have changed now and Western travellers get off lightly but right up until the late 1980's Baedeker's advice would have been accurate.

Customs declaration forms

At the Russian border you will be given a Customs Declaration Form on which you must declare the total amount of money you are carrying (cash and travellers' cheques) and the number of pieces of luggage you have. You must keep this form until you leave, when it may be checked; note that on departure you must fill out another identical form. The purpose of these forms is to deter people from giving away or selling their foreign currency or valuables. Now that the use of foreign currency has been outlawed in Russia it's likely that these forms may be more thoroughly checked than in the last few years when US$ could be spent in shops in Russia. When you exchange money in Russia ensure that you either get given an exchange certificate or have your customs form officially endorsed.

China also requires visitors to fill in a customs form. Don't give away or sell anything you have listed on the form or you may be expected to account for it later. If anything is stolen, get a letter from the local Public Security Bureau (police station) to that effect. Make a photocopy to give to customs, as the original must go to your travel insurance company if you want to claim compensation.

Customs allowances: entering or leaving the country
Russia's customs laws are being reformed so you should check current regulations before arrival. You should not, however, have any problems bringing in a litre of spirits and two litres of wine.

When leaving the country note that you need a special permit to export 'cultural treasures', a term used to include almost anything that looks old or valuable. Paintings in particular attract the attention of customs officials and may be confiscated or charged at 600% duty, if you do not have a permit.

HOTELS

Russian hotels are usually of gargantuan proportions and about as architecturally interesting as the average multi-storey car park in the West. This having been said, some of the old hotels in Moscow and St Petersburg have recently been restored to a very high standard in joint ventures with foreign companies. Many of the 'Soviet modern' hotels can accommodate over 2000 people. Moscow's Hotel Rossiya, once the world's largest hotel, with 3200 rooms and beds for 6000 guests, fell to second place in 1990 with the opening of the 4032-room Excalibur Hotel in Las Vegas.

Checking in
This is not always the swift procedure it should be. After the receptionist has kept you waiting for a while, she will relieve you of your passport and hand you a small pass card without which you will be unable to get into your room; in some of the upmarket hotels, however, you may actually be given your key by the receptionist.

Keys are usually kept by the *dezhurnaya* (floor attendant), very often an elderly female busybody who passes the time drinking tea in her little den, keeping an eagle eye on all that goes on on her floor. You may be able to get hot water or a kettle from her for drinks.

Bedrooms
Unless you are staying in the most expensive accommodation, you will be surprised by the shoddiness of your new home, considering the fact that you probably had to fork out a small fortune for it. In some of the older hotels the rooms are vast and comfortable but they're rather smaller in the more modern places. They are generally furnished in the worst possible taste. In one room I stayed in, one wall was papered with pink roses and the others in a bold orange geometric design; purple nylon curtains completed the schizophrenic decor. Beds are often too short, usually of orthopaedic hardness and bedding consists of blankets in a duvet-cover. There's usually an internal phone and wake-up calls may be arranged at the reception desk; but don't rely on them in the cheaper places.

Bathrooms
Except in the best hotels, bathrooms are equipped with broken fittings, dripping taps, lavatories with dislocated seats and no plugs in either bath or basin. The manager of the Olgina Hotel in St Petersburg was obviously trying to give the place an air of American efficiency: I found a long paper notice that read 'Sanitized' suspended over the unflushed loo in my bathroom. The hot water system is generally reliable in Moscow and St Petersburg but not in Siberia, where you should have a shower wherever you find water above freezing. Don't forget your universal bathplug, soap and loo paper.

INTOURIST

Although the state tourist organisation lost its monopoly in 1990 it still controls a large proportion of the tourist industry and is likely to do so for some time to come. Services offered include tours, theatre ticket booking, travel ticket booking, guides and local transport; the problem is that Intourist generally charges a high price for them. While you will always be able to get what you want cheaper elsewhere, it will usually require a lot more effort, so most people pay up and go along with Intourist. You can, however, be sure that there will always be someone who speaks English at Intourist's hotels.

Tours, guides and interpreters
If you are pressed for time in any city, particularly Moscow or St Petersburg, it may be worth taking a city tour. The problem here

is that you are likely to cover a lot of ground very fast and then spend a large amount of time waiting on the bus for the last couple who want to know 'are we the last?'. Generally it's best to get around on your own: it's much more confusing and takes greater effort and time but you'll learn more on the buses and metro than you will inside a tour bus. You don't have to do this alone, either, as private guides and interpreters can be supplied by Intourist and most other tourist organisations. MNTK (see addresses under hotels in Part 4) can organise guides from US$25 per day. Remember that your guide is probably getting a tiny proportion of what you are actually paying; a present as a tip would be a kind idea.

Sputnik
Basically junior Intourist, Sputnik is Russia's international youth travel bureau. Set up to introduce the youth of the Communist East to the youth of the West it's rather lost its raison d'etre. Sputnik hotels will accept anyone now and are frequently very cheap.

LOCAL TRANSPORT
When you are arranging your trip you may be encouraged to purchase 'transfers' so that you will be met at the airport or station and taken to your hotel. The prices charged for this service can be high (£27/US$40 with Intourist) but it can sometimes be worthwhile. If you are planning to take a taxi from the airport when you arrive it's probably better to arrange a transfer in advance, if only to keep yourself out of the hands of the taxi mafia. Whether you buy transfers for the rest of your trip or not will depend on how enterprising you want to be and what time you'll be reaching each city. It would be foolish to wander around looking for a hotel or guesthouse after dark. Transfers from the hotel to the railway station have less to recommend them. Don't believe that whoever is organising the transfer is responsible if you miss your train; check departure times.

Taxis
Virtually every car in Russia is a taxi: stand in the street with your arm outstretched and within two minutes someone will be pulling over and asking where you want to go. It's illegal, of course, but if drivers are going along your way it makes perfect sense for them to take along a paying passenger. While this may be very convenient, however, it can also be dangerous, as you have no idea of the driver's intentions. For this reason, women travelling alone would be unwise to hitch rides like this and no-one should get into a car that already has more than one occupant. Don't put your luggage into the

boot or your driver could simply pull away when you get out to retrieve it. Russians seem to delight in worrying about crime and if you ask them they'll tell you numerous stories about unwary passengers being driven into the countryside and robbed.

Official taxis are safer but more difficult to find. You'll recognise them by the chequerboard pattern on the door and the green 'for hire' light. Although they have meters, owing to the meteoric decline of the rouble these require recalibration. You should agree on a price before you get in but, of course, once the driver realises you're a foreigner he'll bump up the price accordingly. You're more likely to be charged local rates if you don't pick up taxis outside big hotels or major tourist spots.

Metro

A very cheap way to get around with a flat fare of less that £0.04/US$0.06 and trains every few minutes. In Moscow it's worth using the metro just to see the stations, which are more like subterranean stately homes, with ornate ceilings, gilded statues and enormous chandeliers. There are no tickets: just put a token into the turnstile to get in. Be careful not to fall over getting on the escalators: they move twice as fast as those in the West. Russian metro systems are built deeper underground than their western counterparts, perhaps to act as shelters in the event of nuclear attack. Because they're so far down, escalators need to be extremely long as well as swift. The world's longest escalator is, in fact, in St Petersburg (Ploshchad Lenina), and has 729 steps, rising 59 metres.

In the street, metro stations are indicated by a large blue 'M'. Lines are named after their terminal stations, as on the Paris metro. One peculiarity you'll notice is that where two lines intersect the station is given two names, one for each line. As trains move off, the next station is announced; the counter above the end of each tunnel indicates how long it's been since the last train. In Siberia, there's a metro in Novosibirsk and systems are under construction in Ekaterinburg and Omsk.

Bus

In all cities there's a bus service (fixed fare and often very crowded) and usually also trolley-buses and trams. Some buses have conductors, some ticket machines and in others tickets are purchased from the driver in strips or booklets. If there's no conductor you must punch the ticket yourself, using one of the punches by the window. If the bus is crowded and you can't reach, pass your ticket to someone near the machine and they'll do it for you. Occasionally, inspectors impose on-the-spot fines for those without punched tickets.

Internal flights

These usually involve long delays and far too much sitting around in airports. Try to avoid flying in Russia, not because it's unsafe but because it leaves you with no control over changed circumstances. If you are travelling on the ground there are always alternatives when one form of transport fails.

Getting tickets in Russia can be difficult and time-consuming, too. It's worth trying the Aeroflot office as well as Intourist; always make reservations as far in advance as possible. Foreigners must now pay a price that's roughly twice the local ticket charge.

Boat

Most of the cities you will visit are built on rivers and short trips on the water are usually possible. In St Petersburg the best way to reach Petrodvorets is by hydrofoil. You can also get to Lake Baikal by boat up the Angara from Irkutsk. Possibly the most exciting river trip you can make is from Yakutsk to the Lena Pillars (see p179).

Car Rental

In St Petersburg and Moscow it is possible to rent self-drive cars. Charges are high and you will need an international driving-licence.

ELECTRICITY

In most Russian cities this is 220v, 50 cycles AC. Sockets require a continental-type plug or adapter. In some places the voltage is 127v so you should enquire at the reception desk before using your own appliances. Sockets are provided on the train for electric razors.

TIME

Russia spans ten time zones and on the Trans-Siberian you will be adjusting your watch an hour almost every day. The railway runs on Moscow time and timetables do not list local time. It can be disconcerting to cross the border from China at breakfast-time to be informed by station clocks that it is really only 2.00am. Moscow time (MT) is three hours ahead of Greenwich Mean Time. Siberian time zones are listed throughout the route guide and the main cities are in the following zones: Novosibirsk (MT+4), Irkutsk (MT+5), Khabarovsk (MT+7), Vladivostok (MT+7).

MONEY

(See also p37). The rouble is the basic unit of Russian currency. This is theoretically divided into 100 kopecks but since the exchange rate

rate in early 1994 was 2350/1600 roubles to £1/US$1 you're unlikely to see any kopecks or many of the smaller denomination rouble bills. Roubles come in notes of 1, 3, 5, 10, 100, 200, 500, 5000, 10,000, and 50,000 and in coins of 1, 5, 10, 20 and 50. Note that currency reforms in summer 1993 mean that roubles issued before 1993, apart from notes of 10 or less, are no longer valid; be sure that no-one tries to palm any off on you. All notes are clearly stamped with the date.

Following the reforms of January 1994 the rouble is now the only legitimate currency, and it is illegal for anyone to ask you to pay in US$. People still want dollars for security, however, although as the rouble becomes more steady, they should gain confidence in their own currency. Note that in this guide prices are given in dollars since rapid inflation would render any rouble price out of date almost immediately.

Banks

Most travellers used to change money on the black market simply because the rate was so much better than at the banks. With the ongoing reforms, however, it appears that there may soon be little point in this. It's easiest to change money in your hotel bureau de change but you will probably get a better rate of exchange in a bank. Ensure you are given an exchange certificate/receipt or that the bank stamps your customs declaration form so that you can prove that you haven't been dealing illegally.

Tipping

Soviet policy outlawed tipping. It was seen as nothing less than bribery: the thin end of the corruption wedge. *Glasnost* soon changed all this, though, and you'll find that now certain people (taxi-drivers and waiters etc) have come to accept the practice. It's really up to you but Russians generally don't. If you want to thank your guide or your carriage attendant on the train, the best way of doing so is not with money but with a small gift, preferably something that is obviously Western (ie exotic). Scented soap, perfume, cosmetics, tights, cigarettes, instant coffee and any Western food product will all go down well.

POST AND TELEPHONES

The most reliable postal services are likely to be found in the big tourist hotels, particularly if they are joint-owned with a foreign company. From here you will also be able to make international phonecalls (about £2/US$3 per minute to Europe) and send faxes.

Hotel gift shops sell postcards and stamps and the service bureau will be able to tell you the current postage rates and help you write your country name in Cyrillic. Be warned that letters are likely to be opened in transit by thieves looking for money, so don't send anything valuable or important into or out of Russia. A postcard will take about two weeks to get from Moscow to London.

BROCHURES AND NEWSPAPERS

The service bureaux in hotels will supply you with glossy brochures detailing local sights. Most hotels also have a small bookshop where you can buy a range of Western papers and magazines as well as *Pravda* (English translation), local guide-books and maps. Newspaper kiosks in most towns also stock maps when available.

In Moscow the two papers to look out for are the *Moscow Times* and the *Moscow Tribune*, both of which give good current affairs coverage and the latest information on what's going on in the city.

NATIONAL HOLIDAYS

- 01 Jan: New Year's Day
- 07 Jan: Russian Orthodox Christmas Day.
- 08 Mar: International Women's Day.
- 01 May: International Working People's Solidarity Day. The next working day is also a holiday.
- 09 May: Victory Day, to commemorate the end of World War II (the 1941-45 Great Patriotic War)
- 07 Jun: Independence Day

FESTIVALS

Annual arts festivals in Moscow include Moscow Stars (5-15 May) and Russian Winter (25 Dec to 05 Jan). The most interesting festival is St Petersburg's White Nights, held around the summer solstice, when the sun does not set. The days are separated by only a few hours of silvery light: a combined dusk and dawn. Theatres and concert halls save their best performances for this time and a festival is also held at Petrodvorets.

FOOD

In spite of the recent food shortages in the country visitors are well cared for. No one ever came to Russia for the food alone but that doesn't mean you won't have some really good meals. There's rather more to Russian cuisine than borsch and chicken Kiev but if you're eating most of your meals on the train, you won't have much of a chance to discover this. You will probably leave with the idea that Russian cooking is of the school dinner variety, with large hunks of meat, piles of potatoes and one vegetable (the interminable cabbage), followed by ice-cream.

Although there are food shortages in some parts of the country, Westerners are well catered for in most hotels. A substantial breakfast will provide you with enough energy to tackle even the heaviest sight-seeing schedule. The first meal of the day consists of fruit juice (good if it's apple), cheese, eggs, bread, jam and *kefir* (thin, sour yoghurt). Lunch and dinner will be of similarly large size, consisting of at least three courses. Meat dishes can be good but there is still a shortage of fresh fruit and vegetables except at the best hotels.

Zakuski
Russian hors d'oeuvres, known as *Zakuski*, consist of some or all of the following: cold meat, sausages, salmon, pickled herring, paté, tomato salads, sturgeon and caviare. Large quantities of vodka are drunk with zakuski.

Caviare
The roe of the sturgeon becomes more expensive as it gets rarer. Four species are acknowledged to produce the best caviare: beluga, sterlet, osetra and sevruga, all from the Caspian and Black Seas. To produce its characteristic flavour (preferably not too 'fishy') a complicated process is involved. First the female fish is stunned with a mallet. Her belly is slit open and the roe sacs removed. The eggs are washed and put through strainers to grade them into batches of a similar size. The master-taster then samples the roe and decides how much salt to add for preservation.

Processed caviare varies in colour (black, red or golden) and also in the size of the roe. It is eaten either with brown bread or served with sour cream in *blinis* (thin pancakes). You can get it in most tourist hotels and on the black market. Red caviare is occasionally available on the train.

Soups
Soups are usually watery but good, meals in themselves with a stack of brown bread. Best known is *borsch*: beetroot soup which often includes other vegetables, (potatoes, cabbage and onion), chopped ham and a swirl of sour cream (*smetana*). Cabbage soup or *shchi* is the traditional soup of the proletariat and was a favourite of Nicholas II, who is said to have enjoyed only plain peasant cooking (to the great disappointment of his French chef). *Akroshka* is a chilled soup made from meat, vegetables and *kvas* (thin beer). *Rassolnik* is a soup of pickled vegetables.

Fish

These include herring, halibut, salmon and sturgeon. These last two may be served with a creamy sauce of vegetables. In Irkutsk you should try *omul*, the famous Lake Baikal fish, which has a delicious, delicate flavour.

Meat

The most famous Russian main course is chicken Kiev (fried breast of chicken filled with garlic and butter). Almost as famous is *boeuf Stroganov*, a beef stew made with sour cream and mushrooms, and named after the wealthy merchant family who financed the first Siberian explorations in the 1580s.

Other regional specialities that you are likely to encounter on a trip across Siberia include *shashlik* (mutton kebabs) and *pilov* (rice with spiced meat) from Central Asia, chicken *tabaka* (with garlic sauce) from Georgia, and (to be avoided at all costs) *salo* which is pig's fat preserved with salt, from the Ukraine. From Siberia comes *pelmeni*, small dumplings filled with meat and served in a soup or as a main course. If you're expecting a sirloin when you order *bifstek* you'll be disappointed: it's just a compressed lump of minced meat.

Puddings

Very often the choice is limited to ice-cream (*morozhenoye* - always good, safe, and available everywhere) and fruit compôte (a disappointing fruit salad of a few pieces of tinned fruit floating in a large dish of syrup). You may, however, be offered *blinis* with sour cream and fruit jam; *vareniki* (sweet dumplings filled with fruit) or rice pudding. Unless you are staying in one of the more expensive hotels there will be very little fresh fruit although it is now easily available from street vendors.

Bread

Russian bread, served with every meal, is wholesome and filling. Tourist literature claims that over one hundred different types are baked in Moscow. Communist 'bread technology' was said to be so much in demand in the West that Soviet experts were supposedly recruited to build a brown bread factory in Finland.

Drinks

● **Non alcoholic** Most popular is tea, traditionally served black with a spoonful of jam or sugar. Milk is not always available so you may want to take along some whitener. The Russians have been brewing coffee since Peter the Great introduced it in the 17th century but standards have dropped since then; take a jar of instant with you.

Bottled mineral water is available everywhere but it often tastes rather too strongly of all those natural minerals that are supposed to be so good for you.

There are several varieties of bottled fruit juice (*soc*), of which apple seems to be the most consistently good. The Pepsi and Coca Cola companies fought bitterly over distribution in the USSR and during the 1980s Pepsi was awarded sole rights. Now both are easily available, as are other Western soft drinks.

● **Alcoholic** Vodka predominates, of course, and Russians will be disgusted if you do anything other than drink it straight. It should be served ice cold and drained in one from single shot glasses. Note that a shot of vodka ought to be followed immediately by zakuski (see above): only drunkards drink without food. The spirit originated in Poland (although some say that it was brought back from Holland by Peter the Great) and means 'little water', something of an understatement. If you tire of the original product, there are several flavoured vodkas to sample: lemon, cherry, blackberry or pepper.

Wines tend to be rather too sweet for the Western palate but Russian champagne is surprisingly good and very cheap. Beer is widely available. You should also try *kvas* (a fermented mixture of stale brown bread, malt sugar and water). A popular drink, sold on the streets during the summer, its alcohol content is so low it's hardly noticeable at all.

RESTAURANTS

It used to be very difficult to get a good meal in Russia. Because all restaurants were state-run waiters were not keen to serve you, chefs couldn't be bothered to cook for you and you considered yourself lucky if you managed to bribe your way to a table. With the advent of co-operatives and joint venture restaurants, the situation has improved greatly but for Western service everyone pays Western prices (in US$ until the currency reforms of January 1994).

Until the opening of these joint venture restaurants, hotel restaurants were often the best places to eat and in some Siberian cities they still are. Budget travellers may find the joint venture restaurants too expensive but some have cheaper dining rooms attached serving similar food without the upmarket decor and service. The cheapest places to eat are the self-service cafés found in most shopping

(Opposite) Top: A constant supply of hot water is provided in each compartment of the train by the coal-fired stove-samovar (*batchok*). **Bottom:** Russian Railways restaurant car (see p106).

streets. There are also branches of McDonald's and Pizza Hut in Moscow and St Petersburg.

When Russians go to a restaurant, they go in large groups and they like to make a meal last the evening. Waiters do their best to ensure no dish arrives too quickly and give you more than enough time to try to interpret the menu. Many of the dishes that have prices pencilled against them will in fact be unavailable. While you wait for your food a dance-band entertains with folk-songs and Western hits from the sixties at so high a volume that you can't ignore them. Nevertheless, a visit to a local restaurant can be an entertaining and drunken affair especially if you get invited to join a Russian party. Note that tsarist traditions die hard: if a man wishes to invite a woman from another table to dance he will ask permission of the men at her table before she joins him on the dance-floor

WHAT TO DO IN THE EVENING

If you're expecting a wild nightlife during your stay in Russia, you may be disappointed. There are a few late-night bars in the bigger hotels but for most people it's lights out before midnight. Apart from going to a restaurant, entertainment in the evening is basically of a cultural nature. Tickets for the opera, theatre, ballet or circus can be arranged through the hotel service bureau. It is also possible to buy them from the kiosks in the street or at the box-office on the day of the performance. Touts sell tickets outside theatre entrances just before the show; check the date on the ticket before you buy. Note that there are plans to introduce separately priced tickets for foreigners. Performances usually start early: between 18.00 and 19.00.

Ballet

The season lasts from September to May and you should not miss the experience of a night at the Bolshoi in Moscow or the Kirov in St Petersburg. Apart from the quality of the dancing, tickets cost less than at Covent Garden and the buildings themselves are magnificent. Note that many touring groups dance at the Bolshoi so it may not be the famous company you see the night you go. You may be interested to know that Rudolf Nureyev, Russia's most famous star, was 'shaken out' of his mother's womb on the Trans-Siberian as it was rattling along towards Lake Baikal.

(Opposite) Top: Red Square, Moscow. The Kremlin's Spassky Tower with St Basil's Cathedral on the left and Lenin's Tomb on the extreme right (photo DSJ). **Bottom:** Long players in Russia, Beatles LPs are cheap and widely available.

Opera and theatre

In the past, opera was encouraged more than theatre as it was seen as politically neutral. Glasnost, however, encouraged playwrights to produce drama that reflects Russian life as it is, rather than as the government would like people to see it. This has led to a number of successful new theatre groups opening in Moscow and St Petersburg. Details of plays and operas are available from hotel service bureaux. There are also several puppet theatres which are highly recommended if you have the time.

Cinema and television

In the 1980s the Soviet film industry also benefited from the greater freedoms that came with glasnost. In early 1987, one of the most successful and controversial films was *Is It Easy To Be Young?*, which was deeply critical of the Soviet war in Afghanistan. In the 1990s the pessimism of the people towards life is reflected in films made here. *Little Vera* (1990) is the story of a provincial girl who sinks into small-time prostitution and finally drowns herself. Gorbachev walked out of it saying he disapproved of the sex scenes. In *Executioner* (1991) a female journalist takes on the mafia in St Petersburg and loses.

More Western and American movies are being allowed into the country and censorship laws have been relaxed, with the result that Stallone and Schwartzeneggar are as famous here as they are everywhere else. There are cinemas in every town and shows start early in the evening. Films are shown as a whole programme with a couple of short educational films before the main feature. There is a thriving black market in bootlegged American movies; don't be surprised to find *Total Recall* showing in your restaurant car.

Russian television has evolved fast in the last few years; news and current affairs programmes are now of quite high quality. For the majority of the population there is one programme worth watching at the moment: *The Rich also Cry*, a distinctly mediocre *Dynasty* wanna-be from Mexico. The star, Veronica Castro, has reached cult status unequalled even by the Beatles: a certain Mrs Maslova in Tatarstan made the headlines in 1992 when she stabbed her husband to death after he made a disparaging remark about the actress. Egor Yakovlev, head of Russian state television, commented last year that the programme was probably the only thing holding the CIS together.

SHOPPING

Shopping was an incredibly complicated and frustrating affair in the USSR. Shops were crowded and if they weren't this was a sign that there was nothing worth buying in them. One Russian story tells of the wife of a Soviet official who, visiting London, concluded from the lack of queues that no-one could afford any of the fancy goods for sale. Although things are getting much better regarding the availability of goods the problem is that many people just can't afford them. The common view on market reform is that while twenty years ago there wasn't much in the stores, at least everyone could afford what there was. Now the shelves are overflowing with goods but no-one has the money to buy them. This is the chief reason for the nostalgia for the old days. The situation, one hopes, will improve as wages increase.

Despite the fact that the majority of Russian shoppers tend to flock to the stores with the cheapest prices, you are unlikely to see food queues. Having said this, Russians still carry around their *avoska* (a 'just in case' bag) and are quick to notice a queue forming, joining it even before they know what it is for in the hope that they may snap up a bargain.

For foreigners shopping is no problem at all: you only have to wander into the main street to see the wide variety of goods on sale and if you walk into a privately-owned shop or the electronics section of a department store you'll find quality merchandise on a par with anything available in the West. Whereas previously this was all sold for hard currency, now it's for roubles; the change still doesn't mean that ordinary people can afford it, though.

Making a purchase
The procedure is rather more complicated than in the West and exactly the same as the outmoded purchasing process in the department stores of New Delhi. First you must decide what you want to buy and find out the price (the assistant may write this down on a ticket for you). Then go to the cash desk (where an abacus may be used to calculate the purchase price of the goods you want) and pay, getting a receipt. This must then be taken back to the first counter and exchanged for your purchases.

Department stores
No visit to Moscow would be complete without a visit to GUM, the largest department store in Russia. It comprises an enormous collection of arcades, now partly taken over by upmarket chains and boutiques from the West and is housed in an impressive glass-roofed building, rather like a giant greenhouse. There is another department store chain: TSUM, which has branches in Moscow and most of the larger cities.

Beriozka shops and hotel gift shops

Foreign consumers will find their desires best served by Beriozka shops, which originally sold Western goods for hard currency, with branches in most Intourist hotels and many cities. They always have good supplies of vodka and caviare, as well as Russian handicrafts.

Opening Hours

Large department stores are open from 09.00 to 20.00 Monday to Saturday. Smaller stores have a wide range of opening times, anywhere between 08.00 and 11.00, closing between 20.00 and 23.00, with an hour's lunch-break either from 13.00 to 14.00 or 14.00 to 15.00. Most shops are closed on Sundays.

WHAT TO BUY

Handicrafts

These include the attractively decorated black lacquer *palekh* boxes (icon-painters started making them when religious art lost popularity after the Revolution); enamelled bowls and ornaments; embroidered blouses and tablecloths from the Ukraine; large black printed scarves; guitars and balalaikas; lace tablecloths and handkerchieves; jewellery and gemstones from Siberia and the Urals and painted wooden ornaments, including the ubiquitous *matrioshka* dolls which fit one inside the other. Modern variations on the matrioshka doll include leaders of the former USSR, the Beatles and even American all-star basketball teams. Old communist memorabilia has recently been removed from the shops but is still sold to tourists and makes interesting souvenirs.

Beware of buying paintings, especially if they are expensive, as a 600% duty may be imposed on them when you leave the country. If you are going to buy one, make it a small one so that it will fit into your bag easily. If the painting looks old and as if it might be really valuable it may well be confiscated by customs officials.

Books

You'll find few English-language books in the shops but upmarket hotels usually have a small selection of novels in their gift shops. Russian-language art books are worth buying for their reproductions and they can be very cheap. There are branches of Dom Knigi (House of Books) in Moscow, St Petersburg and most other large cities.

Records and CDs

Whilst the records themselves are not of as high quality as in the West, they are incredibly cheap. There is a fairly wide range of classical records and folk music as well as Beatles oldies and local pop groups blossoming in the aftermath of glasnost. One of the most popular stars in the Soviet pop world was Dean Reed, an American who 'defected' to the East and died under mysterious circumstances in June 1986. Melodiya (the formerly state-run label) also produces, under licence, records by several Western groups. The Beatles have always had a large following in Russia but it was only in March 1986 that their records went on sale outside the black market.

Compact discs are now available, although they are all imported from Europe and the USA. There's no Russian artwork that might make a CD worth buying here rather than at home; one wonders how many Russians can actually afford compact disc players.

Clothes

Most are over-priced and shoddy and unless you have a penchant for nylon shirts and terylene trousers you are unlikely to find anything that's worth buying. Imported clothes are becoming more readily available, however, and there are now a couple of trendy foreign fashion shops in Moscow's GUM, including Benetton. Fur hats and boots are available but can be expensive. Russian/Soviet military clothing is a popular buy for foreigners but this should be concealed as you leave the country or it may be confiscated.

Food and Drink

Basically this means vodka and caviare. The best place to get any alcohol is from the traders in the street kiosks; but check the seal on the bottle before buying to make sure it hasn't been diluted. It is wise to go for the bigger brand names (eg Stolichnaya) as there are reports of the smaller distilleries cutting costs to produce low grade alcohol which has resulted in blindness amongst some drinkers.

Caviare is available on the streets, too, but it may be safer to buy it in the hotel gift shops. Although it will be more expensive, at least you'll know what you're getting.

SPECULATION

Since Western items now have legitimate channels through which to enter the country, you are unlikely to be able to sell anything unless you are bringing it in specifically at someone's request. Moreover, even if you do find a market for something, nobody is likely to have the money to buy it off you at Western prices. You need only go into the street markets and see the number of people hawking things to see how difficult this would be these days. Bring gifts instead - see p36.

The black market

Hard currency is still in demand in Russia. This is partly because while the US$ maintains its value the rouble is constantly slipping, and partly because now that Russians are free to travel around the world they need some easily exchangeable currency to take with them.

When changing money, always deal with someone in a kiosk or in one of the money-changing vans that you'll see in some cities; this way they can't run off with your cash because you'll know where they work. Try not to have any dealings with individuals who just walk up to you in the street; and don't let anyone slip you old rouble notes (see p60).

CRIME

Along with the harmless black-marketeering has grown a disturbing protection racketeer movement. These gangs, using 'heavies' recruited from the army, extort money from black marketeers and the new private enterprises. The owners of co-operatives are forced to pay protection money running into millions of roubles or face their properties being set on fire. Taxi-drivers have been threatened with having their cars damaged or families attacked. There are several gangs operating in the cities and there have been reports of shoot-outs between rival gangs in the streets of Moscow and St Petersburg. It seems that it is not local councils that run Russian cities but the mafia.

Despite the above, Russia is still a safe place for tourists to visit but a little more care should be taken these days. Crimes against tourists were almost unimaginable ten years ago but now a new branch of the police force has had to be set up especially to protect foreigners. The situation is not as bad as in New York or even some other European capitals but you shouldn't wander around late at night, especially in Moscow or St Petersburg. It also helps not to dress too ostentatiously or wear expensive jewellery or watches.

Travellers have reported that petty pilfering from hotel rooms has increased quite considerably over the last few years. Don't take valuables on holiday with you and leave your passport at the hotel reception desk. A money-belt for travellers' cheques and foreign currency you'll be carrying with you is essential.

With many traders using the Trans-Siberian trains theft from compartments is now on the rise. See p109 for more information.

PART 3: SIBERIA AND THE RAILWAY

Historical outline

EARLY HISTORY

Prehistory: the first Siberians
Recent discoveries at Dering Yuryakh (100km south of Yakutsk) have indicated that man may have lived in Siberia for far longer than had previously been thought. Unconfirmed evidence from this site suggests human habitation stretching back as far as 1-2 million years ago, which would place the site on a par with Professor Leakey's discoveries in East Africa. There is evidence of rather more recent human life in the Lake Baikal area. In the 13th millennium BC, Stone Age nomads were roaming round the shores of the lake, hunting mammoths and carving their tusks into the tubby fertility goddesses that can be seen in the museums of Irkutsk today. Several of these sites in the Baikal area have been discovered and the railway passes through one at the village of Malta, 45 miles west of Irkutsk, where a camp dating back to this early period has been excavated.

By the Neolithic Age (twelfth to fifth millennia BC) there is far more archaeological evidence and it shows that the nomadic tribes had reached the Arctic Circle and moved into North America through Alaska. These northern tribes trained dogs to pull their sledges but were left behind technologically, remaining in the Stone Age until Russian colonists arrived in the mid-seventeenth century.

In the south, however, several Bronze Age cultures emerged around the central parts of the Yenisei River. Afanassevskaya, south of Krasnoyarsk, has given its name to the culture of the people who lived in this area in the second millennium BC. They made pottery and decorated it with a herring-bone pattern. The first evidence of permanent buildings has been found near Achinsk, where the Andronovo people built huge log cabins in the first millennium BC. Excavations of sites of the Karassuk culture, also dated to the first millennium BC, have yielded Chinese artifacts, indicating trade between these two peoples.

Early civilisations

The Iron Age sites show evidence of more complex and organised societies. The clear air of the Altai Mountains has preserved the contents of numerous graves of the Tagar Culture which existed here in the second century BC. Their leaders were embalmed and buried like Egyptian pharaohs with all that they might need in the after-life. In their burial mounds archaeologists have found perfectly preserved woollen blankets, decorated leather saddles and the complete skeletons of horses, probably buried alive when their master died.

The Huns moved into the region south of Lake Baikal in the third century BC where the Buryats, their descendants, now live. Their move west continued slowly over the next five centuries when their infamous leader Attila, the 'Scourge of God', having pillaged his way across Europe, reached Paris where he was defeated in 452 AD.

The ancestors of the Kirghiz people were the Tashtyks from west Siberia, who built large houses of clay (one found near Abakan even has an underfloor central heating system), moulded the features of their dead in clay death masks and decorated their bodies with elaborate tattoos. Tiny Kirghizstan in the extreme south of the CIS is all that remains of a once mighty empire that stretched from Samarkand to Manchuria in the twelfth century AD. In the following century, the Kirghiz were taken over by the rapidly advancing Mongols. Genghis Khan's Mongol empire grew to become the largest empire ever, including the Tartars of South Russia, and the peoples of North Asia, Mongolia and China.

The first Russian expeditions to Siberia

In mediaeval times, Siberia was known to Russians only as a distant land of valuable fur-bearing animals. There were occasional expeditions from Novgorod in the fifteenth century. These became more frequent in the sixteenth century, once the lands of South Russia had been released from the grip of the Mongols by Tsar Ivan the Terrible who seized Kazan and Astrakhan, opening the way to Siberia. Yediger, the leader of a small Siberian kingdom just over the Urals, realised his vulnerability and sent Ivan a large tribute of furs, declaring himself a vassal of the Tsar.

Yediger's son, Kuchum, was of a more independent mind and, having murdered his father, he put an end to the annual tribute of furs, proclaiming himself Tsar of Siberia. Since Ivan's armies were occupied on his western frontiers, he allowed the powerful Stroganov family to raise a private army to annex the rebel lands. In 1574 he granted them a twenty-year lease on the land over the Urals as far east as the Tobol River, the centre of Kuchum's kingdom.

Yermak: the founder of Siberia

The Stroganovs' army was a wild bunch of mercenaries led by ex-pirate Yermak, the man now recognised as the founder of Siberia. They crossed the Urals and challenged Kuchum, gaining control of his lands after a struggle that was surprisingly long, since the Rus sians were armed with muskets, the enemy with swords and bows and arrows. On 5th November 1581, Yermak raised the Russian flag in Isker (near modern Tobolsk) and sent the Tsar a tribute of over 2500 furs. In return Ivan pardoned him for his past crimes, sent him a fur-lined cape that had once graced the royal shoulders and a magnificent suit of armour. Over the next few years Yermak was constantly harassed by Kuchum. On 16th August 1584, the enemy ambushed them when they were asleep on an island in the Irtysh. The story goes that Yermak drowned in the river, dragged under by the weight of the armour given him by the Tsar. His name lives on as the top brand of Russian rucksack.

The quest for furs

Over the next fifty years Cossack forces moved rapidly across Siberia, establishing *ostrogs* (military outposts) as they went and gathering tributes of fur for the Tsar. Tyumen was founded in 1586, Tomsk in 1604, Krasnoyarsk in 1628, Yakutsk in 1633 and by 1639 the Cossacks had crossed the width of the country reaching the east coast. Like the Spanish Conquistadors in South America they dealt roughly with the native tribes they met, who were no match for their muskets and cannons. The prize they lusted after was not gold (as it was for the Spaniards in Peru and for later Russian adventurers in Siberia) but furs. In the days before fur farms certain pelts were worth far more than they are today and from the proceeds of a season's trapping in Siberia a man could buy and stock a large farm with cattle and sheep; the chances that such a man would be successful in finding his way into or out of the dark, swampy forests of the taiga were not very high but quite a few did.

Khabarov and the Amur

In 1650, a Russian fur merchant named Khabarov set out from Yakutsk to explore the Amur region in what is now the Far Eastern Territories. He found the local tribes extremely hostile as the Russians' reputation for rape and pillage had spread before him. The land was fertile and rich in fur-bearing animals and Khabarov and his men committed such atrocities that the news reached the ears of the Tsar, who ordered him back to the capital to explain himself. Bearing gifts of fur, he convinced the Tsar that he had won valuable new lands which would enrich his empire. The local tribes, however, appealed to the Manchus, their southern neighbours, who sent an army to help them fight off the Russians. The Tsar's men were gradually beaten back but periodic fighting went on until 1689, when the Russians were forced out of Manchuria and the Amur by the Treaty of Nerchinsk.

Eighteenth-century explorers

Peter the Great became Tsar in 1696 and initiated a new era of exploration in the Far East. By the following year the explorer, Atlassov, had claimed Kamchatka for Russia. In 1719 the first scientific expedition set out for Siberia. Peter commissioned the Danish seaman, Vitus Bering, to try to find a northern sea-passage to Kamchatka and the Sea of Okhotsk (unaware that the route had been discovered by Deshnev eighty years before). However, the Tsar did not live to see Bering set out in 1725.

Between 1733 and 1743 another scientific expedition, comprising naval officers, topographers, geodesic surveyors, naturalists and astronomers, made detailed charts of Russians lands in the Far East. Fur traders reached the Aleutian Islands and the first colony in Alaska (on Kodiak Island) was founded in 1784 by Gregory Shelekhov. (His grave is in the cemetery of the Church of the Holy Saviour in Irkutsk.) The Russian colony of Alaska was sold to the United States in 1868 for the bargain price of two cents an acre.

THE NINETEENTH CENTURY

There were two developments in Siberia in the nineteenth century which had a tremendous effect upon its history. First, the practice of sentencing criminals to a life of exile or hard labour in Siberia was increased to provide labour for the mines and to establish communities around the military outposts. The exile system, which caused a great deal of human misery, (see below) greatly increased the population in this vast and empty region. Secondly, and of far greater importance was the building of the Trans-Siberian Railway in the 1890s (described in a later section).

Colonisation

By the end of the eighteenth century, the population of Siberia was estimated to be about one and a half million people, most of whom belonged to nomadic native tribes. The policy of populating the region through the exile system swelled the numbers of settlers but criminals did not make the best colonists. As a result, voluntary emigration from overcrowded European Russia was encouraged by the government. Peasant settlers could escape the bonds of serfdom by crossing the Urals but Siberia's reputation as a place of exile was not much of an incentive for them to move.

As the railway penetrated Siberia, the transport of colonists was facilitated. Tsar Alexander's emigration representatives were sent to many thickly-populated regions in European Russia in the 1880s. They offered prospective colonists incentives including a reduced rail fare (6 roubles for the 1200 mile journey) and a free allotment of twenty-seven acres of land. Prices in Siberia were high for most things and colonists could expect get up to 100 per cent more than in European Russia for produce grown on this land. Many peasants left Europe for Siberia after the great famine of 1890-91.

Further exploration and expansion

Throughout the century scientists and explorers continued to make expeditions to Siberia, recording their discoveries in the region. In 1829, an expedition led by the German scientist Baron von Humboldt, who had become famous for his scientific explorations in South America, investigated the geological structure of the Altai plateau (southern Siberia).

In 1840, the estuary of the Amur was discovered and colonisation encouraged, after Count Muraviev-Amursky, Governor General of Eastern Siberia, had annexed the entire Amur territory for Russia. This was in flagrant violation of the Russo-Chinese Treaty of Nerchinsk, which had been signed in 1689. However, the Chinese were in no position to argue, being threatened by the French and English as well as by internal troubles in Peking. By the Treaty of Peking (1860) they ceded the territory north of the Amur to Russia, and also the land east of the Ussuri, including the valuable Pacific port of Vladivostok.

THE EXILE SYSTEM

The word 'Siberia' meant only one thing in Victorian England and nineteenth century Russia: an inhospitable land of exiled murderers and other evil criminals who paid for their sins by working in the infamous salt mines. To a great extent this was a true picture of Siberia except that the prisoners were mining gold, silver and coal rather than salt. Some of the first exiles sent over the Urals did indeed work in salt mines which may be why people associated Siberia with salt.

By the year 1900, over one million people had been exiled and made the long march over the Urals to the squalid and overcrowded prisons of Siberia.

George Kennan

In 1891 a book entitled *Siberia and the Exile System*, written by George Kennan, was published in America. It exposed the truly horrific conditions under which prisoners were kept in Siberia and aroused public opinion in both America and Britain. Kennan was a journalist working for the New York *Century Magazine*. He knew Siberia well, having previously spent two years there. He was then unaware, however, of quite how badly the convicts were treated and in a series of lectures before the American Geographical Society he defended the Tsarist government and the exile system.

When his editor commissioned him to investigate the system more thoroughly, the bureaucrats in St Petersburg were happy to give him the letters of introduction which allowed him to venture into the very worst of the prisons and to meet the governors and convicts. The government hoped, no doubt, that Kennan would champion their cause. Such had been the case with the Rev Dr Henry Landsell who had travelled in Siberia in 1879. In his account of the journey, *Through Siberia*, he wrote that 'on the whole, if a Russian exile behaves himself decently well, he may in Siberia be more comfortable than in many, and as comfortable as in most of the prisons of the world.' After the year he spent visiting Siberian prisons, Kennan could not agree with Landsell and the inhumanity of the exile system, the convict mines and the terrible conditions in the overcrowded prisons were all revealed in his book.

The first exiles

The earliest mention of exile in Russian documents of law is in 1648. In the seventeenth century, exile was used as a way of getting rid of criminals who had already been punished. In Kennan's words: 'The Russian criminal code of that age was almost incredibly cruel and barbarous. Men were impaled on sharp stakes, hanged and beheaded by the hundred for crimes that would not now be regarded as criminal in any civilised country in the world, while lesser offenders were flogged with the *knut* (a whip of leather and metal thongs, which could break a man's back with a single blow) and *bastinado* (cane), branded with hot irons, mutilated by amputation of one or more of their limbs, deprived of their tongues, and suspended in the air by hooks passed under two of their ribs until they died a lingering and miserable death.' Those who survived these ordeals were too mutilated to be of any use so they were then driven out of their villages to the lands beyond the Urals.

Exile as a punishment: the convict mines

With the discovery of valuable minerals in Siberia and the shortage of labourers available to mine them, the government began to use criminals to work them. Exile was thus developed into a form of punishment and extended to cover a range of crimes including desertion, assault with intent to kill and vagrancy (when the vagrant was of no use to the army or the community). It was also the punishment for offences that now seem nothing short of ridiculous. According to Kennan, exile became the punishment for fortune-telling, prize-fighting, snuff-taking (the snuff-taker was not only banished to Siberia but also had the septum between his nostrils torn out) and driving with reins. (The old Russian driver had been accustomed to ride his horse or run beside it - using reins was regarded as too Western, too European.)

Abolition of the death penalty

In the eighteenth century demand for labour for the mines continued to grow and the list of crimes punishable by exile was further extended to include drunkenness and wife-beating, the cutting down of trees by serfs, begging with a pretence to being in distress, and setting fire to property accidentally. In 1753, the death penalty was abolished (for all crimes except an attempt on the life of the Tsar) and replaced by exile with hard labour. No attention was given to the treatment of exiles en route, they were simply herded like animals over the Urals, many dying on the way. The system was chaotically corrupt and disorganised, with hardened murderers being set free in Siberia while people convicted of relatively insignificant offences perished down the mines.

Reorganisation in the nineteenth century

In the nineteenth century the system became more organised but no less corrupt. In 1817 a series of *étapes* (exile stations) was built along the way to provide overnight shelter for the marching parties. They were nothing more than crude log cabins with wooden sleeping platforms. Forwarding prisons were established at Tyumen and Tomsk, from where prisoners were sent to their final place of exile. From Tyumen, convicts travelled by barge in specially designed cages to Tomsk. From here some would be directed on to Krasnoyarsk or else to Irkutsk, a 1040-mile, three-month march away. The prisoners would be sent from these large centres to smaller prisons, penal colonies and to the mines. The most infamous mines were on the island of Sakhalin, off the east coast, where convicts dug

The Siberian Boundary Post (circa 1880) In this melancholy scene, friends and relatives bid exiled prisoners farewell by the brick pillar that marked the western border of Siberia, on the Great Post Road.

for coal; the mines at Kara, which Kennan states were producing an annual average of 3,600 pounds of pure gold in the late nineteenth century; and the silver mines of Nerchinsk.

Records were started in 1823 and between this date and 1887, when Kennan consulted the books in Tomsk, 772,979 prisoners had passed through on their way to Siberia. They comprised *katorzhniki* (hard labour convicts) who were distinguishable by their half-shaved heads; *poselentsi* (penal colonists); *silni* (persons simply banished and allowed to return to Russia after serving their sentence), and *dobrovolni* (women and children voluntarily accompanying their husbands or fathers). Until the 1850s hard-labour convicts and penal colonists would be branded on the cheek with a letter to indicate the nature of their crime. More than half of those who crossed the Urals had had no proper trial but were exiled by 'administrative process'. As Kennan states: 'Every village commune has the right to banish any of its members who, through bad conduct or general worthlessness, have proved themselves obnoxious to their fellow citizens.'

Life in the cells

The first prison Kennan was shown round on his trip in 1887 was the Tyumen forwarding prison. He records the experience thus: 'As we entered the cell, the convicts, with a sudden jingling of chains, sprang to their feet, removed their caps and stood in a dense throng around the *nari* (wooden sleeping platforms)...."The prison" said the warden,"is terribly overcrowded. This cell for example is only 35 feet long by 25 wide, and has air space for 35, or at most 40 men. How many men slept here last night?" he inquired, turning to the prisoners. "A hundred and sixty, your high nobility", shouted half a dozen hoarse voices.....I looked around the cell. There was practically no ventilation and the air was so poisoned and foul that I could hardly force myself to breathe it in.'

The hospital cells

None of these dreadful experiences could prepare Kennan for the hospital cells, filled with prisoners suffering from typhus, scurvy, pneumonia, smallpox, diphtheria, dysentery and syphilis. He wrote afterwards: 'Never before in my life had I seen faces so white, haggard, and ghastly as those that lay on the gray pillows in the hospital cells....As I breathed that heavy, stifling atmosphere, poisoned with the breaths of syphilitic and fever-stricken patients, loaded and saturated with the odor of excrement, disease germs, exhalations from unclean human bodies, and foulness inconceivable, it seemed to me that over the hospital doors should be written "All hope abandon, ye who enter here".' From the records he discovered that almost thirty per cent of the patients in the prison hospital died each year. This he compared with 3.8 per cent for French prisons of the time, two per cent for American and 1.4 per cent for English prisons.

Corruption

As well as the grossly inhuman conditions he saw in the prisons, Kennan found that the whole exile system was riddled with corruption. Bribes were regularly accepted by warders and other officials. One provincial administrator boasted that his governor, the Governor of Tobolsk, was so careless that he could get him to sign any document he was given. As a wager he wrote out 'The Lord's Prayer' on an official form and placed it before the Governor who blindly signed it. The government in St Petersburg was too far away to know what was going on in the lands beyond the Urals.

Many high-ranking officials in Siberia were so tightly bound by bureaucratic ties that change was impossible, even if they desired it. An officer in the Tomsk prison confided in Kennan: 'I would gladly resign tomorrow if I could see the (exile) system abolished. It is disastrous to Siberia, it is ruinous to the criminal, and it causes an immense amount of misery; but what can be done? If we say anything to our superiors in St Petersburg, they strike us in the face; and they strike hard - it hurts!'

Political exiles

Life for the so-called 'politicals' and 'nihilists', banished to prevent them infecting European Russians with their criticisms of the autocratic political system that was choking the country to death, was luxury compared to that of the prisoners. Many came from rich aristocratic families and, after the move to Siberia, life for them continued in much the same way as it had west of the Urals. The most famous political exiles were the 'Decembrists': the men who took part in the unsuccessful coup in 1825. Many were accompanied into exile by their wives. Some of the houses in which they lived are now preserved as *Dom* ('house') museums in Irkutsk (see p168).

Kennan secretly visited many of the politicals in Siberia and was convinced that they did not deserve being exiled. He wrote later: 'If such men are in exile in a lonely Siberian village on the frontier of Mongolia, instead of being at home in the service of the state - so much the worse for the state.' A few politicals were sentenced to exile with the native Yakut tribe within the Arctic Circle. Escape was impossible and life with a Stone Age tribe must have seemed unbearable for cultured aristocrats who had until recently been part of the St Petersburg court circle.

Temporary abolition of the exile system

The exile system was abolished in 1900. However corrupt the system and inhuman the conditions in these early Siberian prisons, worse was to come only thirty years later. Under Stalin's regime, vast concentration camps (in European Russia as well as in Siberia) were set up to provide a huge slave-labour force to build roads, railways and factories in the 1930s and '40s. The camps were strictly off-limits to twentieth century George Kennans but former inmates have reported that the prisoners were grossly overworked and undernourished. The mortality rate in some of these camps is said to have been as high as thirty per cent. Reports of the number of people sentenced to these slave labour camps range from between three million and twenty million. Some reports place the death toll up to the late 1950s as high as eighteen million.

Political exiles (circa 1880), many of whom came from aristocratic families, were free to adopt whatever lifestyle they could afford within the confines of Siberia.

Early travellers

VICTORIAN ADVENTURERS

This was the great age of the gentleman (and gentlewoman) adventurer. These upper-class travellers spent the greater part of their lives exploring the lesser-known regions of the world, writing long and usually highly-readable accounts of their adventures and encounters with the 'natives'. Siberia attracted almost as many of this brave breed as did Africa and India. Once they had travelled across the great Siberian plain using the normal forms of transport of the time (carriage and sledge) they resorted to such new-fangled inventions as the bicycle (R.L.Jefferson in 1896), the train (from 1900) and then the car (the Italian Prince Borghese in an Itala in 1907). Some even crossed the country entirely on foot.

THE GREAT SIBERIAN POST ROAD

Before the railway was built, there was but one way for convicts, colonists and adventurers to cross this region: a rough track known as the Post Road or *Trakt*. Posting stations (see photograph opposite p112) were set up at approximately 25 mile intervals along the route, where travellers could rent horses and drivers. Murray, in his *Handbook for Russia, Poland and Finland* (1865 edition) told his travellers: 'Three kinds of conveyances are available: the *telega*, or cart without springs, which has to be changed at every station, and for which a charge of about 8d is made at every stage; the *kibitka* or cart (in winter a sledge) with a hood; and the *tarantass*, a kind of carriage on wooden springs which admits of the traveller lying down full length and which can be made very comfortable at night. The two latter vehicles have to be purchased at Perm, if the *telega*, or postal conveyance be not accepted. A *tarantass* may be bought from £12 to £15.'

George Kennan called the Imperial Russian Post System 'the most perfectly organised horse express service in the world'.

The discomforts of Siberian travel

Since a visit to Siberia could rarely be completed in a single season, most travellers experienced the different modes of transport used in summer and winter. They found the sledge more comfortable than the tarantass and indeed no nineteenth century travelogue would be complete without a detailed description of this unique vehicle. The tarantass had a large boat-shaped body and travellers stored their belongings on the floor, covering them with straw and mattresses on top of which they lay. Although this may sound comfortable, when experienced at speed over atrocious roads and for great distances, by contemporary accounts it was not. S.S.Hill wrote in 1854: 'The worst of the inconveniences arose from the deep ruts which were everywhere...and from the necessity of galloping down the declivities to force the carriage upon the bridges. And often our carriage fell with such force against the bridges that it was unsafe to retain our accustomed reclining position...'

Kate Marsden, a nurse travelling in 1894, recalled the agony of days spent in a tarantass in the following way: 'Your limbs ache, your muscles ache, your head aches, and, worst of all, your inside aches terribly."Tarantass rheumatism" internal and external, chronic, or rather perpetual, is the complaint.'

The yamshchiki
The driver (*yamshchik*) of the tarantass or sledge, was invariably drunk. He had to be bribed with vodka to make good time between the post stations and Murray's 1865 guide-book thoughtfully includes in its 'Useful Russian Phrases' section, the words 'Dam na vodki' ('I will give you drink money'). Accidents were commonplace and R.L. Jefferson (on a trip without his bicycle in 1895) wrote that his yamshchik became so inebriated that he fell off the sledge and died. The same fate befell one of Kate Marsden's sledge-drivers who had gone to sleep with the reins tied around his wrists. She wrote: 'And there was the poor fellow being tossed to and fro amongst the legs of the horses, which, now terrified, tore down the hill like mad creatures.... In a few minutes there was a fearful crash. We had come into collision with another tarantass and the six horses and the two tarantasses were mixed up in a chaotic mass'.

The horses
Sledges and tarantasses were pulled by a *troika*, a group of three horses. These were small furry specimens, 'not much larger than the average English donkey', noted R.L.Jefferson. They were hired between post stations and usually belonged to the yamshchik. S.S.Hill was shocked at the way in which these animals were treated. He remarked: 'The Arab is the friend of his horse. The Russian or Siberian peasant is his severe master who exacts every grain of his strength by blows accompanied with curses....lodges him badly or

not at all, cares little how he feeds him, and never cleans him or clips a hair of his body from the hour of his birth to that of his death.' Horses were worked literally until they died. R.L.Jefferson recalls that two of his animals dropped dead in harness and had to be cut free.

Dangers

Travel in Siberia was not only uncomfortable, it was also dangerous. Wolves and bears roamed the forests and when food was scarce would attack a horse or man (although you were safe in a tarantass). In the Amur region lived the world's largest tiger, the Amur tiger. Just as wild as these animals, and probably more dangerous, were the *brodyagi*, escaped convicts in search of money and a passport to readmit them to Europe.

Dirt and disease

As well as the discomfort of the 'conveyance' and the dangers along the *Trakt*, travellers were warned about the dirt and disease they could encounter. R.L.Jefferson wrote: 'No wonder that Siberia is looked upon by the traveller with abhorrence. Apart from its inhabitants, no one can say that Siberia is not a land of beauty, plenty and promise; but it is the nature of its inhabitants which make it the terrible place it is. The independence, the filth and general want of comfort which characterize every effort of the community, serve to make a visit to any Siberian centre a thing to be remembered for many years and an experience not desirable to repeat.'

Hotel rooms were universally squalid. Kate Marsden gives the following advice to anyone entering a hotel bedroom in Siberia: 'Have your pocket handkerchief ready...and place it close to your nostrils the moment the door is opened. The hinges creak and your first greeting is a gust of hot, foetid air.'

Insects

Especially in the summer months, travellers were plagued by flies and mosquitoes. Kate Marsden wrote: 'After a few days the body swells from their bites into a form that can neither be imagined nor described. They attack your eyes and your face, so that you would hardly be recognised by your dearest friend.'

At night, travellers who had stopped in the dirty hotels or posting stations were kept awake by lice, bed-bugs and a variety of other insects with which the bedding was infested. R.L.Jefferson met a man who never travelled without four saucers and a can of kerosene. In the hotel room at night he would put a saucer filled with kerosene under each bed-leg, to stop the bugs reaching him in bed. However,

(**Above**) Until the building of the Trans-Siberian, the Great Post Road formed the life-line for hundreds of tiny communities such as this. (**Below**) There were few bridges on the Road — crossing frozen rivers and lakes was treacherous in early winter and spring.

Jefferson noted that: 'With a sagacity which one would hardly credit so small an insect, it would make a detour by getting up the wall on to the ceiling, and then, having accurately poised, drop down upon the victim - no doubt to his extreme discomfort.'

Bovril and Jaeger underwear: essential provisions

R.L.Jefferson, who made several trips to Russia (three of which were on his Imperial Rover bicycle) never travelled without a large supply of Bovril and a change of Jaeger 'Cellular' underwear - 'capital stuff for lightness and durability' he wrote after one long ride. Kate Marsden shared his enthusiasm for Dr Jaeger's undergarments: 'without which it would have been quite impossible to go through all the changes of climate; and to remain for weeks together without changing my clothes', she wrote. On the subject of provisions for the trip, Murray recommended taking along basic foodstuffs. Miss Marsden packed into her tarantass 'a few boxes of sardines, biscuits, some bread, tea and one or two other trifles which included forty pounds of plum pudding'.

S.S.HILL'S *TRAVELS IN SIBERIA*

This account of Hill's Siberian adventures was the result of a journey made in the early 1850s to Irkutsk and then Yakutsk (now in the Far Eastern Territories). Armed with a pistol loaded with goose-shot (for the law forbade a foreigner to shoot at a Russian, even in self defence), he travelled by tarantass and existed on *shchi* (soup) and tea for most of the time. He makes some interesting observations upon the culinary habits of the Siberians he met along the way.

He records that on one occasion, when settling down to a bowl of shchi after a long winter's journey 'we found the taste of our accustomed dish, however, today peculiar'. He was made aware of the main ingredient of their soup later, 'by the yamshchik pointing out to us the marks of the axe upon the frozen carcass of a horse lying within a quarter of a verst of the site of our feast'. In some places even tea and shchi were unavailable and they could find only cedar nuts ('a favourite food article with the peasants of Eastern Siberia').

He ate better in Irkutsk, where, at a dinner party, he was treated to *comba* fish, six feet in length and served whole. 'I confess I never before saw so enormous an animal served or cooked whole save once, an ox roasted at a 'mop' in Worcestershire', he wrote later. He was shocked by the behaviour of the ladies at the table, who, when bored, displayed 'a very droll habit of rolling the damp crumb of rye bread... into pills'. He remarks with surprise that in Siberian society ' a glass of milk terminates the dinner'.

KATE MARSDEN VISITS SIBERIAN LEPERS

Miss Marsden was a nurse with a definite mission in Siberia. In the 1880s she learnt, through travellers' accounts, of the numerous leper colonies to the north of Yakutsk. There were rumours of a special herb found there, that could alleviate the symptoms of the disease. After an audience with Queen Victoria, during which she was given useful letters of introduction, she travelled to Moscow. She arrived, in mid-winter, wearing her thin cotton nurse's uniform and a white bonnet, which she immediately exchanged for thick Russian clothes.

Crossing Siberia

When she had met the Empress, who gave her a thousand roubles for her relief fund, she started on her long sledge ride. It was not a dignified send-off - 'three muscular policemen attempted to lift me into the sledge; but their combined strength was futile under the load'. She got aboard eventually and was soon experiencing the extreme discomfort of Siberian travel. She said it made her feel more like 'a battered old log of mahogany than a gently nurtured English-woman'.

Distributing tea, sugar and copies of the Gospel to convicts in the marching parties she encountered along the Post Road, she reached Irkutsk in the summer. She boarded a leaky barge on the Lena River, north of Lake Baikal and drifted down to Yakutsk, sitting on the sacks of potatoes with which the boat was filled. Of this part of the journey she wrote: 'Fortunately we had only about 3,000 miles of this but 3,000 miles were enough'. Her goal was still a 2,000 mile ride away when she reached Yakutsk. Although she had never been on a horse before, this brave woman arranged an escort of fifteen men and rode with them through insect infested swamps and across a fiery plain, below which the earth was in a constant state of combustion, until she reached the settlement of Viluisk.

The Lepers of Viluisk

On her arrival, the local priest informed her that 'On the whole of the earth you will not find men in so miserable a condition as the Smedni Viluisk lepers'. She found them dressed in rags, living in hovels and barely existing on a diet of rotten fish. This was in an area where, in winter, some of the lowest temperatures in the world have been recorded. Unfortunately she did not find the herb that was rumoured to exist there but left all the more convinced that finances must be raised for a hospital.

Although she managed to raise 25,000 roubles towards the enter-prise, her task was not made any easier by several individuals who took exception to her breezy style of writing, accusing her of having undertaken the journey for her own fame and fortune. Some even suggested that the journey was a fiction invented so that Miss Marsden could collect charitable sums for her own use. In the end she was forced to sue one of her attackers who wrote a letter to *The Times* describing her journey as 'only a little pleasure trip'. Nevertheless she achieved her aim: a hospital opened in Viluisk in 1897.

JEFFERSON'S BICYCLE TRIPS

R.L.Jefferson was an enthusiastic cyclist and traveller who made several journeys to Siberia in the 1890s. A year after bicycling from London to Constantinople and back, he set out again from Kennington Oval for Moscow on his Imperial Rover bicycle. Twelve hours out of Moscow, a speeding tarantass knocked him down, squashing the back wheel of his 'machine'. Repairs took a few days but he still managed to set a cycling speed record of just under fifty days for the 4,281 mile journey from London to Moscow and back.

His next ride was to the decaying capital of the Khanate of Khiva, now in Uzbekistan. The 6,000 mile journey took him across the Kirghiz Steppes in south-west Siberia, along the coast of the Aral Sea and over the Karakum Desert. When the bicycle's wheels sank up to their axles in the sand he had the Rover lashed to the back of a camel for the rest of the journey. While in Central Asia he lived on a diet of boiled mutton and *koumis* (fermented mares' milk). He travelled in a camel-hair suit (Jaeger, of course) and top boots, with a white cork helmet to complete the outfit.

Across Siberia
Jefferson then made two more trips to Siberia. In *Across Siberia by Bicycle* (1896), he wrote that he left Moscow and 'sleeping the night in some woodman's hut, subsisting on occasional lumps of black bread, bitten to desperation by fearful insects, and tormented out of my life during the day by swarms of mosquitoes, I arrived in Perm jaded and disgusted...'. He then cycled over the Urals and through the mud of the Great Post Road to Ekaterinburg. Here he was entertained by the Ekaterinburg Cyclists' Club whom he described as 'friends of the wheel - jolly good fellows all'.

Declaring that 'from a cyclist's point of view, Russian roads cannot be recommended', he abandoned his Rover in 1897 for the adventure described in *Roughing it in Siberia*. With three chums, he travelled by sledge from Krasnoyarsk up the frozen Yenisei ('jerking about like peas in a frying pan') to the gold mines in Minusinsk district, spending several weeks prospecting in the Syansk Mountains.

Building the railway

The first railway to be built in Russia was Tsar Nicholas I's private line (opened in 1836) which ran the ten miles from his capital, St Petersburg, to his summer palace at Tsarkoye Selo (Pushkin). The Tsar was said to have been most impressed with this new form of transport and over the next thirty years several lines were laid in European Russia, linking the main cities and towns. Siberia, however, was really too far away to deserve serious consideration since most people only went there if they were forced to as exiles. And as far as the Tsar was concerned, traditional methods of transport kept him supplied with all the gold and furs he needed.

PLANS FOR A TRANS-SIBERIAN RAILWAY

The earliest plans for long distance railways in Siberia came from a number of foreigners. Most books which include a history of the Trans-Siberian give a passing mention to an English engineer, if only because of his wildly eccentric ideas and his unfortunate name. Thus a Mr Dull has gone down in history as the man who seriously suggested the building of a line from Perm across Siberia to the Pacific, with carriages being pulled by wild horses (of which there were a great many in the region at the time). He is said to have formally proposed his plan to the Ministry of Ways of Communication, who turned it down.

The Englishman's name was, in fact, not Dull but Duff and it's not only his name that has been distorted through time. His descendants (John Howell and William Lawrie) have requested that the story be set straight. Thomas Duff was an enterprising adventurer who went out to China to seek his fortune in the 1850s. He returned to England via Siberia, spending some time in St Petersburg with wealthy aristocratic friends. Here he was introduced to the Minister of Ways of Communication and it was probably during their conversation that he remarked on the vast numbers of wild horses he had encountered on his journey. Could they not be put to some use? Perhaps they might be trained to pull the trains that people were saying would soon run across Siberia. It is unlikely that this remark was intended to be serious but it has gone down in history as a formal proposal for a horse-powered Trans-Siberian Express.

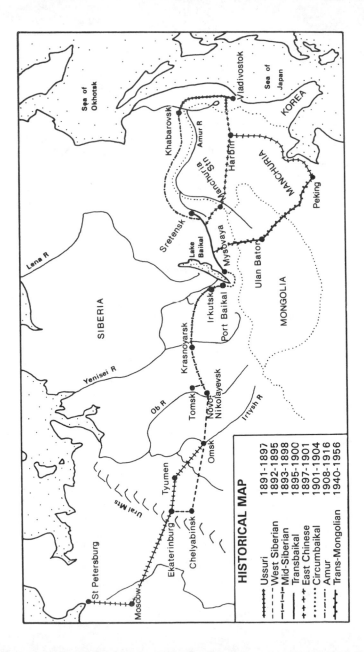

HISTORICAL MAP

++++ Ussuri	1891-1897	
---- West Siberian	1892-1895	
-··-··- Mid-Siberian	1893-1898	
—— Transbaikal	1895-1900	
+++ East Chinese	1897-1901	
········ Circumbaikal	1901-1904	
-··-··- Amur	1908-1916	
++++ Trans-Mongolian	1940-1956	

At around this time the American Perry McDonough Collins was exploring the Amur river, having persuaded the US government to appoint him as their commercial agent in the region. He had been given an enthusiastic welcome by Count Amurski Muravyev, the Governor-General of Siberia, before setting off to descend the Amur in a small boat. Collins envisaged a trade link between America and Siberia with vessels sailing up the Amur and Shilka rivers to Chita, where a railway link would shuttle goods to and from Irkutsk. He sent his plans for the building and financing of such a line to the government but these too were rejected. Collins' next venture, a telegraph link between America and Russia, also failed but not before he had made himself a considerable fortune.

It took a further twenty years for the government to become interested enough in the idea of a railway in Siberia to send surveyors to investigate the feasibility of such a project. Plans were considered for the building of lines to link the great Siberian rivers, so that future travellers could cross Siberia in relative comfort by a combination of rail and ship. European lines were extended from Perm over the Urals, reaching Ekaterinburg in 1878.

Tsar Alexander III : the railway's founder
In 1881 Alexander III became Tsar and in 1886 gave the Trans-Siberian project his official sanction with the words: 'I have read many reports of the Governors-General of Siberia and must own with grief and shame that until now the government has done scarcely anything towards satisfying the needs of this rich, but neglected country! It is time, high time!'

He was thus able to add 'Most August Founder of The Great Siberian Railway' to his many other titles. He rightly saw the railway as both the key to developing the land beyond the Urals and also as the means to transport his troops to the Amur region which was being threatened by the Chinese. When the commission looking into the building of the new line declared that the country did not have the money to pay for it, the Tsar solved the problem simply by forming a new committee, dismissing the first.

THE DECISION TO BUILD

The new commission took note of the petitions from Count Ignatyev and Baron Korf, the Governors-General of Irkutsk and the Amur territories, respectively. They proposed rail links between Tomsk and Irkutsk, Lake Baikal and Sretensk (where passengers could board ships for the journey down the Shilka and Amur Rivers to the coast) and for the Ussuri line to Vladivostok. Baron Korf considered that it was imperative for the Ussuri line to be built as soon as possible if the valuable port of Vladivostok was not to be cut off by the advancing Chinese. The Tsar took note and declared: 'I hope the Ministry will practically prove the possibility of the quick and cheap construction of the line'.

Surveys were commissioned and detailed plans prepared. In 1891 it was announced that the Trans-Siberian Railway would indeed be built and work would start immediately. It was, however, to be constructed as cheaply as possible using thinner rails, shorter sleepers and timber (rather than stone) for the smaller bridges.

The route

The railway committee decided that the great project should be divided into several sections with work commencing simultaneously on a number of them. The West Siberian Railway would run from Chelyabinsk (the railway over the Urals reached this town in 1892) to the Ob River where the settlement of Novo Nikolayevsk (now Novosibirsk) was being built. The Mid-Siberian Railway would link the Ob to Irkutsk, the capital of Eastern Siberia. Passengers would cross Lake Baikal on ferries to Mysovaya, the start of the Transbaikal Railway to Sretensk. From here they would continue to use the Shilka and Amur River for the journey to Khabarovsk, until the Amur Railway could be built between these towns. The Ussuri Railway would link Khabarovsk with Vladivostok. There were also plans for a shortcut from the Transbaikal area to Vladivostok, across Manchuria. This would be known as the East Chinese Railway.

Nicholas lays the foundation stone

After the decision to start work, the Tsar wrote the following letter to his son, the Tsarevich, who had just reached Vladivostok at the end of a tour around the world: 'Having given the order to build a continuous line of railway across Siberia, which is to unite the rich Siberian provinces with the railway system of the interior, I entrust you to declare My will, upon your entering the Russian dominions after your inspection of the foreign countries of the East. At the same time I desire you to lay the first stone at Vladivostok for the construction of the Ussuri line forming part of the Siberian Railway...'

On 31 May 1891, Nicholas carried out his father's wishes, filling a wheelbarrow with earth and emptying it onto what was to become part of the embankment for the Ussuri Railway. He then laid the foundation stone for the station.

RAILWAY CONSTRUCTION: PHASE 1 (1891-1901)

● **The Ussuri, West Siberian & Mid-Siberian Railways (1891-98)**
Work started on the Ussuri line (Vladivostok to Khabarovsk) some time after the inauguration ceremony and proceeded slowly. In July 1892, the construction of the West Siberian (Chelyabinsk to the west bank of the Ob River) was begun. In July 1893 work started on the Mid-Siberian (east bank of the Ob to Irkutsk). The West Siberian reached Omsk in 1894 and was completed when the rails reached the Ob in October 1895. The Ussuri Railway was completed in 1897 and in the following year the final rails of the Mid-Siberian were laid and Irkutsk was linked to Moscow and St Petersburg.

● **The Transbaikal Railway (1895-1900)** The rail link between the Lake Baikal port of Mysovaya and Sretensk on the Shilka River was begun in 1895. In spite of a flood which swept part of the track away in 1897, the line was completed by the beginning of 1900.

Passengers could now travel to Irkutsk by train, take the ferry across Lake Baikal and the train again from Mysovaya to Srtensk, where steamers would take them to Khabarovsk.

● **The East Chinese Railway (1897-1901)** Surveys showed that the proposed Amur Railway between Sretensk and Khabarovsk would be expensive to build because of the mountainous region it would have to pass through and the large supplies of explosives required to deal with the permafrost. In 1894 the Russian government granted China a generous loan to help pay off China's debts to Japan. In exchange for this financial help, a secret treaty was signed between Russia and China allowing the former to build and control a rail link between the Transbaikal region and Vladivostok, across the Chinese territory of Manchuria. Every difficulty encountered in building railways in Siberia (severe winters, mountains, rivers, floods, disease and bandits) were part of the construction of the East Chinese Railway, begun in 1897 and open to light traffic in 1901.

The labour force
The greater part of the Trans-Siberian Railway was built without heavy machinery by men with nothing more than wooden shovels. They nevertheless managed to lay up to two and a half miles of rail on a good day. Most of the labour force had to be imported as the local peasants were already fully employed on the land. They came not only from European Russia but also from as far away as Italy and Turkey. Chinese coolies were employed on the Ussuri Railway but overseers found them unreliable and terrified of the Amur tigers

with which the area was infested. The government soon turned to the prisons to relieve the shortage of labour and gangs of convicts were put to work on the lines. They were paid twenty-five kopecks (a quarter of a rouble) a day and had their sentences reduced - eight months on the railways counted for a year in prison. The 1500 convicts employed on the Mid-Siberian worked hard but those brought in from Sakhalin Island to work on the Ussuri line ran riot and terrorised the inhabitants of Vladivostok.

Shortage of materials
On many parts of the Siberian Plain engineers discovered that although there were vast forests of trees, none of them was suitable for using as sleepers (ties). Timber had to be imported over great distances. Rails came from European Russia and some even from Britain. They were either shipped via the Kara Sea (a southern part of the Arctic Ocean) and up the Yenisei River to Krasnoyarsk, or else right around the continent by boat to Vladivostok (which took two months). From here, when work started on the Transbaikal line in 1895, materials had to be shipped up the Ussuri, Amur and Shilka Rivers to Sretensk (over 1000 miles). Horses and carts were scarce in Siberia and these, too, had to be brought in from Europe.

Difficult terrain
When the railway between St Petersburg and Moscow was being planned, the Tsar took ruler and pencil and drew a straight line between the two cities, declaring that this was the route to be followed, with almost every town by-passed. For the Trans-Siberian, Alexander ordered that it be built as cheaply as possible which is why in some places the route twists and turns so that expensive tunnelling might be avoided.

There were few problems in laying foundations for the rails across the open steppe land of the Siberian plain but cutting through the almost impenetrable forests of the taiga proved extremely difficult. Much of this area was not only thickly forested but swampy in summer and frozen in winter until July. Consequently the building season lasted no more than four months in most places.

In eastern Siberia parts of the ground were locked in permafrost and, even in mid-summer, had to be dynamited or warmed with fires before rails could be laid. The most difficult terrain was the short line around the southern end of Lake Baikal, the Circumbaikal Loop, which required over 200 trestles and bridges and 33 tunnels.

Conditions
For the workers who laboured in Siberia, conditions were hardly the most enjoyable. All were far from home, living in isolated log cabins

that were not much cleaner or more comfortable than the squalid prison in Tyumen, graphically described by George Kennan in *Siberia and the Exile System*. Winters were very long and extremely cold. The brief summer brought relief from the cold but the added discomfort of plagues of black flies and mosquitoes in the swamps of the taiga. There were numerous outbreaks of disease. Workers on the East Chinese Railway were struck first by an outbreak of bubonic plague in 1899 and cholera in 1902. In many places the horses were wiped out by Siberian anthrax.

There were other dangers in addition to disease. In Manchuria and the Amur and Ussuri regions, the forests were filled with Amur tigers for whom the occasional railway labourer no doubt made a pleasant snack. In Manchuria construction camps were frequently raided by bandits (*hunghutzes*) who roamed around the country in gangs of up to seven hundred men. As a result, the Russian government was obliged to allocate considerable sums of money and men to the policing of the region.

There were several set-backs that no one could have foreseen. In July 1897 severe flooding swept away or damaged over two hundred miles of track near Lake Baikal on the Transbaikal line, also destroying settlements and livestock. Damage was estimated at six million roubles. In other areas landslides were caused by torrential rainfall.

RAILWAY CONSTRUCTION: PHASE 2 (1898-1916)

Reconstruction

As the first trains began to travel over the newly-laid tracks, the shortsightedness of the policy of building the railway as cheaply as possible soon became clear. Many of the materials used in its construction were either sub-standard or unsuitable to the conditions they were expected to withstand. The rails were under half the weight of those used in America and fashioned of iron of an inferior quality. They soon bent and buckled and needed replacing. The ballast under the sleepers was far thinner than that put down on the major railways of Europe. As a result, the ride in the carriages was bumpy and uncomfortable and speed had to be kept down to 13 mph for passenger trains, 8 mph for freight. Foreign engineers proclaimed the whole system unsafe and were proved correct by the frequent derailments which took place.

In 1895 Prince Khilkov became Minister of Ways of Communication. On a tour of inspection along the West and Mid-Siberian lines he quickly realised that a massive rebuilding programme would have to be put into operation. Extra trains were also needed to transport the hundreds of thousands of emigrants who were now flooding over the Urals. In 1899 about 100 million roubles were allocated for repairs, work which would have been unnecessary had sufficient funds been made available from the start.

● **The Circumbaikal Loop Line (1901-1904)** In 1901 work began on the 260km Circumbaikal Loop line around Lake Baikal's southern shores. The initial project had been shelved in 1893, since the terrain was considered too difficult. Passengers used the ferry service across the lake but it was soon found that the ships couldn't cope with the increased traffic. The situation became critical at the start of the Russo-Japanese war in 1904, when troops and machinery being sent to the East by rail were delayed at the lake. Construction of the new line continued as fast as possible and by the end of the year the final section of the Trans-Siberian was opened. Passengers were at last able to travel from Calais to Vladivostok entirely by train.

● **The Amur Railway (1907-1916)** The original plans for a railway from Sretensk to Khabarovsk along the Shilka and Amur Rivers were abandoned because the route would entail expensive engineering work. After the Russo-Japanese war in 1904-5, the government realised that there was a danger of Japan taking control of Manchuria and the East Chinese Railway. This was the only rail-link to Russia's naval base at Vladivostok. It was therefore decided that the Amur Railway must indeed be built. Work began at Kuenga in 1908. There were the usual problems of insects, disease and permafrost but with the rest of the railway operational, it was easier to transport men and materials to the Amur area. When the bridge over the Amur at Khabarovsk was finished in 1916, the Trans-Siberian Railway was at last complete. Over 1000 million roubles had been spent on building all the sections (including the East Chinese line) since 1891.

THE FIRST RAILWAY TRAVELLERS

Rail service begins

As each of the sectors of the Trans-Siberian was completed, a rail service was begun. To say that there were teething troubles would be a gross understatement; there was a shortage of engines and carriages, most of the system operated without a timetable and there were frequent delays and derailments along the shoddily constructed line. Nevertheless, in order to attract foreign travellers, luxury trains and 'Expresses' were introduced. Those run by the government were known as Russian State Expresses while another service was operated by the Belgian 'Compagnie Internationale des Wagons-Lits'. In 1900 the Ministry of Ways of Communication published their detailed *Guide to The Great Siberian Railway* in English.

The Paris Exhibition

The Russian government was keen to show off to the world the country's great engineering feat and at the Paris 'Exposition Universelle' of 1900, a comprehensive Trans-Siberian exhibit was staged. Amongst photographs and maps of Siberia, with Kirghiz, Buryat and Goldi robes and artifacts, there were several carriages to be operated by the Wagons-Lits Company on the Great Siberian Railway. They were furnished in the most sumptuous style, with just four spacious compartments in the sleeping carriages, each with a connecting lavatory. The other carriages contained a smoking-room done up in Chinese style, a library and music-room complete with piano.

In the two restaurant cars, decorated with mahogany panelling and heavy curtains, visitors to the exhibition could dine on the luxurious fare that was promised on the journey itself. To give diners the feeling of crossing Siberia, a length of canvas on which was painted a Siberian panorama of wide steppes, thick taiga and little villages of log cabins, could be seen through the windows. In order to complete the illusion that the train was actually chugging across the Great Siberian Plain, the painted panorama was made to move past the windows by mechanical means.

Visitors were intrigued and impressed and more than a few soon set off on the epic trip. The reality, they were to discover, was a little different from what they experienced at the exhibition.

Early rail travellers

When R.L.Jefferson set out to investigate the Minusinsk gold-mining region in 1897, he was able to take the train (travelling for once without his Imperial Rover bicycle but no doubt taking along a good supply of Bovril and 'Cellular' underwear) as far as Krasnoyarsk.

The first English woman to travel the entire length of this route was Annette Meakin, who took her aged mother for company on the journey made in 1900. They travelled via Paris to see the Siberian display at the Paris Exhibition. Having crossed Siberia, they went by ship to Japan and then to North America, crossing that continent by train too. Having circumnavigated the globe by rail, Miss Meakin recorded her experiences in the book she called *A Ribbon of Iron*.

Two years later, in 1902, Michael Myres Shoemaker took *The Great Siberian Railway from St Petersburg to Pekin* (the name of his account of the journey). He wrote enthusiastically: 'This Railway will take its place amongst the most important works of the world .... Russia is awakening at last and moving forward.'

It is interesting to compare the descriptions these travellers give of the trains they took, with the carriages displayed at the Paris Exhibition as well as with the service operated today by Russian Railways.

The carriages

Advertising brochures informed prospective Trans-Siberian travellers, in gushing prose, that the carriages in which they were to be conveyed would be of a standard equal to those used by European royalty. In addition to the luxurious sleeping compartments and dining cars shown at the Paris Exhibition, there would be a bathroom with marble bath-tub, a gymnasium equipped with a stationary bicycle and other exercising machines, a fire-proof safe, a hair-dressing salon and a darkroom equipped with all the chemicals a photographer would need. The carriages would be lit by electric lighting, individually heated in winter and cooled by under-floor ice-boxes in summer.

Although more than a few of those luxurious appointments, which they had seen in the carriages of the Siberian exhibit in Paris, were missing on their train, Annette Meakin and her mother found their accommodation entirely satisfactory. She wrote: 'The Siberian express is a kind of "Liberty Hall", where you can shut your door and sleep all day if you prefer it, or eat and drink, smoke and play cards if you like that better. An electric bell summons a serving-man to make your bed or sweep your floor, as the case may be, while a bell on the other side summons a waiter from the buffet....Time passes very pleasantly on such a train.'

The ride was not so comfortable for the Meakins from Mysovaya on the Transbaikal Railway. Only fourth class carriages were provided and they were forced to take their travelling rugs and picnic hamper to the luggage van, where they spent the next four days.

Travelling in 1902, Michael Myres Shoemaker was very impressed with the bathing arrangements on the train and wrote: 'I have just discovered that there is a fine bathroom in the restaurant car, large and tiled, with all sorts of sprays, plunges and douches. This bath has its separate attendant and all the bath towels you may demand.' He was less enthusiastic about his travelling companions, a French Consul and family whose fox terrier 'promptly domesticated itself in my compartment'.

The restaurant car

At the Paris Exhibition visitors were led to believe that a good part of the enjoyment of travelling on the Trans-Siberian would be the cordon bleu cuisine served in the restaurant car. It was claimed that the kitchens were even equipped with water tanks filled with live fish. The waiters would be multi-lingual and a truly international service was promised.

Travellers found the above description to be something of an exaggeration. Annette Meakin reported the existence of a Bechstein piano and a library of Russian novels in the restaurant car. Shoe-maker wrote: 'The restaurant car is just like all those on the trains of Europe. There is a piano, generally used to hold dirty dishes. There are three very stupid waiters who speak nothing save Russian. The food is very poor.'

Travellers were warned by their guide-books that there were occasional food shortages and advised to take along a picnic hamper. The Meakins found theirs invaluable on their four-day jaunt in the luggage van. In fact, for the first few years after the service began, there had been no restaurant cars. R.L.Jefferson wrote that at meal-times, the train would stop at a convenient station and all passengers (and the engine-driver) would get off for a meal at the station. Trav-elling in 1901, John Foster Fraser reports, in *The Real Siberia*, that locals did good business on the platforms selling 'dumplings with hashed meat and seasoning inside....huge loaves of new made bread, bottles of beer, pails of milk, apples, grapes, and fifty other things'.

The church car
Behind the baggage car was a peculiar carriage known as the church car. It was a Russian Orthodox Church on wheels, complete with icons and candelabra inside, church bells and a cross on the roof, and a peripatetic priest who dispensed blessings along the way. This carriage was detached at stations and settlements where churches had not yet been built and services were conducted for railway workers and their families.

Transport of emigrants
While foreign visitors discussed whether or not their accommodation was all that the Siberian exhibit in Paris had led them to believe, emigrants travelled in the unenviable conditions described by R.L.Jefferson: 'The emigrants' train is simply one of the cattle trucks, each car being marked on the side "Forty men or eight horses". There are no seats or lights provided, and into each of these pens forty men, women and children have to herd over a dreary journey of fourteen or fifteen days...They have to provide their own food but at every station a large samovar is kept boiling in order to provide them with hot water for their tea.'

By the end of the century they were crossing the Urals to Siberia at the rate of about a quarter of a million peasants each year.

Stations
Little wooden station buildings mushroomed along the railway. Russian stations were traditionally given a class number from one to five. Of the stations listed in the official *Guide to the Great Siberian*

Railway, none was of the first class and the majority were no more than fifth class. Beside most stations there towered a water-tank to supply the steam engines. Many of these towers, their eaves decorated with ornate fretwork, can still be seen today. Most of the larger stations also had their own churches and resident priests. If the train did not have a church car, stops would be made for lengthy services at these railside churches, especially on the eve of an important saint's day.

R.L.Jefferson found that in the early years of the railways, the arrival and departure of every train at a Siberian station was quite an event, being 'attended with an amount of excitement that it is hard to associate with the usually stolid Russian. Particularly is this so in Eastern Russia where railways are new and interesting.' A man ' performs a terrific tintinabulation on a large suspended bell. All the conductors blow whistles.' Jefferson goes on to explain that none of the passengers was allowed out of the train until the engine driver had got down and shaken hands with the station-master and his staff.

Delays

Because the original line was so badly laid, the ride in the carriages was rough and uncomfortable and speed had to be kept down. There were frequent derailments and long delays. Annette Meakin complained: 'We stopped at a great many stations; indeed on some parts of the route we seemed to get into a chronic state of stopping'. 'All day long at a dog trot,' wrote Shoemaker, 'Certainly no more than ten miles an hour.' Over some sections the train went so slowly passengers could get out and pick flowers as they walked along beside it. Still, the delays did give one time to catch up on current affairs, as Miss Meakin observes when her train was delayed for four hours ('a mere nothing in Siberia') at Taiga. She writes: 'As we sat waiting in the station the good news was brought that Mafeking had been relieved.'

Bridges

Although the rails were badly laid and of poor quality, the bridges that were made of stone were built to such a high standard that many are still in use today. They were largely the work of Italian masons, who laboured throughout the winter months, the bridge-building season, since no work could be done on the snow-covered line. Many labourers caught hypothermia while they worked in temperatures as low as -40°C, dropping to their death on the ice below.

If a bridge was not finished in the winter when the railway lines reached it, engineers had had the brilliant idea of laying rails across the ice. The sleepers were literally frozen onto the surface of the river by large amounts of water being poured over them. When R.L.Jefferson's train reached the track laid across the Chulim River, passengers were made to get out and walk, in case the train proved too great a weight for the ice to bear. He wrote: 'As it passed us we felt the ice quiver, and heard innumerable cracks, like the reports of pistols in the distance, but the train got across the centre safely.'

Breakdowns

These were all too frequent. A wait of twenty-four hours for a new engine was not regarded as a long delay. Annette Meakin recorded the following incident: 'Outside Kainsk the train stopped. "The engine has smashed up," said a jolly Russian sailor in broken English. "She is sixty years old and was made in Glasgow. She is no use any more"....The poor old engine was now towed to her last berth....I had whipped out my "Kodak" and taken her photograph, thinking of Turner's "Fighting Temeraire".'

Cost of the journey

The *Guide to the Great Siberian Railway* informed its readers that, for the journey from London to Shanghai: 'The conveyance by the Siberian Railway will be over twice as quick and two and a half times cheaper than that now existing' (the sea passage via the Suez Canal). The cost of a first class ticket for the sixteen day journey was to be 319 roubles. From Moscow to Vladivostok the price was 114 roubles.

THE RAILWAY IN THE TWENTIETH CENTURY

After the Revolution

'When the trains stop, that will be the end,' announced Lenin and the trains continued to run, the Trans-Siberian included, throughout these troubled times.

When the new Bolshevik government pulled out of the First World War in early 1918, a Czech force of 50,000 well-armed men found themselves marooned in Russia, German forces preventing them getting back to western Europe. Receiving permission to leave Russia via Vladivostok, they set off on the Trans-Siberian. Their passage was not a smooth one for the Bolsheviks suspected that the Czechs would join the White Russian resistance movement; the Czechs suspected that the Bolsheviks were not going to allow them to leave. Violence erupted, several Czechs were arrested and the rest of the legion decided they would shoot their way out of Russia. They took over the Trans-Siberian line from the Urals to Lake Baikal and travelled the railway in armour-plated carriages.

The Civil War in Siberia (1918-20)

At this time Siberia was divided amongst a number of forces, all fighting against the Bolsheviks but not as a combined unit. Many of the leaders were nothing more than gangsters. East Siberia and Manchuria were controlled by the evil Ataman Semenov, half-Russian, half Buryat and supported by the Japanese. He charged around Transbaikalia murdering whole villages and, to alleviate the boredom of these mass executions, a different method of death was adopted each day. Then there was Baron General von Ungern Sternberg, one of the White Russian commanders whose cruelty rivalled that of Semenov. The Americans, French, English and Japanese all brought troops into Siberia to evacuate the Czech legions and to help Admiral Kolchak, the Supreme Ruler of the White Government which was based at Omsk. Kolchak, however, failed to win the support of the people in the Siberian towns, his troops were ill-disciplined and in November 1919 he lost Omsk to the Bolsheviks. He was executed in Irkutsk in early 1920 and the Allies abandoned the White Russian cause. The Japanese gave up Vladivostok in 1922 and all Siberia was then in Communist hands.

Reconstruction

After the Civil War the Soviet Union set about rebuilding its battered economy. High on the priority list was the repair of the Trans-Siberian line, so that raw materials like iron ore could be transported to European Russia. The First Five Year Plan (1928) set ambitious goals for the expansion of industry and agriculture. It also included new railway projects, the double-tracking of the Trans-Siberian and the building of the Turk-Sib, the line built between Turkestan and Novosibirsk. Work began on two giant industrial complexes known as the Ural-Kuznetsk Combine. Iron ore from the Urals was taken by rail to the Kuznetsk in Siberia, where it was exchanged for coal to take back to the Ural blast furnaces. For all these giant projects an enormous, controllable labour force was needed and this was to a large extent provided by prisoners from the corrective labour camps.

The Second World War

Siberia played an important backstage role in the Great Patriotic War. Many factories were moved from European Russia to Siberia and the populations of cities such as Novosibirsk rose dramatically. The Trans-Siberian's part was a vital one and loads of coal and food were continuously despatched over the Urals to Europe throughout the war years.

The Trans-Siberian today

THE TRAIN

Engines
If you imagined you would be hauled across Siberia by a puffing steam locomotive you will be sadly disappointed. Soviet Railways (SZD), now Russian Railways (RZD), began converting the system to electricity in 1927 (1.5kV dc on suburban routes; 3kV dc 25kV ac 50Hz elsewhere). The Trans-Siberian line is now almost entirely electrified. Engines are usually Czech Skoda ChS2's (line voltage 3kV dc; max output 4620kW; max speed 160kph; weight 126 tonnes) and ChS4T's (25kV 50 Hz; 5200kW; 180kph; 126 tonnes) or Russian-built VL10's or VL60's. On the Moscow-St Petersburg route the latest Czech-built engines are used: the CS200 (3kV dc; 8400kW; 200kph; 157 tonnes) and the CS7 developed from it.

Where electrification has yet to be completed (Eastern Siberia) diesel, rather than steam, engines are used. They are usually Russian-built 2TE10L/M/V types (with overhanging windscreens) or sometimes an Em6Y triple unit. If you're continuing on the Trans-Mongolian or Trans-Manchurian routes to Beijing, it is quite likely that a steam loco will be hitched to your carriages, at least for shunting duties. Although steam engines have officially been phased out in Russia, there were still over 6000 on the books in the early 1990s, many lining the tracks in several stations along the way. Their numbers are shrinking fast now as they are sold off to German scrap merchants for hard currency. See below for identification information and class numbers.

Carriages and carriage attendants
Most of the carriages now used are of East German origin, solidly-built, warm in winter and each staffed by an attendant (*provodnitsa/si* (female) *provodnik/i* (male) in Russian, *fuwuyuen* in Chinese), whose 'den' is situated at one end of the carriage. Their duties include collecting your tickets, letting down the carriage steps at stations, coming round with the vacuum-cleaner each day and providing you with tea (good but without milk) or coffee (utterly disgusting). You pay for what you've drunk on your trip (usually less than £1/US$1.50 in total) just before you reach your destination. The provodnitsi also stoke the solid-fuel boiler which heats the car-

riage and the samovar (*batchok*). Situated opposite the attendant's compartment at one end of the carriage, the samovar provides a continuous supply of boiling water for drinks. There are doors at both ends of the carriages and if you're a smoker the only place on the train where you will be allowed to indulge your habit is in this area between the carriages (unheated in winter).

Carriages are air-conditioned in summer but in order to operate all windows (and doors) must be kept shut, since the system works on the pressure difference between the inside and outside of the carriage and takes about an hour to get going. The initial instinct (and certainly that of the Russian passengers) is to open all the windows, and the carriage attendant wages a constant battle with everyone to keep them closed. Music (either radio or cassettes) is piped to the compartments from the provodnitsa's den; the knob above the window controls the volume.

'On both sectors of the journey we had two *provodniks* and both were husband and wife. A small gift early on smoothed the way and they were all very friendly, helpful and efficient. An example of this was when I discovered one of my small gold earrings was missing. Valia had just hoovered our compartment so she put on rubber gloves, emptied out the contents and found it among the dust'. **Joan Nicholls** (UK).

Compartments

● **Deluxe First Class (Trans-Mongolian train only)** The closest you can get to luxury accommodation while crossing Siberia, these two berth compartments have attached shower-rooms (the only showers on any of the trains), wider bunks, wood panelling, a wind-down window, armchair, table-lamp with frilly shade and plush green carpet. See photo opposite page 113.

● **Soft/First Class** Can be two berths and a washbasin or else the standard hard class four berth compartment, with only two berths used (no wash-basin but more space). On the Trans-Mongolian trains there's a choice between Deluxe First Class (see above) and standard first class which is four people in a hard class compartment with seat covers - not really worth the extra money. Make sure you know what you're getting - I met a honeymooning couple who found themselves sharing a four-berth first class compartment.

● **Hard/Tourist/Second Class** All four berths are used. There is adequate stowage space under the lower bunks and over the door. Bedding is provided and sheets are supposed to be changed every three days. Most travellers find Hard Class perfectly comfortable.

● **Dormitory/Third Class** Foreign travellers are unlikely to be able to get tickets for this class. The carriages are open-plan, similar to Hard Class in China, with doorless compartments containing four bunks in tiers of two with another bunk opposite them, beside the corridor.

Bathroom

Sadly the marble bath-tub (ingeniously designed so that the water would not spill as the train rounded a corner) and the copious supplies of hot water and towels that Michael Myres Shoemaker enthused over on his trip in 1902 are no more. The lack of proper bathing facilities is usually the biggest grumble from people who've done the trip. Apart from in the Deluxe First Class compartments of the Trans-Mongolian there are no showers on the train - a ridiculous oversight. With most of the rail system now electrified there is a cheap power source for heated shower units but no doubt it will be years before they are installed.

Bathing in a Chinese spittoon

A week was a short time to go without a bath in Siberia, we were told, but this didn't make the prospect any more appealing. In pre-Revolution days most Russian peasants spent the whole winter without having a bath. Shopping for supplies on a freezing December afternoon in Beijing before we left, we resolved to find some kind of bucket or basin to facilitate washing on the train. In one shop we found weighty china buckets with bamboo handles and in another a plastic bath designed for a large baby and complete with a little holder for the soap. In the end we settled for something smaller, an enamel spittoon (diameter 9ins/23mm) which turned out to fit the basin in the train exactly. It could be filled from the samovar in the corridor (to the astonishment of the Chinese passengers who knew the true purpose of the utensil we employed for bathing purposes) and it greatly simplified the difficult process of washing.

In every carriage there's a 'bathroom' at each end and it now appears to be standard practice for the carriage attendants to keep one locked for their personal use. Complaining about this is unlikely to achieve anything but a strategic friendly gift might gain you access. This small cubicle contains a basin and a lavatory with a seat that springs up. To flush the lavatory, fully depress the foot pedal, hold it down and lean back out of the way, as the contents have a nasty habit of going the wrong way if the train is moving fast.

The taps on the basin are operated by pushing up the little lever situated in the water outlet. In some carriages a foot pedal operates the taps. If there's a hot tap you'll need to run it for a while before the water warms up. Don't forget to bring along a universal plug (or a squash ball) for the basin, soap and lavatory paper. One of these items is usually available but never all three together. There's a socket for an electric razor but you may need to ask the provodnitsa to turn it on. Best time to visit is early in the morning when the bathroom's just been cleaned. Note that it's locked for the several hours it takes to get across the borders.

Restaurant cars

One of the myths that has sprung up amongst prospective travellers is that you'll get better food if you take the Chinese (Trans-Mongolian) train. As is the custom with international rail travel, restaurant-cars belonging to the country through which the train is travelling are attached to the train at the border. Regardless of which train you're on, when you're travelling through China you'll be eating in a restaurant car supplied by Chinese Railways; at the border with Mongolia this will be replaced by a Mongolian restaurant-car; while the same train is on Russian territory meals will be provided by a restaurant-car from Russian Railways.

Note that on the Trans-Mongolian train there is usually no restaurant car service between the Russian border and Ulan Bator.

● **Russian restaurant-car** You may be feasting on caviare as you rattle across the Siberian steppes but only if you've brought along your own supplies. The food was never much to write home about and financial hardship in Russia has not made things any better but it's true to say that the quality of the food seems to vary very much between one Russian restaurant-car and the next. Comments from recent travellers: 'The restaurant staff buy a lot of fresh produce from local traders at the station stops and are most creative in their use' (Susan Sexton, UK); 'Having flown with Aeroflot many times and experiencing their food, I was pleasantly surprised by the Russian dining-car' (Jacqui Williams, Japan).

On entering the restaurant-car (having averted your eyes from the grubby kitchen to preserve your appetite) you may be presented with the menu, almost invariably in Russian and often running to ten pages or more. The only dishes available will be indicated by a pencilled-in price or added in an almost indecipherable scrawl. The choice includes egg or tomato salad (the white sauce is not mayonnaise but sour cream - actually rather good), *shchi* (thick cabbage soup with meat), *solyanka* (meat soup, thick and nourishing), meatballs and mash or macaroni, smoked *teshka* fish (like hunks of smoked salmon), *skumbria* fish (usually fried and quite good), beef Stroganov, boiled chicken or duck, tea and coffee, and occasionally cakes. Piles of bread and various fizzy drinks (*napitok*) and fruit juice (*sok*) are also on sale. A full meal will cost about £2.50/US$4.

There are usually two people serving, each with their own half of the restaurant-car (one won't serve you if you're in the other half). Small gifts or tips given early on in the trip will help encourage attentive service.

The trend towards free trade means that the restaurant-car staff can now sell all sorts of goodies on the side. Banned for several years, alcohol is now sold on the train again. You should be able to get chilled Russian champagne (£3.25/US$5), vodka, chocolate bars and cartons of fruit juice. Some restaurant-cars even show videos, charging passengers an entry fee to watch bootleg copies of American movies.

Getting better service

The food you're served in the Russian restaurant-car seems to depend entirely on your relationship with the staff. I thought greasy lumps of compressed beef with fried eggs and rice were de rigeur until a recent trip with a flamboyantly friendly Australian/Ukrainian lady, who made a point of introducing herself and her friends to the staff of each car. Not only did she discover that the waiters and cooks were all invariably distant relatives or old family friends but the food was spectacular. Excellent pelmeni, tasty Stroganov: the cooks all rustled up their 'specials' for the crazy Australian and her entourage. Over at the adjacent tables, meanwhile, glum Russians tucked into greasy chunks of beef with eggs on top.

● **Mongolian restaurant-car** The main differences between the Mongolian and the Russian restaurant-cars are that in the Mongolian car you're likely to get a menu in English, you'll have to pay in US$ (bring lots of change because the waiters won't have any) and that there are usually a couple of psychedelically coloured plastic flowers on each table.

Delicacies include 'main course with roast potatoes, main course with rice, main course with noodles and main course with cabbage; all priced from US$3-5. Tea is US$0.50 and coffee US$1; a Pepsi costs US$1. Some Mongolian cars have extensive stocks of duty frees and even souvenirs.

● **Chinese restaurant-car** Travellers tend to agree that the food in the Chinese car is the best. There is more choice, it's true, but it's the most expensive of the three. For US$3 you'll get a breakfast of eggs, bread, jam and tea. Lunch and supper consist of tomato salad (US$2), cold chicken or sauté chicken with hot sauce and peanuts (US$3), fish (US$2.50), sweet & sour pork (US$3), sauté beef or egg plant with dried shrimp. Drinks include beer (US$0.50), cola (US$1) and mineral water (US$1).

LIFE ON THE TRAIN

Most people imagine they'd get bored on so long a journey but you may be surprised at how quickly the time flies by. Don't overdo the number of books you bring: *War and Peace* weighing in at 1,444 pages is a frequent choice, although I know of only one person who actually managed to finish it on the trip. There are so many other things to do apart from reading. You can have monosyllabic conversations with inquisitive Russians, meet the other Westerners on the train, play cards or chess, visit the restaurant car or hop off at the stations for a little exercise. The Trans-Siberian is, as Annette Meakin wrote in 1900, a veritable 'Liberty Hall', and 'time passes very pleasantly on such a train'.

Local travellers
Unlike the Orient Express, the trains that cross Siberia are working trains, not tourist specials. Russian passengers are extremely friendly and genuinely interested in foreign travellers. Sharing her compartment with three Russians, a winter traveller writes: 'Inside the carriage there's interest on both sides. Five hours ago my Walkman was borrowed (with only one tape inside it). It has just been returned with a helpless gesture - the battery (surprise, surprise) has run out. Great concern all round about my travelling unaccompanied and questions as to the whereabouts of my parents. Much shaking of heads and 'tutting'. There's plenty for me to find out. The thin man (with cold eyes that have gradually thawed over the last two days) has five children and is going to Moscow to get stomach medicine for one of them (or for himself?). The large motherly *babushka* in the corner who has been so kind to me is an artist, going to visit her son (or is the son an artist?). The fourth member of the compartment played chess with me last night, totally baffled by my tactics (there weren't any) so that we ended with a stalemate. He hasn't offered again. So much can be achieved with not a word of language in common.' **Heather Oxley** (UK)

The Trans-Siberian time warp
During his trip on the Great Siberian Railway in 1902, Michael Myres Shoemaker wrote: 'There is an odd state of affairs as regards time over here. Though Irkutsk is 2,400 miles from St Petersburg, the trains all run on the time of the latter city, therefore arriving in Irkutsk at 5pm when the sun would make it 9pm. The confusion en route is amusing; one never knows when to go to bed or when to eat. Today I should make it now about 8.30 - these clocks say 10.30 and some of these people are eating their luncheon.'

You will be pleased to know that this is something that hasn't changed, although the system now operates on Moscow time (no different from St Petersburg time). Crossing the border from China after breakfast, the first Russian station clock you see tells you that it's actually 01.00 hours. All timetables quote Moscow time. The restaurant car, however, runs on local time. Passing through anything up to seven time-zones, things can get rather confusing. The answer is to ignore Moscow time and reset your watch as you cross into new time zones (details given in the Route Guide). A watch that can show the time in two zones might be useful, otherwise just add or subtract the appropriate number of hours every time you consult the timetable in the carriage corridor.

Stops

Getting enough exercise on so long a journey can be a problem and most people make full use of the brief stops: 'We even managed to persuade our carriage attendant (never seen out of her pink woollen hat) to take part in our efforts to keep fit on the platforms. Several Russian passengers were happy to participate in our foreign antics while others, dressed in the ubiquitous blue track-suits, watched from the windows of the train. However, if your attendant indicates that you shouldn't get off at a stop, take her advice. At some stops another train pulls in between the platform and yours, making it almost impossible for you to get back on board.' Jane Bull (UK).

Traders' trains

The growth of free trade in Russia has led to some Trans-Siberian routes becoming monopolised by Chinese, Mongolian and Russian traders. Their favoured route is via Ulan Bator on the Chinese train: Second Class compartments are likely to be jammed full of cheap Chinese consumer goods, from imitation Adidas trainers to yellow plastic ducks. There will be scant regard for the 'I paid for the same ticket as you, so I'm entitled to as much space' argument. Luckily, foreigners tend to be lumped together by booking agencies in four-berth compartments, if they're available (they're usually all snapped up by the traders), or advised to travel First Class Deluxe (too expensive for traders).

Safety

As anywhere else when you're travelling, you should take care of your possessions and never leave valuables lying around. Particularly on board the traders' trains, there have been a number of reports of thieves breaking into foreigners' compartments. Some of these trains are now regularly patrolled by the police.

If you're careful, you can virtually eliminate the possibility of theft. Never leave your compartment unlocked and unattended. If you want to get off at a station or to go to the dining car, flick the locking switch and slam the door. If this doesn't lock it, get the provodnitsa to lock it for you; she'll be quite happy to open it again. Luggage inside the compartment should be secured; use a bikelock or a length of chain and a padlock. If you're on the bottom bunk you can stash your bags in the steel box beneath you while you sleep. At night, lock the door and flick open the *secretika* (the safety-latch beside the mirror) to prevent it from being opened more than an inch or so if thieves have a compartment key. In addition, wedge the secretika open with a wad of tightly folded paper or plastic ('a toothbrush handle works well' (David and Siriporn Brian, Hong Kong) so it can't be moved from outside with a piece of wire. A Swiss army knife also fits nicely between the catch and the doorframe.

Finally, always wear your moneybelt, and (especially on traders' trains) watch out for pickpockets, people who bump into you in the corridor for no apparent reason.

STEAM LOCOMOTIVES IN SIBERIA

In 1956, the USSR stopped producing steam engines, and the official policy was to phase out these locomotives by 1970. As with most official plans in the country, this one overran a little and a second official end of steam was announced for the end of 1987, when the number of locos stood at over 6000. Some of these have been sold as scrap to Germany and Korea but many are still stored as a 'strategic reserve' in the yards of larger stations and used occasionally for shunting work. Although the Central Asian Republics are reputed to be the best places for steam engines, there are some to be seen along the Trans-Siberian line (see Route Guide for locations). In Northern China there are large numbers still at work.

In 1837, the first locomotive arrived in St Petersburg, a Hawthorn 2-2-0 to pull the Tsar's private carriages over the fourteen miles of six-foot gauge track to his palace at Tsarskoye Selo. The Russians have always been (and still are) conservative in nature when it comes to buying or building engines. Usually large numbers of a few standard locomotives have been ordered so there's not much of a range to be seen today. They seem to be uniformly large, standing up to 17 feet high, and larger than British locos (partly owing to the Russian gauge being 3½ inches wider than that used in Britain). They are numbered separately by classes, not in a single series as in Britain and not by railway regions. If variations of the class have been built, they are given an additional letter to follow the main class letter. Thus, for example, a 0-10-0 freight locomotive is Class E and those of this class built in Germany are Class Eg. Classes you might see in Siberia should include some of the following (Roman alphabet class letters given in brackets); * = very rare now:

● **Class O (O)*** The first freight trains on the Trans-Siberian route were pulled by these long-boilered 0-8-0 locos (55 tons) which date back to 1889. The 'O' in the class name stands for *Osnovnoi Tip* meaning 'basic type'. Although production ceased in 1923, as late as 1958 there were 1,500 of these locomotives still at work. You would be very lucky to see one of these now, though.

● **Class C (S)*** 2-6-2 (75 tons) A highly successful passenger engine. 'S' stands for Sormovo, where these locos were built from 1911. **Class Cy (Su)** ('u' for *usileny*, meaning 'strengthened') was developed from the former class and in production from 1926-51.

● **Class E (Ye)** 2-10-0 (imported from the USA in 1914). Many of the 1500 Ye 2-10-0s that were reported to be stored at stations east of Irkutsk in the late 1980s have now been scrapped.

● **Class Э (E)** 0-10-0 (American, 80 tons, built in Russia from 1926-52 and also produced in Germany and Sweden).

● **Class CO (SO)** 2-10-0 (97 tons) About 4500 were built between 1934-54: in Ulan Ude from 1938 and in Krasnoyarsk from 1943.

● **Class Ea (YeA)** 2-10-0 (90 tons) Over 2000 were built in the USA between 1944 and 1947 and shipped across the Pacific.

● **ClassФД(FD)** 2-10-2 Over 3200 were built. There's a magnificent example (FD21-3000) preserved on a plinth beside the track in Novosibirsk (km3333-S).

● **Class Л (L)** 2-10-0 About 4130 were built between 1945-56.

BAM: A SECOND TRANS-SIBERIAN

In the 1930s another Herculean undertaking was begun. The project was named the Baikal-Amur-Magistral: a second Trans-Siberian railway, 3140km long, running parallel but to the north of the existing line. It was to run through the rich mining districts of northern Siberia providing an east-west communications back-up to the main line. Work began in Taishet and the track reached Ust Kut on the Lena River when the project was officially abandoned at the end of the war. Much of the 700km of track that had been laid was torn up to replace war-damaged lines in the west. Construction continued in secret, using slave labour until the gulags were closed in 1954.

In 1976 it was announced that work on the BAM was recommencing. Incentives were offered to labourers to collect the 100,000 strong work-force needed for so large a project. For eight years they laboured heroically, dynamiting their way through the permafrost which covers almost half the route, across a region where temperatures fall as low as -60°C in winter. In October 1984 it was announced that the way was open from Taishet to Komsomolsk-na-

Amur. Although track-laying had been completed, only the eastern half of the system was operational (from Komsomolsk to BAM station, where traffic joined the old Trans-Siberian route).

By 1991 the whole system was still not fully operational, the main obstacle being the Severomuisk Tunnel, bypassed by an unsatisfactory detour with a 1 in 25 gradient. It took from 1981 to 1991 to drill 8 of the 10 miles of this tunnel in the most difficult of conditions. Many were already questioning the point of a railway that was beginning to look like a white elephant. Work has more or less stopped now; the main sections of the line are complete but traffic is infrequent. The BAM was built to compete with shipping routes for the transfer of freight but the cost has been tremendous: there has been considerable ecological damage, workers complain of poor housing and there is no money left now for the extraction of the minerals that was the other reason for the building of the railway.

In 1990 the first Western tourists managed to ride part of the BAM line although it is still supposed to be off-limits. If you wish to go you will have to join a special tour, otherwise content yourself with a pack of post-cards available from most stations along the Trans-Siberian. They show smiling female railway workers, happy children in the new towns along the way, vast expanses of birch trees and heroic 'Bamovtsi' labourers hammering in the last sleepers on the 'Baikal-Amur-Magistral: The Road of Courage and Heroism'.

'Along the BAM line the route from Taishet to Severobaikalsk is attractive. It's a long, fairly steep rise from Taishet to Vixorifka (famous for its detoxification centre for alcoholics) with some tight curves where the whole length of the train is visible. There are many logging towns, some impoverished villages and of course the Bratsk Dam to cross with views across the water to the south, with the power station and river gorge to the north.

Beyond Bratsk are large lakes and the Lena River but also plenty of ugly industrial sections. Locals sell hot potatoes, pickles and milk from sledges on the station platforms along the way. **Mary Fox** (UK)

YAKUTIA RAILWAY

Work has been being carried out simultaneously on this branch line from the BAM (from Tynda) pushing north eventually to Yakutsk, to transport the huge reserves of coal and other minerals to be found in Yakutia. The project was scheduled for completion at the same time

---

(Opposite) Post Houses (Posting Stations, see p82) were set up at 25-mile intervals along the Great Siberian Post Road in the 19th century providing travellers with fresh horses, squalid accommodation and inedible meals. This is a fortified example (*ostrog*) to be seen at the open air museum near Irkutsk.

as the BAM but is now at a standstill for lack of funds, although passenger services operate as far as Neryungri. In 1993, with the breakup of the SZD network, a lease to operate a railway between Berkakit and Tommot on this route was sold to a private company.

SAKHALIN RAILWAY

The island of Sakhalin (in the Sea of Okhotsk north of Japan) is currently linked to the Russian mainland by rail ferries operating between Vanino and Kholmsk. Steam specials are occasionally run on the island's 3ft 6in-gauge rail system. In early 1994 the Russian government was reported to be considering proposals for a seven-km rail tunnel between Lazarev and Pogibi (costing R410 billion) to link the island to Khabarovsk oblast.

SECOND ASIA-EUROPE LAND BRIDGE

In September 1990 the rail link between Urumqi in northwest China and the border with Kazakhstan was completed opening a new rail route between east Asia and Europe via the Central Asian Republics. China built this new link to create the shortest rail route (2000kms shorter than the Trans-Siberian) between countries on the western Pacific coast and the eastern Atlantic coast, enabling freight to be transported faster and more cheaply than by ship. It may be many years before it is able to operate efficiently as a freight route, though, because much of the Chinese part is still only single-tracked.

Rail travellers on the Silk Route

Opened also to passenger traffic in 1992, the route offers a new opportunity for those wishing to travel from Moscow to Beijing (or vice versa): a journey along the old Silk Route, through the old Central Asian capitals of Khiva, Bukhara and Samarkand, and the Chinese cities of Dunhuang, Luoyang and Xi'an. Currently there is no through train from Moscow to Beijing via Kazakhstan so organising this trip is more difficult than simply buying a ticket, although some travel agents in the West can make arrangements for you. For the adventurous, however, the trip represents a unique travel opportunity. Full details are given in *Silk Route by Rail* (see p314).

(Opposite) Top: This preserved Class Su steam engine stands by the platform at Ulan Ude station. **Bottom:** The most luxurious way to travel across Siberia is in Deluxe Class on the 'Chinese' train. These are the only compartments on the whole railway system that have showers (photo: Bernard Taylor).

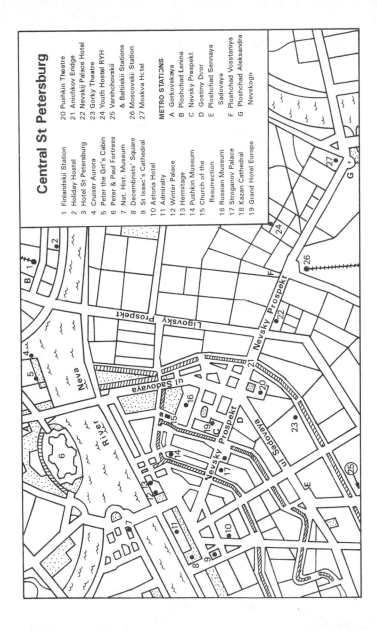

Central St Petersburg

1 Finlandskii Station
2 Holiday Hostel
3 Hotel St Petersburg
4 Cruiser Aurora
5 Peter the Grt's Cabin
6 Peter & Paul Fortress
7 Nat. Hist. Museum
8 Decembrists' Square
9 St Isaac's Cathedral
10 Astoria Hotel
11 Admiralty
12 Winter Palace
13 Hermitage
14 Pushkin Museum
15 Church of the
   Resurrection
16 Russian Museum
17 Stroganov Palace
18 Kazan Cathedral
19 Grand Hotel Europe

20 Pushkin Theatre
21 Anichkov Eridge
22 Nevskij Palace Hotel
23 Gorky Theatre
24 Youth Hostel RYH
25 Varshchovskii
   & Baltiiskii Stations
26 Moscovski Station
27 Moskva Hctel

METRO STATIONS

A Gorkovskaya
B Ploshchad Lenina
C Nevsky Prospekt
D Gostiny Dvor
E Ploshchad Sennaya
   Sadovaya
F Ploshchad Vosstaniya
G Ploshchad Aleksandra
   Nevskogo

PART 4: CITY GUIDES AND PLANS

St Petersburg

Less than 300 years old, St Petersburg is a young city compared to Moscow and yet there is probably as much, if not more, to see here. Many visitors prefer this northern city, perhaps because it is of more manageable proportions than the sprawling capital. It is certainly more beautiful, having been laid out in eighteenth-century Classical style on a grand scale by Peter the Great. A trip to St Petersburg is well worth it if only for a visit to the Hermitage Museum, one of the world's most spectacular collections of European art, which is partly housed in the fabulously ornate Winter Palace.

You can visit Manchester's twin city by taking a side-trip from Moscow on the overnight train and staying a night or two but you really need at least four days to do justice to the sights. Alternatively, you can route your Trans-Siberian journey through St Petersburg by starting (or ending) your trip in Helsinki (200km from St Petersburg) or by travelling directly between St Petersburg and Warsaw (bypassing Moscow). The city is especially attractive in winter, when the snow shows up the brightly painted facades of the buildings. In summer, the most important cultural festival in Russia, 'White Nights', is held here in the last week of June.

HISTORY

'Window on Europe'
Peter the Great decided to build his new capital here to give Russia a 'window on Europe'. He felt that his country was becoming introverted and backward with its capital isolated from the West. The building of this European capital, St Petersburg, was the first step in Peter's crusade for Russia's modernisation. The site selected for the new capital was particularly inhospitable: the marshy estuary of the River Neva. Work began on the Peter and Paul Fortress in May 1703 and in 1712 the capital was moved here from Moscow. St Petersburg grew quickly and stylishly, for Peter employed the finest Italian architects for the palaces and many other important buildings.

Cultural and revolutionary centre

St Petersburg soon developed into the cultural centre of Russia and in the nineteenth century was one of the great cultural centres of Europe. It has been the home of such composers as Tchaikovsky, Glinka, Mussorgsky, Rimsky-Korsakov and Shostakovich, and writers such as Gorky, Pushkin, Turgenev and Dostoyevsky. It was a centre of new ideas and among them, inevitably, were revolutionary ideals. On 14 December 1825, these were translated into actions for the first time in Russia's history, when a group of revolutionaries from the nobility (the 'Decembrists') refused to swear allegiance to Nicholas I and led their troops into Senate Square. Quickly disarmed they were exiled to Siberia.

The Revolutions of 1905 and 1917

The second 'revolution' took place in 1905 when, on 22 January ('Bloody Sunday'), the Tsar's troops fired on a crowd that had marched to the Winter Palace to ask his help in improving working conditions. Ninety-two people were killed and several hundred wounded but more tragic for the country was the fact that the people's faith in their Tsar was finally shattered. Strikes and civil disorder followed and on 25 October 1917 a cannon shot from the cruiser *Aurora* provided the signal for the start of the Revolution proper.

Leningrad: 'Hero City'

In 1914 Tsar Nicholas II changed the city's name to the more Russian-sounding Petrograd; following Lenin's death ten years later, it was renamed Leningrad. In 1945 it was awarded the title 'Hero City' for its stand against the Germans during the Second World War. From September 1941 to January 1943 the city was besieged and bombarded with an average of 250 shells per day. Ultimately, however, most of the 641,803 inhabitants who died during the blockade died of starvation.

St Petersburg today

St Petersburg has been almost entirely rebuilt since the war but fortunately the planners opted for restoration of many of the historic buildings rather than replacement. The building programme continued until the 1980s but is now almost stationary owing to a lack of funds. Work on an ambitious flood barrier around the edge of the Gulf of Finland has recently been halted in its final stages, the best part of US$1 million having been spent.

The modern city is in a chaotic state of flux: a severe shortage of housing means that many inhabitants still live in communal flats, and there is a terrible pollution problem owing to the industrial and chcmical plants on the city's outskirts. Inefficient sewage systems occasionally infect tap water with giardia and on no account should you risk drinking it.

In June 1991, after a heated public debate, 55% of Leningrad's citizens voted to change the city's name back to St Petersburg. Opponents of the change included the Russian Supreme Soviet, headed by Mikhail Gorbachev, for whom 'Leningrad' was symbolic of the siege during the war. Yeltsin and the city's younger inhabitants were all for it, and on 6 September 1991 the Congress of Peoples' Deputies ratified the decision.

Throughout its short history, St Petersburg has always been at the forefront of change in the country. Since 1990 the city's council has been attempting to turn it into a free economic zone; and as you wander through the streets you'll come across numerous Western-standard joint-venture collaborations. The windows of the ornate shops of Nevsky Prospekt, once filled with stacks of tinned fruit juice and bottled beetroot that nobody wanted, now glitter with Western delicacies few can afford.

ARRIVAL AND DEPARTURE

By air
There are two airports: **Pulkovo II** (20km south of the city) for international and some domestic flights (bus 13 from Moskovskiy metro station) and **Pulkovo I** for domestic flights (bus 39 from Moskovskiy metro station or express bus from the Aeroflot terminal just off Nevsky Prospekt at 13, Ul Gertsena). If you're travelling independently you can probably join one of the groups going by bus from your hotel. Although the flight between Moscow and St Petersburg takes only one hour, what with getting to and from airports and the usual delays you are better off taking the train.

By train
There are five stations, three of interest to foreign travellers. Their names are self-explanatory: **Finlandskii** (metro station: Ploshchad Lenina) for trains to and from Helsinki; **Moskovskii**, (metro: Ploshchad Vosstaniya) for Moscow trains; and **Varshchovskii** (metro: Frunzenskaya) for trains to Warsaw, Berlin and other Western cities. Do not confuse this last station with Baltiiskii station next door to it. Check departure times with the hotel service bureau and arrive half an hour before the train is due to leave. Russian trains rarely depart late and have been known to roll out of the station a few minutes ahead of schedule.

ORIENTATION AND SERVICES

St Petersburg stands at the mouth of the Neva, where the river meets the Baltic Sea's Gulf of Finland. The centre of the city is the 4km Nevsky Prospekt; the Hermitage Museum and the top hotels are at its north-western end.

Intourist has been replaced by a number of independent travel organisations, some of which have service desks in hotels. The *Traveller's Yellow Pages Saint Petersburg* (US$8) is a good source of information. Revised editions are produced twice a year and each entry includes a useful introduction. *The Fresh Guide to St Petersburg* is an entertaining and informative locally-produced guidebook.

Visas and extensions

The OVIR office is at 4 Ul Saltkova-Shchedrina (metro Chernishevskaya) and is open 10.00-12.00 (Monday and Wednesday) and 14.00-16.00 on Friday. Transit visas are generally not extended for longer than five days and it can be tricky to get more than three days, so it may be necessary to leave the country and go to Tallinn (Estonia) or Finland to get a new visa.

Note that if you plan to return to Europe bypassing Moscow, the train crosses Latvia, Lithuania and Belorus so you'll need visas. These countries have embassies in Moscow but not in St Petersburg.

WHERE TO STAY

Upmarket hotels

The two most centrally located hotels have recently been completely refurbished and now offer luxury facilities at seriously luxurious prices. The **Grand Hotel Europe** (tel 312 00 72 or 119 60 00), at 1/7 Nevsky Prospekt/Mikhailovskaya, is reputed to be the best hotel in the country; doubles here start at US$245. The **Astoria Hotel** (tel 311 42 06), built in 1913 and furnished in beautiful Art Nouveau style, is now a Finnish/Russian joint venture. It's opposite St Isaac's Cathedral and prices are from US$180 for the simplest double. Good tours can be arranged from here. The **Nevskij Palace** (tel 311 63 66), a new five-star hotel, is at the other end of Nevsky Prospekt (number 57). A standard single costs US$180 and a double US$215.

Slightly further away and of a lower standard, you might want to try the **Pribaltiskaya** (tel 356 41 35, rooms from US$120), at 14 Ul Korablestroiteley (metro Primorskaya) or the floating hotel **Olympia**, from US$165, at Ploshchad Morskoi Slavy 1 (metro Primoskaya, then bus Nos 7, 30 or 128). The Finnish-built **Pulkhovskaya** (tel 264 51 22) is at Ploshchad Pobedy 1, (metro: Moscovskaya).

Midrange hotels

There are numerous three and two-star hotels in the city. The **Hotel St Petersburg** (tel 542 94 11), at Nab Pirogovskaya 5/2, only a five minute walk from Finlandskii railway station (metro Ploshchad Lenina) is now a UK/Russian joint venture; rooms start at US$120.

Cheaper options include the **Hotel Oktyabrskaya** (tel 277 63 30) at 10 Ligovsky Prospekt (metro Ploshchad Vosstaniya) and the **Hotel Karelia** (tel 226 35 15) at Ploshchad Chernishevskogo (metro Park Pobedy). It may be worth checking the prices at the recently-opened floating hotel, the **Commodore** (tel 119 66 66), Morskaya Voksal. Proposed prices were as low as US$30 for accommodation (with breakfast) in a small inner cabin. **MNTK** (tel 178 95 36) is at 21 Ul Yaroslava Gashcka. Rooms here are US$65 single or US$90 double.

Budget accommodation

There are two youth hostels in St Petersburg. The first (the original) is the **Russian Youth Hostel** (tel 277 05 69, fax 277 51 02), at 28, Ul 3rd Sovietskaya (soon to be renamed Rozhdestvenskaya). A bed in a three-bed dormitory costs US$16. The building is clean and well-organised and it's an excellent place to meet other travellers and pick up the latest travel information. Ticket bookings are handled here at reasonable rates, as are visa invitations and extensions (they can only help extend your visa if you have booked it through them - see p26). They don't book Trans-Siberian tickets but will fax the Travellers Guest House Moscow and get them to reserve one for you. Unfortunately the fact that RYH is good means that it's often full; it seems likely that trying to get a room here will become more difficult when the establishment joins the YHA and becomes part of the new international booking network. Calling in advance will increase your chances of getting a bed.

If this hostel is full they will make a booking for you at the **Holiday Hostel** (tel 542 73 64). It's more basic but cheaper (US$12) and is beautifully located on the waterfront (there are even rooms overlooking the river) near the Finlandskii railway station at 1 Ul Mihaylova. Don't be put off by the neighbours in the Victorian-looking Christ's Prison next door (constantly surrounded by crowds hollering over the walls to their unfortunate relatives inside), and make sure you've got the three-figure code to open the front door or you could be in for a long wait till someone comes out. TGH Moscow are negotiating to move into this building. If they do, expect all the usual ticket-booking and visa advice services.

Finally, note that many companies, including TGH Moscow and other foreign agencies (see pp20-33) can organise homestays here.

TRANSPORT

In this city of canals and rivers, the 'Venice of the North', you might expect the local transportation system to be dominated by gondolas or punts but it's just like any other city in Russia. There's a good metro system as well as buses, trams and trolley-buses. The metro stations rival Moscow's in their Baroque decor and trains run from 05.35 to 00.30.

The same flat fare (2½ US cents) is payable on the metro, trolley-buses, buses and trams. A taxi ride to the airport should cost around US$8 but if you pick one up at the airport on arrival you are likely to pay two or three times this amount. There are also buses to and from the airport (see p117). In summer, hydrofoils to the palace of Petrodvorets go from Pier No. 2 behind the Hermitage.

It's possible to rent a car at Innis (tel 210 58 58, at the Hotel Astoria), or Interavto (tel 277 40 32) at 9/11 Ispolkomskaya.

ST PETERSBURG METRO PLAN (ROMAN SCRIPT)

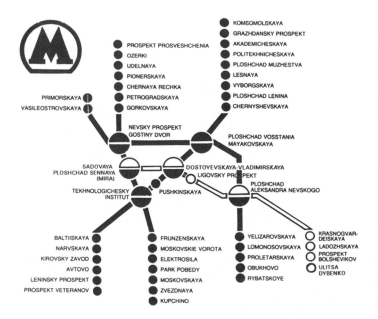

TOURS

Independent sightseeing is easy enough to organise, while the service bureau in your hotel should be able to arrange the following: the **Hermitage** (about US$12); **Peter & Paul Fortress** (US$11); **city tour** (US$10). There are also architecture tours, metro station tours and excursions to **Petrodvorets** (US$15), or to **Pushkin** and **Pavlovsk** (US$12 each).

Between May and September, **boats** leave Anichkov Bridge Pier (just off Nevsky Prospekt) from 10.00 for 70-minute tours. Boat trips can be arranged from the other bridges, too. The larger boats charge less but you may be stuck with a Russian commentary or, worse, Russian pop music. Private boats will cost around US$20 per hour but give you the freedom to go wherever you want. During the 'White Nights' festival boats leave the pier near Decembrists' Square at 21.00 and passengers are entertained by musicians during the trip.

ST PETERSBURG METRO PLAN (CYRILLIC SCRIPT)

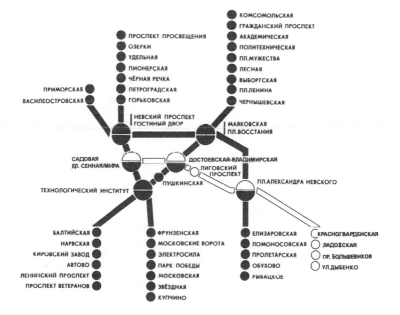

WHAT TO SEE

The State Hermitage Museum

Bigger than the British Museum or the Louvre, this museum surpasses both in the lavishness of its setting and the comprehensiveness of its collection of paintings. It comprises two huge buildings, the **Winter Palace** and the **Hermitage**. The Winter Palace, designed by the Italian architect, Rastrelli, was completed in 1762. The thousand rooms and halls contained within its Baroque exterior were decorated in the reign of Catherine the Great who favoured the Classical style. Catherine ordered the building of the Hermitage, next door to her palace, as a place of retreat where she could contemplate the art collection she had begun.

The Hermitage is so large it would be impossible to see more than a small part of it in one visit. The museum comprises the following departments:

1. The History of Russian Culture

2. Ancient History (Don't miss the exquisite goldwork in the Scythian collection. You may be allowed in only if you are with a tour group. It's worth checking this in advance.)

3. Central Asian Department

4. The Middle East, China and Japan

5. Ancient Greece and Rome

6. European Art This is the section that draws the tourists. There are works by Leonardo da Vinci, Raphael and Michelangelo (Halls 207-30); El Greco, Velazquez, Murillo and Goya (Halls 239-40); Van Dyck, Rembrandt and Rubens (Halls 245-54). French artists are well represented in Halls 272-297 and the Impressionists can be seen in Halls 317-345. The works of Reynolds, Gainsborough and other English artists are displayed in Halls 289-303.

Rules for social conduct in the Hermitage

When Catherine the Great held a dinner party the lucky few who were honoured with an invitation were bound by a list of social rules displayed by the doors to the dining room. Guests were ordered to 'put off their title and rank as well as their hats and swords'. Pretensions were to be left outside; guests were to 'enjoy themselves but break nothing and spoil nothing'; be sparing with their words; eat and drink with moderation and avoid yawning. Those who violated the above rules were obliged to undergo the following punishment: the drinking of one glass of fresh water (ladies not excepted) and the recital of a page of poetry.

The setting for these masterpieces could not be more magnificent: grand marble halls with gilded columns, mosaic floors and vast crystal chandeliers. If you have the time, it is better to make several short visits to the Hermitage, rather than one extended one.

It's open daily (except Monday) 10.30 to 18.00 but entrances close at 17.00. Note that Sunday is 'groups only' day but it's often possible to bribe your way in. Entrance is US$7, or US$2.50 with a student card. (It's US$0.40 for Russians). Queues for tickets at the front entrance can be long (not too bad around 12.30).

Decembrists' Square and St Isaac's Cathedral

In this square, the scene of the uprising by the group of officers who came to be known as the Decembrists (and were sent to Siberia for their treachery), stands the **Bronze Horseman**, the monument to Peter the Great. The statue was commissioned by Catherine II and the work carried out by the French sculptor Falconet, in 1782.

South of the square is **St Isaac's Cathedral** (built between 1819 and 1859) with its vast gilded dome and ornate interior. You can climb part of the way up the dome for a good view over the city. In pre-Revolutionary days, the Cathedral would be packed with up to 14,000 people for major celebrations like Easter and the Saint's birthday. Recently reconsecrated, services are held here only at major Christian festivals but it's possible to view the spectacular interior daily (except Wednesday) from 11.00 to 1800. There's a US$3 admission charge for foreigners.

A walk down Nevsky Prospekt

This has been the main shopping street and most fashionable place to be seen in St Petersburg since the foundation of the city. A walk along this once grand street, past palaces and churches, over canals and beside faded buildings is a walk through the history of the city itself. Nevsky Prospekt starts near the Admiralty Building and, as you walk south-east from here, you can identify the buildings by the numbers beside the doors. The following may be of interest:

7 Gogol wrote *The Government Inspector* here in the 1830s. The lower floors now house a large **Beriozka** shop.

9 This building was modelled on the Doges' Palace in Venice, for the Swedish banker, Wawelberg. Now it's the **Aeroflot** office and air terminal.

14 Note the blue and white sign here which dates from the Siege of Leningrad in World War Two and advises pedestrians to walk on the other side of the street during shelling.

17 This impressive building, designed by Rastrelli and built in 1754, was once the palace of the wealthy Stroganov family. Although they are more famous for the beef stew named after them, it was the Stroganovs who initiated the conquest and colonisation of Siberia by sending their private army to the Urals in the 1570s.

20 The former **Dutch Church**, built in 1837, now an art gallery.

22 Good pizzas and snacks from the basement café here.

24 Once the showrooms of the court jewellers Fabergé (creators of the golden Easter eggs now on display in the Kremlin).

27 Nevsky 27 Café (coffee US$2, pizza US$9, steak and chips US$15). German-Russian joint venture.

28 The former showrooms of the Singer Sewing Machine Co. with their trademark (a glass globe) still on the roof. Now the **Dom Knigi** (House of Books), the largest bookshop in the city.

Kazan Cathedral was designed by Voronikhin and completed in 1811. Prince Peter Kropotkin writing in 1911, called it 'an ugly imitation on a smaller scale of St Peter's in Rome'.

The large, domed cathedral is approached by a semi-circular colonnade. There is a statue at each end of the colonnade, that on the left being of Mikhail Kutuzov, who prayed here before leading an army to battle against Napoleon. After the victory over the French in 1812, the cathedral became a monument to Russia's military glory. In an act of supreme tastelessness, the Soviets turned it into a Museum of Atheism, later renamed the Museum of Religions. The cathedral will soon be reconsecrated.

Looking north along the Griboyedov Canal, you'll see the onion-domed **Church of the Resurrection** (reminiscent of St Basil's in Moscow). It was built on the spot where Alexander II was assassinated in 1881. **Gino Ginelli** and **Chayka** (see p127) are on the right.

31 This housed the City Duma (Municipal Council) in tsarist times. The tower was used as a fire-lookout. The little portico around the corner is the **theatre box-office**. Foreigners may buy tickets here. Opposite the Duma, Ul. Brodskogo runs north into Arts Square (Ploshchad Iskusstv) where the **Russian Museum** (in the Mikhailovsky Palace (this is one of the largest art galleries, with 300,000 paintings, drawings and sculptures; open 10.00-18.00, closed Tue)), the **Maly Opera House** and the **St Petersburg State Philharmonia** are situated. The **Grand Hotel Europe/Yevropeiskaya** is a short distance down Ul. Brodskogo.

32 Church of St Catherine Stanislaw Poniatowski, the last king of Poland and one of the lovers of Catherine the Great, is buried here. Local artists sell their sketches and watercolours outside.

40 Nevsky 40 Café This is a branch of Nevsky 27 above.

Gostiny Dvor, the city's largest department store, fills the whole of the next block (south side). It's intriguing to browse around inside just to see what's on offer and prices are fixed so it's a good place to buy souvenirs (matrioshkas from US$2-12).

'Designer' labels are popular here (just the labels: stitch them into the clothing yourself). 'Clock House', 'Bemsi' and 'Kessi Life' are all big names; serious street-cred is available with 'World Platoon Natural Products A New Jeans Spirit'. The shop's only well-stocked areas are the off-licence sections, where real champagne is on offer (US$48 for a bottle of Moet).

Gostiny Dvor is, however, looking severely weather-beaten these days; it's all rather a mess, as if the stalls moved in before the decorators had finished or vice versa. Some have suggested that this represents a microcosm of Russia itself.

Opposite Gostiny Dvor is **Passazh**, a smaller rather more upmarket department store which also sells antiques and icons.

The **statue of Catherine the Great**, surrounded by her lovers (or 'associates' as some guides coyly put it) and other famous people of the time, stands in a park in front of the Pushkin Theatre.

56 Yeliseyev's, the delicatessen, rivalled the Food Hall at Harrods in tsarist days when it was presided over by Mr Yeliseyev. After the Revolution it became Gastronom Number One and the ornate showcases of its sumptuous interior were heaped with jars of ugly boiled vegetables. Exotic Western fare is now taking their place.

The building on the south side of the street beside the Fontanka Canal became known as the **Anichkov Palace** (after the nearby **Anichkov Bridge** with its famous equestrian statues). Continuing east along the Nevsky Prospekt, it's one km from here to Ploshchad Vosstaniya where Moskovskii railway station (for trains to Moscow) is situated.

From Ploshchad Vosstaniya it's a further two km to the end of the avenue at Ploshchad Alexandra Nevskogo. The **Alexander Nevsky Monastery**, with seven churches in the grounds, is situated here across the square from the **Hotel Moskva**.

Peter and Paul Fortress

In 1703 work began on this fortress, situated on an island at the very heart of the city. It was used as a maximum security prison until 1921, when it was turned into a museum. If you're here at mid-day don't be surprised by the sound of a cannon. It's the daily noon-day cannon that St Petersburgers check their watches by. At the centre of the fortress is the **St Peter and St Paul Cathedral**, with its soaring, needle-like spire (122m). It now serves as a mausoleum for Peter the Great and his successors and is crammed with their ornate tombs. The remains of Nicholas II, Russia's last monarch, have yet to be buried here. The cathedral is open daily except Wednesday.

Leaving the fortress, crossing the bridge and walking east along the river (see map) you will come to a small brick building amongst the trees in a square. This outer shell protects **Peter the Great's log cabin**, the earliest surviving building in the city (built in 1703) and now preserved as an interesting little museum (closed Tuesday).

Other sights

Since the city boasts a total of sixty museums, it is impossible to give details of more than a few in a guide of this type. As well as those places of interest listed above there are art museums (**Monastery of the Holy Trinity and Alexander Nevsky**); museums of social history (the **cruiser *Aurora*** from which was fired the signal for the Revolution); literary museums (homes of **Dostoyevsky** and **Pushkin**) and scientific museums (the history of rail transport in the CIS at the **Railway Museum** at 50 Ul Sadovaya; the **Arctic and Antarctic Museum** and the **Natural History Museum**, where a fully preserved baby mammoth dug out of the Siberian permafrost, is on display).

Excursions

Thirty kilometres west of the city lies **Petrodvorets** (Peterhof), built as Peter the Great's Versailles by the sea. It is most famous for its spectacular fountains, whose gilded figures appear in all the tourist literature. Open daily (though the main palace is closed on Monday) from 11.00 to 20.00. In the summer you can get there by hydrofoil from the landing stage near the Hermitage (several boats each hour, US$1.50 each way) or go by train from Baltiiskii railway station (metro: Baltiiskaya). At **Pushkin** (25km outside St Petersburg) is the grand palace (closed Tuesday) that was the home of the Imperial family. Set in a beautiful park, it was formerly known as Tsarskoye Selo (the Tsar's village). Four km south of here is **Pavlovsk**, built by Catherine the Great for her son Paul. Trains for Pushkin and Pavlovsk leave from Vitebskii railway station (metro: Pushkinskaya). **Lomonosov (Oranienbaum) Palace** with its beautiful park attracts far fewer tourists than the above three and is a peaceful place to visit. Trains leave from Baltiiskii railway station (metro: Baltiiskaya). Ilya Repin's house **Penaty** (closed Tuesday) is at Repino and can be reached by train from Finlandskii station.

WHERE TO EAT

You'll find it easier to get a good meal in St Petersburg than in Moscow as so many joint-venture restaurants and bars have sprung up in the last few years, many along Nevsky Prospekt.

The city's top restaurants charge anything from US$20 to US$50+ per course and include the **Aphrodite** (86 Nevsky Prospekt, tel 275 76 20) for seafood, the **Tbilisi** (10 Ul Sitninskaya, tel 232 93 91) for Georgian food including excellent shashlik, the **Imperial** (53 Kamenovstrovsky Prospekt, tel 234 17 42) for good Russian food, and the **Europe Restaurant** (tel 113 80 66) at the Grand Hotel Europe. The Bacchanalian Sunday brunch (12.00 to 15.00) at the Europe, with live jazz, is popular.

The **Cafe Literaturnaya**, where Pushkin had his last meal before his fatal duel, is at 18 Nevsky Prospekt. It offers classical music and traditional Russian fare with a standard set meal for US$20, not including drinks. It's best to reserve in advance here (tel 312 85 36). Also on Nevsky Prospekt **Le Cafe**, at No 142 has been recommended. It's a German-Russian joint venture that serves a variety of dishes from Vienna sausages (US$9) to tenderloin steak (US$30). **Sadko's**, in the Grand Hotel Europe, is good value and popular. A large main course costs US$9. The **Korean House**, at 20 Naberezhnaya Reki Fontanka (metro Gostiny Dvor) has been highly recommended, as has **Pizza Express** at 23 Ul Podolskaya (metro: Technologichesky Institut). US$14 gets a pizza delivered to your door (tel 292 26 66).

On Kanala Griboyedova (just off Nevsky Prospekt) **Gino Ginelli's** serves frozen fare from the godfather of ice cream but note that cheaper ice creams (US$0.20) are hawked on most street corners.

Bars

Shoestring travellers rave about the **Beer Garden** at 86 Nevsky Prospekt because the beer's reasonably cheap, it stays open late and and it's full of other travellers looking for a bar that serves reasonably cheap beer that stays open late. The German **Chayka Bar** (14 Kanala Griboyedova) is another foreigners' haunt, a bit pricier than the Garden (US$4 for a beer). At 79 Nevsky Prospekt is the almost-English **John Bull Pub** which certainly looks the part despite a few inconsistencies (the staff is Russian and the bitter's ice-cold).

NIGHTLIFE

St Petersburg is probably the most interesting city in Russia for nightlife: everything from sitting around in the bars mentioned above to a night out at the ballet. Ask at the service bureau for a programme of **ballet** (Kirov US$50, Maly US$20), **opera**, **concerts** and the **circus**. You can buy tickets, if available, for just US$0.50 at the kiosk off Nevsky Prospekt (see p124) or from the RYH at US$5. Alternatively try the touts outside the theatre just before the show.

The **St Petersburg Jazz Club** at 27 Zagorodny Prospekt is the best place to go for jazz. You can buy tickets (US$3) here in the afternoon for the evening sessions. Nightclubs have been springing up in the city recently, the best of which is currently **Joy**, at 28 Kanala Griboyedova. Other clubs can be somwhat seedy, especially the new strip bars you'll see advertised around town.

WHAT TO BUY

Nevsky Prospekt is the main shopping street and here you will find the **Beriozka** (Nos.7-9), the department store **Gostiny Dvor** (No.35) and **Dom Knigi** (the House of Books, for good-value art books and posters). Next door to Sadko's Restaurant is **Melodiya**, the Russian music store. Here you can buy a copy of 'Sgt Pepper's' with Russian artwork for just US$2. Other Western LPs are as cheap as US$0.35. Most of the larger hotels have shops selling imported goods.

MOVING ON

Several airlines have offices here. American Express has a travel agency in the Hotel Grand Europe. You'll probably get the best deals on flights from the Russian Youth Hostel and you'll also save yourself some hassle on train tickets by getting them here. Alternatively visit the Central Railway Agency near Kazan Cathedral. Approximate prices for tickets are: Berlin US$140, Prague US$65, Helsinki US$67. (Note the information on visas on p118).

If you've had enough of trains, Finnord Bus Agency (37 Ul Italianskaya) operates an overnight coach service to Helsinki for US$52 (US$37 with student card). It may also be worth checking prices at Express Bus Service (Hotel Pulkovskaya). Finally, there's also a daily ferry service (US$20) from Tallinn (Estonia) to Helsinki.

(Opposite) Top: Outside the Hermitage Museum in St Petersburg horse-drawn carriage rides around the Alexander Column are offered for US$3. **Bottom:** The golden statues of the Grand Cascade at Petrodvorets (Peterhof).

Moscow

All railway lines in Russia lead to the capital, so you'll be spending some time here, even if it's just a quick visit to Red Square as you change stations.

Moscow is a fascinating city to explore, made more so by recent tumultuous political events, so any time here is well spent: bank on three days as a minimum to see the main sights. Finding a place to stay, whatever your budget, is not a problem and extending a transit visa is currently a straightforward process.

HISTORY

The archaeological record shows that Moscow has been inhabited since Neolithic times. However, the first written mention of the city was not until 1147, when Prince Yuri Dolguruky was said to have founded the city by building a fort on a site beside the Moskva River, in the principality of Vladimir. The settlement which grew up around the wooden fort soon developed into a major trading centre.

The Mongols
Disaster struck the Russian principalities in the early thirteenth century in the form of the Mongol invasion. Moscow was razed to the ground in 1238 and for the next two and a half centuries was obliged to pay an annual tribute to the Mongol Khan. During this time the principality of Muscovy (of which Moscow was capital) emerged as the most important state in Russia. In 1326, Moscow became the seat of the Russian Orthodox Church. Prince Dimitri Donskoi strengthened the city's defences and built a stone wall around the Kremlin. In 1380 he defeated a Mongol-Tatar army at Kulikovo but it was not until 1476 that tributes to the Khan ceased.

The years of growth
The reign of Ivan III (the Great: 1462-1505) was a period of intensive construction in the city. Italian architects were commissioned to redesign the Kremlin, and many of the cathedrals and churches date

(Opposite) St Basil's Cathedral, Moscow's most famous landmark, is situated on Red Square. A museum during the communist period, the Cathedral has now been reconsecrated and regular services are held here.

from this period. Prosperity continued into the sixteenth century under Ivan IV (the Terrible) and it was at this time that St Basil's Cathedral in Red Square was built.

The early seventeenth century was a time of civil disorder, and a peasant uprising culminated in the invasion of Moscow by Polish and Lithuanian forces. When they were driven out in 1612 the city was yet again burnt to the ground. Rebuilt in stone, Moscow became the most important trading city in Russia by the end of the century. It remained a major economic and cultural centre even after 1712 when Peter the Great transferred the capital of Russia to St Petersburg.

The final sacking of the city occurred in 1812 when Napoleon invaded. As much of the damage was probably caused by retreating Muscovites as by the French armies but three quarters of all the buildings were destroyed. Recovery was swift and trade increased after the abolition of serfdom in 1861.

Revolution
Towards the end of the century Moscow became a revolutionary centre and factories were hit by a series of strikes and riots. Michael Myres Shoemaker, who was here in 1903, wrote in *The Great Siberian Railway from St Petersburg to Peking*: 'Up to the present day the dissatisfaction has arisen from the middle classes especially the students, but now for the first time in Russia's history it is spreading downward to the peasants... but it will be a century at least before that vast inert mass awakens to life.' In 1905 there was an armed uprising and twelve years later 'that vast inert mass' had stormed the Kremlin and established Soviet power in the city. The civil war saw terrible food shortages and great loss of life.

The capital once more
In March 1918 Lenin transferred the government back to Moscow. In the years between the two world wars the city embarked on an ambitious programme of industrial development and the population doubled to four million by 1939. During the Second World War many of the factories in the European part of the USSR were re-sited over the Urals, a sensible move as it turned out, for by October 1941 the German army had surrounded the city and the two-month Siege of Moscow had begun.

Moscow today
The only thing that can be said with certainty about Moscow is that the changes that have transformed it over the last five years are not about to stop now. On the one hand the restructuring here seems to be part of a beneficial transition to a market economy: new hotels

spring up, joint-venture restaurants open and private shops flourish. On the other hand it's impossible to ignore the raging poverty: old women in the streets stand for hours trying to hawk their one hairbrush or plastic bag, ragged war veterans sleep in the subways and everywhere, it seems, there are beggars. The fact that the new generation of foreign shops, bars and restaurants offer all the latest in Western luxuries highlights the contrasts. Most Muscovites can afford only to window shop in such places.

Crime, ranging from petty pilfering to gang warfare on the streets is on the increase and many businesses are forced to pay protection money to local 'mafia' gangs. Certain areas in the city are being compared to Chicago in the 1930s. There is also a chronic shortage of housing which has worsened with the arrival of thousands of ethnic Russians from the other CIS republics.

Moscow is currently in a complete state of flux. Just what will be the final result of this metamorphosis remains to be seen.

ARRIVAL AND DEPARTURE

By air

International flights land at **Sheremetyevo International Airport**, 35km from the city centre. Buses from just across the parking lot here will ferry you to or from the metro stations Rechnoi Vokzal (bus No 551) or Planernaya (bus No 517), departing every half hour (6am to 11pm). There are also special orange airport buses. Taxis charge US$20 or more to the city centre; for your own safety take an official cab rather than just any car whose driver offers you a lift.

Domestic flights use **Domodedovo airport**, to the south of the city. Buses connect the airport with Domodedovskaya metro station.

Buses to either airport are also available from the air terminal office at 37 Leningradski Prospekt (metro station Dinamo).

By train

There are nine railway stations, the four you are most likely to use being: **Belorusskii/Smolenskii** (metro: Belorusskaya), for trains to and from Western Europe (note that in late 1993 it was announced that Belorusskkii would be renamed Smolenskii but as yet no change has been made); **Leningradskii** (metro: Komsomolskaya) for Helsinki and St Petersburg; and, next door to it, **Yaroslavlskii** (metro: Komsomolskaya) for Trans-Siberian trains (except No 26 to Novosibirsk via Kazan, which leave from Kazanskii) and **Kazanskii**, opposite Leningradskii, for trains to Central Asia. **Kievskii** (metro: Kievskaya) is for trains to Budapest; note that departures from here require a Ukrainian visa. See p145 for **leaving Moscow**.

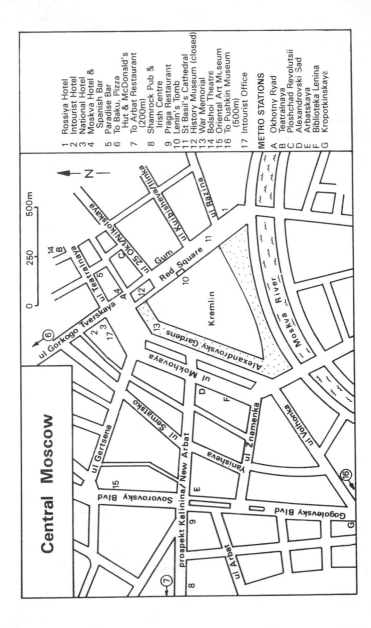

Central Moscow

N

0   250   500m

1   Rossiya Hotel
2   Intourist Hotel
3   National Hotel
4   Moskva Hotel &
    Spanish Bar
5   Paradise Bar
6   To Baku, Pizza
    Hut & McDonald's
7   To Arbat Restaurant
    (200m)
8   Shamrock Pub &
    Irish Centre
9   Praga Restaurant
10 Lenin's Tomb
11 St Basil's Cathedral
12 History Museum (closed)
13 War Memorial
14 Bolshoi Theatre
15 Oriental Art Museum
16 To Pushkin Museum
    (500m)
17 Intourist Office

METRO STATIONS

A   Okhotny Ryad
B   Teatralnaya
C   Ploschad Revolutsii
D   Alexandrovski Sad
E   Arbatskaya
F   Biblioteka Lenina
G   Kropotkinskaya

ORIENTATION AND SERVICES

At the very centre of the city are the Kremlin, Red Square and St Basil's Cathedral. The most conveniently placed (and mainly expensive) hotels are in this area. The metro system is efficient, however, so it's not vital to have a hotel right on Red Square.

The main branch of **Intourist** (tel 292 23 65) is located at Ul Mokhovaya 13, around the corner from the National Hotel. Open daily from 9am to 8pm, it offers tours and books rail and air tickets.

Money
Hard currency used to be the number one requirement for travellers in Moscow but as the currency reforms take effect there's less of a demand for it. Travellers' cheques are becoming more widely accepted but are time-consuming to cash. If you need hard currency, go to the **Radisson Slavyanka Hotel** (2 Berezovskovskaya Emb., metro Kievskaya), or the **Olympic Penta** (18 Olympski Ave, metro Prospekt Mira). Both will change leading travellers cheques (2% commission) and give cash advances on credit cards (5% commission). **American Express**, on Ul Sadovo Kudrinskaya (Bank for Foreign and Economic Affairs), will change only their own cheques.

Russian visa extensions
OVIR, the state visa office, is at 42 Ul Chernishevskogo (metro Kurskaya) and is open daily except Wednesday, Saturday and Sunday. Opening hours are 10.00-13.00 and 15.00-18.00 (17.00 on Friday). The visa extension situation changes from month to month but five-day extensions (US$5 in roubles) are currently easy to get. Longer extensions or a second extension are not so straightforward, usually requiring a ticket out of the country. Note that extensions start from the day of application.

Embassies
● **Australia** (tel 956 6070), Kropotkinskii Per 13.
● **Canada** (tel 241 58 82), Starokonyushenni Per 23.
● **China** (tel 143 15 43), Ul Druzhby 6 (metro: Universitet). Open weekdays 09.00-11.30. Service here is extremely slow so you will have to queue: get here at least by 07.00 in order to get a place (some will be here by 05.00). If there are more than 20 people in front of you in the queue you are unlikely to get in that day. Most travellers think it's worth paying the extra US$20 on-the-spot express fee so that they don't have to return and go through the queuing process again.
● **Czech** (tel 251 05 40) Ul Yul Fuchika 12 (metro: Mayakovskaya).

- **Estonia** (tel 290 46 55) Kalashny Per 8 (metro: Tverskaya).
- **Hungary** (tel 143 86 11), Ul Mosfilmovskaya 62 (Kievskaya).
- **Mongolia** (tel 244 78 67), Staropesovsky Per 7/1 (metro: Smolenskaya). Open weekdays 10.00-12.00, 15.00-17.00.
- **Latvia** (tel 925 51 82), Chaplygina 3, (metro: Chistye Prudy).
- **Lithuania** (tel 291 75 86) Ul Pisemskogo 10 (metro: Arbatskaya).
- **New Zealand** (tel 290 12 77), Ul Vorovskogo 44.
- **Poland** (tel 254 36 21), Bolshoi Tishinskiy Per 1 (metro: Barri kadnaya).
- **Ukraine** (tel 299 64 75) Ul Stanislavskogo 18 (metro: Tverskaya).
- **UK** (tel 230 63 33), Naberezhnaya Morisa Toreza 14.
- **USA** (tel 252 24 51), Novinskii Blvd 19/23.

It's worth explaining how to use the combination-lock luggage lockers at Russian stations because they're not as straight-forward as they look. Find an empty locker and put your luggage in it, taking care not to leave any valuables. Before you close the door set the dials (1 letter, 3 numbers) on the inside of the door to your desired combination, insert the required token (available from the attendant) and close door. Note down the number of the locker as well as the number of the combination.

WHERE TO STAY

Upmarket hotels

The luxurious **Hotel Metropol** (tel 927 60 00), close to Red Square at 4 Teatralny Proezd, is as much a historic monument as a hotel for it was here that Rasputin is said to have dined, and Lenin to have made several speeches. Its beautiful Art Nouveau interior featured in the film of *Dr Zhivago*. Rooms cost from US$330 for the cheapest single to US$1500 for the suites. Other hotels of this ilk (five star international) include the **Hotel Savoy** (tel 929 85 00) at 3 Rozhdestvenka, also close to Red Square, with rooms from US$255/380 for a single/double; the **Hotel Pullman Iris** (tel 203 01 31) at 10 Korovinskoye Chausse, with swimming-pool and single rooms from US$180; and the similarly-priced **Marco Polo** (tel 202 28 48) at 9 Spiridonevsky Sidest. The **Hotel Aerostar** (tel 224 80 00), at 37 Leningradsky Prospekt (seven km from the centre of town towards the airport), has rooms from US$215.

The **Hotel Intourist** (tel 203 01 31), at 3 Ul Tverskaya, is a popular choice since it's very close to Red Square. It's US$135/155 for a single/double room. You can see the Kremlin and Red Square from the windows of the **Hotel National** next door but it's undergoing extensive renovations at present.

Mid-range accommodation

Hotel Moskva (tel 292 29 94), on Ul Tverskaya, is well located; singles are US$70, doubles US$80. The **Hotel Rossiya** (tel 298 15 25), at 6 Ul Razina, is the world's second biggest hotel and also the closest hotel to Red Square; rooms are US$30/40. Both of these hotels are renowned mafia hangouts, however, and there have been numerous reports of petty pilfering from rooms here.

At US$33/66 for a single/double room, the **MNTK budget guesthouse** (tel 483 04 60), at 59a Beskudnikovsky Blvd, is good value. Being right next door to the Hotel Pullman Iris, even a taxi driver should be able to find it.

Budget accommodation

Currently the best budget place to stay in town is the **Travellers Guest House Moscow** (tel 971 40 59, fax (+7)-095-280 76 86), where a bed in a four-bed room costs US$15. Singles are US$30 and doubles US$35. There's a restaurant and bar, kitchen and laundry facilities and a travel agency. TGHM is a magnet for the city's budget travellers; it's an excellent place to pick up the latest travel tips and visa information. The staff will book tickets for you even if you're not staying here but they'll be unable to do anything about extending your visa unless you've booked it through them (see p26). They can also make free bookings for you for accommodation in St Petersburg and Irkutsk and they sell Trans-Siberian tickets and stopover packages. It's fairly easy to find, at 50 Ul Bolshaya Pereyaslavskaya on the tenth floor: take the metro to Prospekt Mira and then walk north out of the station for ten minutes. Take the third turning on the right (Banniy Per.) which leads to a T-junction. At the junction turn left and the building is immediately on your right.

If the TGHM is full, try the **Molodezhnaya** (tel 210 45 56), a big blue monster of a hotel built for the 1980 Olympics, at 27 Dmitreyevskoe Shosse. Ask at reception and you'll be quoted prices of US$25-40 for a double but go straight up to the 20th floor and there you should be offered a bed in a triple room for under US$10. It's a ten-minute walk from Timiryazevskaya metro station and is visible from the station itself.

Cheaper and more basic is the **Hotel Ipkir** (tel 210 71 48) where a single bed will cost you US$7; there's a communal kitchen between every two rooms. It's 400m south of Dmitreyevskaya metro station at 79 Ul Butirskaya, opposite the cluster of trees.

TRANSPORT

The best way to get around is on the palatial **metro** system, a tourist attraction in itself. It's cheap (less than US$0.06 for a token that takes you to any destination, no matter how far) and the trains are frequent (every 90 seconds at peak times).

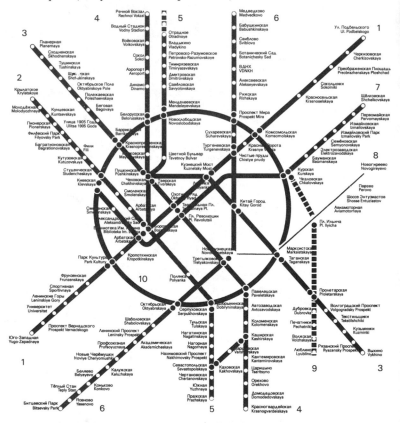

Moscow Metro - line names and colour codes **1** (Red) Sokolnicheskaya **2** (Light blue) Filovskaya **3** (Purple) Tagansko-Krasnopresnenskaya **4** (Light green) Zamoskvoretskaya **5** (Grey) Serpukhovsko-Timiryazevskaya **6** (Orange) Kaluzhsko-Rizhskaya **7** (Dark blue) Arbatsko-Pokrovskaya **8** (Yellow) Kalininskaya **9** (Dark green) Lyublinskaya (under construction) **10** (Brown) Circle

Bus and **tram** services are comprehensive but overcrowded. Virtually any Russian car will be a **taxi** but don't get in if there are already passengers (see p57). Self-drive **hire cars** (from hotel service bureaux) might be worth considering for some of the sights outside the city but are not recommended for city sightseeing.

There's a pleasant **river trip** (Route 1, frequent departures) which leaves from the Kiev terminal (Kievskaya metro station) and passes Lenin Hills and Gorky Park on its way towards the Kremlin. The 1½-hour trip ends at the Novospassky Bridge terminal.

TOURS

Tours of the main sights can be arranged in any of the upmarket hotels or at the Intourist office, at 13 Ul Mokhovaya. The Intourist Hotel offers the following: **Armoury and Kremlin** (2½ hours, US$22, not Tues), **Kremlin diamonds** (1½ hours, US$20, not Thurs) **city sightseeing** (2½ hours, US$20, daily), **Kremlin grounds tour** (1½ hours, US$10, not Thurs), a **metro tour** and tours to many **museums**. Cheaper tours are offered by guides who hang around at the Tomb of the Unknown Soldier; if they are qualified they will have ID cards to prove it.

It's worth enquiring about the mysterious **KGB Tour** that is occasionally offered by Intourist. If this is running you'll be treated to demonstrations of miniature cameras, microdots, bugging techniques and more. Highly recommended.

WHAT TO SEE

Red Square

This wide cobbled square, *Krasnaya Ploshchad* in Russian, extends across the area beside the north-eastern wall of the Kremlin. The main sights around the square are St Basil's Cathedral, Lenin's Mausoleum, the GUM Department Store and the Kremlin.

St Basil's Cathedral

Also known as the Church of the Saviour and nicknamed the Pineapple Church by Victorian travellers, this whimsical architectural creation is as much a symbol of Moscow as Tower Bridge is of London. Commissioned by Ivan the Terrible, it was completed in 1561 and so pleased with the result was the Tsar that he had the architect's eyes put out (the guides tell you) so that he would never be able to produce anything to equal or surpass it. Apparently the architect went on to produce other buildings, so perhaps this is a tall story; but it's a good one fitting the Tsar's character perfectly. St

Basil's is a quite incredible building, with its nine brightly-painted, dissimilar domes and the stone-work decorated with the intricate patterns more usually found on the wooden buildings of the time. For many years a museum, it has been returned to the Church.

Lenin's Mausoleum

Built onto the side of the Kremlin in 1930, the red granite mausoleum and its mummified occupant are something of an embarrassment to the current regime. In October 1993 the hourly guard-changing ceremony was stopped but in early 1994 the tourists were still queuing up to file past the once-revered corpse, laid out in its dark suit and polka-dot tie. Lenin currently receives visitors from 10.00-13.00 on Tue, Wed, Thurs and Sat; and from 10.00-14.00 on Sun; but the doors may soon close forever on this ghoulish tourist attraction.

The mausoleum was the centre of a cult that flourished for almost 70 years. The cubist design is the work of A.V.Shchusev who envisaged the cube, like the pyramid, as a symbol of eternity and it was his plan that every Soviet home would have its own little cube to the memory of the dead leader. Until the early 1990s no Soviet town was without a Lenin statue, no public office lacked a Lenin portrait.

There are plans to move Lenin's body to the family plot in St Petersburg after the more important reburial of the Tsar and his family has been completed. Behind the mausoleum are the graves of other communist heroes, including Brezhnev and Stalin, and these will be moved to Novodevichy Cemetery. The fate of the building itself is unsure. Campaigners want it demolished and replaced with the statue of Kuzma Minin and Prince Pozharsky (famed for saving Moscow during the 'Times of Troubles' in the early 17th century) that originally stood here but is now in front of St Basil's.

Mummification for the masses
The Centre for Biological Researches, responsible for the preservation of Lenin's body, recently announced the offer of full mummification services to anyone for a mere US$300,000.

Previous clients are a testimony to their considerable skill. An independent team of embalmers recently inspected Lenin's corpse and declared it to be in perfect condition. After his death on 21 January 1924 an autopsy was carried out and a full report published in *Pravda*. The public were treated to a list of weights and measurements of most of the internal organs of their dead leader (his brain weighed 1340g - far larger than average). Then the embalmers began their work. One wonders if the decision the Central Executive Committee took in 1924 to preserve Lenin's body, had anything to do with Howard Carter's discovery of the Pharaoh Tuthankamun fourteen months earlier. Indeed, Dr Zbarsky, who headed the Russian team of embalmers boasted that Lenin's body would remain unchanged indefinitely. This claim is reiterated by Dr Yuri Denisov-Nikolsky, who hopes to attract rich American corpses.

GUM

The remarkable glass-roofed GUM building (pronounced 'goom') was constructed in 1894 as a shopping mall where individual traders could set up their stalls. It was nationalised after the Revolution and turned into a huge state store, a monument to Soviet shortages, but following the recent market reforms it's attracting Western chains. You can now buy anything from a Benetton sweater to the latest compact disc but most Muscovites can afford only to browse. There are a couple of bars and restaurants here (see p143), as well as fast-food stands.

The War Memorial

It is traditional for bridal couples to visit this monument in the Aleksandrovsky Gardens on their wedding day to be photographed beside the eternal flame. Beneath the marble lies the body of one of the soldiers who helped to stop the German advance on Moscow in 1941. The changing of the guard ceremony which used to take place outside Lenin's tomb should be held here soon.

The Kremlin (See map on p140)

The heart of Moscow and the seat of the Russian government, the Kremlin is, in fact, a large walled castle. Although the site has been continuously occupied for at least the last 800 years, the walls and many of the cathedrals date from the fifteenth century. There are 20 towers, the most famous being the **Spassky Tower** above Red Square. The Kremlin's main entrance and ticket office is in Kutafya Tower, on the opposite side to Red Square. Note that you may not take large bags or rucksacks in, and that you won't get past the guards if you are wearing shorts.

There are now different prices for foreigners and Russians. Entry costs Russians US$0.05 plus US$0.80 to visit all of the cathedrals; and another US$1 to visit the Patriarch's Palace. The ticket office is open 10.00-16.00 daily. Intourist will charge US$6 for entrance and US$4 per cathedral.

Cathedral Square

In the centre of the Kremlin is a square around which stand four cathedrals and the **Bell Tower** of Ivan the Great (81m/263ft high), which Napoleon attempted to blow up in 1812. Beneath the tower stands the **Tsar Bell**, at 200 tons the heaviest in the world. The piece of the bell that stands beside it broke off during the fire of 1737. Nearby is the largest calibre **cannon** in the world.

The Cathedral of the Dormition/Assumption (Uspenski Sobor), the work of an Italian, was completed in 1479 and was the traditional place of coronation for Russia's tsars. During the last coronation, on 26 May 1896, something happened that was taken by those who saw it as a bad omen: as Nicholas II walked up the steps to the altar, the chain of the Order of St Anthony fell from his shoulders to the floor. Inside are three thrones; the wooden one to the right as you enter belonged to Ivan the Terrible.

The Cathedral of the Archangel (1505-09) looks classically Russian from the outside but the hand of its Italian architect Alevisio Novi can be seen in the light interior. Forty-six tsars (including Ivan the Great and Ivan the Terrible) are buried here. The smaller **Cathedral of the Annunciation** (1484-89), the private chapel of the tsars, was the work of Russian architects and contains icons by the great master, Andrei Rublyev. The **Church of the Deposition of the Virgin's Robe** (1484-5) was designed as a private chapel for the clergy. The Patriarch worshipped in the **Church of the Twelve Apostles** (1656) next door to his residence.

Moscow - The Kremlin

Red Square
Lenin's Mausoleum
Gardens
Aleksandrovsky
Moskva River

1 War Memorial
2 Kutafya Tower
3 Trinity Tower
4 Palace of Congress
5 Church of the Twelve Apostles
6 Church of the Deposition of the Virgin's Robe
7 Cathedral of the Assumption
8 Tsar Cannon
9 Bell Tower of Ivan III
10 Tsar Bell
11 Cathedral of the Archangel
12 Cathedral of the Annunciation
13 Faceted Palace
14 Saviour Cathedral
15 Terem Palace
16 Grand Kremlin Palace
17 Armoury
18 Poteshny Palace
19 Arsenal
20 Senate
21 Supreme Soviet
22 Spassky Tower
23 Ticket Kiosks
24 Patriarch's Palace

Other buildings The **Great Kremlin Palace**, now a government building, is not usually open to visitors. One wall of the Italian-designed **Faceted Palace** (so-called because of its facade of pointed stone blocks) faces Cathedral Square. The **Golden Tsarina Palace** or Terem Palace with its striking red and white tiled roof is one of the oldest parts of the Kremlin and dates from the seventeenth century. The seat of Russian government is the modern **Palace of Congresses**. The **Armoury Museum** should not be missed (although admission may only be possible if you go on a previously arranged tour) as it contains a dazzling display of various tsars' jewellery and regalia, weapons and armour. Of special interest to Trans-Siberian passengers is the ornate **Great Siberian Easter Egg** (probably the finest of the 56 famous Imperial Easter Eggs made by Carl Fabergé), which contains a clockwork model of the train, complete with golden engine (with a ruby for the headlight), five gold coaches and a church-car (Hall III).

Tretyakov Art Gallery
The best collection of icons and sculpture in Russia is housed here. There are icons painted by Andrei Rublyev; *Christ's First Appearance to the People* which took Alexander Ivanov 20 years to complete and two halls devoted to the great Russian masters, Ilya Repin and Vasily Surikov. The gallery is at 10 Lavrushinsky Perelok, (Metro: Tretyakovskaya). Open daily (except Mon) 10.00 to 19.00.

Pushkin Museum of Fine Arts
Most interesting for its large collection of Impressionist paintings including many famous canvases (Manet's *Déjeuner sur l'Herbe* for example, and Monet's *Boulevard des Capucines*). There are also galleries of Egyptian antiquities and Old Masters. Well worth a visit, the gallery is at 12 Ul Volkhonka, (metro: Kropotkinskaya). Open daily (except Mon) 10.00 to 19.00.

Arbat Street
This pedestrianised shopping street is very popular with tourists. As in Covent Garden there are buskers, street artists and swarms of souvenir sellers hawking everything from matrioshkas to military jackets. Bargain hard and watch out for pickpockets. At the western end there's a branch of McDonald's.

Novodevichy Convent
This beautiful sixteenth century walled convent is well worth visiting. Dating back to the sixteenth century it has been used at various times as a fortress (it held out against the Poles during a siege in 1610) and a prison (among others, Peter the Great banished his sister

Sophia here). Although Napoleon tried to destroy it in 1812 it remained undamaged: one brave nun rushed in and extinguished the fuses to the powder kegs at the last minute. The **cathedral** is famous for its frescoes and highly ornate, multi-tiered iconostasis (the backdrop to the altar), all recently restored. It also contains a small museum. Novodevichy is open 08.00-17.00 daily but closed Tuesday and the first Monday of the month. (Nearest metro: Sportivnaya).

Behind the convent is the famous **cemetery**. As well as the graves of many influential people (Khrushchev, Chekhov and Prokofiev among them) there are some outlandish gravestones: one soldier lies beneath a large model tank. Stalin, Gagarin and Brezhnev will probably be moved here from Red Square.

Other museums, galleries and churches in Moscow

North of the centre is what remains of the **USSR Economic Achievements Exhibition** (metro: VDNK). At the entrance is the impressive 100m monument to the Russian space programme. Beyond the showgrounds are the 18th century **Ostankino Palace**, now a museum of serf art in an enchanting building that's well worth a visit (closed Tue and Wed), and the Ostankino TV tower with its revolving restaurant.

There is simply not room in a guide-book of this type to give details of more than a few of Moscow's 150 museums and exhibitions. There are museums devoted to Gorky, Tolstoy, Dostoyevsky, Pushkin, Chekhov, Gogol, Glinka, Lermontov and the icon painter Andrei Rublyev; museums of science, folk art, anthropology, the theatre and famous battles (the Battle of Borodino Museum). Further information from the service bureau in your hotel.

Excursion to Sergiyev Posad (Zagorsk)

A visit to the cathedrals and churches of the town formerly known as Zagorsk (see p224), 75km from Moscow, makes a very worthwhile day trip. For many years this was the seat of the Russian Orthodox Church (it was moved back to Moscow in 1990) and it is still the site of one of the most important seminaries in the country.

To get to Sergiyev take a local train from Yaroslavskii station (about every half hour) for the 1½ hour journey, or join a tour. Entry is free although there are camera charges (US$4, or US$10 for a video-camera). The impressive museum costs another US$1.

WHERE TO EAT

The restaurant scene in Moscow is changing very fast with new places opening daily. The food you are likely to get, however, will either be the standard Russian fare ('cutlet', very cheap) or something served up by joint-venture restaurants: ie foreign food, about the same price as in the West.

Upmarket restaurants

The best restaurants are still to be found in the expensive hotels (see above). Other places to try include **La Cantina**, the Tex Mex bar by the Hotel Intourist. Service is provided by American language students, giving an almost authentic Texan atmosphere. The food's not bad but quite expensive at US$12-16 for a main course and beer at US$3. There's another Tex Mex bar, **Armadillo**, behind GUM. **Patio Pizza**, opposite the Pushkin Museum, is highly recommended.

The **Spanish Bar and Restaurant** is on the ground floor of the Hotel Moskva. A main course should cost about US$8 here. Just around the corner, the **Paradise Restaurant** is more expensive (US$6 for a gin and tonic or US$15 for a hamburger). Other foreign restaurants include the **Shamrock Pub** in the Irish Centre on New Arbat St, where you can get draught Guinness for US$4 and various bar snacks. **Rosie O Grady's**, at Ul Znamenka 9 (metro: Biblioteka Lenina) is another Irish place. A large meal here will cost you US$8, with Guinness also at US$4. It really does look authentic and is a good place to meet homesick travellers. Credit cards are accepted for orders over US$50 and it's open at weekends until 1am. **Pizza Hut** on Ul Tverskaya serves some fairly average pizzas. Unless you buy a slice on the street, however, this is the expensive branch, so bank on paying US$6-12 for a small pizza. Russian beer is US$3. A cheaper outlet is at Kutusovsky Prospekt 17 (metro: Kievskaya).

Budget restaurants

These generally fall into two categories: cheap Russian and fast food outlets. Restaurants in the former category can be very cheap if you're with a Russian speaker but if not you may well be ripped off. Some serve champagne and caviare, so bills can mount up if you're not careful. In this group, try the **Praga**, a Soviet-style vault on the edge of Arbat St, the **Arbat** further up (there's a big Aeroflot globe above the entrance) or the **Cafe Margarita** (by Patriarch's Pond, metro: Mayakovskaya) - excellent value, with blinis and caviare for US$4, but it can get very crowded. For a meal with a view, try the revolving **Seventh Heaven Restaurant** on the top of the Ostankino television tower (metro: VDNK) where prices, surprisingly, are quite reasonable (under US$10 for a big meal).

If you simply want cheap fast food, try **Rostik's** fried chicken bar in GUM: Col Sanders has little to worry about but it's not bad and is considerably more interesting than a visit to one of the ever-multiplying branches of **McDonald's** (Big Mac for US$1.50 from one of three outlets: Arbat St, and two on Ul Tverskaya). There are several new cafes and bars on **Arbat St** which might be worth a look. Those staying at the TGHM will doubtless make use of the **Kombis** sandwich bar on Prospekt Mira, which produces excellent filled rolls (US$2-4), or the **Flamingo** chicken restaurant next door (more expensive). A little further up the street is an **Italian bar** which even serves cappuccino (US$4). Finally, the restaurant on the second floor of the **Hotel Intourist** (entrance opposite the casino) has an eat-all-you-can buffet for US$7. Supposedly it's for residents only, so keep a low profile.

NIGHTLIFE

Tickets for the **Bolshoi** are easy to come by if you don't mind paying US$50 for them: try the service bureau in your hotel or the Intourist office. There's a ticket office at the theatre but all tickets are usually bought up by black marketeers. If you want a cheap ticket, stand around outside the opera house before the performance and they'll find you. You'll be quoted prices of US$10-40 depending on how gullible they think you are. Barter and remember that the later you leave it before the performance the more anxious they'll be to get rid of their tickets. Check the date and time of the performance on the ticket before you hand over any cash.

The **Moscow State Circus** performs two shows daily at the arena beside Tsvetnoye Blvd metro station. Tickets are readily available and cost US$2. The human performers are generally excellent but Western visitors tend to be dismayed by the animal acts.

The major hotels generally have some sort of evening entertainment and a couple run casinos. There's a Moscow **Hard Rock Cafe** in the basement of the Zilnoye Theatre in Gorky Park. The jazz at **Arkadia Jazz Club** (3 Teatralnaya Proezd) is considered very good. Open till 5am; the US$10 entry fee includes a cocktail and coffee.

WHAT TO BUY

Most foreigners end up buying their matrioshkas, ceramic boxes and furry hats from street sellers, although you'll need to check quality first and then bargain hard. The underpass outside the Intourist Hotel is always busy and there are some reasonable paintings for sale here. The best place to go, however, is Ismailovsky Park at a weekend: you'll find a massive market selling everything from stolen icons to Skippy peanut butter. **GUM**, the **Irish Centre** on New Arbat St and the **Garden Ring** Irish supermarket, at 1 Bolshaya Sadovaya (metro:

Mayakovskaya) are all good places to stock up on Western instant coffee, biscuits and other essentials for the train. Shops in the larger hotels offer a reasonable but expensive selection of consumer goods.

MOVING ON

By rail

Trains from Siberia arrive either at Yaroslavskii or Kazanskii stations (both at Komsomolskaya Square). If you're on a transit visa you are supposed to go direct to the station for your onward train (see p131) to make your reservations for departures the same day. If you want to avoid the queuing, it's easier to get someone else to buy tickets for you: the Travellers Guest House will do this for a small commission; otherwise try Intourist, at 13 Ul Mokhovaya, or Intourtrans, near the Bolshoi Theatre, at 15 Ul Petrovka (see map; second floor for reservations or confirmations, third for bookings).

Train numbers, times, journey length and fares for first/second class are as follows: Budapest (35hrs) No15: 16.38, US$222/130; Helsinki (16hrs) No32: 18.17, US$122/80; Berlin (26hrs) No13: 13.28, US$221/135; Prague (33hrs) No21: 19.07, US$95/73, Warsaw (19hrs) No9: 15.20, No21: 19.07, US$90/70. All of the above trains go daily. There are departures for London via Ostend (51hrs) on Mon, Wed, Sat on train No15: 18.21, US$503/342; Beijing US$242/157 and Ulan Bator US$149/95: for **Trans-Siberian** timetables see p297.

Rail destinations within the CIS include St Petersburg (8hrs) US$44/US$25, train No2: 23.55 is recommended; Ekaterinburg US$100/57; Novosibirsk US$168/91; Irkutsk US$238/126; Ulan Ude US$264/138; Khabarovsk US$385/199; Vladivostok US$419/216. Trains to Central Asian cities including: Samarkand US$181/97, Tashkent US$168/91 and Alma Ata US$200/107.

By air

Moscow is not the best city in which to buy international air tickets. Numerous airlines have offices here (many situated on Ul Petrovka, behind the Bolshoi Theatre). Aeroflot is generally the cheapest and has two offices on this street: the international flight centre at No 20, the domestic centre at No 15. Sample prices are: London US$1065, LA US$2066 and New York US$1702. Intourist or the Travellers Guest House should be able to offer better prices.

From Domodedovo airport there are frequent flights to St Petersburg (US$89), and many cities in Siberia including Ekaterinburg (US$128), Irkutsk (US$249), Khabarovsk (US$341), Novosibirsk (US$185), Ulan Ude(US$253) and Vladivostok (US$378): all daily.

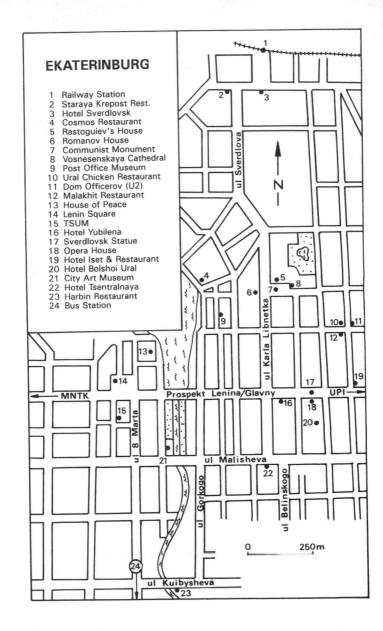

EKATERINBURG

1 Railway Station
2 Staraya Krepost Rest.
3 Hotel Sverdlovsk
4 Cosmos Restaurant
5 Rastoguiev's House
6 Romanov House
7 Communist Monument
8 Vosnesenskaya Cathedral
9 Post Office Museum
10 Ural Chicken Restaurant
11 Dom Officerov (U2)
12 Malakhit Restaurant
13 House of Peace
14 Lenin Square
15 TSUM
16 Hotel Yubilena
17 Sverdlovsk Statue
18 Opera House
19 Hotel Iset & Restaurant
20 Hotel Bolshoi Ural
21 City Art Museum
22 Hotel Tsentralnaya
23 Harbin Restaurant
24 Bus Station

ul Sverdlova

N

ul Karla Libnetka

MNTK

Prospekt Lenina/Glavny   UPI

ul 8 Marta

ul Gorkogo

ul Malisheva

ul Belinskogo

0   250m

ul Kuibysheva

Ekaterinburg

Ekaterinburg's role in shaping Russian history has been both immense and paradoxical: ushering in the Socialist era in 1918 with the murder of the Romanov family, providing the setting for 1960's 'U2 Affair' (effectively a caricature of the Cold War itself), and giving the country Boris Yeltsin, who played a key role in dismantling the Soviet myth. The city seems to act as Russia's litmus paper: as a harbinger of whatever is to come.

Its historical significance alone justifies a visit and while there is not much to see here in real terms, the wealth of pre-Stalinist architecture makes a change from other Siberian cities, harking back to the days before the Revolution, when Ekaterinburg was already the centre of a rich mining region.

From 1924 to 1992 the city was known as Sverdlovsk.

HISTORY

The earliest settlers in the area were the 'Old Believers', religious dissidents fleeing the reforms of the Russian Orthodox Church in 1672. They created the *Shartash* township here and were the first to discover that the area was rich in iron ore. This discovery was the key to later development: Peter the Great, in the process of fighting the Great Northern War against Sweden, gave instructions for new sources of iron to be found, and the first ironworks were established here just as the war ended in 1721. A fortress was built a year later and the town was named Ekaterinburg in honour of Peter's new wife, Catherine. The railway reached the town in 1888 bringing foreign travellers on their way to Siberia.

The murder of the Romanovs

The Romanov family was moved from Tobolsk to Ekaterinburg in May 1918 and imprisoned in a house belonging to a rich merchant. Here they spent the last two months of their lives being tormented by the guards, who openly referred to Nicholas as the 'Blood Drinker' and scrawled lewd pictures on the walls depicting the Tsarina with Rasputin.

Several attempts were made to save the royal family and eventually the Bolshevik government, deciding that the Tsar was too great a threat to its security, ordered his elimination. Shortly before midnight on 16 July Nicholas, Alexandra, their four daughters and their haemophiliac son, Alexis, were taken down to the cellar where they were shot and bayonetted to death. The bodies were then taken to the Four Brothers Mine, 40km outside the city, where the guards spent three days destroying the evidence. The corpses were dismembered with axes, doused with petrol and burned.

A week later the White Army took Ekaterinburg and their suspicions were immediately aroused by the sight of the blood-spattered walls of the cellar. In the garden they found the Tsarevich's spaniel, Joy, neglected and half starved. However, it was not until the following January that investigators were led to the mineshaft, where they found fragments of bone and pieces of jewellery that had once belonged to members of the Imperial Family. They also found the body of Jimmy, Anastasia's dog, that the murderers had carelessly flung down the mineshaft without bothering to destroy. All the evidence was identified by the Tsarevich's tutor, Pierre Gilliard. At first the Bolsheviks would not admit to more than the 'execution' of Nicholas, accusing a group of counter-revolutionaries of the murders of his family. Five of them were tried, 'found guilty' and executed. However, in 1919 after the death of Party official Yacob Sverdlov, it was acknowledged that it was, in fact, he who had arranged the massacre. In his honour the town was renamed Sverdlovsk.

The U2 Affair
The next time the town became the focus of world attention was in May 1960 when the American U2 pilot, Gary Powers, was shot down in this area. US Intelligence was no doubt unhappy to hear that he had survived the crash, parachuting into the arms of the Soviets and confirming that he had been spying. The ensuing confrontation led to the collapse of the Summit conference in Paris.

The city today
Ekaterinburg is now one of Russia's most important industrial cities, with a population of nearly 1½ million. The city's most famous son is, of course, Boris Yeltsin: coup-buster, economic reformer, referendum winner, dissolver of parliament and Russian President.

Industries here include heavy engineering, chemical production and the cutting and setting of gemstones. The industrial base used to be armaments research and production but munitions factories, including the vast 'Pentagon' building in the eastern part of the town, are now being closed down or converted. If Ekaterinburg is an indicator of the state of affairs in Russia, things don't look too good: I asked if anything important had happened here recently and was told only that there had been 'a number of mafia funerals'.

ORIENTATION AND SERVICES

The main street (Prospekt Lenina, recently renamed Glavny) runs from east to west through the city and is bisected by the River Iset. The point where the road and the river cross is more or less the city centre and most of the hotels, restaurants and sights are within walking distance of it.

Tourism is new to Ekaterinburg, there's no Intourist service here yet and even hotel staff are unlikely to speak English. MNTK (see below) may be able to help with tours.

WHERE TO STAY

Hotels worth trying include the **Tsentralnaya** (tel 55 11 09) on Ul Malisheva: doubles from US$30-100; the **Yubilena** (tel 51 57 58) on Prospekt Lenina, cheaper at US$8-80 but with an extensive collection of pornographic literature for sale in the foyer; and the **Bolshoi Ural** (tel 55 68 96), right next door to a 'secret' weapons technology plant and at US$20 for a double probably the best of the bunch.

More interesting architecturally but less likely still to be standing in 10 years time is the **Hotel Iset** (tel 55 69 43). This dilapidated construction was built to resemble a hammer and sickle from above. The sickle, which one imagines would be the tricky bit, turned out well but the hammer never really quite happened. The entrance is a small unmarked door around the back and rooms range from US$7/8 (for a single/double) to US$85. Directly opposite the railway station is the **Hotel Sverdlovsk** (tel 53 62 61) which is a more conventional, Intourist-style place. The cheapest rooms are US$10/20 and there's even an independent water heater in the bathrooms.

MNTK (tel 28 91 45) is a 20-30 minute bus ride from the city centre, at 4a Ul Bardina. To get here, take bus No 18, which starts opposite UPI (see p152) and stops right outside the building (it's on the right). The spotless rooms are US$65 single or US$90 double.

The best place to stay can be difficult to arrange, although with luck you might just be able to walk in off the street and get a room: **Dom Mir-y-Druzhba** (House of Peace and Friendship) is at 1/2 Nab Pabochei Molodeshi, on the western bank of the river, 200m north of Prospekt Lenina. They have luxurious apartments or rooms at knock-down prices (eg a flat with three double bedrooms, two bathrooms, kitchen, hall and dining-room for US$60). When the 18-room hotel here is full they can also arrange homestays. Call or fax in advance (tel 51 77 52, fax 51 86 47). If you do manage to get in here you have the added bonus of knowing that you're staying in the former residence of one B Yeltsin.

TRANSPORT

Getting around the town is easy as there are extensive bus, trolleybus and tram services but getting to the more distant sights will require a little planning. Bus No 31, trolleybus Nos 1, 5 and 9 and trams Nos 4, 14, 25 and 32 run between the station and the city centre. Taxis are easy to find and a metro system is under construction.

WHAT TO SEE

The Romanov House

The site of the murder of the Imperial family is simply a patch of bare earth marked by a white metal cross. Yeltsin had the original building demolished in 1976. There are plans for a church here but until it's built there's not much to see: just the plain cross with some rather moving photographs of the Tsar's family pinned to it. The site is occasionally the scene of small pro-monarchy demonstrations.

Next door to the cross is a small wooden **chapel** dedicated to St Elizabeth (Elizabeth Fyodorov), Alexander II's sister-in-law, who was also brutally killed by the Bolsheviks. Following the Romanov murders she was thrown down a mineshaft and left to die. Local villagers claimed to have heard her miserable wailings for two days as she prayed for the souls of her attackers who, when they realised that she was still alive, piped poisonous gas into the well and then filled the hole with earth.

The grand building opposite the Romanov site now houses the headquarters of the Children's Movement. It was commissioned by one of Ekaterinburg's wealthy merchants, Rastoguiev, and legend holds that he was so rich that he used to mint his own gold coins in the basement. Apparently he was a cruel man: having bailed an architect out of jail, he offered to buy the man's freedom if he designed him a beautiful enough house. The architect laboured hard to complete his side of the bargain but, when Rastoguiev did not keep his promise, hanged himself.

Next door to this building is **Vosnesenskaya Cathedral**, impressive from the outside but containing nothing of particular note. It was closed following the Revolution, its treasures removed and its murals painted over.

Gary Powers' U2 plane

It is difficult to get to see the remains of Powers' aircraft. They are exhibited in the Officers' Club (Dom Officerov) near the city centre but staff here are sometimes unwilling to let foreigners in or occasionally seem to be ignorant of the fact that the plane is even here at all. I managed to buy an entrance ticket but was then ushered into an evangelical faith-healing meeting that was being held here. The exhibit itself is impressive but what was state-of-the-art espionage equipment in 1960 is today only the remains of an old aeroplane. Pride of place goes to the U2 camera which so impressed Nikita Khrushshev: 'It must be said that the camera is not a bad one,' he said, 'the photographs are very accurate. But I must say that our cameras take better pictures and are more accurate'.

Dom Officerov is easily recognisable by the massive armoury outside, and around the back is a collection of Soviet military hardware including a couple of fighter planes, a helicopter, a long line of tanks and the cosmonauts' re-entry capsule from the rocket Soyuz.

Lenin Square
This small square, which marks the centre of the city, is the site of the original city cathedral; there is talk of building a new one but lack of funds will delay this for some time. More likely is the idea that Lenin and his out-of-favour Communist colleagues will be collected up and put into a new 'Soviet Museum'. Further up the street is Sverdlov; he is regularly daubed with graffiti and red paint. Kirov stands outside the Polytechnical Institute.

Opposite Lenin is the 18th century government building, originally housing shops. The clock tower above it is a copy of one of the towers of the Moscow Kremlin.

The discovery of the Romanov remains
The story behind the discovery of the Romanov remains is almost as bizarre as that of their 'disappearance'. In July 1991 it was announced that parts of nine bodies had been found and that these were almost certainly those of the Imperial Family. Perhaps the most intriguing aspect of the discovery was the fact that three of the skulls, including that of the Tsar himself, had been placed in a wooden box. In fact the bodies had been discovered some 20 years before by a local detective thriller writer named Geli Ryabov. He deduced, by the skulls' immaculate dental work, that these were indeed the bodies of the Royal Family, but later reburied them for fear of persecution by the secret police.

In December 1992, testing at the Forensic Science Service laboratory in Aldermaston matched DNA samples from the bodies with DNA taken from a blood sample from Prince Philip (Tsarina Alexandra's sister was Philip's maternal grandmother). DNA matching is currently being carried out on samples from a lock of Anna Anderson's hair. Anderson, who died in the USA in 1984, claimed to be the Tsar's daughter Anastasia but was never able to prove it. Her bones (and those of Alexei, the heir to the throne) were not amongst those found.

The state burial of the royal remains has been delayed following a disagreement between surviving members of the Romanov family, who want the bones to be returned to Ekaterinburg as a memorial to the millions killed by the Communists, and the government, who favour burial in St Petersburg.

City art museum

There's a fine collection of nineteenth century iron sculpture here, a gallery of Russian paintings including works by Ivanov and Tarakanova, a portrait of PA Stroganov (of Beef Stroganov fame), and a famous portrait of Christ by Polenov. Pride of place in the museum goes to the iron pavilion, which won first prize in the Paris Exposition in 1900. It's very impressive but you can't but wonder what it's for. The museum is open daily from 09.00-17.00.

Museum of regional history

The museum of regional history is something of an enigma since everyone will assure you that it does exist but few know where it is. It's actually in the process of being relocated but a large proportion of the exhibits are still in the old museum, in Alexander Nevsky Cathedral. The cathedral is worth visiting even if you can't get into the museum; it was built by the architect Molachov in 1814-52 to commemorate the French retreat from Moscow. Strewn around this impressive, rather decrepit building is an array of miscellaneous items including a snow plough, a couple of anchors and large gun.

Post office museum

This small museum, depicting the life of postmen in tsarist Russia (see p249), is relatively uninteresting unless you manage to get onto a tour with its chief custodian. If you can arrange this, together with an interpreter, you're in for a wacky afternoon, as she delights in demonstrating how everything works, singing and even telling people's fortunes ('You have travelled a long way, yes? You are only passing through Ekaterinburg' etc). Exhibits include a bedroom laid out as it would have been for a nineteenth century postmaster's family, an original post carriage and a small display in the stables. It's at 6 Ul Proletarskaya and open 11.00-18.00, not Sat.

Other things to see in Ekaterinburg

The **Geology Museum** at 39 Ul Kuibysheva is good; try to track down the curator, who speaks perfect English and seems to enjoy showing visitors around. The **opera house**, directly beside the statue of Sverdlov on Prospekt Lenina/Glavny is the third most important in Russia after Moscow and St Petersburg. The troupe here has a repertoire of 25 ballets and 20 operas and the programme changes every night. At the eastern end of Prospekt Lenina is **UPI**, the Urals Polytechnical Institute, an impressive building which often features on postcards. In fact it was recently re-termed a university but the old name has stuck. The building beside it with the cannons outside is the city's military college.

Excursions from Ekaterinburg

● **Europe/Asia marker** Forty km to the west, beside the main road to Moscow (*Novi Moscovski Trakt*), is a marble and granite obelisk marking the continental border. There's not much else to see here but villages along the way are attractive.

● **Museum of wooden architecture** It's a long way away (60km to the north) and not as good as the one outside Irkutsk, so you might be justified in giving it a miss. The most interesting building here is the old church. Closed since the Revolution, craftsmen began its restoration recently and were surprised to find many of the carved floor tiles missing. As work proceeded, the lost tiles began to show up, brought in by pensioners who had long ago removed pieces of their church as mementos. Incredibly, all the tiles have now been returned. Bus No31 from the railway station will get you here.

● **Other sights** Visitors are occasionally taken to either the **Alapayevsky jade mines** 300km to the east, or to **Tchaikovsky's house** 300km to the north-east. A visit to either of these sites could take in the mineshaft where Elizabeth Fyodorov (see p150) was murdered but there's nothing to see at this rather grim site.

WHERE TO EAT

The best, most interesting and most expensive restaurant in town is the Chinese **Harbin**. There's hardly a chopstick in sight but the food is surprisingly good. US$15 will get you a set four-course meal for one which will probably be more than enough for two. It may well be topped off with the restaurant's pièce de resistance - a large deep-fried fish flambéed at the table. I asked my wide-eyed Russian companion what the fish was: 'It's...on fire!' was the reply. Harbin is very near the circus and the concrete communications tower to the south of Prospekt Lenina (both visible from the river). To get here take tram Nos 4, 14, 26 or 34 from the centre to the stop on Ul Belinskogo, or trolleybus Nos 1, 5 or 9 from the railway station.

Next best bet is the **Cosmos**, a trendy ex-Party restaurant with a casino (and a large neon sign). Food is standard Russian/European fare: bank on US$5-10 per person. Smaller and cheaper is the **Ural Chicken Restaurant**, opposite Dom Officerov. It tends to be pretty busy (always a good sign) and a set meal will cost you about US$3. Opposite this is the **Malakhit** which is cheaper but the food is not nearly as good. The pelmeni at **Iset** is good, although the place is a bit dingy and service can be casual. Near the railway station, the **Sverdlovsk Hotel** restaurant has been recommended but the **Staraya Krepost** just across Ul Sverdlova, is better.

Novosibirsk

With a population of over 1.6 million people, this is the largest city in Siberia and its industrial centre but, of the cities along the Trans-Siberian that foreigners usually visit, Novosibirsk has the least to offer the tourist. It's a relatively young city and has few buildings of historic interest.

You can visit the enormous opera house, the museums and the nearby town of Akademgorodok, the Scientists' City where three thousand scientists live in a purpose-built town, a Soviet academic experiment. Winters here are particularly harsh, with temperatures falling as low as -50°C. Novosibirsk is the starting point of the 'Turksib' railway line; enterprising travellers could catch a train from here to Alma Ata in Kazakhstan and then continue west into China.

HISTORY

Novosibirsk didn't exist before the Trans-Siberian was built and its spectacular growth this century is largely due to the railway. In 1891 it was decided that a railway bridge over the Ob should be built here. A small settlement grew up to house the railway workers and named Novo Nikolayevsk in honour of the accession of the new Tsar.

By 1900 over 15,000 people lived here and the numbers grew as railway and water-borne trade developed. As far as tourists were concerned, there was only one reason for getting off the Trans-Siberian in Novo-Nikolayevsk as Baedeker's 1914 *Guide to Russia* points out: 'It is a favourite starting point for sportsmen in pursuit of the wapiti, mountain sheep, ibex and other big game on the north slopes of the Altai'. The town suffered badly during the Civil War when 30,000 people lost their lives. During the first four months of 1920 a further 60,000 died of typhus. In 1925 Novo-Nikolayevsk was re-christened Novosibirsk ('New Siberia').

Between 1926 and 1939 the population grew exponentially. The coal-fields of the Kuznetsk Basin were developed and Novosibirsk became the transit base after a rail link was built. The town of Novokuznetsk, in the centre of the Kuznetsk region, grew quickly and iron ore arrived by rail from the Urals for its blast furnaces. In the early 1930s the 900-mile Turksib Railway was completed linking

Novosibirsk with Turkestan in former Soviet Central Asia, via Semipalatinsk and Alma Ata. Grain from the lands around Novosibirsk could then easily be exchanged for cotton, which grew best in Central Asia. The building of this railway, the jewel in the new government's first five-year plan, was recorded on movie-film and is still shown today as a fascinating early example of documentary film.

During World War II large numbers of civilians and complete factories were moved here from European Russia, and the city has been growing ever since. It's now the busiest river port in the area and the major industrial centre in Siberia, most people being employed in engineering or metallurgy factories. In spite of the wealth generated by the area's natural resources, Novosibirsk is no better run than other Russian cities. On almost every occasion that I've visited the place there's been no hot water not just in the hotel but in most of the city. Apparently it's been like this on and off since 1917!

1990 saw pro-democracy rallies here, with a number of students staging hunger strikes in the square in front of the opera house. In October 1993 during the Yeltsin/Congress struggle, there were once again political demonstrations in the square, this time pro-Soviet. Novosibirskians who've had enough of politics have been concerning themselves with the problem of raising money for a statue in honour of Mexican starlet Veronica Castro (leading lady in the soap opera, *The Rich Also Cry* - see p66).

Novosibirsk's centenary, in 1993, was marked with major celebrations, including the official opening of a church closed after the Revolution (see p158).

ORIENTATION AND SERVICES

The third largest city in Russia, Novosibirsk was designed on a grand scale. Krasny Prospekt, its main street, extends for over ten kilometres. The mighty River Ob bisects the city, leaving the main hotels, sights and the railway station on the east bank. Although there were plans to rid the city of its Communist-era street names, the signs are still in place.

Intourist can be found in the Hotel Sibir, although the larger hotels all have service bureaux.

WHERE TO STAY

Not many tourists stop here so there are only a few hotels. By far the most upmarket is the **Hotel Sibir** (tel 23 12 15), a new Polish/Russian joint venture and Intourist's standard pad. Rooms are US$80 single or US$90 double and are clean and well maintained. There's a classy souvenir shop in the foyer. The **Hotel Novosibirsk** (tel 20 11 20) is well located right opposite the railway station but that, unfortunately, is the best thing about it; don't leave valuables lying around your room here. It's US$61 single or US$74 double. Much cheaper, and probably better, is the **Hotel Tsentralnaya** (tel 22 72 94) right in the city centre on Ul Lenina. Room prices here are from US$9/18 for a single/double without bath, right up to US$96 for a suite. Hot water is said to be reliable. Few of the staff speak English.

MNTK is some way from the centre of town to the west of the river, at 10 Ul Kolkhidskaya (tel 41 01 55); rooms are US$65 single and US$90 double. To get here, take bus Nos 2 or 37 from Ploshchad Stanislavskaya.

1 Rwy Station
2 H. Novosibirsk
3 Cafe
4 Beriozka
5 Circus
6 Church
7 Okean Rest.
8 Sobek Rest.
9a/b Folk Museum
10 TSUM
11 Bus to Akadm.
12 Korean Rest.
13 Hotel Sibir
14 Bakery
15 Lenin Sq.
16 Kafe Jazz
17 Opera House
18 Post Office
19 H.Tsentralnaya
20 Druzhba Rest.
21 Preserved Loco
22 Art Gallery
23 Church
24 Cathedral

METRO STATIONS
A. Pl. G. Mikhailovskogo
B. Sibirsk/Krasny Prospekt
C. Ploshchad Lenina

NOVOSIBIRSK

TRANSPORT

On foot, Lenin Square is about twenty minutes from the railway station, straight down Vokzalnaya (Station) Magistral. Novosibirsk has a good **metro** system (some stations lined with Siberian marble).

To get to Lenin Square (metro: Ploshchad Lenina) from the station (metro: Ploshchad Garina Mikhailovskogo), go one stop to Sibir-skaya/Krasny Prospekt, change to the Studentskaya line and it's one stop to Ploshchad Lenina.

There's an extensive **bus** service which you can use for Akademgorodok (see p159). Take bus Nos 2 or 22 from the railway station, or Nos 2 or 8 from the metro station Studentskaya. Route taxi No15 from the railway station will also take you here. It's also possible to catch the train to Obskoye More, the station for Akademgorodok; but it's easier to go out by taxi and take the train back.

Novosibirsk's **airports**, Tolmachovo (international) and Gorod-skoye (domestic) are situated on opposite sides of the city but are linked by bus No122.

TOURS

The service bureaux in the hotels offer a morning tour of the city as well as tours to the sights and museums described below. Tours to Akademgorodok usually include a visit to the geological museum and a boat-trip on the Ob Dam in summer. They will also arrange tickets for the circus (closed in summer) and for opera and ballet at the Opera House. You can organise your own boat trip from the landing stage near Retsnoy Vokzal metro station to Korablik Island, which is popular with Novosibirskians for swimming and sunbathing from May to Sep.

WHAT TO SEE

Lenin Square and the Opera House

This is the centre of the city and the square is dominated by the vast **Opera House**, one of the largest in the world, with its silver dome. It was completed in 1943, when most of the builders had been sent off to join the war effort. Its completion is seen as all the more heroic in that it was to some extent due to the women and children, who helped the few remaining builders.

In the middle of the square is a **statue of Lenin**, his coat blowing behind him in the cold Siberian wind, a rather more artistic represen-tation of the man than the many others produced. He is flanked by three soldiers on his right and by two 'Peace' figures on his left, who look as if they are directing the traffic that flows around the great square. In the winter there are troika rides around the square, and people build ice-sculptures. The low building above the metro station is the oldest stone structure in the city and houses part of the local Folklore Museum.

The Folklore Museum

The bulk of this collection is housed in the ground floor (entrance at the side) of the block right behind TSUM but eventually displays will be moved to the Lenin Square building. It's an interesting museum, although you will need a guide to explain the significance of some of the historical exhibits. There's a display showing life before the Revolution including a Singer sewing machine, a rusty British Norton motorbike (built in 1909) and an early piece of rail (stamped 'Birmingham 1899'). There's also a special section recording the troubled times during the civil war, when the city was occupied by the White Russians and then the Bolsheviks before being devastated by an outbreak of typhus in 1920. The extensive display of Siberian flora and fauna includes some of the 50 species of mammals, 30 species of fish and 30 species of birds that are found only in Novosibirsk oblast. There's also a collection of Siberian trees and grasses, a geological display and the skeleton of a mammoth. The labels on the natural history exhibits are in Latin as well as Russian: for a translation see p304. The museum is open 10.00-18.00, closed Tuesday.

Other things to see

The **Cathedral** at the far end of Krasny Prospekt near the river is now fully restored and is well worth a look. Closer to the centre of town, however, is **Russia's most central church**, opened during the 1993 centenary celebrations and built on the spot that marks the exact centre of the country. The original church here was destroyed after the Revolution. The **Dom Museum Kirov** is devoted to Kirov, the Party leader that everyone had assumed would succeed Stalin but who was assassinated in 1934. It is housed, next to the new Sibir Hotel, in an attractive log cabin, one of the few that have survived. In the neighbouring apartment block there is a small exhibition of local handicrafts, mainly wood-carvings. There is a good **Art Gallery**, along Krasny Prospekt, on Sverdlovsk Square.

WHERE TO EAT

The best restaurants in Novosibirsk are in the **Sibir Hotel**. In the restaurant downstairs service is good, as is the food (the *chicken Kiev* is recommended); but it tends to fill up with leather-jacketed, shell-suited 'businessmen' in the evenings. Directly above it, the second floor restaurant is better and also has live Dixieland jazz every night. Expect to pay US$5 without drinks; if you want wine it's best to buy it in the kiosk outside the restaurant. The **Druzhba** (Friendship) Restaurant is next door to the Hotel Tsentralnaya and has been highly recommended. It's cheaper than the Hotel Sibir.

If you want seafood, the **Okean** is said to be the best place to get it.

A night at the **Sobek**, a Russian/Korean joint venture restaurant, could be exciting. It's an intimate little place that's packed with racketeers and mafia men. The food's not bad, about US$3 per person, live ammunition extra. For more authentic Korean food and a less threatening atmosphere, it might be worth trying out the new **Korean restaurant** on Voksalnaya Magistral.

For snacks, go to the **Jazz Cafe** where there's live jazz every evening and great mounds of chocolate cake every afternoon. It's very much a bar rather than a restaurant so you won't be able to get a meal here. There's a surprisingly good snack bar in **TSUM** where the pastries are excellent and the coffee thoroughly drinkable. The **cafe/bar** on Ul Cheluskintsev near the station isn't bad, either, if you avoid the coffee. **Zolotoye Kolos** is an excellent bakery opposite the Hotel Tsentralnaya.

WHAT TO BUY

There are the usual souvenir shops in the hotels and a Beriozka shop on Cheluskintsev Street near the circus. The main streets for shopping are Vokzalnaya Magistral but you'll do better in Akademgorodok. The market is one block east of Krasny Prospekt.

When the circus is not in town there's a clothing market in the building. If you're feeling cold this is a good place to buy Chinese down-filled jackets. The central department store (TSUM) next door to the Folklore Museum is surprisingly well stocked with Western goodies, although one wonders how many Russians can afford the Lego sets priced at US$246.

EXCURSION TO AKADEMGORODOK

Established in the 1950s to house the scientists of the Siberian branch of the USSR's Academy of Sciences, Akademgorodok now comprises 26 special research institutes and a staff of over 10,000. In this pleasant sylvan setting, students spend five years studying Physics, Chemistry, Mathematics, History or Economics (a recently restructured course, no doubt). They're amongst Russia's most intelligent young people: Akademgorodok is ranked third in the university tables after Moscow and St Petersburg.

It is worth visiting if only to see how the elite of the Soviet system lived. As with its Olympic athletes, the Soviet Union believed in training its academics from a very early age, spiriting them away from home to attend special boarding schools for the gifted. It's also worth visiting for the walks through the forests and around the dam.

The **Geological Museum** in the Institute of Geology & Geophysics is open to tours only. You could follow one in or just say 'Moozay' to the doorman and the museum is straight ahead, up the stairs. The overpowering mineral wealth of Siberia is displayed here, including the purple mineral chaorite found only in this part of the world.

It's interesting to wander round the well-stocked shops, just one of the perks provided for the scientists and their families. The **bookshop** has maps, posters and books in English. There's a good restaurant at the **Zolotaya Dolina Hotel** but you may need to book.

After looking round Akademgorodok you can walk through the birch forest and over the railway-track (hourly trains back to Novosibirsk, 06.02-23.17, from Obskoye More station) to the beaches of the **Ob Dam**. It was created by the building of the Novo-sibirskaya power station, Siberia's first large hydro-electric project. This is a good place to swim as the water is surprisingly warm. If you want to picnic on the beach, the bakery sells bread and pastries and sometimes has delicious fish stew in take-away plastic bags.

AKADEMGORODOK

1 Bus Station
2 Bus to Novosibirsk
3 Supermarket & bookshop
4 Bakery
5 Cafe
6 Geological Museum
7 Market
8 Zolotaya Dolina Hotel
9 Obskoye More Station

Irkutsk

If you can afford only one stop on the Trans-Siberian, you should make it in Irkutsk. In this city, which was once known as the 'Paris of Siberia', you will find the people rather more friendly and relaxed than in European Russia. Along many of the streets you can still see the cosy-looking log cabins (eaves and windows decorated with intricate fretwork) which are typical of the Siberian style of domestic architecture. Sixty-four kilometres from Irkutsk is Lake Baikal, set amongst some of the world's most beautiful countryside. Trekking, camping, boat excursions and riding are just a few of the pursuits that are now available in this outdoor paradise.

HISTORY

Military outpost

Irkutsk was founded as a military outpost in 1652 by Ivan Pakhobov, a tax-collector who had come to encourage the local Buryat tribesmen to pay their fur tribute. By 1686 a church had been built and a small town established on the banks of the Angara. Tea caravans from China passed through Irkutsk, fur-traders sold their pelts here and the town quickly developed into a centre for trade in Siberia. By the beginning of the nineteenth century, Irkutsk was recognised as the administrative capital of Siberia. The Governor, who lived in the elegant white building that still stands by the river (opposite the obelisk), presided over an area twenty times the size of France. At the time when prisoners were being sent to Siberia, political exiles often chose to live out their lives here. The most celebrated exiles were the Decembrists, who had attempted a coup in St Petersburg in 1825, and the houses in which some of them lived can now be visited. With the discovery of gold in the area in the early 1800s, 'Gold Fever' hit Irkutsk. Fortunes were made in a day and lost overnight in the gambling dens.

Boom town

By the end of the century, in spite of a great fire in 1879 which destroyed 75 per cent of the houses, the city had become the financial and cultural centre of Siberia. Its cosmopolitan population included fur traders, tea merchants, gold prospectors, exiles and ex-convicts. Irkutsk had become 'a city of striking contrasts, with the magnificent mansions of the rich at one end of the pole and the dilapidated shanties of the poor at the other' as an Intourist brochure pointedly remarks. Those prospectors who were lucky became exceedingly rich, some amassing personal fortunes that would be equivalent to £70 or £80 million today. Often no more than illiterate adventurers or ex-convicts, they spent their money on lavish houses, French tutors for their children and clothes from the Paris fashion houses for their wives.

By far the most exciting occasion in the Irkutskian social calendar for 1891 was the visit of the Tsarevich (later Nicholas II) who only stayed a day but still had time to visit the museum, the gold-smelting laboratory and the monastery, to consecrate and open the new pontoon bridge over the Angara (replaced only in 1936), to review the troops and to attend a ball at the public club. On 16 August 1898 Irkutsk was linked by rail to Europe with the arrival of the first Trans-Siberian Express.

The first rail travellers arrive
The train brought more European tourists than had dared venture into Siberia in the days when travelling meant weeks of discomfort bumping along the Trakt (the Post Road) in a wooden tarantass (carriage). Their guide books warned them of the dangers that awaited them in Irkutsk. Bradshaw's *Through Routes to the Capitals of the World* (1903) had this to say about the town: 'The streets are not paved or lighted; the sidewalks are merely boards on crosspieces over the open sewers. In summer it is almost impassable owing to the mud, or unbearable owing to the dust. The police are few, escaped criminals and ticket-of-leave criminals many. In Irkutsk and all towns east of it, the stranger should not walk after dark; if a carriage cannot be got as is often the case, the only way is to walk noisily along the planked walk; be careful in making crossings, and do not stop, or the immense mongrel mastiffs turned loose into the streets as guards will attack. To walk in the middle of the road is to court attack from the garrotters with which Siberian towns abound.'

The dangers that Bradshaw warned his travellers against were no exaggeration for at the time the average number of reported murders per year in Irkutsk was over four hundred, out of a population of barely 50,000. There were also reports of criminals who roamed the streets in sledges, lassoing their victims and dragging them off to murder and rob them in the quieter back-streets.

Irkutsk today
Today's Irkutskians are rather better behaved, although mafia-related crime is on the increase. A city of over half a million, Irkutsk is still

one of the largest suppliers of furs to the world markets, although engineering is now the main industry.

For too long Irkutskians have had to allow Moscow to make all their political, economic and environmental decisions for them. Control is slowly being decentralised and there have been a number of victories recently. The wood pulp mill built on the edge of Lake Baikal is still an eyesore but filtration systems now ensure that waste water is purified before being returned to the lake. The city now needs to have direct access to the hard currency earned by its exports, so that the money can be spent improving the lot of the people of Irkutsk rather than disappearing into the bottomless coffers of Moscow. It seems likely, however, that the city will benefit from tourism with the increasing numbers of visitors stopping off on their way to Lake Baikal.

ORIENTATION AND SERVICES

Irkutsk railway station is on the west bank of the river; the city centre and the tourist hotels are on the east. Any bus heading north from the railway station should take you over the bridge (ask for Ploshchad Kirova); from here all hotels are within walking distance.

The **Intourist office** is at the Intourist Hotel; the people here are helpful and speak good English.

Irkutsk has a **Mongolian Embassy** (tel 34 21 45: consul, or 37 27 47: front desk) at 11 Ul Lapina. It's open 09.00-18.00. In theory, it's possible to get a transit visa here in only 45 minutes (bring two passport photographs, US$30 and your ticket out of Mongolia). In fact, it's likely to be more difficult than this unless you speak Russian or Mongolian.

WHERE TO STAY

The **Hotel Intourist** (tel 29 63 35) is the best in town. At US$60 for a single or US$80 for a double (all with attached bathrooms) rooms are expensive but they're clean and pleasant. There are two restaurants and as far as the locals are concerned, this is the liveliest spot in Irkutsk and the scene of rowdy wedding receptions.

The **Hotel Angara** (tel 24 16 31) was the main hotel used for foreigners until the Intourist was built in the late 1980s. It then declined rapidly but is now improving. Singles are US$30, doubles US$40, all with attached bathrooms. Rather more basic is the **Hotel Sibir** (tel 29 37 51) just across Kirov Square from the Angara. It's not as nice, and the management occasionally turns foreigners away but it's only US$8.50 single or US$17 double.

On the western side of the river there's **MNTK** (see p26), at 337 Ul Lermontova (tel 46 25 69), which charges US$65 single or US$90 double although rates may be cheaper if you manage to get one of the four-bed rooms. You'll have to take a taxi from the station, as it takes about a hour to walk here.

TRANSPORT

Since most of the sights, restaurants and shops are within walking distance of the hotel, this is the most pleasant and interesting way to get around. There's no metro but the usual bus service operates. Bus No 20 runs between the station and the airport down Lenin Street. Trams 1 & 2 go from the station over the bridge and into the centre of town. Tram No 4 goes out to the airport (25 mins) from outside the Hotel Sibir Hotel, and back.

Getting to Listvyanka

Most people take the **'Raketa'** (hydrofoil) to get to Listvyanka on Lake Baikal (US$1.40, one hour, 3-4 departures a day). It's best to get a ticket for the earliest trip (usually 09.30). To get to the terminal, take bus No16 south from Ploshchad Kirova and ask to be let off at Raketa, which is a couple of stops beyond the Angara steamship. Alternatively, you could take a local **bus** (departures every 1½hrs for the 1½hr journey) from the bus station. If you can get a few people together a **taxi** is worth considering. Note that you'll probably be charged for the return trip even if you only want to take the taxi one way. It might be better to pay the driver to wait at Listvyanka and then bring you home, too.

TOURS

Intourist offers a two-hour **city tour** (US$20 not including the churches) and a **Baikal tour** (US$50 for a car but if there's a bus tour going you may be able to join it for US$15). The tour to Baikal leaves at 08.00 and gets back at around 18.00. Intourist occasionally runs its own boat trip to Listvyanka and this might be worth enquiring about if you don't want to arrange things yourself.

WHAT TO SEE

Cathedrals and War Memorial

In Irkutsk in 1900 there were two cathedrals. The splendid Cathedral of Our Lady of Kazan, bigger than Kazan Cathedral in St Petersburg, was damaged during the civil war. It was demolished and now

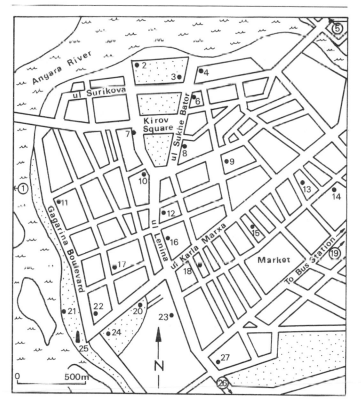

IRKUTSK

1 Railway Station
2 War Memorial
3 Church of Our Saviour
4 Cathedral of the Epiphany
5 Znamensky Convent
6 Catholic Church
7 Buses to Listvyanka
8 Hotel Angara
9 Circus & Aura Restaurant
10 Hotel Sibir
11 Hotel Intourist
12 Art Gallery
13 Synagogue
14 Decembrists' Museum

15 OVIR
16 Natural History Museum
17 Chinese Restaurant
18 Mongolian Embassy
19 Maria Volkonsky's House
20 Drama Theatre
21 Boat Trips
22 Governor's House
23 Fichtelberg Restaurant
24 Museum of Regional History
25 Explorers' Obelisk
26 To Listvyanka
27 Church of the Holy Cross

the ugly bulk of the **Palace of Pioneers** (the Central Government Building) stands in its place, opposite the **war memorial**. Here, in summer, you may be able to witness the strange spectacle of children dressed in army uniforms wielding rifles and guarding the memorial. Only children who get good marks in school are allowed the privilege of goose-stepping around the eternal flame. In 1993 this stopped but there are plans for it to restart.

The second cathedral, the **Cathedral of the Epiphany** (1724), is across the road, beside the river. In the great fire of 1879 it was badly damaged and the heat was so intense that it melted one of the 12-ton bells. It has recently been repainted inside and is now an icon museum and art gallery (exhibitions here change every few months). The cathedral is often used as a concert hall because of its excellent acoustic properties: a whisper towards one corner will be carried along the curved ceiling to the opposite one. It's sometimes permitted to climb up into the bell tower. Open 11.00-18.00.

Church of Our Saviour

This boat-shaped church is now a museum but may soon be reconsecrated. There are some interesting frescoes on the exterior which depict, from left to right, Buryats being baptised, Christ being baptised and the local bishop, Innocenti, being canonised. The museum inside contains a small display of stuffed local animals (see p304). Upstairs there's an interesting religious history display including the robes, rattle of human bones and feathered head-dress of a *shaman* (see below); masks and robes used in Tibetan Buddhist mystery plays; prayer wheels and Buddhist texts from the monasteries south of Irkutsk. Up a very narrow staircase here is a small exhibition of bells. Open 09.00-17.00, not Tuesday. Entry is US$0.40 and there's a camera charge of US$1.

Catholic Church

Opposite the Church of Our Saviour is a church with a tall steeple, the Catholic church. It is the only (mock) Gothic church in Siberia and was built in 1883 by exiled Poles; it is now used for organ concerts.

Museum of Regional History

This museum, situated beside the river just south of the Intourist Hotel, has some interesting exhibits. Upstairs is a 'local achievements' gallery including a model of part of the BAM (see p111). Above the stairs is a panorama showing the Great Fire of 1879. The ethnographic galleries are downstairs and exhibits include flints and bones from the archaeological site of Malta, just outside Irkutsk. ls1 where evidence of human habitation has been found dating back 24,000 years; the inside of a settler's house earlier this century with carved wooden side-board and HMV gramophone and 78s; a set of robes worn by a *shaman*, together with his antlers and drum; photographs showing what life was like for past inhabitants and the convicts; and also a most peculiar article of clothing: a suit made completely of fish skins, the standard summer costume of the Goldi tribe who lived in the Far Eastern Territories. The museum is open 10.00-16.00, not Mon. Entry is US$0.20.

Shamanism

This is a primitive form of religion centred around the shaman, a kind of medium and healer. Although the concept of the shaman is fairly common throughout the world, the word itself originally derives from the Tungus tribes of Siberia.

Wearing spectacular robes, the shaman would beat his drum and go into a trance in order to communicate with the spirits. From them he would discover the cause of an illness, the reason for the failure of the crops, or he would be warned of some approaching disaster. Commonly spirits were thought to select their shamans before they were born and brand them with distinguishing features: an extra finger or toe or a large birthmark. During their adolescence they would be 'tortured' by the spirits with an illness of some kind until they agreed to act as shaman. Often such people were epileptic, mentally disordered or physically weak. Through their spiritual power they gained authority and often large amounts of money for performing rituals.

'Shamanism played an extremely negative role in the history of the Siberian peoples... In status, activity and interests, the shamans were hand in glove with the ruling cliques of the indigenous populations', wrote the Marxist anthropologists M.G.Levin and L.P.Potapov, in *The Peoples of Siberia*. Other anthropologists have been less severe, noting that shamanism gave those with mental and physical disorders a place in society at a time when most other societies shunned the handicapped.

Other Churches

At the turn of the century, Irkutsk boasted fifty-eight places of worship. This fell to only three or four after the Revolution but with glasnost has risen to ten today.

The **Church of the Holy Saviour** at Znamensky Convent lies to the north-east of the city, over the bridge. The frescoes inside are very impressive but recent restoration has left the interior looking rather modern, a bit like the bizarre centre of some 60s sect. Don't wear shorts or you won't be allowed in. Services are held here regularly (check with Intourist for times). Note that the adjacent 'hotel' is for the clergy only. Beside the church are the graves of Yekaterine Trubetskoi (see p168) and also Gregory Shelekhov, who founded the colony of Alaska in 1784 (sold to the USA in 1868). His grave is marked by an obelisk decorated with cartographic instruments.

Orthodox services are also held at the **Church of the Holy Cross** which is reputed to have the best choir in the city.

It's also interesting to visit the **synagogue**, a large blue building, the lower storey of which has been converted into a factory. Enter through the door on left with the three stars above it. You may need to knock loudly to get the caretaker's attention and he'll then shuffle down in shirtsleeves and braces to open up. He'll check that you have some kind of head covering (there are a few caps you can borrow) and may give you a photocopy of the Ten Commandments.

Art Gallery

This is the most impressive art gallery east of the Urals and includes works by eighteenth and nineteenth century Russian, German, Flemish, French, Italian and English painters. The collection was begun by Vladimir Sukachev in the 1870s and 'donated' to the city after the Revolution. There are, however, the inevitable modern Soviet galleries where you can see such socialist masterpieces as A.A.Plastov's *Supper of Tractor Operators* and A.V.Moravov's *Calculating of Working Days*. The gallery devoted to nineteenth century local scenes is particularly interesting and in the gallery of the Western Art (XV-XIX centuries) you will find a small canvas with the label 'Landsir 1802-73' which is *The Family of Dogs* by Sir Edwin Landseer, who designed the lions in Trafalgar Square. Open daily (except Tue) from 11.00 to 16.00; entry is US$0.50.

Decembrists' 'Dom' Museum (Trubetskoi House)

The wooden house once occupied by Sergei and Yekaterine Trubetskoi (who is buried in the graveyard of the Church of the Holy Saviour) and other nobles involved in the unsuccessful coup in 1825 is preserved as a museum, kept as it was when the exiles lived here. The beautiful white porcelain fireplace in the drawing-room came from the old Grand Hotel. In the cellar there is an interesting display of old photographs showing life in the Nerchinsk silver mines and a prison cell in Chita. There is also a picture of Maria Volkonsky (see below) and her child. At 64 Ul Dzerzhinsky, it's open daily (except Tuesday) from 10.00-18.00. Entry is US$0.20. ('With thermopane windows it would be a great place'. Louis Wozniak (USA): Visitors' book in this museum.)

Maria Volkonsky's House

The large and attractive blue and white house of this famous Decembrist who followed her husband into Siberian exile is open to the public. If you've read Caroline Sutherland's *The Princess of Siberia* then you must visit Maria Volkonsky's house. It is a grand old building but it's a pity it's so sparsely furnished as it doesn't have the lived-in feel of the other 'Dom' museum. Displays include Maria's clothes, letters, furniture, and church robes of 18th and 19th centuries. In the yard there are several wooden buildings and a well. Open daily (except Monday) 10.00-18.00.

Angara steamship (Museum of Baikal Navigation)

The *Angara*, commissioned in 1899, was partially assembled in England and then sent to Irkutsk in pieces by train. Until the completion of the Circumbaikal line she ferried rail passengers across the lake, together with her bigger sister, the *Baikal*. Following the line's completion in 1904, the *Angara* performed a series of menial tasks before being abandoned, partially submerged, in 1958. Now lovingly restored, she houses the Museum of Baikal Navigation, containing displays of early bone harpoon tips and fishing equipment, nets, fish-traps and a small hoard of ship's navigational instruments.

To get here by bus: take bus No16 south from Kirov Square (towards the hydrofoil terminal) and be sure to keep an eye out for the ship on the right when the Angara River comes into view. Get off at the next stop and walk back towards the river (10 mins). The bus ride takes about 45 mins. The museum is open 10.00-17.30, daily except Monday; entry is US$0.20.

Other sights

In the summer, touring companies perform in the imposing **Drama Theatre**, built at the turn of the century, in Karl Marx Street. There are also **boat trips** (1-2hrs) along the river to the dam and power station. They leave daily from the landing-stage near the **Explorers' Obelisk** (Yermak and Count Muravyev-Amursky on its sides and the double-headed Imperial eagle on the railings surrounding it). The building beside the obelisk may look like a mini Sydney Opera House but its main use is for dog shows.

In the **Fur Distribution Centre**, on the southern outskirts of the city, visitors are shown some of the 18 varieties of mink and also the pelts of the Barguzinsk sable, which sell for over £500/US$750 each. It's open to tours only, and only between October and May.

The **Natural History Museum** has been closed 'for refurbishment' for the last three years and there is some debate as to whether it will ever reopen. Check the current state of play with Intourist. The collection used to contain examples of local animals that are trapped for their fur, the skeleton of a mammoth and a large collection of stuffed animals.

WHERE TO EAT

The newly-opened **Aura Restaurant**, on the first floor of the circus building, is currently the best place to eat in Irkutsk. It's a clean, well-organised private restaurant whose only drawback is the fact that there are striptease shows here on weekends. (An entry fee will indicate that there's a show in progress). The food is good, authentic Siberian fare: their pelmeni is recommended.

Next best but much less interesting is the **Hotel Intourist**. There are three restaurants here: an expensive Chinese place that's usually full in the evenings, the 'Irkutsk' and the 'Siberian Tract' restaurants. All serve reasonable food but service can be very slow unless you're with a group. Try the delicious *omul*, from Lake Baikal, if it's on the menu here.

The **Fichtelberg Restaurant**, on Ul Lenina isn't bad at all and serves an excellent steak with sour cream and wild garlic sauce for US$4. Unfortunately there's a house band, and it gets rather hot and stuffy here on summer evenings. The best oriental food is to be had at the **Chinese Restaurant** at 67 Fifth Army St but it's difficult to get in for dinner without a reservation.

Cafes and snack bars are common along Ul Karla Marxa.

WHAT TO BUY

The heart of the city is the market, which extends for several hundred metres behind the main shopping street, Ul Karla Marxa. It's not hard to find: long before you see it you'll hear the many bootleg cassette dealers demonstrating their 'latest' releases. Tapes sell for US$2-3, current favourites being REM and any dance track with a rhythm that goes 'whumpa-whumpa-whumpa'. Other stalls sell everything from Sindy dolls and Snickers bars to sports shoes and switchblades. It's also a good place to change money. Detsky Mir is the best proper shop in the market area. You can buy Kodak film here, or have your photographs processed in an hour.

The area outside the Intourist Hotel used to be the big black market hang-out but now there are only a few kids selling matrioshkas. Rip-off of the Year Award goes to the Intourist shop for selling Baikal water ('saturated with pure ozone-containing oxygen' (?) 'Bring a piece of Baikal to your home') at US$5 per litre. For US$5 you could take a taxi to Baikal and go swimming in the stuff.

Lake Baikal

The world's deepest lake

Sixty-four kilometres (forty miles) south of Irkutsk, Lake Baikal is 1637 metres (5371 feet) deep and is estimated to contain more than 20,000 cubic kilometres of water, roughly 20% of the world's freshwater supplies. If all the world's drinking water ran out tomorrow, Lake Baikal could supply the entire population of the planet for the next 40 years.

Known as the 'Blue Eye of Siberia' it is also the world's oldest lake, formed almost 50 million years ago. It's among the largest lakes on the planet, being about 400 miles long by between 20 and 40 miles wide. The water is incredibly clear and, except around Baikalsk and the Selenga delta, completely safe to drink owing to the filtering action of the numerous types of sponge which live in its depths, along with hundreds of other species found nowhere else.

Holy Sea

Russian colonists called Baikal the 'Holy Sea' since there were so many local myths and legends surrounding it. The Buryats believed that the evil spirit Begdozi lived on Olkhon Island in the middle,

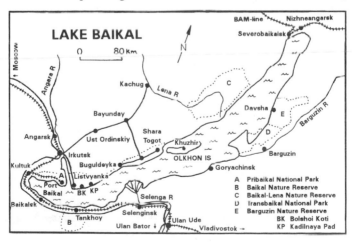

though the Evenki shamans held that this was the home of the sea
god, Dianda. It is hardly surprising that these primitive tribes were
impressed by the strange power of the lake for at times sudden
violent storms spring up, lashing the coast with waves up to seven
feet high. It freezes to a depth of about ten feet for four months of
the year, from late December. The Angara is the only river that
flows out of the lake and since the dam and hydro-electric power
station were built on the Angara in 1959, the water-level of the lake
has been slowly rising.

Environmental threats
The remoteness of the lake kept it safe from the threat of environmental damage until the building of the Trans-Siberian at the end of
the last century. Damage to the environment is increasing following
the building of the new towns on the northern shores for the construction of the BAM line, and also owing to industrial waste from
Ulan Ude (the Selenga River flows past the city into the lake via one
of the world's last large wetlands, the Selenga delta). The most
famous campaigner for the protection of the lake is author Valentin
Rasputin. Demonstrations in Irkutsk in 1987 resulted in filtration
equipment being installed in the wood pulp mill at Baikalsk, on the
edge of the lake but current reports suggest that it is inefficient and
that pollution is continuing. A coastal protection zone was established around the edge of the entire lake in 1987 but campaigners
bemoan the fact that the government's anti-pollution laws have no
teeth. They believe that the lake should be placed under the independent protection of UNESCO.

GETTING TO LAKE BAIKAL

The road from Irkutsk takes you through taiga forests to the lakeside
village of Listvyanka. Intourist offer day-long tours (see p164) with
guide, lunch, visit to the Limnological Institute and a short boat-trip
on the lake. You can travel out here independently from Irkutsk by
hydrofoil or local bus (see p164). It's easy to get a bus back from
Listvyanka: just stand at the stops by the port or by the Limnological
Institute and flag the bus down. It leaves Listvyanka at 07.00, 11.50,
14.40, 18.00, plus an extra bus at 15.50 (Fri, Sat, Sun) and there
may be an additional bus at 09.45 daily in the summer.

Open Air Museum
Beside the road between Irkutsk and Listvyanka is the Museum of
Wooden Architecture, an interesting collection of reconstructed,
traditional wooden houses. It is located at the km47 marker from

Irkutsk, the km23 marker from Listvyanka - ask the bus driver for the 'Moozay'. There is a large farmhouse, a bathroom with a vast wooden tub and, a short way along a path, a water-mill and a post-house, complete with the Imperial crest on its roof-top. When the only way to cross Siberia was by road and river, fresh horses and simple accommodation were available from post-houses. The museum is open only in the summer but you can wander round outside in spring and autumn.

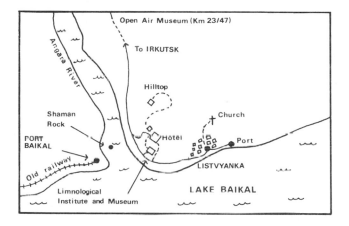

LISTVYANKA

This attractive village of wooden houses lies at the end of the road right beside the lake. There's a shop, two small restaurants and the jetty. The Limnological Institute and the Hotel Baikal above it are about one kilometre before the village on the road from Irkutsk.

Where to stay

Above the road and just before the village is the pleasant **Intourist Hotel** (tel 11 22 34) where most tours stop for lunch. Rooms are from US$21/28 for a single/double with attached bathroom up to US$130 for a suite. Various services are offered here including bike hire (US$6 per day), skiing, sleigh rides, boat trips and riding. There is an expensive sauna, too. Behind the hotel is a hill that gives a good view over the water to the Khamar Daban Mountains. The half-hour hike up is well worth it. At the top there's a little shelter and a tree decorated with paper ribbons that people have tied to it for good luck, a very old Siberian superstition.

Cheaper places to stay should be opening soon in the Listvyanka area. The Travellers Guest House Moscow (see p135) is about to open a new hostel here offering accommodation to budget travellers.

The Limnological Institute and Museum

This was set up for the study of the unique marine life and animals in the Baikal area. Over 80 per cent of the species here cannot be found anywhere else in the world. The exceptionally high oxygen levels in the lake create the ideal environment for many creatures which have long since become extinct elsewhere. These include the freshwater seals, found only here and until recently threatened with extinction by the Buryats who turned them into overcoats. They are now a protected species, listed in the 'Red Book' and currently number about 60,000. A unique Baikal fish is the tiny *golomyanka* which, composed almost entirely of transparent fat, lives at extreme depths. Surprisingly, like a mammal, it gives birth to its young alive and fully formed. The museum also contains a model of the *Angara*, some examples of the tasty *omul* (which appears on local menus) and a collection of the sponges which keep the water so clean. The colonists' wives discovered that they were also very useful for polishing the samovar. There are ambitious plans for a new ecology centre to be built here and a model is on display. Entry is US$1.

Listvyanka Church

A pleasant ten-minute walk through the village takes you to a tiny church in which an old woman sells cheap-looking icons. Although the village is worth seeing, one feels that this church has been part of the Intourist 'milk-run' for a long time. 'No smoking on the territory of the Church', warns a sign in English. Concessions to tourists have their advantages: five-star lavatories are thoughtfully located behind the building.

Life-enhancing waters

Guides never fail to recount the superstition concerning the power of Baikal water. Dip your hands in, they say, and you will live a year longer than you otherwise would. Dip your feet in too and this will be extended to five years. Brave the icy waters for a swim and, if the shock doesn't kill you instantly, you'll be around for twenty-five extra years.

A world record was set in here in 1991, as a team of relay swimmers managed to cross the width of the lake in 17 hours. Even these intrepid athletes had trouble, though: because of the extreme cold, the longest period any one of them could spend in the water at one time was 30 minutes.

Shaman Rock

In the stretch of water between the Limnological Institute and Port Baikal it's just possible to make out the top of a rock sticking out of the water. The legend relating to its origin is as follows: Old Man Baikal had 336 sons (the number of rivers which flow into the lake) and one daughter, the beautiful but headstrong Angara. She enraged him by refusing to marry the weak and feeble Irkut, preferring the mighty Yenisei (Russia's longest river). The old man chained her up but one stormy night she slipped her bonds and fled north to her lover. As she ran her furious father hurled a huge boulder after her. She got away but the rock remained to this day, a small point showing above the water. The level of the lake has since risen and very little of Shaman Rock is now visible.

Port Baikal

Across the water the dilapidated station and warehouses of old Port Baikal lie rotting. Until the railway line around the south of the lake was completed in 1904, passengers crossed by steamer to Mysovaya. The largest ship was a 290 foot ice-breaker, the *Baikal*, which transported the carriages from the train on her deck. She was built by the English firm of Sir W.G.Armstrong, Whitworth and Co. in Newcastle, delivered by train in kit-form and she sank in 1919 during the Civil War. Her sister ship, the smaller *Angara*, supplied by the same firm, survived and is now a museum (see p169).

It's possible to visit Port Baikal, and *Babushkin* makes the half hour crossing (May-Dec) from Listvyanka at 07.35, 9.10, 11.45, 16.10, 18.10, 19.40, 20.45 and back from Port Baikal at 06.25, 8.05, 10.00, 14.00, 17.05, 18.40, 20.05. Tickets are available on the quay.

Intourist occasionally organises an all-day excursion to see the old railway line by boat, landing for lunch on a beach. Tunnels and viaducts are still in perfect condition and a train is reputed to run at night along the track from Port Baikal to Kultuk on the main Trans-Siberian line. It would be difficult to try to ride this railway as there seem to be numerous guards in the area.

Bolshoi Koti and Kadilnaya Pad

Visits to these two Baikal villages have been recommended by a number of readers. Guides offer organised excursions including a 25km hike through the taiga to **Bolshoi Koti**, then by boat to **Kadilnaya Pad**, where tourists stay in hunters' lodges and can have authentic Siberian Baths (see overleaf).

You could do part of this trip independently as there's a boat that makes the trip to Bolshoi Koti from Listvyanka daily. It's only a small fishing village but it's considerably less touristy than Listvyanka. There's a small beach and the locals are especially friendly. (Two English visitors in 1993 stopped a villager to enquire whether it was possible to arrange a boat trip, and he insisted that they borrow his boat and fishing rods for the weekend!). There are no hotels here but it may be possible to arrange homestays in advance (see pp20-33). If the Travellers Guest House is operating in Listvyanka they should be able to give more details.

Trips can also be arranged to **Olkhon Island**, ideal for those who like lying around in the sun and doing nothing but daydreaming or fishing. Be warned that the only food you are likely to get here is omul.

Siberian bath rituals with birchen besoms
In the words of an Intourist brochure: 'Siberian bath is an incomparable experience. Its heat is milder than in sauna, it is lighter and not scorching. A birchen besom exuding forest fragrance is its traditional accessory. In the steam room bath lovers lightly lash each other with birchen besom for hours on end, and then plunge into a snow-drift or into a cold stream, depending on the season. This makes the ritual complete'.

Other Siberian excursions

BRATSK

Three hundred miles north of Irkutsk lies one of the largest dams in the world. The enormous hydro-electric power station at Bratsk, second largest in the Russia after the one at Krasnoyarsk, is the chief attraction of this town. Originally founded in 1631 it was never more than a tiny village until construction started on the dam in 1955. It reputedly produces 4.5 million kW of electricity. It's estimated that eventually the new Russian power station on the Tungusku River will be able to produce 20 million kW. The Raul Leoni plant in Venezuela is currently the world's largest power station, producing 10.3 million kW.

Bratsk is on the BAM railway but unless you're stopping off on this line, or unless you're especially interested in power stations, there seems little reason to come here. In the words of one visitor: 'The dam is a dam. You can go down into the bowels of the Hoover Dam and be over-awed. This one just has a posh reception centre with a huge mural of Lenin. It's really not worth the effort to visit the dam or even to go to Bratsk at all'. Bob Helling (UK).

The town of Bratsk is actually four separate communities arranged around the vast dam and connected by a road which runs right over the five-kilometre-long dam wall. Tourists stay at the bleak **Taiga Hotel**, the best of the three in the town, located in the centre of Bratsk, or else in the **Bratsk**.

After the **power station**, the town's other sights are the **open-air museum** (which has some interesting reconstructions of traditional houses, a Cossack watchtower and an abundance of azaleas in spring), the wooden **puppet theatre** and the **toboggan slide**.

Getting to Bratsk

From Irkutsk, you could take the hydrofoil, which leaves Irkutsk at 08.30, arriving in Bratsk at 20.55. On the return journey it leaves at 07.50 arriving at 20.45 in Irkutsk.

If you're coming by train from the west, the BAM line branches off the Trans-Siberian at Tayshet (650km west of Irkutsk). There are daily connections to Moscow.

ABAKAN

Founded at the end of the 18th century as Ust Abakanskoye, the town became Abakan in 1931 and has now developed into an industrial city of 165,000 people, the administrative centre of the Khakassia Republic. Its main attraction is its pleasant location among rolling hills, and hiking trips can be organised from here.

The main tourist accommodation is in the **Intourist Hotel**, at 54 Ul Khakasskaya. Sights include the **Local Lore Museum** with its unique collection of outlandish stone sculptures, many just rough-hewn heads on huge long necks. Found along the banks of the Abakan and Yenisei Rivers, they are reminiscent of the Easter Island statues. There's also a **zoo** with Siberian fauna.

Several excursions can be organised from Abakan. **Sushenskoye**, on the banks of the Yenisei, is where Lenin began his married life. Exiled in 1897, he was joined by Krupskaya and they stayed in the village until 1900. The Russians are good at open-air museums and whole streets are recreated here: houses of rich traders, poor peasants, shop, tavern and bathhouse.

Minusinsk is a small town 20km from Abakan, with a well-preserved central part, a museum and the Cathedral of Our Saviour. You may also be taken to the **Sayano-Sushenskoye Dam and Hydro-electric Station**, the old mining settlement at **Maina** and the tourist centre on the banks of the Yenisei.

Getting to Abakan

There are flights from several cities including Moscow and Irkutsk. To come by train you leave the main Trans-Siberian line at Krasnoyarsk (Train Nos 23/24 & 657/658) or Achinsk (Nos 193/194 & 659/660) and it's about 12hrs from either station.

YAKUTSK

This is the capital of the vast Yakut Autonomous Region (see p262). Lying only 600km south of the Arctic Circle, it is one of the world's coldest cities (average temperature in January is minus 32°C) although summers are pleasantly warm (plus 19°C in July). It is also one of Siberia's oldest settlements, founded in 1632 on the banks of the mighty Lena River as a base for exploration and a trading centre for gold and furs. There is little left of historic interest in this polluted city but it is worth visiting for the excursions on the Lena and to see the effects of permafrost. All the buildings here have to be built on massive stilts or they would sink into the ground, the heat from them melting the permafrost.

Only about 30% of the people are Yakut, the majority of the rest being Russians and Ukrainians. Like other minority groups in Russia the Yakuts are now making themselves heard in Moscow. They have been exploited since the region was first colonised 350 years ago and even now most of the foreign exchange earned from their fabulously rich region stays in Moscow.

Getting to Yakutsk

Until the rail link is finished (which will be many years from now as there is still 800km to cover) the only way in is by plane from Irkutsk, Moscow or several other cities. There are sometimes direct flights between Yakutsk and its twin city, Fairbanks in Alaska.

Where to stay

The new hotel in the town centre may now be open. If not, the best hotel is the **Yakutsk**, although visitors complain about the shortage of lavatory seats. The **Lena** is also sometimes used for foreigners.

What to see

The most interesting place to visit in Yakutsk is the **Permafrost Institute**. You are taken 12 metres underground to see part of the old river bed, where the temperature never varies from -5°C. Permafrost is said to affect 25% of the earth and 50% of Russia. Outside the Institute is a model of the baby mammoth (now in St Petersburg Natural History Museum) that was found preserved in permafrost.

The **Yakutian State History and Culture Museum**, housed in what was formerly the Bishop's Palace, is one of the oldest museums in Siberia. It is said to include over 140,000 items illustrating Yakut flora, fauna and anthropology. Outside is an *ostrog* (wooden fort). The **Museum of Yakut Music and Folklore**, at 8 Ul Kirova, has an interesting display about Yakut shamanism. There's also the **Yakut Literature Museum**, with a large yurt outside it and the **Geological Museum**, crammed full of all the geological wealth of Yakutia. A Museum of the Mammoth is planned. Tours can be arranged to Yakut and Evenk reindeer breeding farms.

Several churches are now open: the Russian Orthodox (5, Ul Ushakov) and the Baptist (14, Ul Pilotov). The **Church of St Nicholas**, visible from the Hotel Yakutsk, was built in 1852 and until recently served as the Communist Party archives.

Intourist (at the Hotel Yakutsk) and Yakutintour (6 Ul Arzhakova) in Yakutsk are very helpful and keen to develop tourism in their region. Possible future excursions may include trips to the Arctic and even the North Pole.

Excursions on the Lena River

The geological formations known as the **Lena Pillars** have fascinated travellers since the 17th century. About 140km upriver from Yakutsk, the rock of the cliffs alongside the river has been eroded away into delicate shapes of a reddish brown colour. Hydrofoil excursions leave around 08.00, often with breakfast (followed by vodka and cognac) on board. You reach the landing spot about four hours later and it takes about an hour's strenuous climb to reach the top for a magnificent view of the river and the cliffs. A picnic is usually organised. Be very careful disembarking: one of our party (who'd overdone the vodka at breakfast) toppled off the flimsy gang-plank into the chilly waters.

On the way to the Lena Pillars you pass the archaeological site of **Dering Yuryakh**, where, in 1982, evidence of man dating back 1-2 million years was discovered, putting the site on a par with Professor Leakey's excavations in Africa. There's not much to see but there are plans for a museum.

Cruise ships *M/S Demyan Bedny* and *M/S Mikhail Svetlov* do 7-10-day trips along the Lena River starting from Yakutsk, passing the Lena Pillars and continuing to the river port of Lensk before returning.

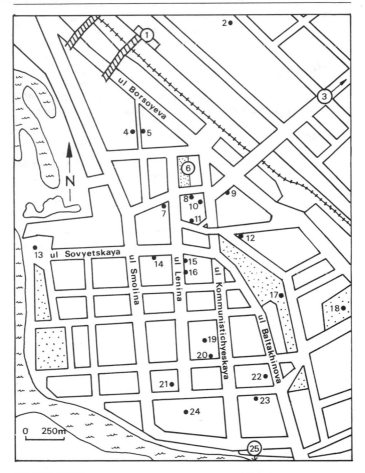

ULAN UDE

1 Railway Station
2 Hotel Odon
3 Open Air Museum
4 Hotel Geser
5 Intourist
6 Main Square
7 Opera House
8 Hotel Baikal
9 Book/Poster Shop
10 Coffee Shop
11 Hotel Buryatia
12 Buryat Lit. Museum
13 Main Bus Station
14 Hotel Barguzine
15 Natural Hist. Museum
16 Bookshop
17 War Memorial
18 Troitskaya Church
19 Department Store
20 Art Museum
21 Bus Park
22 Market
23 Hotel Zolotoye Kolos
24 Historical Museum
25 Church

Ulan Ude

Ulan Ude is well worth a stop if only to visit the **Datsan** (35km outside the city), the centre of Buddhism in Russia and until recently one of the few operating Buddhist monasteries in the CIS. Rail enthusiasts may also be interested in a visit to the **locomotive repair workshops**. The people of Ulan Ude are very friendly and hospitable and the place has a relaxed atmosphere to it, with quite a few traditional Siberian wooden buildings still standing. Tourist facilities are still fairly basic but are improving as more foreigners become interested in adventure tours around Lake Baikal, 100km (62 miles) to the north.

Ulan Ude is a 45-minute flight, or a 7½-hour train journey, from Irkutsk. Air links with Ulan Bator have been established and a new service to Beijing is planned.

HISTORY

Military outpost
In 1668 a military outpost was set up here in the valley between the Khamar Daban and Tsaga Daban mountain ranges. Strategically located beside the Selenga and Ude rivers, it was named Verkhneudinsk. A cathedral was built in 1745 and the town became a key trading centre on the route of the tea caravans from China. The railway reached the town in 1900 and in 1949 the branch line to Mongolia was opened.

Ulan Ude today
Capital of the Buryat Republic, Ulan Ude is now a pleasant city of nearly 400,000 people (only 21% of whom are Buryats, the rest mainly Russians). Local industries include the large railway repair workshop and locomotive plant (which until 1956 produced steam engines), food processing, helicopter assembly and glass making.

Buildings here require firm foundations since the city is in an earthquake zone. The most recent 'quake, measuring 9.5 on the Richter scale, was in 1959 but because its epicentre was directly beneath Lake Baikal nobody was killed.

The military bases in the area kept Ulan Ude off-limits to foreigners until the recent thaw in East-West relations. Princess Anne led the tourists in in 1990 with the first royal visit to Russia since the

Tsar's execution in 1918. A local official declared that her visit was probably the most exciting thing to have happened in the region since Genghis Khan swept through on his way to Moscow in 1239.

ORIENTATION AND SERVICES

To reach the centre of town from the railway station, cross the line on the pedestrian bridge. It takes about 15 minutes to walk to Lenin Square. The main hotels and the Intourist office are all in this area.

The Intourist office, staffed by charming and helpful people, is currently to be found in the Hotel Geser.

WHERE TO STAY

The **Hotel Buryatia** (tel 21 835) is at last open, having taken the best part of 15 years to be completed, although it'll probably be another couple of years before all the floors are furnished. Rooms are US$22/50 for a single/double with attached bathroom but prices are sure to go up as more facilities open. The old Communist Party hotel, the **Hotel Geser** (tel 25 954) is, at the moment, much better organised. Singles are US$40 and doubles US$50. The main Intourist office is located here, too.

There are numerous cheaper hotels but none is particularly good. The best of them seems to be the **Hotel Barguzine** (tel 28 103) with rooms for US$8/10. It doesn't always have hot water but does have friendly staff and a stuffed bear in the foyer. The **Hotel Baikal** (tel 23 718) is popular with black marketeers and offers double rooms for US$15. Less pleasant hotels include the **Hotel Odon** (tel 43 480) and the **Zolotoye Kolos** (no phone at all).

Intourist and foreign travel companies can book homestays, and this is probably the best option if you are on a tight budget. Charges are about US$10-20 per night but you should book in advance; don't just show up at the office and demand a bed for the night.

TRANSPORT

Most places, except the Datsan and the Open-air museum, are within walking distance but there's also a **tram** and **bus** service that operates as in any other Russian city. **Taxis** congregate in the usual places: outside the hotels and by the railway and bus stations but are not in great supply.

To get to the **Datsan** either get a taxi or take local bus No 104 (Kolonova) from the main bus station. There are four buses daily and the ride takes about 45 minutes. Alternatively bus No 130 (every 30 mins) goes as far as the village of Yevolga from which it's a 4½ mile/7½km walk across the plain to the Datsan (walk straight ahead out of the village, then turn right after about 2 miles/3km; you can see the Datsan from there).

To reach the **Open-air museum** (20mins) take bus Nos 8 or 35 from the bus park near the old church (see map).

TOURS

There are tours to all of the major sights, and also a number of excursions to places you will never have heard of. The resurgence of Buddhism in the area has resulted in the reopening, reconstruction, or construction of a large number of Buddhist temples and monasteries. Intourist is quite willing to take you to any of them. Notable examples include the **Tamcha Datsan** (150 km from Ulan Ude) founded in 1741. The ten-hour tour costs US$80 for a car or US$20 if you go as part of a group on a bus tour. A tour to **Atsagat Temple** (50km) costs US$50 for a car or US$12 on a group tour.

Other tours go to **Lake Baikal**, some of the old cities along the tea route to China (**Kyakhta, Novoselenginsk** etc), or to remote villages with interesting ethnic roots (**Bolshoi Kunali**). They will also arrange **helicopter trips** for US$400 per hour.

WHAT TO SEE

Ivolginsky Datsan (monastery)

The centre of Russian Buddhism stands on a wide plain 35km outside the city and it's a fascinating place to visit. Before the Revolution there were hundreds of similar monasteries in the area with the largest and most important at Selenginsk (see p271). Almost all were closed and the monks sent to the gulags but when Stalin sanctioned greater religious tolerance in the 1940s, astrologers selected this site for a new monastery and it was built in 1946. There are now 30 lamas, some of them very elderly but novices still join each year and most spend up to five years studying in Ulan Bator. Tibetan Buddhism is practised here and the Dalai Lama has visited the Datsan five times, most recently in September 1992 when the crowds that came to see him filled the entire monastery enclosure.

Visiting the Datsan See p182 for how to get here. As you walk around the Datsan don't forget that you should walk clockwise around objects of Buddhist veneration (prayer wheels, temples and stupas); hats must be taken off inside the buildings. The largest temple, a three-storey building built in 1971, burnt down four months after completion, with the loss of numerous valuable *thang-kas* (paintings). It was rebuilt in just seven months. Inside, its joyous technicolour decoration seems rather out of place in grey Russia: golden dragons slide down the sixteen wooden columns supporting the upper galleries (where there is a library of Tantric texts), and hundreds of incarnations of the Buddha line one wall. Easy to recognise is Manla, with the dark blue face, the Buddha of Tibetan medicine. The largest thangka hanging above the incarnations is of the founder of this 'Yellow Hat' (Gelukpa) sect. Juniper wood is burnt and food and money offered to the incarnations. Visitors are shown round by a smiling monk. Be sure to make a donation, bearing in mind the tremendous cost of the rebuilding projects that are now being carried out of old monasteries throughout the region.

Beside this is a smaller pagoda, and the **green temple** behind it is the oldest building in the complex, constructed in 1946. The octagonal white building houses a model of **Paradise** (*Devashin*) and a library of several hundred Tibetan and Mongolian texts, each wrapped in silk. In the big **white stupa** nearby are the ashes of the most famous former head lama of the Datsan, Sherapov, who died in 1961. There is even a **Bo tree** growing very successfully in its own greenhouse from seeds brought in 1956 from Delhi. Visiting Buddhists stay in the 'hotel' and students now come from all over the CIS to spend time studying Buddhism here.

Snacks are available at the kiosk outside, which is where the buses go from. You could also try hitching a ride back in a tour-bus.

Cultural/Historical Museum
A new home has still not been found for this fantastic collection devoted to Lamaism (Tibetan Buddhism) and the spiritual culture of the Buryats. Assembled mainly from monasteries closed after the Revolution, it is stored in the old cathedral by the river and visits are only possible by special arrangement through the Intourist office (US$5). Ask to visit the *fond* (museum warehouse).

Packed into the dilapidated building there are numerous Buddha figures; the robes of a Buryat shaman; musical instruments (conches and horns and a beautiful guitar with a carved horse's head); a large collection of masks used in Buddhist mystery plays; icons dating back to the 17th century; a display of day-to-day objects from the houses of the rich traders of Kyakhta (see p271) including a Roger & Gallet shaving-cream mug; a large and valuable collection of Tibetan thangkas including healing thangkas used by those monks practising Tibetan medicine. There is also a unique *Atlas of Tibetan Medicine*. The fact that it's all just piled up and collecting dust only adds to the

Indiana Jones atmosphere of the place. If you can't get a tour with Intourist try the door anyway but if you're looking for someone to let you in watch out for the extraordinarily vicious dogs round the back.

Natural History Museum
Some of the interesting displays here include a Lake Baikal panorama with flora and fauna (ask an attendant to turn on the 'authentic Siberian' soundtrack for you) and a model of the mini-submarine Pisces XI which reached a depth of 1410m in the lake in 1977; there are two large galleries of local wildlife: eagles, wolves, bears and reindeer etc. Since one of the world's few remaining wetlands is the Selenga Delta on the edge of Lake Baikal, there is also a comprehensive display of local birds. Labels are in Cyrillic and Latin (see p304). Entry is US$0.20 and the museum is open daily except Monday.

Open-air/Ethnographic Museum
One of the best of the numerous open-air museums in the country, this collection of reconstructed buildings lies on the northern outskirts of the city (see p183 for how to get there). Exhibits include a Bronze Age stone circle; Evenki camp with birchwood wig-wam, implements including a sable trap, skis and sledges, and a shaman's hut with wooden carvings outside it: birds on poles, animals and fish. There is a dreadful zoo with camels standing in the mud, bears in tiny cages and disconsolate reindeer (the more people that complain to the guides about this the better). The Buryat area contains *ghers* (yurts) of felt and wood and also a log cabin in which there are silk robes and day-to-day items. There are also houses of Kazakhs, Cossacks and 17th century Orthodox Christians, built around large brick ovens with sleeping platforms above them. Except in midsummer it gets very cold walking round here; bring warm clothing.

Locomotive Works
Between 1938 and 1956 steam locomotives were built here and there is a preserved example of one (SO17u) mounted on the right-hand side of the road to the open-air museum, not far past the railway bridge. The works are situated at the northwest end of the railway station. Visits (US$5) may be arranged through Intourist.

Troitskaya Church
This small, attractive church, built in 1798, has recently reopened and is undergoing renovation. Only a small section of the interior is currently open but it looks good; new bells were fixed in 1993. As at many Russian churches, begging babooshkas crowd around the entrance.

Other sights

Check with the service bureau to find out if there is anything on at the impressive **opera house** (the season is Oct-May). It's on the square dominated by the sinister bulk of **Lenin's head**, the biggest in the world; standing in front of him you feel like Dorothy meeting the Wizard of Oz. It's worth spending some time wandering around the town and there are still quite a few ornate wooden buildings to be seen here. Over the bridge at the south end of town is the **Russian Orthodox church** where services are held regularly. Marriages take place at the **Wedding House** next door to the Hotel Baikal. The **Art Museum** contains both Buryat and classical Russian art but is currently closed. The **Buryat Literary Museum** is probably of limited interest but upstairs there are two exhibits explaining a 17th century Tibetan canon of medicine.

WHERE TO EAT

The best restaurants in Ulan Ude are still the ones in the hotels. The **Geser** serves reasonable food and the service is quite good. A large meal including a couple of drinks will cost US$5-8; the over-friendly women who drift up to your table and ask if you're 'hungry' will probably cost rather more. The restaurant in the **Baikal** is similar, though it's a bit bigger and US$2 will buy you a reasonable two course meal without the harassment. If it ever fully opens, the **Hotel Buryatia** should be more upmarket. The **coffee bars** in the Hotel Barguzine and behind the Hotel Baikal have been recommended, and the snack bar in the Hotel Geser isn't bad, either.

A new restaurant, **Myth**, serves good Russian and Buryat dishes but is quite far from the main hotels, near the football stadium at 1A Ul Myokovsky, on the way to the open air museum. Buses 3, 8, 29 and 30 stop nearby - ask for the stop 'Kinema Oktyabra'. A meal here will cost you about US$5 without drinks.

WHAT TO BUY

Fresh fruit and vegetables are available in the market. There's a good bookshop with a wide selection of posters, books in English and also sheet music near the main square, and another down Ul. Lenina, which is the main shopping street.

Interesting Siberian alcohol is brewed at 1 Ul Novokuznetskaya. Under the brand name 'Crystal' it comes in a range of colours and it's worth buying a bottle just for the label: 'The smell of Siberian taiga which you'd never visited givs you a happy recollection of last summer!'. Sounds rather like a crossword clue.

Khabarovsk

Khabarovsk is a relaxed provincial city of 600,000 people, pleasantly located beside the Amur River. In the summer, holiday crowds flock to the sandy river banks, giving the place the atmosphere of a friendly English seaside resort; (but for some reason sunbathing in Russia is often done standing up). It's bitterly cold here in winter and when the river freezes, people drive their cars onto it and fish through holes chopped in the two-foot thick ice. Apart from the river, the other sights include an interesting Regional History Museum, a Military Museum and the arborctum, which was founded over one hundred years ago to supply the numerous parks and gardens in the city.

Until recently, rail passengers bound for Japan were required to change trains here, spending the day in Khabarovsk before catching the overnight 'tourist special' to the coast. The two reasons for this were both security-related. Because Vladivostok was home to the USSR's Pacific fleet, the port was out of bounds to foreigners and boats to Japan left from Nakhodka, 90km to the east; since the line east of Khabarovsk passed very close to the border with China, foreigners were required to make this journey at night to discourage them from taking photographs. Now most boats to Japan leave from Vladivostok so travellers need not get off here, although Khabarovsk is a pleasant enough place to spend a day or two.

HISTORY

In 1858 a military settlement was founded here by Count Muravyev-Amurski, the governor general of East Siberia who did much to advance Russia's interests in the Far East. It was named Khabarovka, in honour of the Cossack explorer who conquered the Amur region in the 17th century, and whose statue now stands in the square in front of the railway station. By 1883 the town was known as Khabarovsk and the following year, when the Far Eastern Territories were made a region separate from Eastern Siberia, it became the administrative centre and home of the governor general of the area.

Until the railway arrived, the town was just a trading and military post picturesquely situated on three hills on the banks of the Amur River, where it is joined by its tributary, the Ussuri. It was a junction for passengers who arrived by steamer from west Siberia, along the Shilka and Amur rivers. Here they would transfer to another ship for the voyage down the Amur and Ussuri to Vladivostok.

From 1875 onwards several plans were submitted for the building of the Ussuri Railway, which now runs along the great river between Khabarovsk and Vladivostok. Work began in 1893 and on 3 September 1897 a train completed the first journey between these two towns. A railway technical school was opened in the following year on the street that is now named Ul Karla Marxa.

Early visitors
As more of the sections of the Trans-Siberian Railway were built, greater numbers of foreign travellers arrived in Khabarovsk. The *1900 Guide to the Great Siberian Railway* did not encourage them to stay long, reporting that: 'The conditions of life in Khabarovsk are not attractive, on account of the absence of comfortable dwellings, and the expensiveness of some products and of most necessary articles ..... Imported colonial goods are sold at a high price and only fish is very cheap.' Tourists at the time were also advised against trying Mr Khlebnikov's locally produced wine, made from the wild vines that grow in the area because: 'it is of inferior quality and without any flavour'. Recommended sights included the wooden triumphal arch (now demolished) erected in commemoration of the visit of the Tsarevich Nicholas in 1891 and the bronze statue of Count Muravyev-Amurski on the promontory above the river. After the Revolution the count was traded in for an image from the Lenin Statue Factory but he has recently been replaced.

The city today
The railway brought more trade than tourists and though it suffered during the Civil War, the town quickly grew into the modern city it is today. Few of the old wooden cabins remain but there are some attractive stone buildings from Imperial times. It is the capital of Khabarovsk kray (territory) and one of the regions with the richest mineral deposits in the CIS, although the land is little more than a gigantic swampy forest. Khabarovsk is now a major industrial centre involved in engineering, petroleum refining and timber-working.

ORIENTATION AND SERVICES
Khabarovsk is a large city; the railway station and the Hotel Intourist are about 3-4kms (2 miles) apart, a half-hour walk.

The Intourist office is at this hotel and many of the tourist sights are within walking distance of it.

WHERE TO STAY

The main tourist hotel is the **Intourist** (tel 33 65 07) which is expensive (singles/doubles at US$112/114) but is, however, surprisingly well organised and pleasant. There's a number of good shops on the ground floor, an excellent restaurant on the eleventh, and the service bureau on the second offers a wide range of excursions. In its brochure, the hotel is described as 'a twelve storey modern style building with a clear-cut architectural silhouette'.

There are two hotels that are even better than the Intourist but since neither has more than seven rooms and both are popular with business travellers, you're unlikely to be able to get in unless you book well in advance. The **Hotel Sapporo** (tel 33 27 02) charges US$105/158 and the **Hotel Parus** (tel 33 72 70) US$175/300.

MNTK (tel 39 94 01) is situated a fair way away from the centre of town, at 211 Ul Tikhookeanskaya but is easily accessible by tram No 5 (45 mins from the railway station). The comfortable rooms here are US$60/90.

The older, less plush hotels are cheaper than the above. The **Hotel Turist** (tel 34 04 17) is probably the best of these, at US$17/34. It's a 15 minute walk from the station. The **Hotel Tsentralnaya** (tel 33 47 59) may be worth a try, too. It's well located on Freedom Square (formerly Lenin Square) next to the telegraph office and costs US$20 for a single or US$26 for a double. The **Hotel Amur** (tel 39 43 73), on Ul Lenina, charges US$34 for a double but they rarely have hot water. When I visited they had no water at all.

TRANSPORT

There's no metro but there are regular bus, trolley-bus and tram services. Bus No1 goes from the station to Komsomolskaya Square. Bus No3 and trolley-bus No1 run the length of Ul Karla Marxa to the airport. Taxis are available from hotels, the airport and the station. Boat trips go from the jetty below Amurski Cliff.

TOURS

The service bureau (tel 39 99 19) in the Hotel Intourist offers the following tours: **city tour** (2½hrs by car: US$29); **museum tours** (US$8); the **arboretum** (1hr: US$8); **city sightseeing from above** (2 hrs: US$220 for the flight); **Nanai village folk show** (4hrs: US$39).

They will also arrange **tickets** for the Drama Theatre, the Musical Comedy Theatre and the circus. Note that these are all closed on Mondays and that tickets must be booked before 13.00 on the day you wish to go to a performance. Additional entertainments that can be organised are **boat trips**, with a folk group performing on deck; and traditional **Russian tea parties** at which you will be served the local delicacy, the *booblick*, which is a kind of dough-nut.

WHAT TO SEE

Museum of Regional History
The museum, based on the extensive collection of Baron Korff, a former governor general of the Amur region, was opened in 1894. In 1897 it was moved into the three-storey building in which it is now housed. With donations made by hunters and explorers over the last 90 years, the collection has grown into an impressive display of local history, flora and fauna. Labels are in Cyrillic and Latin (see p304).

Among the animals in the galleries on the ground floor are two Amur tigers. Also known as the Siberian or Manchurian tiger (*Felis/Panthera tigris altaica*), this is the largest member of the cat family and can weigh up to 350 kg, about twice the average weight of an African lion. In the same gallery are various fur-bearing animals including the large sea-otter or Kamchatka beaver (*Enhydra lutris*) from which come the highest-priced pelts in the world. Before protection of the animal began in the early 1900s single pelts were selling for over £1300/US$2,000.

The upper galleries are devoted to local history and ethnography. The area was inhabited by several tribes at the time of the Revolution. The Goldi and Orochi lived near the mouth of the Ussuri; the Olchi and the Giliak beside the Amur. All tribes had their *shamans* and some of their robes and equipment are on display as well as a suit made entirely from fish-skins. The skin of a common fish, the *keta*, was not used only for clothing but also for tents, sails and boots. There's also a display of early settlers' furniture, samovars and other utensils, including some bread baked by the original colonists.

Military Museum
Fifty metres up the street from the Museum of Regional History, this museum provides a record of military activity here since the city was founded. There are numerous pictures of Russian soldiers, as well as photographs of British, French, Italians and Americans in Vladivostok in 1918. There's also a picture of the British cruiser, HMS Suffolk. The museum's walls are decorated with medals and old weapons, including a weather-beaten Winchester rifle and a few Smith and Wesson pistols. There's a small display on Mongolia including a picture of Lenin and Sukhe Bator sharing a joke. Upstairs is a large

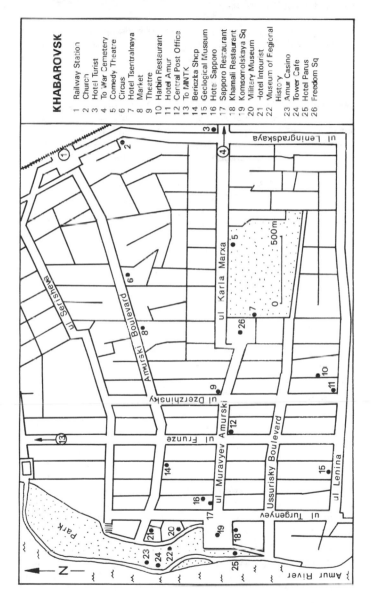

KHABAROVSK

1 Railway Station
2 Church
3 Hotel Turist
4 To War Cemetery
5 Comedy Theatre
6 Circus
7 Hotel Tsentralnaya
8 Market
9 Theatre
10 Harbin Restaurant
11 Hotel Amur
12 Central Post Office
13 To MNTK
14 Beriozka Shop
15 Geological Museum
16 Hote Sapporo
17 Sapporo Restaurant
18 Khamali Restaurant
19 Komsomolskaya Sq
20 Military Museum
21 Hotel Intourist
22 Museum of Regional History
23 Amur Casino
24 Tower Cafe
25 Hotel Parus
26 Freedom Sq

quantity of WWII memorabilia. Behind the building there's a row of armoured vehicles and tanks, a lone train carriage and a Mig fighter plane. The museum is open 10.00-17.00 daily except Monday and costs US$0.50.

Other sights and things to do

The **Geological Museum**, on the corner of Ul Lenina and Ul Push-kina, contains a well laid-out display of local minerals. You've heard how rich Siberia is in natural resources, now come and see what they actually look like. Paradoxically, pride of place goes to some rocks from the moon, small fragments under a microscope. Open 10.00-17.00 daily (not Monday) and entry is US$0.50.

Founded long before the railway arrived in Khabarovsk, the **arboretum** is an interesting place to visit. Originally set up to provide trees and shrubs for the new town's parks, it now claims to have a specimen of every plant species found in the Far Eastern Territories. A visit is usually possible only with a tour group.

The **Amur River** is a focus of interest in both winter and summer. In the winter when it freezes local men drill holes through the ice and set up little tents to sit in while they fish. In the summer the beaches along the banks become crowded with swimmers. The water is certainly not crystal clear but it's refreshing on a hot summer's day. You should watch out for the strong current though. There are also boat trips on the river.

There are regular services at the **church** on Ul Leningradskaya, the interior of which is beautifully decorated.

WHERE TO EAT

The two best restaurants in town are both foreign. The **Harbin**, long renowned as the best Chinese restaurant in Siberia (the *Washington Post* commented that 'You have to go all the way across the USSR for good mu-shu pork'), has two halls. The one on the right is cheaper. Food can be excellent but the service is variable. The Japanese restaurant, **Unikhab**, on the top storey of the Hotel Intourist, is more reliable. For some reason the floor here slopes to the right on the southern side of the building, promoting a somewhat unsteady feeling even before the vodka appears but the food more than makes up for this. Try their steamed crabs, good value at US$9 for a huge pile of claws and legs.

(Opposite) Top: There are still some traditional wooden buildings to be seen in Siberian cities, such as this in Irkutsk (see p161). **Bottom:** Crosses mark the site of the murder of the last tsar and his family in Ekaterinburg (p150; photo DSJ).

The **Sapporo Restaurant** on Ul Muravyev Amurski is the next best place to eat. It's clean and comfortable and they can even produce a reasonable bottle of Spanish wine. Main courses cost US$3-4; both the crab and the sturgeon are recommended. Not far from here, on Komsomolskaya Square, is **Khamali** which is certainly different. Flashing Christmas tree lights and plastic foliage make for an interesting and intimate atmosphere; prices are about US$4 for a main course. If you're staying at MNTK, the closest restaurant is the **Chinese Samovar** (Kitayski Samovar). There are some dubious dealings going on behind the scenes but the food's not bad. Despite being only 50m from the main road, it's difficult to find. Take tram No5 to Avtodorozhny Technikum.

By far the best snack bar here is the **Tower Cafe**: good coffee, excellent ice cream and meringues. Take a chair out onto the balcony for a superb view over the river.

NIGHTLIFE

Khabarovsk doesn't offer much in terms of nightlife but gamblers may be interested to know that there is now a casino, the **Amur**, at 15 Ul Shevchenko (just opposite the Tower Cafe). This is almost certainly the main rendezvous of all the petty criminals, hangers-on and hookers in the city, so watch your wallet if you go. The casino's literature offers comfort to worried punters, promising 'True service and guarantee of safety' which is not exactly reassuring. It's open every night from 20.00 to 06.00.

WHAT TO BUY

Interesting local products include ginseng and a special blend of vodka and herbs known as *Aralievaya Vodka*. The attractive, tree-lined Ul Muravyev Amurski is the place to go shopping, although the shops close from 14.00 to 15.00 for lunch. The Beriozka on Amurski Boulevard doesn't sell much of interest apart from wine (US$10) and expensive ceramic boxes (US$300). There's a far better selection in the Hotel Intourist and this is also the best place to stock up on snacks for the next leg of the journey.

(Opposite) Top: The library at Ivolginsky Monastery (Datsan), 25km outside Ulan Ude (see p183) contains priceless Buddhist texts and a colourful model of the Buddhist paradise. **Bottom left:** Count Muravyev-Amurski, the founder of Khabarovsk, is now back in place in the city (photo DSJ). **Bottom right:** All over the country cathedrals and churches are being reopened. Restoration should now be complete at Troitskaya Church in Ulan Ude (see p185; photo DSJ)

Excursions from Khabarovsk

Khabarovsk is an ideal base from which to start trips into the Siberian outback. The service bureau at Hotel Intourist here offers special interest tours to various distant and not so distant regions and can be contacted in advance on tel 4212-39 99 19; fax 1-509-689 42 22 51. Some of the excursions and tours currently being offered are listed below but as the region opens up to tourism many other places will become available.

Sakhalin is an island just off the East Siberian coast. The main attraction here is the great variety of wildlife which foreigners may explore, photograph, study, ride horses amongst, or kill. The most popular tours are the hunting and fishing trips, US$700 for 5-10 days salmon fishing or as much as US$6000 for bear hunting.

Excursions to **Birobidzhan**, the capital of the Jewish Autonomous region, 170km from Khabarovsk, have been possible for some time, although many of the Jewish people once here have now emigrated to Israel. The town grew up after it was decreed that all spare lands in the Amur River basin should be given to the Jews; and it became the capital of the region in 1937. There's not much to see but the drive through the countryside (2 hrs) is attractive. Trans-Siberian trains pass through Birobidzhan about 3 hours west of Khabarovsk.

Other destinations in eastern Siberia and the Far Eastern Territories that can be visited from Khabarovsk include **Yakutsk** (see p178), **Kamchatka** (for fishing and hunting), **Perelk** in the Arctic Circle (to see the Northern Lights) and **Magadan** (a former gulag centre). Weekly flights now link Magadan with Anchorage.

Now that the boat for Japan leaves from Vladivostok there's little reason to visit **Nakhodka** unless you enjoy exploring docks or looking at fishing boats. There is a hotel here.

The ultimate in self-catering holidays
The world's zaniest package holiday is to Sakhalin Island on Intourist's *Robinzonada* tour 'for people who wish to live with nature and repeat the experience literature hero Robinson Cruso' (sic). Basically what this means is that you get abandoned in some desolate spot and are expected to provide yourself with food from the rivers and forests. A qualified guide watches over you, concealed in some tree (presumably) and you pretend he's not there. The holiday costs US$2000 per person and lasts 15 days.

Vladivostok

Vladivostok, eastern terminus of the Trans-Siberian line and home of the Pacific Fleet, was off-limits until 1990. Soviet citizens needed special permits to visit and foreigners, with a few notable exceptions (Gerald Ford, 1975), required nothing short of divine intervention.

Ferries for Japan now leave from Vladivostok (from the dock next to the railway station). Whether you're coming from the east or heading that way it's well worth stopping off to explore one of the former USSR's major Cold War secrets.

HISTORY

The Vladivostok region has been inhabited for many thousands of years, certainly back at least to the second millennium BC; inhabitants were largely nomadic, however, so few relics remain. Eastern chronicles reveal that this area was considered part of the Chinese empire at a very early stage but that it was so remote and conditions so harsh that they left it well alone.

The Russians arrive

In the mid-19th century the Russians were concentrating on expanding their territory eastwards at China's expense. At the head of the exploratory missions was Count Muravyev-Amurski (see p75) who, in 1859, chose the site for a harbour here from his steamer, the *Amerika*. A year later a party of forty soldiers landed to secure the region. The port was named Vladivostok, or 'Rule the East'.

In 1861 the first shipments of soldiers arrived to protect Russia's new eastern frontier and settlers were not far behind. It soon became apparent just how important a find this city was: one of the few deep water ports on the east coast, Vladivostok's coastline remains unfrozen for longer than other parts of Siberia, being inaccessible for only 72 days per year compared with Nakhodka's 98. The city's strategic location resulted in the movement of the Russian eastern naval base here in 1872 from Nikolaevsk-na-Amur (where the water remains frozen for an impressive 190 days per year).

Conflict in the east

In 1904 the Russo-Japanese war broke out. Vladivostok was heavily bombarded during the fighting and trade virtually ceased but while

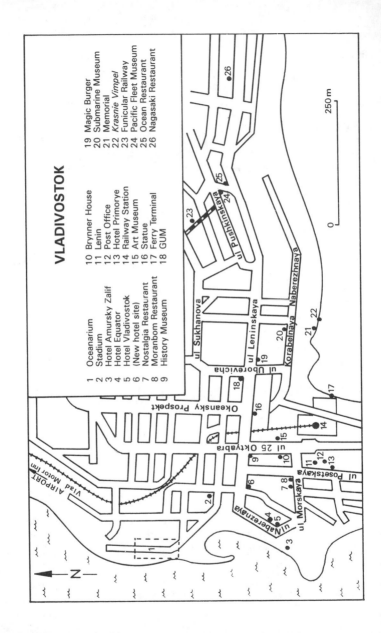

VLADIVOSTOK

1 Oceanarium
2 Stadium
3 Hotel Amursky Zalif
4 Hotel Equator
5 Hotel Vladivostok
6 (New hotel site)
7 Nostalgia Restaurant
8 Moranbom Restaurant
9 History Museum

10 Brynner House
11 Lenin
12 Post Office
13 Hotel Primorye
14 Railway Station
15 Art Museum
16 Statue
17 Ferry Terminal
18 GUM

19 Magic Burger
20 Submarine Museum
21 Memorial
22 *Krasnie Vimpel*
23 Funicular Railway
24 Pacific Fleet Museum
25 Ocean Restaurant
26 Nagasaki Restaurant

250 m

0

large parts of the port were destroyed, the war was ultimately to prove beneficial: peace settlements with Japan left Vladivostok as Russia's prime east coast port although Japan gained Port Arthur and parts of Sakhalin Island.

During the First World War the city served as the chief entry point for supplies and ammunition from the USA. At the same time, foreign troops (British, Japanese, American, Canadian and Italian) flooded in to support the White Russians' struggle against the Bolsheviks. The most notorious foreign 'visitors' were the Czech legions which had fought their way east all the way from the Ukraine in a desperate bid for freedom (see p101). Many of their graves, and those of the foreigners, can still be found in the cemetery here.

Ultimately, as it became clear that the Bolsheviks were gaining the upper hand, the foreign forces departed. Most troops had left by 1920 although some Japanese stayed on until October 1922. Finally, on 25 October, the city was 'liberated' and Soviet power established, prompting Lenin's only known edict about Vladivostok: 'It's a long way away. But it's ours'.

The Soviet period

The Soviet period was good for the city. Money poured in, along with orders to develop the port and build more ships. In the last days of the Great Patriotic War Vladivostok assumed a key role as the centre of operations from which the fight against the Japanese in Manchuria was co-ordinated. Twenty-five ships from here were sunk in four years and some 30,000 sailors perished.

The city was then sealed off completely from the outside world as the Cold War set in, and the Pacific Fleet expanded fast. The West heard little more of this protected port until 1986 when Gorbachev made his 'Vladivostok Initiative' speech, in which he highlighted a grand new plan for Soviet economics and military commitments in the Far East. Echoing Peter the Great, he announced that Vladivostok was to become 'A wide open window on the East'.

Vladivostok today

The city is keen to establish itself as a major player on the Pacific Rim. There are even periodic murmurs of an independence movement whereby the entire Primorsky region would become an independent economic zone; attempts to encourage this have included the offer of free passports to Hong Kong Chinese. While there is, doubtless, enormous potential in the area, mafia gangs from all over Russia have been drawn here by the availability of hard currency; and there's a thriving criminal underworld dealing in every commodity imaginable.

ORIENTATION AND SERVICES

Vladivostok is built along the Muravyev Peninsula, which stretches south-west into the Sea of Japan. Scattered around it is a series of islands, of which Russky Island remains the most important. It's still very much off-limits and protected by ferocious guard dogs so don't try any sightseeing here.

The focal point of the city is Golden Horn Bay, so called because of its resemblance to the Golden Horn of Istanbul, and it's here that most of the ferries, warships and fishing boats dock. The railway station is conveniently located on the waterfront, ideal if you're transferring directly to the ferry terminal. Opposite this is Lenin Square and between the square and the station is Ul 25 Oktabrya (now renamed Aleutskaya), one of the main shopping streets. The central hotels are within walking distance of the station, to the east.

A number of countries have **embassies** here, including Australia (tel 22 87 78), Japan (tel 26 75 13), Korea (tel 22 78 22) and USA (tel 21 58 54).

Those staying here for any length of time will find Eric Azulay's *Vladivostok - Your Essential Guide* (US$4) useful. It's packed with helpful information and is on sale in hotel shops.

WHERE TO STAY

The most central hotels are not the best but this looks set to change when the new business-class joint-venture hotel on Ul Leninskaya/Svetlanskaya opens. Intourist directs most visitors to the **Hotel Vladivostok** (tel 22 22 08) where charges are US$46/70 for a single/double with attached bathroom. Although the rooms are clean and the dezhurnayas charming, the foyer seems to attract sleazy characters at night. Right next door is the **Hotel Equator** (tel 21 28 64), a step or two downmarket but cheaper, at US$24 for a single. Better than these two and closer to the seafront is the nearby **Hotel Amursky Zalif** (tel 22 55 20), at US$50/75 for a single/double. At the **Hotel Primorye** (tel 21 31 82), which is very close to the station and charges US$30/36, conditions are somewhat basic.

The top hotels are all about 20km from the centre in the Sanatornaya district. The best is the **Vlad Motor Inn** (tel 21 58 54), a Canadian/Russian joint venture. Service here is very good and the restaurant serves excellent steaks. It's US$150 for a double. The **Hotel Enkai** (tel 21 54 22) is an old Communist Party hotel and charges US$100 for a double; the **Hotel Pensionat** (tel 21 56 39), just up the same street, is slightly cheaper, at US$70.

TRANSPORT

It you are arriving at the airport (30km to the north), you'll need to take a taxi or bus No 101 to the main terminal (1hr; tickets must be bought before boarding) and then change to the *electrichka* (local train) heading south for three stops (about 15 mins).

If you are staying at one of the three upmarket hotels, take the electrichka six stops north from the railway station to Sanatornaya.

TOURS

All of the sights are within easy walking distance so there's not really any need for a tour. If you want to see something further away, however, contact Intourist (tel 25 88 39), at 90 Prospekt Okeansky. **Boat trips** around the harbour are highly recommended: the chance to take pictures of Russian nuclear submarines doesn't arise that often. Boats leave from the pier (see map) every half hour.

WHAT TO SEE

The Pacific Fleet

Don't miss this unique opportunity to see some of the world's finest naval technology, although owing to a lack of funds it's beginning to look a little weatherbeaten now. Locals will tell you that it's all right to take photographs but telephoto lenses and hundreds of pictures of radar fittings may arouse suspicion; a touch of caution is advised. A good place to watch the ships is from the Eagle's Nest Hill (*Orlinoye Gnezdu*). There's no charge for the funicular railway trip to the top.

Arsenev history museum

This is the biggest and best of Vladivostok's museums, recounting the history of both the city and the region, and named after a local writer. The wildlife display is interesting: local sea life, a Ussuri leopard, a large Amur tiger and a couple of moose locking antlers in the corner. There's a display of the belongings of the early settlers, the robes of a Tungus shaman and the safe from the first bank here, stuffed with old rouble notes. Upstairs there's a small Yul Brynner exhibition (his family lived here before the Revolution), naval memorabilia and local art (the wood carvings are particularly attractive). Open 10-16.30 daily except Monday, entry is US$0.20.

Pacific Fleet Military Museum

In an old church surrounded by pieces of heavy artillery, torpedoes, anchors and bombs, this museum isn't difficult to find. The display inside is small but interesting with miscellaneous items from various conflicts: muskets, model ships, propaganda posters, a flamethrower, an ejector seat and the twisted propeller and gun from a ditched fighter plane. Open 09.30-17.45 daily except Monday and Tuesday.

Submarine Museum

On the waterfront right beside Korabelnaya Naberezhnaya and next to the eternal flame is an old C56 submarine housing a display covering the history of submarines in Vladivostok. There are early uniforms, ships' instruments, pictures of the earliest submarine (1865) and the first flotillas (1906). The display is largely made up of old photographs, although you can also see some of the gifts made to submarine commanders from foreign hosts including, strangely enough, the key to the Freedom of the City of San Diego and (Tom Cruise fans, take note) a USN Fighter Weapons School Top Gun shield. Open daily 09.00-13.00, 14.00-18.00, entry is US$0.50.

Krasnie Vimpel

Although marginally less interesting than the Submarine Museum, the first ship in the Soviet Pacific Fleet is moored just opposite and can also be visited. The *Krasnie Vimpel* was launched on 24 January 1923. Displays include lots of photographs of early crew members, medals, uniforms and various other pieces of salty memorabilia. Some of the machinery is preserved down below. If you're interested in buying bits and pieces of naval uniforms (belt buckles, cap badges etc) the sailors who run the museum may be able to help out. Open daily from 09.30-17.45.

Other things to see

The **Primorskaya Art Museum** (open 10.00-18.00 daily, not Monday) at 12 Ul 25 Oktabrya/Aleutskaya is worth a visit. There's a lot to see in here, most of the art having been donated by the Tretyakov Gallery in Moscow. Almost directly opposite, at No 15, is the **Brynner House**. You can't get inside the former residence of Yul Brynner's family but it's a real pilgrimage for some. On Karabelnaya Nazerbezhnaya, opposite the submarine, is the **parabolic monument**, dedicated to the founders of the city. In the well-tended **Naval Cemetery** are the graves of the Russians and people from other countries who died fighting the Communists in 1919-20. Unfortunately it's a fair way away, on the hill overlooking the Golden Horn Bay, so you would be wise to take a car.

The **Oceanarium** is interesting, with displays of stuffed birds and marine life and many species of live fish in tanks. Entry is US$0.30. Animal lovers might want to avoid the whale pool (400m past the oceanarium) where the whales perform tricks for their food.

WHERE TO EAT

The best restaurant within easy reach of the railway station is **Nostalgia**. The cafe here serves genuinely good coffee (most unusual in Russia) and the tiny restaurant next door is clean and has zakuski for about US$3 and main courses for US$5. Right next door, through the ornate Oriental doorway, is the Korean restaurant **Moranbom** which is probably better known for being difficult to get into than for its good food. Main courses are US$3-4, although the crab zakuski will set you back US$20!

Three other restaurants which charge similar prices to the above are the Japanese **Sakua** (in the basement of the Hotel Vladivostok), the **Volna** (above the ferry terminal) and the **Nagasaki**, at 115 Leninskaya/Svetlanskaya (recognisable by the bright mosaic on the doorway).

The cheapest meal in town seems to be at the **Magic Burger**, a Russian McDonald's wanna-be. Service is reasonably fast although you'll have to queue outside to get in; burgers cost US$1.

The city's best places to eat are further away, in the Sanatornaya district. The **Vlad Motor Inn** serves deluxe hamburgers that actually taste like deluxe hamburgers, for US$6, and some of the biggest steaks you'll ever see for US$10. An advance booking and reasonably smart dress would be a good idea in the evening. Begin the night with an unforgettable cocktails (US$6) from the bar here. Around the corner in the Hotel Pensionat is the **Captain Cook Restaurant**, an Australian/Russian joint venture that has been highly recommended.

WHAT TO BUY

The best souvenirs in town are sold in the Nostalgia shop (in the same building as the restaurant). Many of the things sold here are expensive but they do seem to be of a high standard. There are the ubiquitous matrioshkas, jewellery, paintings and locally-made rag dolls (from US$36). The gift shops in the Art Museum or the Arsenev History Museum are also worth a look.

General items are to be had from GUM on Ul Leninskaya/Svetlanskaya. According to Eric Azulay the shop was built by a two Germans in the late 19th century and claimed to be able to order literally anything for customers, including live Amur tigers.

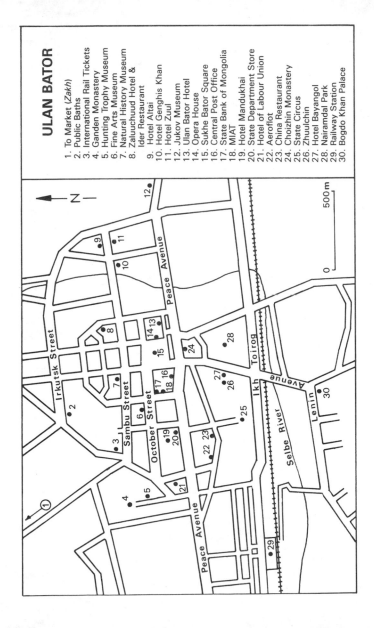

ULAN BATOR

1. To Market (*Zakh*)
2. Public Baths
3. International Rail Tickets
4. Ganden Monastery
5. Hunting Trophy Museum
6. Fine Arts Museum
7. Natural History Museum
8. Zaluuchuud Hotel &
   Ider Restaurant
9. Hotel Altai
10. Hotel Genghis Khan
11. Hotel Zuul
12. Jukov Museum
13. Ulan Bator Hotel
14. Opera House
15. Sukhe Bator Square
16. Central Post Office
17. State Bank of Mongolia
18. MIAT
19. Hotel Mandukhai
20. State Department Store
21. Hotel of Labour Union
22. Aeroflot
23. China Restaurant
24. Choizhin Monastery
25. State Circus
26. Zhuulchin
27. Hotel Bayangol
28. Nairamdal Park
29. Railway Station
30. Bogdo Khan Palace

— N —

0   500 m

Ulan Bator

The world's coldest capital city is a fascinating place to visit even if it does, at first sight, look like just another Soviet-style city. Amongst the industrial suburbs and concrete tower blocks there are vibrant splurges of colour in the temples and old palaces. The Mongolian people are charming and cheerful (Luigi Barzini, driving across the country in 1907, was amazed at their high spirits; the nomads he encountered galloped alongside his car roaring with laughter). Against all this, arranging a visit cheaply (see p18) is still not easy. There are, however, some short stopover tours which are good value and currently the best way to visit the city.

HISTORY

Home of the Living Buddha
Until 1911 Ulan Bator was known as Da Khure to the Mongolians and by its Russian name, Urga, to foreigners. Although nomadic herdsmen had been erecting their yurts here for a few months each year for many preceding centuries, a permanent settlement did not materialise until 1639, when the Da Khure Lamasery was built. This was the abode of the 'Living Buddha' or Dalai Lama, one of three incarnations of the Buddha, the other two being in Tibet and Beijing. The Dalai Lama in Urga was usually a child, who died, or rather was murdered, shortly before reaching maturity, since it was believed that the soul of a deity could dwell only in the body of a child.

Independence
When Mongolia declared herself independent of China in 1911, the city was renamed Niisled Khurehe, and by this time it had become a large trading centre on the route between China and Russia. There were, in fact, three separate cities here: the Chinese, the Russian and the Mongolian. The Chinese and Russian were engaged in the tea and silk trades but the Mongolian city's concern was the salvation (or rather the liberation) of souls. There was a population of 30,000 Buddhist monks in the many lamaseries here.

Ulan Bator today
After the Communist Party came to power in 1921, the capital was renamed Ulan Bator, meaning 'Red Hero'. With considerable help

from the USSR, the city was redesigned and the architectural origins of the austere tower blocks and municipal buildings are recognisably Soviet. The result of this influence from their overbearing neighbour to the north is that the city is now in serious financial trouble, with a huge foreign debt. The Russian Federation alone is demanding some US$900 million. The streets are lined with shoddy buildings, the city's industrial base is collapsing, the factories and lignite burning power stations are causing severe pollution problems and the chronic housing shortage means that many people still live in yurts, in large groups around the edge of the city.

Soviet influence ended with the breakup of the USSR and the democracy movement in Mongolia. In the country's first democratic elections in 1990, the communist government was re-elected, repeating their victory in the next elections in 1992. Conscious efforts are now being made to bring back the Mongolian culture, with the revival of Mongolian script in place of Cyrillic and the renaming of city streets after Mongol heroes rather than Soviet ones.

ORIENTATION AND SERVICES

It's about 1½km from the railway station to Sukhe Bator Square. The majority of people arriving here have prebooked accommodation and will be met at the station. Taxis are also available but they're not in great supply.

Information

The state tourist organisation, **Zhuulchin** (tel 328428/fax 320246) is located just around the back of the second Bayangol building. They can book tours and rail and air tickets. Note that they no longer have a monopoly and a number of independent organisations (see 'Tours' below) are providing much needed competition.

Pick up a copy of the *Mongol Messenger*, a weekly English-language newspaper, for information about local events for the week. The most impressive festival is *Naadam*, held between 11 and 13 July. It involves traditional sports like wrestling and archery.

The **Central Post Office** is on Sukhe Bator Square but it's better to buy stamps (see p211) from the hotels which have a greater range. Telephone calls can be made from the Post Office. Note that all telephone numbers here are in the process of being changed.

Although Ulan Bator is relatively safe compared to some cities in the West, crime is on the increase. You're advised not to wander round the streets after dark and to take particular care at the railway station, where **pickpockets and bag-slitters** operate on the crowded platforms.

Banks and currency

The Mongolian unit of currency is the tugrik, divided into 100 mungos. Exchange rates in March 1994 were US$1 to 350 tugrik (about £1 to 520 tugrik). The rates are similar at the banks and on the black market but you should check the latest situation with other travellers. Black marketeers hang around outside the larger hotels, if you use their services take care that you're not shortchanged. Don't change too many dollars into tugrik since much of what is worth buying in the shops is available only for dollars.

Travellers' cheques can be cashed for tugrik or US$ (at unfavourable rates) at the Ulan Bator Hotel, the Bayangol hotel, the State bank (which also accepts credit cards) or the Post Office (open Mon-Fri 09.00-13.00, 14.00-21.00, until 18.00 on Sat, closed Sun; travellers' cheques for over US$50 only).

Embassies

Countries which have embassies in Ulan Bator include China (tel 23940), Russia (tel 25207), UK (tel 51033) and USA (tel 29639).

WHERE TO STAY

Upmarket hotels

The city's accommodation situation is improving, although construction of its most upmarket hotel, the **Ghengis Khan** appears to have ground to a halt. Local estimates are that it will be finished in 1997 which means that it probably won't be open until the next century. The Holiday Inn is said to be heading negotiations for the rights to this building. Until it opens, the best place in town is the **Ulan Bator** (tel 20237) where a single is US$32 and a double US$42. There's a bureau de change and a hard currency shop selling Western alcohol and soft drinks (Coke US$1.20, Smirnoff US$9).

Although recently refurbished, the **Bayangol** (tel 326781), is not such good value, at US$64 single, US$81 double. There's also a hard currency store here (open 09.00-14.00, 17.00-20.00) and a bureau de change.

The **Zaluuchuud** (tel 324594) is much more basic but it's quite pleasant. The rooms are US$24 each, although some travellers have managed to bargain prices down as low as US$7. No English is spoken here.

Budget accommodation

The centrally located **Mandukhai** (tel 322204) charges US$10/12 for a single/double with common bathroom, or US$25 for a deluxe suite with separate sitting room. The **Altai** (tel 50110) is further from the centre but good value with rooms for US$10/16 (common bath) and three room suites with attached bathroom from US$20.

Across the road from here is the **Zuul** (tel 51438). There's no sign; look for the entrance with the yellow railings and the black padded door. Rooms here are cheap at 1000 tugrik, and 16,000 tugrik will get you a double room with attached kitchen, bathroom and sitting room. Much less pleasant, though better located and ridiculously cheap is the **Hotel of Labour Union** on Partizani Gudmz. It's got no sign and is very basic (no hot water) but it's just 500 tugrik for a double, 700 tugrik for a triple.

TRANSPORT

There are buses, trams and trolley-buses but Ulan Bator's sights are generally either within walking distance or too far away for a local bus. Taxis should charge about 100 tugrik per km.

TOURS

Package tourists with Zhuulchin and other groups will be offered trips to the main sights in Ulan Bator; other travellers will find them easy enough to visit independently. Zhuulchin also has tours to places beyond the capital (see p212) including the following: **Terelj** (US$70 for a car and US$25 for a hotel room), **Udornov** (US$50 for a car, US$25 for a night in a yurt) and trips to the **Gobi Desert** (US$149 by air).

Independent travel agencies are now springing up here and it may be possible to arrange tours that are better value. **Blue Sky Travel** (tel 24865) at the Ulan Bator Hotel have been recommended by several readers. Another operator is **Cana Service** (tel 321974) which offers not only excursions and guides but also bed and breakfast accommodation for US$6 per person, 'including electricity'.

To protect and serve
The following excerpt from the *Mongolian Independent* ('Fearless and Free') would suggest that foreigners, drink-drivers and other minority groups should avoid unnecessary contact with the Mongolian security department:

'Why is it that the police bash the bejesus out of drunks? There are too many cases to describe all in detail. But here's a taster. Take fellow A. Perhaps a little tipsy, he gets dragged from his car. Police decide to lock him up. But not before stripping him naked and throwing him into a cell with, it turns out, a homosexual. In the dark. Fending off his friendly cell-mate was only part of the joy. Every hour, along came the guards to beat him again. The fact that he is a citizen of a rich Western country is largely irrelevant - except to show that cops don't discriminate.' (Edition No 5, 1993)

WHAT TO SEE

Sukhe Bator Square

The mounted statue of Sukhe Bator in heroic pose stands in the centre of this large square, opposite his mausoleum (modelled on Lenin's in Red Square). His preserved body does not receive visitors but newly-weds queue up to have their photos taken at the foot of his statue. In 1990 the square was the scene of the pro-democracy demonstrations that led to the first free elections.

Ganden Monastery

Mongolia once had 700 monasteries but virtually all were destroyed in the communist crackdown at the end of the 1930s. More than 14,000 monks were killed and tens of thousands forced to give up their vows. With the pro-democracy movement in 1990 restrictions have been eased allowing some monasteries to reopen and Ganden to operate less as a show-piece for tourists.

The first group of buildings here was put up in 1938 and as well as the main temple there are stupas, a library and the accommodation for the monks. Powdered juniper, thrown into the big burner outside the temple for good luck, is dispensed in a side building. It's best to go in the morning (09.00-12.00) when services take places.

Bogdo Khan Palace & Museum

This is a wonderful old place, full of ghosts and rather like Beijing's Forbidden City on a human scale. Exploring the palace one gets the impression that the owners walked out a few years ago, leaving it in the hands of rather relaxed caretakers who've forgotten to mow the lawn. Entered through a gateway guarded by four fierce-looking incarnations, the palace comprises two courtyards with small pavilions on each side. There are exhibits of thangkas (Buddhist paintings), musical instruments and Buddha figures, as well as the day-to-day furnishings of the buildings.

The museum is beside the palace complex and exhibits include Bogdo Khan's throne, fur-lined robes and crown, and his luxurious yurt (covered with the skins of 150 snow leopards and containing stove and portable altar). His collection of stuffed animals is also displayed somewhat haphazardly: a moth-eaten lion sharing the same quarters as a grubby polar bear. Outside is an interesting display of conveyances (palanquins and carriages).

Open Mon, Fri, Sat and Sun from 10.00-18.00; Tues, Wed from 10.00-16.00, closed Thurs and the last Wed of each month. Entry is US$1. To get here take any bus heading south from the Bayangol Hotel and get off when you see the tank memorial (five minutes).

Natural History Museum

Mongolia is well known for its dinosaur graveyards and some of the discoveries are on display here, including several fossilised nests of dinosaur's eggs. These come in a fascinating range of shapes: cannon balls, ostrich-eggs, even Cornish pasties. Also worth seeing are the displays of stuffed animals arranged in quite imaginative panoramas of the Gobi and the mountains in the west. Here are many of the animals in the Red Data Book (endangered species) including snow leopard, wild Bactrian camel, Gobi bear, hulan (wild ass), red wolf, northern otter, snow griffon and Przhevalsky's horse. On the top floor are displays of national dress (smelling strongly of moth-balls) and a number of yurts.

Housed in a large building with creaky floor boards, a notice on the door warns: 'Closed last Monday of the month for cleaning'. Hardly surprising that the displays are rather dusty. Open Mon 10.00-16.00 (but not last Mon of the month); closed Tue; other days open 10.00-18.00. Entry is 40 tugrik and there's a US$5 charge for a camera, US$10 for a video camera.

Choizhin Monastery/Religious Museum

Preserved for many years as a museum of religion, this temple complex has been handed back to the monks in the new spirit of religious freedom. The temple is brightly decorated and houses a large collection of ornate masks for Buddhist mystery plays. Take a close look at the golden seated Buddha figure, no statue but the mummified body of a lama, encased in gold. The northern pavilion houses a number of statues graphically depicting Tantric rituals (ie sexual union).

Open daily (except Tues) 10.00-17.00, entry is US$1. Immediately to the south of the museum is a statue of the Mongolian writer Natsagorj, surveying the dilapidated funfair before him.

Fine Arts Museum

The museum includes a comprehensive display of thangkas, one more than 15m long. There are copies of prehistoric cave paintings, robes and masks from Buddhist mystery plays and a gallery of modern paper-cutting art. Open 10.00-17.00. Entry is US$1.

(Opposite) Top: The mounted statue of Mongolia's revolutionary hero, Sukhe Bator, in Ulan Bator's central square, makes a traditional backdrop for wedding photographs. Bottom Duck-billed dinosaur at the Natural History Museum, Ulan Bator.

Other museums and sights

Many of the city's smaller, less significant museums have been closing down recently, a fact which seems to have disappointed few visitors. Thus it is no longer possible to visit the Ulan Bator Museum in Sukhe Bator's bungalow, the Revolutionary Museum (soon to become another history museum), or the Lenin Museum, which has recently suffered the humiliation of being turned into a shopping centre.

The **Jukov Museum** is still open, although since it commemorates the Soviet military commander it's unlikely to be packing in the tourists for much longer. This small museum is filled with military and Soviet memorabilia and is easily recognised by the tank outside the front door.

The **Hunting Trophy Museum** near Ganden Monastery focuses on a highly controversial issue: the lucrative industry the Mongolians have set up selling hunting packages to foreign tourists (see 'Hunting trips' below). It's open daily (except Mon) 09.00-17.00 but closes at 14.00 at weekends.

It would be worth checking to see if the **Janraisag Temple** is open yet. Built in 1911 at a reputed cost of 45 tons of silver in order to commemorate the formation of the sovereign Mongolian state, this temple has been undergoing extensive restoration since 1989.

Nairamdal Park (opposite the Bayangol Hotel) is where locals go to relax and it has a boating lake, ferris wheel, camel rides and model dinosaurs.

Evening activities may include a visit to a ballet or opera in the State Theatre on Sukhe Bator Square; enquire at reception in your hotel for tickets and times, or buy tickets from the box office on the night. There is also a circus. The bar at the Ulan Bator Hotel is popular amongst foreigners. A disco is occasionally held in the Bayangol Hotel.

Public Baths

No hot water in your hotel? Can't face the prospect of another day without soap, shampoo and disinfectant? Then the public bath is the place for you. Entry is 100 tugrik and for this you get the use of a sauna and a good hot shower. See map for location.

(Opposite)   Lost in a time warp, the Bogda Khan Palace (see p207) is a fascinating place to visit.

WHERE TO EAT

Mongolian cuisine

The standard comment you'll get if you say you're off to Mongolia is 'Hope you like boiled mutton'. This is the main ingredient of the Mongol diet and consumption is currently at 8kg per person per month (96kg per year). As a visitor, you will be treated to the best food there is, which is, of course, mutton and you're likely to get heartily sick just of the smell of it, let alone the sight and the taste.

Fresh vegetables are rarely seen so there's not much of an alternative but some Mongolian restaurants do have eggs and bread, so eggs on toast or even omelettes are sometimes possible. Milk, cheese and yoghurt are often unavailable so vegetarians can have a very hard time in Mongolia and should bring supplies with them.

Restaurants

The best restaurants in Ulan Bator are in the hotels. The current favourite is the **Ulan Bator Hotel**, which has two: make sure you get into the tugrik restaurant on the ground floor or you'll be paying US$ for your meal. The same applies in the **Bayangol**: the restaurant downstairs is gaudy but cheap (the equivalent of US$2 for a meal) but upstairs you'll pay US$12 for a plate of eggs.

Right next door to the Zaluuchuud Hotel is the **Ider Restaurant**, a Russian place serving mutton stews, cold zakuski, potatoes and pasta. The food is reasonable and very good value at 300 tugrik. The **China Restaurant** serves a good almost-Chinese meal (without mutton) for about 2000 tugrik. It's just south of Peace Ave, on the first floor of the building with the ornate Chinese doorway. The Chinese restaurant inside the **Mandukhai Hotel** is not quite as good and accepts only hard currency.

Mongolian liquor
The national drink is *koumiss* (fermented mare's milk). *Mongolia Magazine* gives the following tip: 'Before drinking shake *koumiss* well. Keep it in a skin suspended on the wall of your yurt and periodically shake it with a special beater'. Every year 22 million litres are produced in late summer and early autumn, it's a seasonal drink.

Mongolian beer is rather weak and gassy, 'Arkhi' vodka expensive at about 800 tugrik a litre. Unfortunately this price doesn't act as a deterrent: the country has a serious drinking problem and you would be wise to give people who look drunk a wide berth. The intoxicated Mongolian is not a particularly friendly character and there have been a few attacks on foreigners by drunks here. The reported excuse for these unprovoked assaults was that the travellers 'looked Russian'.

WHAT TO BUY

Things to buy include leather goods, cashmere shawls and sweaters, sheepskin, carpets, jewellery, dinosaur cards and models. The country is also noted for its wonderfully bizarre, oversize **postage stamps** with naive representations of cars and trains. So many are needed for air-mail postage that there is little room left on the postcard for a message. Buy these at the hotels as they're not always available at the post office.

The best place to pick up a bargain, or just to mingle and explore, is the city **market** (*zakh*) some 10km to the north-east of the railway station. Here you can buy anything from a cowbell to a camel and, of course, heaps of imported Russian and Chinese goods fresh off the train. It's open Wed, Thurs, Sat and Sun.

Less exciting but more convenient, the **State Department Store** is interesting to look around and claims to satisfy the retail needs of 25,000 people a day. Here you can buy simple Mongolian toys and souvenirs or a even pair of the black riding boots (2-3000 tugrik - sizes up to 42) which the men wear with their *del*, the national costume. These are also available here (fur-lined in winter, cotton in summer) as well as knitted Mongolian hats. There's a bakery selling bread and cakes. The usual Russian system of payment prevails: choose, then pay taking your receipt to exchange for the goods. There's a bookshop opposite the department store.

The 'duty-free' shops in hotels sell Western products and liquor. (Open 10.00-15.00, longer in some hotels). The best shop is next to Zhuulchin, a good place to stock up on food for the train journey.

MOVING ON

Rail tickets for travel within Mongolia may be booked at the station. International trains must be booked at the **railway office** on Sambu St (see map). It's not easy to find and even harder to buy tickets as few of the staff can be bothered to help and even fewer speak English. The office is open 09.00-14.00 weekdays and until 13.00 on Saturday. Prices quotes from here for Hard Class are: Moscow US$120 and Beijing US$78. Zhuulchin can organise tickets for you but make a service charge of about 5%.

Air tickets can be arranged at MIAT, the state airline, although you're supposed to book 10 days in advance. Prices are: Moscow (US$841, twice weekly), Beijing (US$150, three times weekly) and Irkutsk (US$99, twice weekly). Alternatively, try Aeroflot but prices here are very similar.

Excursions from Ulan Bator

ULAN BATOR AREA

If you really want to see Mongolia you must get out into the countryside. There's no better antidote to the polluted city than a night or
two camping in a yurt and a few days trekking or riding. Get a copy
of Robert Storey's *Mongolia - a travel survival kit* for the practical
details of exploring beyond Ulan Bator.

Terelj

Most travellers are shipped off to Terelj, some 85km from Ulan
Bator, where they sleep out under the stars, drink mare's milk for
breakfast and sit around campfires lulled by the sound of gently siz-
zling mutton kebabs. There are also two hotels here. Zhuulchin will
charge US$25 per person for theirs but one kilometre along the road,
the second hotel is considerably cheaper at 1000 tugrik (US$3) per
person. This is certainly the great outdoors but don't expect to have
it all to yourself.

Since there's no public transport, you'll have to come with a tour
group or by car. Zhuulchin charges US$70 for a car and driver.

FURTHER AFIELD

Excursions requiring more time (and only possible between May and
October) include a visit to the **South Gobi** for game viewing (camels, gazelles, bears etc), Zhuulchin charges US$149 for a short tour
by air; the hot springs of **Khangai**; **Khuzhirt**, where tourists stay in
a *yurt* camp and visit the ruins of the 14th century capital **Karakorum** (450km west of Ulan Bator); the 400 year old monastery at
Erdene-dzu and the **Orkhon Falls**.

Hunting trips can be organised here and they are big foreign-currency earners
for the Mongolians. In their tourist brochure Zhuulchin see nothing amiss with
the following statements four paragraphs apart: 'The South Gobi, the habitat of
rare animals entered in the Red Data Book, such as....the snow leopard', and
'Most foreigners are attracted by the chance to get rare hunting trophies: the skin
of a snow leopard...'. This seems slightly out of key with the 17th century law
of Halkh Juram which enforced a caring attitude to nature in Mongolia. The
country may need hard currency but there are better ways to attract tourists than
by inviting them to contribute to the extinction of rare species.

Beijing

Both the Trans-Manchurian and Trans-Mongolian routes, by far the most popular with travellers crossing Siberia, start or finish in Beijing, so you'll probably be spending some time here. The city is well worth exploring and most travellers stay for at least three or four days. You'll find, however, that no matter how much time you allow yourself, you'll still leave having missed some of the sights. The range of accommodation here is far superior to what's currently on offer in Russia and Mongolia; budget accommodation is very cheap.

HISTORY

Remains of China's oldest known inhabitant, Peking Man, were unearthed some 50km to the south of present-day Beijing in 1921, proving that life in this region dates back at least to 500,000 BC. Chinese records go back only as far as the Zhou dynasty (12th century BC - 771BC) but indicate that by this period this region was acknowledged as the country's capital.

The city and its environs were to remain at the heart of Chinese culture and politics, although the role of capital was often lost to other cities, including Xi'an (where the Terracotta Army now draws the tourists) and Luoyang. Beijing's strength, however, lay in its proximity to China's northern frontiers: by ruling from here emperors could keep a close eye on military developments to the north, where 'barbarians' were constantly threatening invasion.

Despite the construction of the Great Wall (a continuous process dating from the second century BC) Genghis Khan marched in in 1215, sacked the city and then proceeded to rebuild it as his capital; the Mongols called this Khanbalik (City of the Khan). It was at this stage that the first Westerners visited, including Marco Polo, who liked the place so much that he stayed for 17 years.

The Mongol collapse; further developments

The Mongol empire fell in 1368 and the Chinese shifted their capital to Nanjing. Following a coup led by the son of the first Ming emperor, the government was moved back here and the city renamed Beijing (Northern Capital). The Manchurian invasion in 1644 established the final Chinese dynasty, the Qing, which was to rule from here until the abdication of Pu Yi, the 'Last Emperor', in 1912.

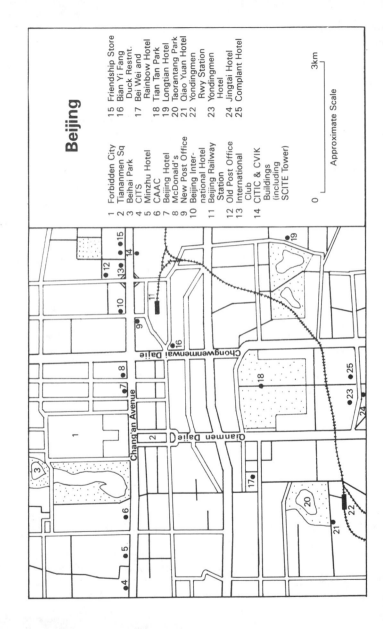

Beijing

1 Forbidden City
2 Tiananmen Sq
3 Beihai Park
4 CITS
5 Minzhu Hotel
6 CAAC
7 Beijing Hotel
8 McDonald's
9 New Post Office
10 Beijing International Hotel
11 Beijing Railway Station
12 Old Post Office
13 International Club
14 CITIC & CVIK Buildings (including SCITE Tower)
15 Friendship Store
16 Bian Yi Fang Duck Restnt.
17 Bei Wei and Rainbow Hotel
18 Tian Tan Park
19 Longtian Hotel
20 Taorantang Park
21 Qiao Yuan Hotel
22 Yondingmen Rwy Station
23 Yondingmen Hotel
24 Jingtai Hotel
25 Complant Hotel

0   3km

Approximate Scale

Although the early years of Qing dynasty rule were successful, corruption, opium and foreign intervention soon undermined Chinese authority and there were major rebellions in the city in the late 19th century.

The Civil War and beyond
The Kuomintang, under Chiang Kai Shek, relocated China's capital to Nanjing in 1928, although following the Communist victory it was moved back here in 1949. In October of that year, Chairman Mao declared the foundation of the People's Republic of China in Beijing. The city has hardly been quiet in the meantime: every major movement in the country since then, notably the mass conventions of the Cultural Revolution and the Democracy rallies (culminating in the Tiananmen Square Incident of 1989, when over 2000 civilians were killed), has had its roots here.

ORIENTATION AND SERVICES

Although Beijing is a large city, finding your way around is not too difficult owing to the fact that most streets head either north-south or east-west. The streets are, however, very crowded.

Embassies
See p32 for information on Mongolian and Russian embassies in Beijing. Note that if you plan to travel through the Baltic Republics (Estonia, Latvia or Lithuania) you'll need another visa unless passing directly through from Moscow. If you are heading west from St Petersburg you'll need a visa. These are best organised in Moscow.

- **Australia** (tel 532 2331) 15 Dongzhimenwai Dajie
- **Canada** (tel 532 3536) 10 Sanlitun Lu
- **Czech Republic** (tel 532 1531) 2 Xiushui Beijie, Jianguomenwai
- **Germany** (tel 532 2161) 5 Dongzhimenwai Dajie
- **Hungary** (tel 532 1431) 10 Dongzhimenwai Dajie, Sanlitun
- **Mongolia** (tel 532 1203) 2 Xiushui Beijie Jianguomenwai
- **Netherlands** (tel 532 1131) 1-15-2, Ta Yuan Office Building
- **New Zealand** (tel 532 2732) 1 Dong Er Jie, Ritan Lu
- **Poland** (tel 532 1235) 1 Ritan Lu, Jianguomenwai
- **Russian Federation** (tel 532 2051) 4 Dongzhimen Beizhong Jie
- **Slovakia** (tel 532 1531) Ritan Lu, Jianguomenwai
- **Sweden** (tel 532 3331) 3 Dongzhimenwai Dajie
- **Ukraine** (tel 532 63 59) Chaoyang Apartment House (near the Great Wall Sheraton Hotel), flat 3, 2nd floor
- **UK** (tel 532 1961) 11 Guanghua Lu
- **USA** (tel 532 3831) 3 Xiushui Beijie, Jianguomenwai

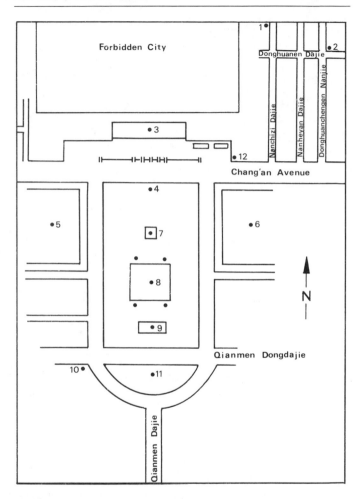

TIANANMEN SQUARE

1 PSB
2 Bank of China
3 Tianan Gate
4 Flagstaff
5 Great Hall of the People
6 Museums of Chinese History and the Revolution
7 Monument to the People's Heroes
8 Mao's Mausoleum
9 Qianmen Gate
10 Kentucky Fried Chicken
11 Arrow Castle
12 Bicycle Park and lavatories

Services
CITS, China International Travel Service, has representatives in many of the larger hotels in Beijing. CITS China head office (tel 601 1122) is at 103 Fuxingmennei Dajie; the Beijing head office (tel 515 0231) is at 28 Jianguomen Wai, the other end of Chang'an Ave. **CITS ticketing offices** are in the Beijing International Hotel (see map, p214). The air ticket office is inside the hotel; the rail office is on the south-western corner.

The airline office, **CAAC** (tel 601 7755) is on the western side of Chang'an Ave at 15 Fuxingmen Dajie, and there's an efficient bus service to the airport from the stop just across the street. Note that there's a departure tax of US$8 on international flights.

The main **post office** is on Chaoyangmennan Dajie, the street that runs north off Jianguomen Dajie on the east side of the Beijing International Hotel.

Banks and currency
The unit of currency is the *yuan* (Y) which is divided into 10 *jiao* or *100* fen. In March 1994 there were about Y8.50 to US$1, Y12 to £1; but this is likely to alter, given the changes below. For many years there were two types of yuan circulating in China, Renminbi (RMB) used by the majority of the population, and Foreign Exchange Certificates (FEC) used by tourists, diplomats and the few Chinese who could get hold of them. Certain luxury items could only be bought for FEC and a black market developed. Now FEC are being phased out and the humble RMB is legal tender everywhere. Check with other travellers before changing any money and when FEC become redundant ensure you don't get landed with them when changing money. (They are clearly marked). If you need hard currency the CITIC Industrial Bank will change travellers' cheques into US$ and allow credit card withdrawals in US$.

WHERE TO STAY

Upmarket and mid-range hotels
If you want a really comfortable stay, try one of the following: **The Palace Hotel** (tel 512 8899), the **Grand Hotel** (tel 513 7788), the **Great Wall Sheraton** (tel 500 5566), the **Beijing International Hotel** (tel 512 6688) or the famous **Beijing Hotel** (tel 513 7766) which is very well located close to Tiananmen Square. All are fairly central and offer first class accommodation. A double in a hotel of this standard will cost you at least US$100.

The **Minzhu Hotel** (tel 601 4466), on Fuxingmen Dajie charges US$75 for a double. Cheaper but still perfectly comfortable, there's the **Hua Dua Hotel** (tel 500 1166) at 1, Xinyuan Nan Lu, with doubles for US$25-45. The **Qiamen Hotel** (tel 301 6688) at 175 Yongan Rd, the **Hademen Hotel** (tel 701 2244) on Chongwenmen Dajie and the **Xiaqiaou Hotel** (tel 513 3366) on Dong Jiao Min are all similarly priced.

Budget accommodation

The standard travellers' haunt is the **Qiao Yuan Hotel** (tel 301 2244) on Yong Anmen Dongbinhe Lu, opposite Taoranting Park. Service here can be atrocious but the place is always packed. A room in a dormitory will cost you Y30 and a three-bed room is Y110. Watch out for the hotel bank, where staff are quite happy to let you sign a travellers' cheque before telling you that they have no cash. Trans-Siberian specialists, Monkey Business (tel 301 2244, ext 716) have an office in the room 716 of the new building and there's **alternative accommodation** on the 7th floor here, which is worth checking out. To get here, take bus Nos 20 or 54 from the railway station to Yondingmen terminal (the end of the line) and walk west along the canal for 800m. Alternatively, get a taxi and ask for 'Qiao Yuan Fandian'.

There are three other popular travellers' hostels, of which the cheapest is the **Longtian Hotel** (tel 771 2244) on Zuoanmen Xibinhe Lu, at Y45 for a basic triple room. Bus No51 goes right past it; look for the hospital just next door. Alternatively, try the **Yondingmen Hotel** (tel 721 3344) on Anlelin Lu, where a double room will cost you Y58 and a triple Y75, both with common bathrooms. Very near here is the **Jingtai Hotel** (tel 722 6688) with doubles for Y60; to find it go left out of the Yondingmen and then up a tiny side street on the right. Bus No 40 will drop you off at the end of Anlelin Lu and these two hotels are only a five-minute walk from there.

TRANSPORT

The metro system is good but stations are not always where you need them. Buses and trolley-buses are cheap but very crowded; watch out for bag-slitters and pick-pockets. Most travellers join the rest of the city's population on two wheels; there are many places to rent bikes from. Taxis are easiest to get outside hotels. They're metered and good value when shared.

TOURS

There are tours on offer from most of the larger hotels to all the major sights but you can easily visit the Forbidden City, the Temple of Heaven and Beijing's other tourist attractions independently. It is, however, probably worth taking a tour to see the Great Wall and the Ming Tombs (see below).

WHAT TO SEE

Tiananmen Square

Just as Red Square is the best place to start a tour of Moscow, so is Tiananmen Square for a trip around Beijing. In the centre is **Chairman Mao's Mausoleum** (open 08.30-11.30 daily) in which, after joining a long queue which moves surprisingly fast, you can see the great man himself. To the east is the **National Museum of Chinese History**, which also houses the **Museum of the Chinese Revolution**. Both are well worth a morning exploring if you have the time, and are open 08.30-15.30, closed Mon. Opposite the museums on the other side of the square is the **Great Hall of the People**, used for meetings of the National People's Congress and containing an impressive 10,000 seat auditorium.

To the north of the square is the Imperial Palace , better known as the **Forbidden City**, entered through **Tiananmen Gate**. This enclosure, comprising over 178 acres and 1000 buildings takes at least a day to explore to get even a bare impression; there's so much to see here that really you need much longer.

The palace was erected by the Ming emperor Yong Le in the early 15th century and since then has been the home of the last 24 emperors, up until the abdication of Pu Yi in 1911. The best way to get around is to hire a cassette tour at the main gate and have everything explained to you by Peter Ustinov. It's a good idea to wander round again afterwards, soaking up the atmosphere. The palace is open 08.30-16.30 daily but ticket offices close at 15.30. Entrance is Y45 and the cassette tour costs Y22.

The Great Wall

China's most famous attraction makes an ideal day trip from Beijing. Most tourists visit the Wall at **Badaling** but it's less crowded at **Mutianyu**. The Wall itself was not built in one massive construction project as many believe; in fact the original scheme under Emperor Shih Huang (first century BC) was simply to join extant stretches of individual defensive walls together. It was hoped that the resulting fortification would protect China from marauding foreigners but this was not the case. It's currently responsible for drawing more foreigners to China than ever, as those who visit at Badaling will see. It's possible to get there independently by train (the Trans-Siberian route passes through Badaling - see p280) from Xizhimen station but otherwise you'll have to go with a tour group. This is easy to arrange for Badaling: go to any large hotel or CITS and you'll be able to book a tour the next day. There are fewer excursions to Mutianyu: your best bet is to go with Monkey Business, who run a daily trip from the Qiao Yuan Hotel for Y40.

Tian Tan - the Temple of Heaven
This is the site from which China's emperors conducted the country's most important religious rituals, upon which depended the wellbeing of the population. The temple in Tian Tan Park is open from 08.00-17.00 and entry is Y10. Sights worth noting here include the **Hall of Abstinence**, the marble **circular altar**, the **Imperial Vault of Heaven** (where a whisper towards the surface on one side is perfectly audible around the opposite side). The most famous building of the complex is the **Hall of Prayer for Good Harvests**, to the north, built entirely without the use of glue or nails.

The Summer Palace
The palace (summer retreat of the Imperial family since 1750) covers an area about four times the size of the Forbidden City. Virtually everything in the grounds apart from the lake dates back only to the start of this century, as there has been repeated destruction by foreigners: the entire area was razed in 1860 as retribution for the Opium Wars and then again in 1900 after the Boxer Rebellion. It's a great place to explore slowly and if the weather is good it's well worth spending a whole day here wandering around the **Royal Residence**, the **Dragon King Temple**, the **Long Corridor**, the **Tower of Buddhist Virtue** and the **lake**.

WHERE TO EAT
Peking Duck is, of course, the local speciality and there are numerous restaurants to try it at: good places include the **Bian Yi Fang** restaurant on Chongwenmenwei Dajie near the railway station (Y50 for two), the first floor of the **Hong Bin Lor** on Chang'an Ave (Y40 for two) and the **Beijing Duck Restaurant** just west of Vie de France (see below), south-west of Tiananmen Square.

Cheap food is generally easy to find in Beijing: try any backstreet for noodles or dumplings. There's a cheap **night market** on Donghuamen Dajie, just to the east of the Forbidden City. Spicy food fans usually head for the **Sichuan Restaurant** in Xirongxian Alley, just to the other side of the City. Those staying at the popular Qiao Yuan Hotel tend not to venture that far, though, since there's a number of friendly restaurants just outside the door or around the corner which all serve 'Western' Chinese food.

Finally, if you're homesick, visit **McDonald's** on Chang'an Ave, **Kentucky Fried Chicken** on Tiananmen Square, or **Pizza Hut** (two branches, one on Dongzhimenwai, the other south of Tiananmen Square on Zhushikou). For cakes, pastries and croissant go to **Vic de France** (two branches, one on Chang'an Ave, the other to the south-west of Tiananmen Square).

WHAT TO BUY

Most people tend to buy souvenirs in the large **Friendship Store** on Jianguomen Dajie (Chang'an Ave), which has an enormous range. For a more challenging time, visit the shops in the **Wangfujing district** directly east of the Forbidden City. Another good place is the **Qianmen district**, where you're likely to have to fight your way through the crowds; bartering is in order here.

MOVING ON

By air

A good place to get flight information is the **air ticketing office** at the Beijing International Hotel. Many major airlines maintain offices in Beijing, so it's usually not difficult finding a seat; the problem is that it can be very expensive. Most airline offices are in the SCITE Tower on Chang'an Ave. Sample prices include London (US$1150) and Berlin (US$1380), both on British Airways; Paris (US$1380); Singapore (US$475), Tokyo (US$460), and Hong Kong (US$230) on CAAC. If you want to fly the first leg of your Trans-Siberian journey, **MIAT** (tel 501 8888, ext 807; room 807, Jing Guang World Hotel, Jing Guang Center, Hujialou, Chaoyanou) charges US$150 for Beijing to Ulan Bator and US$99 for Ulan Bator to Irkutsk.

By rail

● **Domestic** Tickets can be bought from the railway station at the foreigners' ticket office on the ground floor. Alternatively CITS will book for you for a small fee, saving you the queuing.

● **International** Tickets must be booked either from the international train booking office in the Beijing International Hotel, or from a registered ticket agency (see p31).

If you've just arrived on the Trans-Siberian and feel like clocking up a few more kilometres on a train you could follow the Silk Route back to Europe by rail (see p314).

PART 5: ROUTE GUIDE AND MAPS

Using this guide

Introduction
This route guide has been set out to draw your attention to points of interest and to enable you to locate your position along the Trans-Siberian line. On the maps, stations are indicated in Russian and English and their distance from Moscow is given in the text. Note that on the maps there is an orientation symbol (M), indicating the direction towards Moscow.

Stations and points of interest are identified in the text by a kilometre number. Note that in some cases these are approximate so be ready for a particular point a few kilometres before the stated position. Where something of interest is on only one side of the track, it is identified by the letters N (north or left-hand side of the train, going from Moscow east) or S (south or right-hand side) after the kilometre number. The altitude of major towns and cities is given in metres and feet beside the station name. Time zones are indicated through the text (MT = Moscow Time). See inside back cover for **key map**.

Kilometre posts
These are located on the southern side of the track. They are sometimes placed so close to the train that they're difficult to see. The technique is either to hang out of the window (dangerous) or press your face close to the glass and look along the train until a kilometre post flashes by. Note that there is a difference of one kilometre between one side of the sign and the other.

Station name boards
These are almost as difficult to catch sight of as the kilometre posts since they are usually posted only on the station building and not along the platforms as in most other countries. Rail traffic on the line is heavy and even if your carriage does pull up opposite the station building you may have your view of it obscured by another train. For the station name in Cyrillic script see the strip-maps.

Stops

Where the train stops at a station the length of the stop is indicated by ● (short stop: 1-5mins), ●● (medium stop: 6-10 mins) or ●●● (long stop: 11-15 mins). The carriage attendant will tell you the precise amount of time as this may be reduced if the train is running late. Don't stray too far from the train as it moves off without a signal or whistle (except in China) and passengers are occasionally left behind. Three of us, our carriage attendant included, were once almost left in sub-zero temperatures on the platform of some tiny Siberian station, when the train left five minutes ahead of schedule.

Speed calculations

Using the kilometre posts and a watch, it's possible to calculate how fast, or more usually how slowly, the train is going. Note the time that elapses between one post and the next and consult the table below. Since the average speed of the train over the seven day journey between Moscow and Vladivostok is only 69 kph (43 mph), you are unlikely to use the higher figures on this table.

Seconds	kph	mph	Seconds	kph	mph
24	150	93	52	69	43
26	138	86	54	66	41
28	129	80	56	64	40
30	120	75	60	60	37
32	113	70	64	56	35
34	106	66	68	53	33
36	100	62	72	50	31
38	95	59	78	46	28
40	90	56	84	43	27
42	86	53	92	39	24
44	82	51	100	36	22
46	78	49	120	30	18
48	75	47	150	24	15
50	72	45	180	20	12

Precautions against invaders

In 1940s' Britain, with the fear of German invasion, road signs were removed to make orientation difficult for the invader. Soviet cartographers attempted a similar sort of deception with deliberate errors and misspellings. Russian maps are notorious for their inaccuracies. On the Trans-Mongolian route, just before reaching the border I noticed an inconsistency between the name of a small station whose signboard read 'Azhida' and the name as it appeared on my Russian map, 'Dzhida'. It could have been just a printer's error but as the train reached the southern part of the town a large military airfield came into view. Note that the distances sometimes given on train timetables are also unreliable, usually out by 5-8km. If you notice any inaccuracies in the distances given in this book please write to the author - address on page 2.

MAP 1

Trans-Siberian route

Km0: Moscow: Yaroslavskii Station

(See p297 for timetables). If you're arriving from Siberia and leaving Moscow by train the same day, you may need to take the metro or a taxi to one of Moscow's nine other stations (see p131). If your journey begins here make sure you get to the station early as trains invariably leave on time. Yaroslavskii station and Kazanskii station (which is used by a few trains bound for Siberia) are both on Komsomol Square (metro: the palatial **Komsomolskaya Ploshchad** with its marble pillars and mosaic ceilings). Yaroslavskii station is very distinctive; it was built in 1902 as a stylised reproduction of an old Russian *terem* (fort), its walls decorated with coloured tiles. Trains have destination plates fixed to their sides but any railway official will point you in the right direction if you show them your ticket.

In about twenty minutes, the smoking factories and suburban blocks of flats will have been left behind and you'll be rolling through forests of pine, birch and oak. Amongst the trees there are picturesque wooden *dacha* (holiday homes where many of Moscow's residents spend their weekends). You pass through little stations with long, white-washed wicket fences and empty platforms. About 1-1½hrs out of Moscow you come to Sergiyev Posad (Zagorsk).

Km73 (N): Sergiyev Posad (Zagorsk)

Have your cameras ready for the stunning sight of the blue and gold domes of the cathedrals of Sergiyev Posad, known as Zagorsk between 1930 and 1993. Look north back to the city just after you leave the station. For many years this was the seat of the Russian

Orthodox Church (until it was moved back to Moscow in 1990) and one of the most important seminaries in the country is here. The beautiful buildings of the seminary are much visited by tourists.

Sergiyev Posad is named after St Sergius of Radonezh who founded the *lavra* (monastery) here in 1340. The fortified monastery complex now comprises nine cathedrals and churches. The most striking is the **Cathedral of the Assumption** (Uspenski Sobor) with its four blue cupolas dotted with golden stars and, in the centre, a larger gold cupola. It was built between 1559 and 1585. The **Cathedral of the Holy Trinity** (1422) stands beside it and in spite of its gilded roof, seems quite plain in comparison. The 285ft **bell-tower** was designed by Rastrelli, the principal architect of the Winter Palace and many other buildings in St Petersburg.

Until the time of the Revolution, literally millions of people made the pilgrimage to this sacred city. After the Revolution, the monks were disbanded and sent out into the fields and the churches became museums. With the slightly more relaxed religious climate that came after Stalin's time, the monastery was re-established. Now that the church has been fully embraced again by the state, the monastery is reported to be taking in record numbers of novices.

Km112: Aleksandrov (●) There is usually a one minute stop here which just gives you time to see the six old **steam locomotives** that lie rotting in the station yard.

Km121-1266: Time zone MT + 1 After Aleksandrov you cross into the next time zone. Local time is now Moscow time + 1 hour.

The train now enters Yaroslavlskaya *oblast* (administrative district), an area of 36,000 square kilometres in the upper Volga basin, famous for its cheeses. Apart from dairy farming, oats, flax and vegetables are grown in this region.

Km240 (N): Amidst the fields and quite close to the track is a sadly neglected but **picturesque church** with five dilapidated domes and a tower.

Km280 (N): Another dilapidated church, this one with a soaring steeple (like a more humble version of the Cathedral of St Peter and St Paul in St Petersburg) and a clock with no hands.

Km284: Yaroslavl (●) Travelling past factories that look as if they've been deserted with piles of rusting machinery left outside them, you come to the large industrial city of Yaroslavl, population 690,000. It is said to have been founded in 1010 by the Christian

King Yaroslavl the Wise. It grew quickly into an important trading centre on the Volga shipping route. Many of the ancient cathedrals still stand in spite of the heavy fighting that went on here during the Civil War. The **Spassky Monastery**, badly damaged in the fighting, dates from the thirteenth century. Most of the other large religious buildings, including the **Cathedral of St Elias** with its five large green domes, were built in the seventeenth century. The theatre, founded in 1750, is the oldest in Russia. Since the early eighteenth century, Yaroslavl has been a major textile centre. The production of petroleum products is the other important industry in the city today.

Km289: Volga River In times gone by Russians regarded this river with such high respect that they would stand and take off their hats to Mother Volga, as the train rattled onto the first spans of the long bridge. Rising in the Valdai hills, Europe's longest river meanders 3,700km down to the Caspian Sea. It is to Russia what the Nile is to Egypt: a source of life and a thoroughfare. You get a good view of the city of Yaroslavl and its cathedrals looking back south as you go over the bridge.

Km357: Danilov (● ● ●) There's usually a fifteen minute halt here for an engine change. The platform is crowded with little fat women wearing overcoats and scarves, selling bunches of gladioli, buckets of purple onions and small paper bags of potatoes, freshly boiled with herbs. Waddling up and down the train with their produce, they look like animated matrioshka dolls.

Km370-378 Some quite good views on both sides of the train in the breaks between the trees. The train soon enters Kostromskaya oblast, a 60,000 sq km plain in the middle Volga basin. Most of the northern part of the oblast is covered with taiga (swampy forest). There is some cultivation (flax and oats) in the south. Main industries are linen-making and timber-processing.

Km447: Over the Kostroma River and into **Buy (●)** (pronounced B'wee) station. The two minute stop here will give you more than enough time to view the silver-painted statue of Lenin on the platform, although by the time you read this he may well have gone the way of most other silver-painted statues of Lenin.

Km501: Galich A large town beside the equally large Lake Galichskoye.

Km700: Shariya (● ●) There is usually an 8-10 minute stop at this station where some **steam locos** are stored (L & Er classes).

Km818: Svetcha Roughly mid-way between Shariya and Svetcha, you enter Kirovskaya oblast. Most of the 120,000 square kilometres of this region are within the basin of the Vyatka River. Since the greater part of the *oblast* is made up of taiga, the main industry here is logging.

Km870: Kotelnich Junction with the line down to Gorky. A few kilometres east of the town you cross the Vyatka River, which rises in the foothills of the Urals and flows 1,300km down to the Kama River

Km957: Kirov (●●●) Standing on the banks of the Vyatka River, the city was founded in 1181 and named Klynov. It developed into a fur-trading centre entirely dependent on the river for transport and communication with the rest of the country. In the eighteenth century it fell under the rule of Moscow and was renamed Vyatka, soon gaining a reputation as a place of exile. In 1934 its name was changed once more and it became Kirov, in honour of the communist leader assassinated earlier in the same year. Kirov was, at one time, so close to Stalin that most people assumed that he would eventually succeed him as General Secretary of the Party. However, in the 1930s he broke away and it is more than likely that Stalin had a hand in his murder. His death served as the excuse for Stalin's Great Purge in the mid-1930s during which several million people died in labour camps.

Modern Kirov is a large industrial and administrative centre with a population of over 400,000. There are saw-mills, chemical plants, tanneries and a tyre-making factory.

For the next 300km after Kirov the line follows the Vyatka River (for a short distance) then the Cheptsa, climbing into the foothills of the Urals.

MAP 2

MAP 3

Ардаши
ARDASHI
Зуевка
ZUYEVKA
Коса
KOSA
Фаленкн
FALENKI
Яр
YAR
Кожиль
KOZHIL
Рехино
REKHINO
Глазов
GLAZOV
Балезино
BALEZINO
Пибаньшур
PIBANSHUR
Чепца
CHEPTSA
Кез
KEZ
Кабалуд
KABALUD
Кузьма
KUZMA
Бородулино
BORODULINO
Субботники
SUBBOTNIKI
Верещагино
VERESHCHAGINO
Зюкай
ZYUKAY
Менделеево
MENDELEYEVO
Григорьевская
GRIGOREVSKAYA
Чайковская
CHAYKOVSKAYA
Шабуничи
SHABUNICHI
Оверята
OVERYATA
Курья
KURYA
ПЕРМЬ
PERM
Ферма
FERMA
Мулянка
MULYANKA
Юг
YUG
Ергач
YERGACH
Кунгур
KUNGUR
Кишерть
KISHERT
Шумково
SHUMKOVO
Тулумбасы
TULUMBASI
Кордон (KORDON)
Шамары (SHAMARY)
Шаля (SHALYA)
Сарга (SARGA)
Сабик (SABIK)
Кузино (KUZINO)
Первоуральск
PERVOURALSK

KIROVSKAYA OBLAST
Чепца R.
UDMURT REPUBLIC
PERMSKAYA OBLAST
SVERDLOVSKAYA OBLAST

Km1127: Yar About twenty kilometres before this station you leave Kirovskaya oblast and cross the administrative frontier into the Udmurt Republic. This region was settled by the Udmurts, a people of Finno-Ugric extraction, and was established as an autonomous republic in 1920. It is now a heavily industrialised area.

Km1190(N): Note the large number of well-preserved **steam locomotives** behind the trees, just before Balyezino station (W).

Km1162: Glazov (●) Some trains make a short stop at this station.

Km1190: Balyezino (●●) Between Yar and Balyezino there are many farms specialising in market-gardening in this rolling, open countryside. You pass vast fields of grey-green cabbages, and long rows of greenhouses covered in plastic sheeting line the track in some places. There are tiny villages of log cabins with brightly painted front doors.

Km1216: Cheptsa A few kilometres west of this station, the line crosses the Cheptsa River which the route has been following for the last 250kms. The train begins to wind its way up towards the Urals.

Km1267-2510: Time zone MT + 2
About 40kms east of Cheptsa you enter a new time zone (Moscow Time + 2).

Km1315 (S): Vereshagino There's a **preserved tender loco**, high up on embankment plinth about 1km west of the station. Between Cheptsa and this station is the frontier between the Udmurt Republic and Permskaya oblast. Permskaya's 160,000 square kilometres are, like those of Kirovskaya oblast, lost to the swampy forests of the taiga. However, Permskaya has greater prizes than its millions of pine and birch trees, for the region includes the mineral-rich Ural Mountains. Main industries therefore include mining, logging and paper-making. Agriculture is confined to market-gardening. There are some quite good views south, a few kilometres after Vereshagino. Other views are at km1365 (S); km1375 (N) and kms1397-1402 but there's nothing really spectacular.

Km1431: Kama River This mighty river flows over 2,000kms from the Urals into the Volga and is one of the great waterways of the CIS. Its power has been harnessed by the Perm hydro-electric power station. Near the bridge, the banks of the Kama are lined with cranes and warehouses. A short distance west of Perm station (to the north of the line) there's a turntable and beside it an ancient green **'O' Class locomotive** (OB 14). Engines of this type were hauling the Trans-Siberian at the turn of the century.

Km1433: Perm (●●●) This city of more than one million inhabitants was founded in 1723 when the copper smelting works were established here. From its important position on the Kama River, the Great Siberian Post Road and later the Trans-Siberian Railway, Perm quickly grew into a major trading and industrial centre.

Before the railway reached Perm most travellers would arrive by steamer from Nizhny Novgorod (now Gorky) and Kazan. R.L.Jefferson (see Part 3) cycled here from London in 1896 on his Siberian ride and was entertained by Gospodin Kuznetsoff, the 60 year old president of the Perm Cycling Club, and fifty enthusiasts. On 20 July 1907, the cyclists came out to escort an equally sensational visitor, the Italian Prince Borghese who had just driven across Siberia from Peking in his Itala and was on his way to Paris, where he would win the Peking to Paris Motor Rally. One of the wheels of the car was damaged and, when the Prince's chauffeur had replaced some of the wooden spokes, he declared that the wheel needed to be soaked to make the wood expand before the repair could be completed. A local official advised them to send it to one of the bathing establishments along the Kama River. A bathing-machine (of the type used by Victorian swimmers at English sea-side resorts) was hired and the wheel spent the night taking the waters.

Between 1940 and 1957 the city was called Molotov, after the communist official who fell from favour after the Stalin era. Modern Perm is a vast industrial metropolis (the suburbs extend east to the oil refineries at km1452) and its population is engaged in producing heavy machinery, petroleum products and chemicals. Several old steam locos may be seen around the station.

Km1458 (S): The attractive green domed church here might make a good photograph.

Kms1460-1777: The train winds its way up to the highest point in the Urals. One would expect the range of mountains that divides Europe from Asia to be rather more impressive than these hills but they rise up not much more than 500m/1640ft above sea level in this area. R.L.Jefferson wrote in 1896: 'The Urals certainly are not so high or majestic as the Alps or the Balkans but their wild picturesqueness is something to be seen to be appreciated.' Their wild picturesqueness is somewhat marred and scarred today by open-cast mines (km1507 (N) and km1509 (N)). There is a large timber-mill at km1523 (N).

Km1534: Khungur Founded in the mid-seventeenth century as a military outpost, this large town lies away from the track to the north. Of less importance now than in the past, Khungur has six large churches, each built in a different style, and a large cathedral with a gold dome.

Km1537(N): A picturesque church stands alone on the hill across the Sylva River. The line follows this river up the valley to km1556 where it cuts across a wide plain. The trees close in again from about km1584 but there are occasional clearings with villages and timber-mills (km1650 (N)).

Km1672: Shalya Fifty kilometres west of here, you enter Sverdlovskaya oblast. It covers 195,000 square kilometres, taking in parts of the Urals and extending east onto the Siberian plain. Like most of the other oblasts you have passed though, this one is composed almost entirely of taiga forests. From the rich deposits in the Urals are mined iron ore, copper, platinum, gold, tungsten, cobalt, asbestos and bauxite as well as many varieties of gemstones. The soil is poor and consequently there is very little agriculture in the region.

Km1727-9: Kuzino East of the large marshalling yard here the line rises once more, passing a little town built around a freshly whitewashed church with a green dome.

Km1748: A large factory, with rows of apartment blocks for its workers, looks a little out of place amongst the forests up here in the Urals. There are several more factories and mining complexes around the town of Pervoralsk, about 15km east of Kuzino. From km1764 east the area becomes quite built up.

Km1777 (S) Europe/Asia Obelisk

People begin collecting in the corridor long before you reach this white stone obelisk which marks the continental division at this point in the Urals. Just before you get to it, when travelling east, there is a large brick tower beside the track at km1775-6(S). Two kilometres east you reach the obelisk which has 'Europe' written on the west-facing side, 'Asia' on the east side and 'Asia Europe' on the side facing the train. It stands on the south side of the line.

When R.L.Jefferson reached the point near here where the road crosses the Urals (also marked with an obelisk) he wrote enthusiastically of the view: 'Hills piled upon hills, shaggy mountains and gaunt fir trees, and beyond them dwindling away into the mist of the horizon the great steppe lands of Siberia.' George Kennan wrote in 1887: 'The scenery of the Urals where the railroad crosses the range resembles in general outline that of West Virginia where the Baltimore and Ohio railroad crosses the Alleghenies; but it differs somewhat from the latter in colouring, owing to the greater preponderance in the Urals of evergreen trees.' Unfortunately you won't get much of a view from the train today.

Km1813: Ekaterinburg (● ● ●)

After a large lake (kms1807-9) the train halts in this, the largest of cities in the Urals (formerly known as **Sverdlovsk**), for a change of engine. See p147 for more information about the city where the last Tsar of Russia and his family were executed in 1918.

For about 70km east of Ekaterinburg, the train winds down and out of the Urals to the Great Siberian plain. You are now in Asia (not quite in Siberia yet) but the scenery and houses look no different from those on the European flank of the mountains.

MAP 4

Km1915: Bogdanovich The *1900 Guide to the Great Siberian Railway* drew its readers' attention to the Kurinsk mineral springs 'situated 15 *versts* (a verst is slightly longer than a kilometre) from the station.....They are efficacious for rheumatism, paralysis, scrofula and anaemia. Furnished houses and an hotel with good rooms are situated near the baths. There is a garden and a promenade with band; theatricals and concerts take place in the casino'. Such frivolous jollities are hard to imagine in this rather gloomy region today.

The U2 Affair: USSR, 1: USA, nil

The U2 affair represented an unprecedented Cold War embarrassment for the West. On 1 May 1960, an American U2 spyplane was shot down from a height of 68,000 feet some 45km south of Sverdlovsk (as Ekaterinburg was then known). Its pilot, Gary Powers, baled out without activating the plane's self-destruct mechanism for fear that he would blow himself up (criticisms were later raised in Congress that he had not killed himself, either by destroying the aircraft or by pricking himself with the poisoned needle so thoughtfully provided by the CIA). He was picked up shortly after reaching the ground.

Four days later the USA announced that a U2 'meteorological aircraft' had 'gone missing' just north of Turkey after its pilot had reported problems with his oxygen mask. In a detailed press announcement it was speculated that he had fallen unconscious while the plane, automatic pilot engaged, might possibly have flown itself over Soviet territory. Shortly after this announcement, Khrushchev told the Supreme Soviet that a U2 'spyplane' had been shot down over Sverdlovsk. US presidential spokesman Lincoln White commented that 'this might be the same plane', and did his best to cool the situation by explaining the oxygen supply theory again. He concluded: 'there was absolutely no deliberate attempt to violate Soviet airspace and never has been', and he grounded all other U2s to 'check their oxygen systems'.

On 7 May Khrushchev addressed the Supreme Soviet again: 'I must tell you a secret. When I made my first report I deliberately did not say that the pilot was alive and well ... and now just look how many silly things they (the Americans) have said'. Khrushchev exploited his position, revelling in the details of the American cover-up: he was in possession of the pilot ('alive and kicking'), the 'plane, the camera, and had even had the photographs developed. He also had Powers' survival pack, including 7500 roubles, other currencies and gold rings and gifts for women. 'Why was all this necessary?' he asked, 'Maybe the pilot was to have flown still higher to Mars and was going to lead the Martian ladies astray?' He laughed at the US report that the U2 had a maximum height of 55,000 feet: 'It was hit by the rocket at 20,000m (65,000 feet). And if they fly any higher we will also hit them'.

The U2 Affair brought the 1960 Paris Summit to a grinding halt. Following the arrival of the first U2s in England in August 1962, Moscow remarked that they ought to be 'kept far away from us'. In the USSR, Powers was sentenced to ten years but released in exchange for Rudolph Abel, a KGB spy, in 1962. Soviet press maintained that Powers had been sent home as an 'act of clemency'. No mention was made of the exchange. The wreckage of the plane is now on display in Ekaterinburg (see p150).

Km2078: Siberia begins here (ends here, for those going west). This is the frontier between Sverdlovskaya and Tyumenskaya oblasts. Tyumenskaya comprises 430,000 square kilometres of flat land, tundra in the north, taiga in the south. Until oil was discovered in the region twenty years ago, the inhabitants were engaged in reindeer-herding in the north and farming in the south. Many people have been brought into the oblast recently to work in the petroleum and construction industries.

South of the line, the point where the Great Post Road crossed Siberia's frontier was marked by 'a square pillar ten or twelve feet in height, of stuccoed or plastered brick', wrote George Kennan (on his way to research *Siberia and the Exile System* in 1887). He added: 'No other spot between St Petersburg and the Pacific is more full of painful suggestions, and none has for the traveller a more melancholy interest than the little opening in the forest where stands this grief-consecrated pillar. Here hundreds of thousands of exiled human beings - men, women and children; princes, nobles and peasants - have bidden good-by (sic) forever to friends, country , and home.....The Russian peasant even when a criminal is deeply attached to his native land; and heart-rending scenes have been witnessed around the boundary pillar.....Some gave way to unrestrained grief; some comforted the weeping; some knelt and pressed their faces to the loved soil of their native country and collected a little earth to take with them into exile.....Until recently the Siberian boundary post was covered with brief inscriptions, good-bys and the names of exiles.....In one place, in a man's hand, had been written the words "Prashchai Marya" (Goodby Mary!) Who the writer was, who Mary was, there is nothing now left to show.....' (see p78).

Km2140: Tyumen (●●) The oldest town in Siberia, founded in 1586. It was built on the banks of the Tura River, the site of the former Tatar town of Chingi Tura, said to date back to the fourteenth century. The Russian town was named by Tsar Feodor Ivanovich after Tyumen Khan, who formerly ruled this region. It grew quickly as a trading centre with goods arriving and being shipped on from the large port on the Tura River.

At least one million of the people who passed through this town before 1900 were convicts and exiles. Many were lodged, under the most appalling conditions, in the Tyumen Forwarding Prison (See Part 3: 'The Exile System'). When George Kennan visited the prison in 1887, he was horrified by the overcrowded cells, the dirt and the terrible smell. He wrote: 'The air in the corridors and cells.....was

MAP 5

laden with fever germs from the unventilated hospital wards, fetid odors from diseased human bodies and the stench arising from unemptied excrement buckets.....' After a miserable two-week stay here, convicts were sent on prison barges to Tomsk. Conditions were not much better for the 500,000 emigrants who flooded through the town between 1883 and 1900, but they at least had their freedom.

When the new railway reached Tyumen in 1888 prisoners from Russia were no longer herded over the Urals in marching parties but travelled in relative luxury in box-cars used also for the transport of cattle and horses.

Tyumen is growing again now, in population (at present about 400,000) and in importance because of oil and gas discoveries in the *oblast*. Other industries include ship-building and timber-processing.

Steam engines may still be used for shunting in this station.

Km2431: Ishim (●●) The town lies beside the Ishim River, which is a tributary of the Irtysh. This is the centre of the fertile agricultural region known as the **Ishim Steppe**. George Kennan recounts an amusing incident that occurred here in 1829, when Baron von Humboldt was conducting a geological survey for the Tsar. The famous explorer (who gave his name to the Humboldt Current off the west coast of South America) had by then become more than a little annoyed by the petty Siberian officials who kept him from his studies. He must have been rather short with the police prefect in this little town for the man took great offence and despatched an urgent letter to his governor-general in which he wrote:

'A few days ago there arrived here a German of shortish stature, insignificant appearance, fussy and bearing a letter of introduction from your Excellency to me. I accordingly received

him politely; but I must say I find him suspicious and even dangerous. I disliked him from the first. He talks too much .... despises my
hospitality .... and associates with Poles and other political criminals .... On one occasion he proceeded with them to a hill overlooking the town. They took a box with them and got out of it a long
tube which we all took for a gun. After fastening it to three feet they
pointed it down on the town .... This was evidently a great danger
for the town which is built entirely of wood; so I sent a detachment
of troops with loaded rifles to watch the German on the hill. If the
treacherous machinations of this man justify my suspicions, we shall
be ready to give our lives for the Tsar and Holy Russia.' Kennan
adds: 'The civilised world is to be thanked that the brilliant career of
the great von Humboldt was not cut short by a Cossack bullet ....
while he was taking sights with a theodolite in that little Siberian
town of Ishim.'

North of Ishim, up the Ishim and Irtysh Rivers, lies the city of
Tobolsk, one of the oldest settlements in Siberia. Yermak (see p73)
reached the area in 1581 and established a fort here. The Tsar hoped
to develop the region by encouraging colonisation but as far as the
Russian peasant was concerned, Siberia was as far away as the moon
and no voluntary mass exodus over the Urals occurred. The policy
of forced exile was rather more successful. The first exiles that
arrived in Tobolsk were former inhabitants of the town of Uglich
where they had been witnesses to the murder of Tsarevich Dimitri.
With them was banished the **Uglich church bell** which rang the
signal for the insurrection following the assassination. The bell was
reconsecrated in Tobolsk church but in the 1880s the Uglich Town
Council decided it would like its bell back. Tobolsk Council refused
and the case eventually went to court. The judge ruled that as the
bell had been exiled for life, and it was still calling the people to
prayers, it had not yet completed its sentence and must therefore
remain in Tobolsk.

Km2520: Administrative frontier between Tyumenskaya and
Omskaya oblasts. **Omskaya** is on a plain in the Irtysh River basin,
occupying 140,000 square kilometres. The thick forests of the taiga
cover the northern part of the oblast. In the south there is considerable agricultural development, the main crops being spring wheat,
flax and sunflowers. As well as sheep and cattle farms, there are
many dairy-farming co-operatives. This has been an important but-
ter-producing region since the nineteenth century, when butter was
exported to as far away as Turkey and Germany. It is said that but-
ter-making was introduced to the region by the English wife of a

Russian landowner. There are many swamps and lakes in the oblast which provide the habitat for a multitude of water birds, including duck, coot, grey goose, swan and crake.

Km2521-2870: Time zone MT + 3 Local time is now Moscow Time + 3 hours.

Km2565: Nazevayevskaya (●●) This area is famous as much for its insects as for its dairy produce. In 1887, Kennan found that travelling through this marshy region was a singularly unpleasant experience. He wrote: 'We were so tormented by huge gray mosquitoes that we were obliged to put on thick gloves, cover our heads with calico hoods and horse hair netting and defend ourselves constantly with leafy branches.' You, however, should be quite safe in your compartment.

Km2707: Irtysh River which is joined here by the Om. The Irtysh rises in China and flows almost 3,000km into the Ob River.

Km2712: Omsk (●●●) (87m/285ft) Founded in 1719 when a small fortress was set up on the west bank of the Om. At the centre of a fertile region, Omsk soon developed into an important agricultural market town. By the beginning of the nineteenth century it had become a regional administrative centre and had been accorded city status.

Omsk was the military headquarters of the Cossack regiments in Siberia. The fortress had been considerably enlarged and included a large *ostrog* (prison). It was here that Dostoyevsky did four years hard labour for political crimes in 1849. His unenviable experiences were recorded in *Buried Alive in Siberia*. He was twice flogged, once for complaining about a lump of dirt in his soup; the second time he saved the life of a drowning prisoner, ignoring a guard who ordered that the man be left to drown. Dostoyevsky received so severe a flogging for this charitable act that he almost died and had to spend six weeks in the hospital.

Annette Meakin and her mother had a more amusing time in Omsk in 1900. Visiting the German pastor and his wife they asked what the strange crying sounds were that they heard each morning, to be told that they were made by the camels. 'So you have camels in Omsk!' was the excited Mrs Meakin's response to this news. 'I have always wished to mount a camel.' The German lady replied frostily: 'Intelligent people do not mount camels. They are beasts of burden.'

The vast **Cathedral of the Ascension** was completed in 1898 and the 1900 Guide to the Great Siberian Railway advised its travellers to see the banner of Yermak (the sixteenth century conqueror of Siberia) which was kept in the cathedral: 'This banner was brought from the town of Beriozov and is two *arshins* and six *vershoks* long (66ins/1.7m; 1 *arshin* = 28ins, 1 *vershok* = 1.75ins). On one side is represented the Archangel Michael on a red winged horse, striking the Devil with his spear and precipitating houses and towers into the water; on the other is seen St Demetrius on a dark horse thrusting Kuchum, mounted on a white horse, into an abyss.'

During the Civil War, Omsk was the capital of the White Russian government of Admiral Kolchak, until November 1919 when the Red Army entered and took the city. The population grew fast after the war and now more than a million people live here. Textiles, food, agricultural machinery and timber-products are the main industries. There is also an important petro-chemical industry here, supplied by a pipeline from the Ural-Volga oil region.

There are often good snacks to buy from the babushkas on the platform (chicken US$2, sour cream US$0.20, bread, eggs etc). If you're travelling on a 'trading train' (see p109) this is one of the rougher stations; take care of your possessions and yourself.

Km2761(S): In 1990 there were about **50 locos** in strategic reserve beside the line here but their numbers are now falling as they are sold off for scrap.

Baraba region Between Omsk and the Ob River (which flows through Novosibirsk) you cross a vast area of swampy land known as the Baraba region (sometimes wrongly referred to as the Barabinsk Steppe, according to the *1900 Guide to the Great Siberian Railway*). The scenery is monotonous: wide grassy plains interspersed with groves of birch trees. There are numerous shallow lakes and ponds which form a perfect breeding ground for the gnats and mosquitoes which terrorise the local population during the summer months. Before the Russian settlers arrived in the eighteenth century, the region was occupied by Tartar and Kirghiz tribes (see p239).

The West Siberian Railway (kms2716-3343)
The original line started in Chelyabinsk, south of Ekaterinburg, and ran through Kurgan and Petropavlovsk (both south of the modern route) to Omsk. Work began in July 1892 under the direction of chief civil engineer, Mikhailovski. His task was beset by problems that were to be experienced along other sections of the line: a shortage of labour and animals, a complete lack of suitable trees for sleepers and inhospitable working conditions (swamps that swarmed with insects). However, the first section (Chelyabinsk to Omsk) was completed in 1894 and the Omsk-Novo Nikolayevsk (now Novosibirsk) section opened in October 1895. The total cost of the line was 46 million roubles, one million roubles fewer than the original estimate.

MAP 6

Km2870: The administrative frontier between Omskaya and Novosibirskaya oblasts. The 178,000 square kilometres of **Novosibirskaya oblast** extend across the Baraba region of swamps and lakes. Some of the land has been drained and is now extremely fertile. Crops include spring wheat, flax, rye, barley and sun-flowers with dairy farming in many parts of the Baraba region. You may see cowherds rounding up their cows on horseback.

Km2871-4475 Time zone MT + 4 Local time is now Moscow Time + 4hrs.

Km2880: Tatarskaya (●) A rather uninteresting small town of apartment blocks and log cabins. The *1900 Guide to the Great Siberian Railway* was not enthusiastic about the place. 'The country is swampy and infested with fever. The water is bad, supplied by a pond formed by spring and bog water.' There was a church, a centre for emigrants, a school and 'the butter manufacturies of Mariupolsky, Padin, Soshovsky, Popel and Weiss, producing annually about 15,000 *puds* (250,000 kg) of cream butter'.

Km2883(N): Attractive group of brightly painted log cabins. About fifty kilometres south of the line between Chany and Barabinsk lies Lake Chany, the centre of a fishing industry. Catches are smaller now but in the nineteenth century it was famous for its abundant stock of large pike (weighing up to 14kg/30lbs) and carp.

Km3035: Barabinsk (●) There is a short stop by this ugly station building and fish (from the surrounding lakes) are often sold on the platform (not always cooked). Other possible purchases might include Western chocolate bars or Bruce Lee badges from the kiosks. At the centre of the swampy **Baraba region**, Barabinsk was founded in 1722 when a field fortress was built here and the town which grew up around it was, until after the Revolution, called Kainsk. Cossacks were stationed here to try to encourage the nomadic Tatars, Kirghiz and Kalmyks to pay their taxes. For the 300km east of Barabinsk to Novosibirsk the rural scenery continues: fields of sunflowers or pastures dotted with cows and sheep, small clumps of birch trees or swamps and ponds.

The Kirghiz
South of Omsk and the Baraba region lie the **Kirghiz Steppes**, the true home of the Kirghiz people. The area extends from the Urals in the west to the mineral-rich Altai Mountains in the south. The Kirghiz are direct descendants of the Turco-Mongol hordes that joined Ghengis Khan's armies and invaded Europe in the thirteenth century AD. When S.S.Hill paid them a visit in 1854, they were nomadic herders who professed a mixture of Shamanism and Mohammedanism and survived on a diet of boiled mutton and *koumiss* (fermented mare's milk). They lived in *kibitkas* (felt tents or yurts), the doors of which were arranged to face in the direction of Mecca. Fortunately this alignment also kept out the southern winds that blew across the Steppe. Of these people Hill wrote: 'The Kirgeeze have the high cheek bones.....of the Mongol Tatars, with an expression of countenance that seemed at least to us the very reverse of agreeable.' However he warmed to his 'new half wild friends' when they shared their 'brave mess of *stchee*' (soup) with him.

George Kennan found them equally hospitable in 1887. Inside the tent he was offered a large container filled with about a litre and a half of koumiss. For fear of causing offence he swallowed the lot and to his horror, his host quickly refilled the container. Kennan wrote 'When I suggested that he reserve the second bowlful for my comrade, Mr Frost, he looked so pained and grieved that in order to restore his serenity I had to go to the *tarantas*, get my banjo and sing "There is a Tavern in the Town"'. This did not have quite the desired effect and they left shortly after.

Km3204: Chulimskaya A large junction.

Km3319: Ob station The city of Novosibirsk can be seen to the northeast of here.

Km3332: Bridge over the Ob River The original bridge, built at the end of the nineteenth century, still stands. The writers of the **Guide to the Great Siberian Railway** were clearly very proud of this tremendous feat of engineering, which at the time had only just been completed. They devote almost a whole page of their book to a detailed description of the bridge, beginning: 'At the 1,328 *verst*, the line crosses the Ob by a bridge 327.50 *sazhens* long, having 7 spans, the I and VII openings are 46.325 *sazhens*, the II, IV and VI, 53.65 *sazhens*, and III and V, 53.15 *sazhens*. The upper girders of the bridge are on the Herber's system.' If you are unfamiliar with the

MAP 7

Russian Imperial units of measurement, a *verst* is 1.06Km or 3500ft and a *sazhen* is 2.1m or 7ft. For those interested, the bridge is therefore about 690m in length.

The Ob River is one of the world's longest rivers, flowing more than 4000km north across Siberia from the Altai Mountains to the Gulf of Ob, below the Arctic Ocean.

After you cross the bridge there is a **preserved steam loco** mounted on a plinth at km3333(S)

Km3335: Novosibirsk (●●●) (183m/ 600ft) is the capital of Western Siberia. See p154 for further information.

The suburbs of Novosibirsk stretch out east to about km3348. Travelling east you pass through flat land of fields and swamps with the dachas of Novosibirskians in little groups amongst the trees. Some are particularly photogenic (km3409 (S)). The line traverses an area of thin taiga to Oyash (km3424)

Km3485: This is the **administrative frontier** between Novosibirskaya and Kemerovskaya oblasts.

Km3498: Yurga A few kilometres east of here, the train crosses the River Tom, which flows an unimpressive (by Siberian standards) 700km (or twice the length of the Thames) from the Kuznetsk basin into the Ob.

Km3565: Taiga (●●) Junction of the branch line to Tomsk. R.L.Jefferson was here in 1897 and wrote later: 'This little station was bang in the midst of the most impenetrable forest I had ever set eyes on.....in the centre of a pit it seemed, for the great black trunks of pines went up all around and left only a circular space of blue sky visible.' Annette Meakin wrote a few years later: 'We thought Taiga one of the prettiest stations in Siberia. It is only a few years old, built something after the style of a Swiss chalet.'

Unfortunately it has since been replaced by a building that is rather more substantial but aesthetically less pleasing.

If you were to take the other line from Taiga, you would come after about 80km, to the ancient city of **Tomsk**, once the most important place in Siberia. It was founded in 1604 on the River Tom and developed into a large administrative, trading and gold-smelting centre on the Great Siberian Post Road. When it was bypassed by the railway (although later connected by a branch-line) Tomsk began to lose out to the stations along the main line. However, it is still a sizeable city of almost half a million people, the administrative capital of Tomskaya oblast and a large centre of industrial engineering.

Tomsk was visited by almost every nineteenth century traveller who came to Siberia. The city was an important exile centre and had a large forwarding prison. Having almost succumbed to the stench from the overcrowded cells in 1887, Kennan wrote: 'If you visit the prison my advice to you is to breakfast heartily before starting, and to keep out of the hospital wards.' By the time Annette Meakin visited it fourteen years later, the railways had removed the need for forwarding prisons and she could write: 'It was not unlike a group of alms houses. We found very few prisoners.'

Tomsk, perhaps like many other cities in the CIS, has a number of satellite 'cities' around it, hidden in the Siberian forests. The exact whereabouts of some of these military bases was kept secret from the West until 1992 when a nuclear accident in 'Tomsk-7' made world headlines.

Between Taiga and Mariinsk there are deposits of coal. The CIS has no shortage of this fossil fuel: 25 per cent of world supplies. It has been mined around the town of Yar since the nineteenth century. The centre of the coal-mining district, however, lies 300km south of here, around the city of **Novokuznetsk**, in the Kuznetsk (or Kuzbass) Basin. In the early 1900s a plan had been put forward to link these coal-fields with the Ural region where iron-ore was mined and coal was needed for the blast furnaces. This plan was not put into action until the 1930s when the so-called Ural-Kuzbass Kombinat was developed. Trains bring iron-ore to the Kuzbass furnaces and return to the iron foundries of the Urals with coal. You will have met (or will meet if you're going west) a good deal of this traffic on the line between Novosibirsk and the Urals. According to Eric Newby this stretch of the line has more freight traffic than any other in the world, with a train every couple of minutes.

Kms3613-3623: Several long views south across the fields. The line climbs slowly through birch forests and small fields to Mariinsk.

MAP 8

Km3715: Mariinsk (● ●)   Just west of the station there are large engine repair yards (S). Two kilometres east of the town you cross the Kiya River, a tributary of the Chulim. East of the river the line rises to cross the watershed at km3760, where there are good views south. The line descends through the market town of **Tiazhin** (km3779) to the river of the same name and then climbs over the next watershed descending to **Itat**, another agricultural town.

Km3820:   This is the administrative frontier between Kemerovskaya oblast and Krasnoyarskiy *kray*. A kray is a large oblast, usually found in less developed areas like Siberia. This is also the border between West and East Siberia. **Krasnoyarskiy** is large, covering 2½ million square kilometres (an area the size of Saudi Arabia) between the Arctic Ocean in the north and the Sayan Mountains in the south. Most of the kray is covered with taiga, though there is tundra in the region within the Arctic Circle and some agricultural land in the south. The economy is based on timber processing but there are also important mineral reserves.

Km3848   A number of **steam locos** can be seen (S) as you approach Bogotol.

Km3849: Bogotol (● ●)   Market town. About 30km east of here the line begins to descend, crossing the **Chulim River** at km3917. R.L.Jefferson arrived here in the winter of 1897 and described the river as 'rather a small stream when compared to the Obi, Tom or Irtish but still broad enough to make two of the River Thames at London Bridge'. The bridge had not been completed but engineers had had the brilliant idea of freezing the rails to the thick ice, thus enabling the train to cross the river.

Km3917: Achinsk (●) (214m/700ft) Founded in 1642 when a stockaded outpost was built here, on the banks of the Chulim. It was burnt down by the Kirghiz forty years later but was soon rebuilt. In the eighteenth and nineteenth centuries Achinsk was an important trading centre, linked by the Chulim to Tyumen and Tomsk. Tea arrived by caravan from China and was forwarded in barges. To the north, in the valleys around the Chulim basin, lay the gold mines. The most valuable and productive mines today, however, are those producing lignite (brown coal). Achinsk is also an agricultural centre.

Kms3932-33(S): The half-way point on the line from Moscow to Beijing (via Mongolia). There is a **white obelisk** to mark it on the south side of the line but it is difficult to see. The line continues through a hilly region of taiga winding round sharp curves (kms4006-12) and past picturesque groups of log cabins (km4016). There are occasional good views at km4058(N) and after the village of Minino (km4072) at 4078(N).

The Mid-Siberian Railway (kms3343-5191)

Work began on the line at the River Ob in the summer of 1893. Since Tomsk was to be bypassed, part of the route had to be hacked through the thick forests of the taiga regions around the station aptly named Taiga. It would have been far easier to have followed the route of the Great Siberian Post Road through Tomsk but some of the city's administrators wanted nothing to do with the railway, since it would break their trade monopolies and bring down prices, damaging the economy as far as they were concerned. By the time they realised that the effect was quite the opposite it was too late to change the route of the line. Besides, the engineers had discovered that the bypass would save 90km. The tiny village of Novo Nikolayevsk (now Novosibirsk) situated where the railway crosses the Ob, grew quickly and soon eclipsed Tomsk as an industrial and cultural centre.

This was difficult territory to build a railway across. The swampy taiga is frozen until mid-July, so the building season was barely three months long. There was the usual labour shortage and 1,500 convicts had to be brought in to help. In 1895 a branch line from Taiga reached Tomsk. Although only about 80km long, it had taken a year to build, owing to the virtually impenetrable taiga and the terrible swamps. In 1896 the line reached Krasnoyarsk and work began on the eastern section to Irkutsk. Numerous bridges were needed in this hilly country but by the beginning of 1898 the mid-Siberian was complete and the first trains rolled into Irkutsk. Total cost was about 110 million roubles.

Km4098: Krasnoyarsk (●●●) (159m/520ft) A major industrial city of 850,000 people. It was founded in 1628 beside the Yenisei River. (*Yenisei* is also the name of the Moscow-Krasnoyarsk Express which you may see standing in the station). A fort was built and named Krasny Yar. As an important trading centre on the Great Siberian Post Road and the great Yenisei waterway, the town grew fast in the eighteenth century. The railway reached Krasnoyarsk in 1896, some of the rails for this section of the line having been brought from England by ship via the Kara Sea (within the Arctic Circle) and the Yenisei. By 1900, the population was 27,000 and the town boasted 20 churches and two cathedrals, a synagogue, 26 schools, a railway technical college and a botanical garden reputed to be the finest in Siberia.

Murray would not recognise the town he described as 'pleasantly situated and sheltered by hills of moderate elevation', in the 1865 edition of his *Handbook for Russia, Poland and Finland*. R.L.Jefferson wrote in 1897: 'Its situation cannot fail to elicit admiration - the tall mountains rear up around it.' Most of the townsfolk he met here were ex-convicts. So used were they to their own kind, that they were particularly suspicious of anyone who lacked a criminal record. He was told of a certain merchant in the city who found it difficult to do business, never having been behind bars. To remedy the situation he travelled all the way to St Petersburg and deliberately committed a crime that was punishable by exile to Siberia. After a short sentence in Irkutsk he returned to his business in Krasnoyarsk and 'got on famously' thereafter.

Travelling intellectuals were advised to visit the library of the Krasnoyarsk merchant, Yudin. This bibliophile assembled a collection of 100,000 volumes, including almost every publication ever issued in Siberia. At the end of the nineteenth century, while sentenced to exile in Krasnoyarsk, Lenin spent several months working in this library. In 1906 Yudin sold his valuable collection to the Library of Congress, for less than half of its true worth. By this act of generosity he said that he hoped closer relations between the United States and Russia would be established.

During the Second World War, many factories were evacuated from European Russia and rebuilt here. Industrial growth has continued since then and the long list of things the city now produces includes aluminium, chemicals, ships, televisions, fridges and heavy machinery.

Km4100-2: Yenisei River Good views (N) & (S). Leaving Krasnoyarsk, travelling east, the train crosses the great river that bisects Siberia. The Yenisei (meaning 'wide water' in the language of the local Evenki people) rises in Mongolia and flows into the Arctic Ocean, 5,200km north of its source.

This bridge, which is almost a kilometre in length, dates from the 1890s and had to be built on heavy granite piers to withstand the huge icebergs which steamroller their way down the river for a few weeks each year. The cement was shipped from St Petersburg, the steel bearings from Warsaw.

MAP 9

For several kilometres after you've crossed the river the lumber mills and factories blight the countryside. Open-cast mining has slashed ugly gashes into the hills around km4127(N). Between Krasnoyarsk and Nizhneudinsk the line crosses hilly, picturesque countryside, and the train climbs out of one valley and descends into the next. There are numerous bridges on this section. There are some good places for photographs along the train as it curves round bends at km4165-7 and km4176-4177, then the land becomes flatter.

Km4227: Uyar Large strategic reserve of working **steam locos** at west end of station (N) where there is also a dump of about ten engines rusting away amongst the weeds. This town's full name is something of a tongue-twister. Try saying 'Ular-Spasopreo-brazhen-skoye' after a few glasses of vodka. Before the Revolution the station was called Olginskaya in honour of Grand Duchess Olga Nikolaevna.

Km4343: Kansk Another ancient Siberian settlement. A fort was built here in 1604 beside the River Kan. By 1900 it was an important station on the railway and a stopping point on the Great Siberian Post Road. The original station building has been replaced by a modern concrete eyesore. Leaving Kansk you cross the River Kan at km4346.

Km4375: Ilanskaya (●●) Several rusting **steam locos** in this station: one at the west end (S) and a further three quite ancient types at the east end (N). This agricultural town was founded in the early nineteenth century beside the Ilanka River. Between here and Tayshet, there are large deposits of lignite (brown coal). Our provodnitsa was well aware of this last bit of information and issued four of us with buckets to collect coal (for the carriage boiler) from the piles lying about the platform.

Km4453: Reshoti Junction for the line south to Abakan, an industrial centre in the foothills of the Sayan Mountains. There is good hiking in the area from Abakan (see p177).

About nine hundred kilometres due north of here lies the town of Tura, the capital of the **Evenki National Okrug**, 745,000 square kilometres of permanently frozen land, specially reserved for the indigenous population. The **Evenkis** belong to the Tungus group of people (the names are often used interchangeably) and they were originally nomadic herders and hunters. After the Buryats and the Yakuts, they form the next largest ethnic group in Siberia but they are scattered into small groups, right across the northern regions. They used to live in wig-wams or tents and survived off berries and reindeer-meat (a great delicacy being the raw marrow sucked straight from the bone preferably while it was still warm). They discovered that Christianity fitted in well with their own Shamanistic religion and worshipped St Nicholas as deputy to the Master Spirit of the Underworld. After the Revolution they were organised into collective farms and although most of the population is now settled, there are still some reindeer-herders in the extreme north of the region.

Km4475: This is the administrative frontier between Krasnoyarskaya and Irkutskaya oblasts.

Km4476-5755: Time zone MT + 5 Local time is now Moscow Time + 5hrs.

Kms4501-02: The river here conveniently marks the **half-way point** for the Moscow to Beijing (via Manchuria) run.

Km4516: Tayshet (●) (317m/1040ft) Junction for the line to Bratsk and the Baikal Amur Magistral Railway (BAM).

Km4555(S): Razgon A small, poor-looking community of log cabins. About a kilometre east of here, the line rises and there are views across the taiga at km4563(S), km4569(N) and km4570.

Km4631: Kamyshet It was here that George Kennan stopped in 1887 for repairs to his tarantass. While the wheel was being replaced, he watched the amazing spectacle of a Siberian blacksmith shoeing a horse. 'The poor beast had been hoisted by means of two broad belly-bands and suspended from a stout frame so that he could not touch the ground', he wrote. Three of the horse's legs had been secured to the frame and 'the daring blacksmith was fearlessly putting a shoe on the only hoof that the wretched and humiliated animal could move.'

Kms4640-4680: The train snakes its way through the foothills of the Eastern Sayan Mountains. The Sayan Range forms a natural frontier between Siberia and Mongolia.

The **half-way point** on the line from Moscow to Vladivostok is at kms1618-9.

There are some good views and a number of chances to take photographs of the whole length of the train as it winds around the valleys. The best spots are around km4657(S), km4660(S), kms4662-5 and km4667. The line descends to Nizhneudinsk.

Km4680: Nizhneudinsk (● ●)

(415m/1360ft) There's not much more than saw-mills, swamps and insects in this area. Of the mosquitoes, Kennan complained 'I found myself blotted from head to foot as if I were suffering from some eruptive disease.'

About 800km due north of here, on 30 June 1908, one of the largest (pre-atomic era) explosions took place, in the Tunguska River region. Two thousand square kilometres of forest were instantly destroyed in what came to be known as the **Tunguska Event**. The sound of the explosion was heard up to 350kms away; the shock waves were registered on seismic equipment right around the world, and the light from the blast was seen throughout Europe.

Newspapers of the time proposed all kinds of theories to explain its cause - from the testing of new explosives to crash-landing Martian space-ships. Scientists now believe that the explosion was caused by a fragment of Encke's Comet, which disintegrated as it entered the Earth's atmosphere, creating a vast fireball.

Between Nizhneudinsk and Irkutsk the country becomes flatter and the taiga not so thick. The train passes through numerous timber-yards.

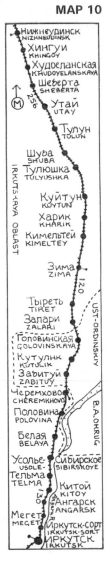

MAP 10

Km4789(S): Large **graveyard** with a blue fence around it, standing close to the line. Some of the graves are topped with red stars, some with red crosses. Kennan wrote in 1887: 'The graveyards belonging to the Siberian settlements sometimes seemed to me much more remarkable and noteworthy than the settlements themselves.....Many graves (are) marked by three armed wooden crosses and covered with narrow A-shaped roofs.'

Km4794: Tulun An agricultural and wood-processing centre on the Uya River. The line follows the river, crossing it at km4800 and passing a large saw-mill at km4804(S) which might make a good photo with the town behind it. For once there are no wires to get in the way. At km4809(S) there is a large open-cast mine. You pass through an area of large cultivated fields.

Km4875: Kuytun The town's name means 'cold' in the language of the local Buryat people (see below). There are cold springs in the area.

Km4940: Zima (● ● ●) (460m/1500ft) Founded by exiles in the early nineteenth century. When the Tsarevich Nicholas visited Zima on 8 July 1891, the Buryats presented him with a model of one of their yurts (tents) cast in silver. Three kilometres east of the town, the line crosses the River Oka, a tributary of the Angara. As the line rises out of one valley, crosses the watershed and drops down to the next river you get several reasonable views: km4958(S), km4972(N), km4977(S) and km4990(S).

Kms5000-40 You pass through the Ust-Ordinsky Autonomous Okrug. There's another graveyard close to the track at km5010(S).

Km5061: Cheremkhovo The centre of the coal-mining district of the same name.

Km5100: Near here is the village of **Malta**, on the banks of the Belaya River. It was in a house in Malta, in February 1928, that farmer Platon Brilin was helping a comrade to build a cellar. While he was digging, his spade struck a white object which turned out to be a mammoth tusk carved into a female form. Excavations revealed dwellings with walls made from mammoth bones and roofs of antlers. He had discovered the remains one of an ancient settlement, dating from the thirteenth millennium B.C. A grave yielded the body of a child, still wearing a necklace and headband of bones. He may have been a young shaman (see p167) for the gods were thought to select their earthly representatives by branding them with some kind of deformity: the boy has two sets of teeth. Numerous figurines made of ivory have been found at Malta and also at the site in **Buret**, eight kilometres from here. Many of the excavated artifacts may be seen in the museums in Irkutsk. The oldest settlement in the CIS that has so far been discovered is at Dering Yuryakh (1-2.5 million years old) in northern Siberia near Yakutsk.

Between km5100 and Irkutsk (km5185) there are fields interspersed with large industrial areas. In the distance, at km5130(N) there is a large oil refinery.

How the post was sent to Siberia

'The building of the Trans Siberian Railway revolutionised the carrying of mail across the vast Siberian steppes. By 1902 a letter could be carried from St Petersburg to Vladivostok in less than two weeks instead of several months as previously. The first Siberian letter on record was that carried to Moscow in 1582 by some of Yermak's Cossacks, informing Tsar Ivan the Terrible that Siberia was now his. A regular postal system had been established in Siberia by 1600, Russian peasants being encouraged to emigrate to Siberia to work as Post House keepers and post-riders or *yamshchiki* (see p83). The post always had priority for the supply of horses and for right of way on the new post roads. Each Post House keeper had to keep some horses permanently in reserve in case the post should arrive, and on the road a blast of the courier's horn was enough to make other road users pull over and allow the post to pass. Indeed, the yamschiki were not averse to using their whip on the drivers of carts which were slow to move out of the way.

In April 1829 the German writer, Adolph Erman, travelling down the still-frozen Lena River from Irkutsk to Yakutsk, wrote that he had "the good luck of meeting the postman from Yakutsk and Kamchatka. At my desire he waited until the frozen ink which I carried with me had time to thaw, and a few lines to friends in Berlin were written and committed to his care. The courier, or paid overseer who attended the mail from Yakutsk to Irkutsk carried, as a mark of his rank and office, a sword and a loaded pistol, hanging by a chain from his neck. In winter he obtains from the peasants the requisite supply of sledges and horses; and when the ice-road is broken up he takes boats, sometimes, to ascend the Lena" (*Travels in Siberia*).

By the time Annette Meakin travelled along the Trans-Siberian Railway in 1900, she was able to send letters home speedily by train, but she had evidently heard about dishonest postal officials and she took pains to register all her letters. In *A Ribbon of Iron*, she wrote "If you do not register in Siberia there is every chance that the stamps will be taken and the letter destroyed long before it reaches the border. You cannot register after 2 p.m., in which case it is advisable to use a black-edged envelope. Superstition will then prevent its being tampered with". Black-edged envelopes were used during a period of mourning.

Much of the mail still travels by train, and passenger trains in Siberia often include a travelling post office coach in which mail is sorted. These have an aperture at platform level, through which letters and cards can be posted'. **Philip Robinson** (UK). Philatelists may be interested to know that Philip Robinson is the author of *Russian Postmarks* and *Siberia - Postmarks and Postal History of the Russian Empire Period*. Enquiries concerning these books will be forwarded to the author (address p2).

Km5160: Angarsk (●) Known as Sukhovskaya before the Revolution, the town is on the banks of the Angara River, the only river which flows out of Lake Baikal.

Just north of **Meget**, travellers have reported a large strategic reserve (N) of L and Ye 2-10-0s.

Km5179: Irkutsk Sort. (Irkutsk marshalling yard) The station used to be called Innokentievskaya, in honour of St Innocent, Archbishop of Irkutsk, who was said to have been the first miracle-worker in Siberia. The **St Innocent Monastery of the Ascension** near here was founded in 1672.

The Tsarevich looked in on his tour of Siberia in 1891. The visit was thus described: 'After having listened to the singing, the Tsesarevich (sic) knelt at the shrine of the Siberian Saint, kissed the relics and received the image of Innocent, presented to him by Agathangelius, Vicar of Irkutsk. At the same time a deputation from Shaman Buryats expressed the desire of 250 men to adopt the orthodox religion and to receive the name of Nicholas in commemoration of the Tsesarevich's visit to Siberia, which was thus to be preserved in the memory of their descendants. The Imperial traveller graciously acceded to this request.'

Km5185: Irkutsk (●●●) (440m/1450ft)
See p161 for information and a description of this city, once known as the 'Paris of Siberia'.

Lake Baikal Leaving Irkutsk, travelling in the direction of Khabarovsk and Vladivostok, the line climbs up into the hills before giving magnificent views over Lake Baikal. It then winds down through a series of tunnels and a Swiss-style horse-shoe bend to follow the mountainous shore of the lake. At many points the rails lie right beside the water and some of the best views of the whole trip are along this section of the line, over this immense stretch of water. (See p171 for information on Lake Baikal).

Winding through valleys of cedar and pine, and crossing numerous small streams, the train passes **Kultuk**, the junction for the old line from Port Baikal. At km5228(N) a giant etching of Lenin waves nonchalantly from the hill above. The line climbs steeply to km5254 and then snakes downwards giving you your first glimpses of Lake Baikal from kms5274-8. After the tunnel (km5290) there is a splendid view over the lake at km5292(N).

Km5297-8: Tunnel as the line curves sharply round the valley and descends to the water's edge. After the junction and goods yard at

Slyudyanka II (km5305) the train crawls slowly along a part of the line that is liable to flooding from the lake, and into the main station.

Km5312: Slyudyanka (●●●) As the station is only about 500m from the lake there is just enough time to run down to the water and dip your hand in for good luck (see p174). Check with the carriage attendant that the train is stopping for the usual 15mins and hurry down between the log cabins to the lake. You must be quick since people have been left behind. If you're not feeling energetic there's usually lots to buy on the platform - breadsticks and bags of *orecha* (cedar seeds, the classic Siberian snack).

Although there are some photogenic log cabins near the station, Slyudyanka is a rather unattractive mining town and port. Fur-trappers hunt sable and ermine in the forests around this area.

For the next 200km the line is never far from the lake, occasionally running right beside it.

Km5397: This is the **administrative frontier** between Irkutskaya oblast and the Buryat Republic. This region, which is also known as **Buryatia**, comprises an area of 350,000 square kilometres (about the size of Italy). It was set aside for the Buryats (see p254), an indigenous ethnic group once nomadic but now adapted to an agricultural or urban life. Their republic is composed of mountainous taiga and the economy is based on fur-farming, stock-raising, food and timber-processing and the mining of gold, aluminium, manganese, iron, coal, asbestos and mica. In fact almost all the elements can be found here.

When Prince Borghese and his team were motoring through this area in 1907, taking part in the Peking to Paris Rally, they found that since the building of the railway the Great Siberian Post Road had fallen into disrepair.

MAP 11

Most of the post-stations were deserted and many of the bridges were rotten and dangerous. The Italians were given special permission by the governor-general to use the railway bridges. In fact they covered a considerable part of the journey here by driving along the railway line. However, their 40 h.p. Itala was not the only unorthodox vehicle to take to the rails. On his cycle-tour through south Siberia in 1896, R.L.Jefferson found it rather easier to pedal his Imperial Rover along the tracks than along the muddy roads.

Km5421(N): The lonely looking collection of ramshackle buildings by the water's edge might make a good photograph.

Km5477: Mysovaya This port was where the *Baikal* and *Angara* delivered their passengers (and their train). Also called Babushkin in honour of an Irkutsk revolutionary, it was the western starting point of the Transbaikal railway (see p255).

When Annette Meakin and her mother disembarked from the *Baikal* in 1900, they were horrified to discover that the awaiting train was composed entirely of fourth class carriages. The brave ladies commandeered seats in the corner of one compartment but soon they were hemmed in by emigrating peasants. When two dirty moujiks climbed into the luggage rack above them, the ladies decided it would be better to wait at Mysovaya than spend four days in such claustrophobic conditions, and got out. However, the station-master allowed them to travel in an empty luggage-van, which gave them privacy but not comfort.

Between Mysovaya and Petrovskiy Zavod the line skirts around the lower reaches of the Khamar Daban mountain range. The train passes through Posolkaya (km5524) where there was once a large walled monastery, set up by an abbot and a monk in 1681. Around km5536, the line enters the wide valley of the River Selenga, which it follows as far as Ulan Ude (km5642).

Km5562: Selenginsk Founded as a stockaded outpost in the seventeenth century. Unfortunately the wood-pulping factories are rather more in evidence than the sixteenth century monastery which was the centre for missionaries attempting the conversion of the Buryats. From about km5515 east, the line begins to climb, crossing the Selenga River at kms5617-8. At km5633-4(N) there's an army camp with some abandoned tanks.

Km5642: Ulan Ude (●●●) (544m/1785ft) A city of 400,000 people, this is the capital of the Buryat Republic. Stretch your legs on the platform where there is a **steam loco** (see photo opposite p113) preserved outside the locomotive workshop (N) at the western end of the station. See Part 4 for further information about the city and sight-seeing possibilities if you're staying here.

Turn to p270 for the **Trans-Mongolian route to Beijing**.

The Circumbaikal Line (kms5191-5483)

Until 1904, passengers crossed Lake Baikal on ferries which took them from Port Baikal to Mysovaya. In 1893 it had been decided that this short section of line along the mountainous southern shore of the lake would be impossibly expensive to build, and the plan was shelved in favour of the ferry link. From the English company of Armstrong and Mitchell a specially designed combined ice-breaker and train-ferry was ordered. The 4,200 ton ship, christened the *Baikal*, had three pairs of rails laid across her decks for the carriages and could smash through ice up to four feet thick. A sister ship, the *Angara*, was soon brought into service. This ship has now been converted into a museum and is moored in Irkutsk (see p169).

The ferry system was not a great success, however. In mid-winter the ships were unable to break through the ice and in summer the wild storms for which the lake is notorious often delayed them. Since they could not accommodate more than 300 people between them, many passengers were subjected to a long wait beside the lake. The Trans-Siberian Committee realised that, however expensive it might prove, a line had to be built to bridge the 260km gap between the Mid-Siberian and the Transbaikal Railways. Further surveys were ordered in 1898 and in 1901 ten thousand labourers started work on the line.

This was the most difficult section to build on the entire railway. The terrain between Port Baikal and Kultuk (near Slyudyanka) was virtually one long cliff. Thirty-three tunnels and more than two hundred bridges and trestles were constructed, the task being made all the more difficult by the fact that in many places the labourers could reach the route only by boat. Work was carried on simultaneously on the Tankhoi to Mysovaya section.

The labour gangs hacked out embankments and excavated seven kilometres of tunnels but the line was not ready at the time it was most needed. On 8 February 1904, Japan attacked the Russian Navy while it lay at anchor in Port Arthur on the Pacific. Troops were rushed by rail from European Russia but when they arrived at Port Baikal, they found the *Baikal* and *Angara* ice-bound in the severe weather. The only way across the lake was a seventeen-hour march over the ice. It was then that the Minister of Ways of Communication, Prince Khilkov, put into action a plan which had been successful on several of Siberia's rivers: rails were laid across the ice. The first train to set off across the frozen lake did not get far along the forty-five kilometre track before the ice gave way with a crack like a cannon and the locomotive sank into the icy water. From then on the engines had to be stripped and their parts put on flat-cars that were pulled over the ice by gangs of men and horses.

Working as fast as possible, in all weathers, the Circumbaikal line was completed in September 1904 at a cost of about 70 million roubles. The first passengers found this section of the line particularly terrifying, not on account of the frequent derailments but because of the tunnels: there were none in European Russia at that time.

In the 1950s a short cut was opened between Irkutsk and Slyudyanka, which is the route followed by the train today. The line between Irkutsk and Port Baikal is now partly flooded and no longer used. Much of the Port Baikal to Kultuk section, however, is still operational and can be visited by boat from Listvyanka.

East of Ulan Ude the line crosses the River Uda and from Onokhoi follows the valley of a river named Brian. From Zaigraevo, the train begins to climb to Ilka, a town on the river of the same name. It continues to ascend the Zagon Dar range, reaching the highest point (882m/2892ft) at Kizha, near the administrative frontier.

Km5675(N): Onokhoy Large number (about 40) of **steam locos** kept at the west end of this station.

Km5755: This is the **administrative frontier** between Buryatia and **Chitinskaya** oblast. The 432,000 square kilometres of the Chitinskaya oblast comprise a series of mountain ranges interspersed with wide valleys. The dominant range is the Yablonovy (highest peak: Sokhondo, 2,510m/8,200ft) which is crossed by the Trans-Siberian near Amazar. The mountains are covered in a vast forest of conifers and the climate is dry. The economy is based on mining (gold, tungsten, tin, lead, zinc, molybdenum, lithium, lignite), timber-processing and fur-farming.

Km5756-8150: Time zone MT + 6 Local time is Moscow Time + 6hrs.

The Buryats
The largest ethnic minority group in Siberia, these people are of Mongolian descent. When Russian colonists arrived in the lands around Lake Baikal, the Buryats were nomads who spent their time herding their flocks between the southern shores of the lake and what is now northern Mongolia, in search of pastureland. They lived in felt-covered *yurts* and professed a mixture of Buddhism and Shamanism.

The Buryats lived on fish from Lake Baikal, bear-meat and berries. However, their favourite food was said to be *urme*, the thick dried layer of scum skimmed from the top of boiled milk. They hunted the Baikal seal for its fur and in winter, when the lake was frozen, they would track these animals on the ice wearing white clothing and pushing a white sledge as a hide. Back in their *yurts* the Buryats were not the cleanest of Siberian tribes, lacking even the most basic of social graces as the anthropologists Levin and Potapov point out in *The Peoples of Siberia*. Describing an after-dinner scene, they wrote: 'The vessels were not washed, as the spoons and cups were licked clean. An unwashed vessel was often passed from one member of the family to another as was the smoking pipe. Customs of this kind promoted the spread of various diseases.' Most of the diseases were probably brought by the Russian colonists.

Although at first hostile to the Russian colonists, the Buryats became involved in the fur-trade with the Europeans and a certain amount of inter-marriage occurred. Some gave up their nomadic life and felt-covered *yurts* in favour of log cabins in Verkhneudinsk (now Ulan Ude) or Irkutsk. The Buryats, who number about 350,000, now have their own **Buryat Republic**, around the southern part of Lake Baikal. The capital, Ulan Ude, was opened to tourists in 1990 and is an interesting place to visit.

Km5784: Petrovskiy Zavod (Works) (●●●) The line descends from Kizha to this town which is also known as Petrovsk-Zabaikalskiy. It was named after the Imperial ironworks set up here in 1790 and still going strong today. A monument and large mural (see overleaf) at the station commemorates the fact that the town was a place of exile for several of the Decembrists, including the Princes Trubetskoi and Volkonsky. Their wives received special permission from the Tsar to join their husbands in exile. They arrived in 1830 and spent the next ten years imprisoned here. For a very readable account of the life of Maria Volkonsky and the Decembrist Exiles see *The Princess of Siberia* by Christine Sutherland. Maria Volkonsky's house in Irkutsk is now a museum.

East of Petrovskiy Zavod, the line turns north-east into the wide, picturesque valley of the River Khilok, which it follows for almost 300kms to Sokhondo, crossing the Yablonovy Range between Mogzon and Chita.

Km5883: Look out for the large graveyard of about 40 old **steam locomotives**.

Km5884: Bada Aerodrome The little town is clearly a product of the aerodrome and not vice versa: it's built around a large Soviet monument, a Mig fighter plane facing skyward. The runway (N) is interesting for the large numbers of old Soviet aircraft that congregate here. These might make an interesting photograph but discretion is advised.

The Transbaikal Railway (kms5483-6532)
Work was begun in 1895 to connect Mysovaya (the port on Lake Baikal) with Sretensk, on the Shilka River near Kuenga, where passengers boarded steamers for the voyage to Khabarovsk. Materials were shipped to Vladivostok and thence by boat along the Ussuri, Amur and Shilka Rivers. There was a shortage of labour, for it proved impossible to get the local Buryats to work on the line. Gangs of reluctant convicts were brought in, although they became more interested in the operation after it was decided that they should receive 50 kopecks a day in return for their labour.

The terrain is mountainous and the line meanders up several valleys and over the Yablonovy Range. Owing to the dry climate work could continue throughout the winter, although water was in short supply during these months. Workers were also faced with the problem of permafrost which necessitated the building of bonfires to thaw the ground, or dynamite to break it up. A terrible set-back occurred in July 1887, when 350km of track and several bridges were swept away in a freak flood.

The line was completed in early 1900 by which time it had cost over 60 million roubles.

Km5899(S): Good place for a photo along the train as it travels on higher ground beside the river. Also at km5908(S), when the train winds slowly along the water's edge.

Km5932: Khilok (●) (805m/2,640ft) A small industrial town. East of here you continue to climb gently up the valley beside the Khilok. There are pleasant views over the wide plain all along the river. North of the line are the Khogoy and Shentoy mountains, part of the Tsagan Khuntei Range.

Km6053: Mogzon (●●) (907m/2,975ft) There's a large **steam dump** here and, for several kilometres around this town there are a number of heavily guarded prisons (km6055 (N) is one example). Conditions within the prisons must be abysmal if the economic conditions currently endured by the local people are anything to go by. The train I was on in late 1993 was boarded by hungry townsfolk who bought up every scrap of food in the restaurant-car, including the plate of bread that the diner beside me was about to tuck into.

Km6093: Sokhondo (944m/3,095ft) Named after the highest peak (2,510m/ 8,230ft) in the Yablonovy Range. The line leaves the river valley and climbs over the Yablonovy. There is a long view at km6097(N). About 7km east of here you reach the highest point on the line (989m/ 3242ft). In the 1914 edition of his *Russia with Teheran, Port Arthur and Peking*, Karl Baedeker drew his readers' attention to the '93 yard tunnel inscribed at its western entrance "To the Great Ocean" and at its eastern entrance "To the Atlantic Ocean" in Russian', that was here. The line has now been re-routed up onto a huge grassy plain. It then descends steeply through Yablonovaya and there are several good views (kms6107-6109).

Km6116(S): There was a vast graveyard of **steam locomotives** here (I counted fifty-two along the siding in 1986) but now most of the engines have been dismantled. West of the town of Ingoda, the train enters the narrow winding valley of the River Ingoda, which it follows for the next 250km east. The line passes through Chernovskaya, where lignite is mined.

Km6131(S): The line crosses a picturesque meadow with a stream meandering across it. Good for a photograph when the flowers are out in May and June.

(Opposite) Top: Lake Baikal, the world's deepest lake, does not freeze over until the end of December, in spite of the extreme cold. **Bottom:** At Petrovskiy Zavod station (km5784) there is a mural commemorating the exiled Decembrists, some of whom were sent here following the conspiracy in 1825 (photo DSJ).

Km6199: Chita (●●●) (655m/2150ft)

Founded in 1655, the capital of the Chitinskaya oblast stands beside the Chita and
Ingoda rivers, surrounded by low hills. A
stockaded fort was built here by the Cossacks
at the end of the seventeenth century and the
town became an important centre on the
Chinese trade route. In 1827 a large group of
exiled Decembrists arrived here and spent the
first few months building the prison that was
to be their home for the following three years.
Many stayed on after they had served their
sentence and the development of the town in
the nineteenth century into an industrial and
cultural centre was largely due to their efforts.

George Kennan was here in 1887 and
wrote: 'Among the exiles of Chita were some
of the brightest, most cultivated, most sympa-
thetic men and women we had met in Eastern
Siberia.' By 1900 more than 11,000 people
lived here. There were nine churches, a
cathedral, a nunnery, a synagogue, thirteen
schools and even a telephone system. The
modern city is near the junction for the line to
China and there are large repair workshops
here. Other industries include light engineering and the production of food and textiles.

East of the city of Chita, the train continues to
follow the left bank of the Ingoda River
downhill, for the next 250kms. The train
passes through **Novaya**, where the original
community and the whole of the town were
wiped out in the great flood of 1897. At
Km6225 (S) there's a collection of log cabins
(some of them quite photogenic) which look
rather vulnerable being built on the edge of
the river flood plain.

Km6265: Darasun (●) About 1km east of
the station there's a good view as the train
snakes along the river.

MAP 12

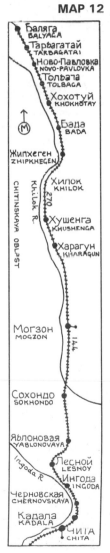

Km6270: Army supply base surrounded by a wooden stockade.

Km6293: Karymskaya (●●●) (605m/1985ft) Small industrial town first settled by the Buryats.

Km6312: Tarskaya   Formerly known as Kaidalovo, this is the junction for the **railway to Beijing via Manchuria** (see Map 21, p281). A whitewashed church stands on the hill (S) above the village. Good views along the river at km6316(S) and across the wide plains for the next 100km, especially around km6332(S) and km6369(S). There are large fields around the river and bare hills to the north. The best views are all to the south, across to Mongolia.

Km6417: Onon   (515m/1690ft) A few kilometres east of here the clear waters of the Ingoda River are joined by those of the muddy Onon, on whose banks the great Mongol leader, Genghis Khan (see p276), was born in 1162. The Onon and the Ingoda together form the Shilka River, a tributary of the mighty Amur. The railway follows the picturesque valley of the Shilka for the next 120kms.

Km6446: Shilka Pass (●●●)   (505m/1655ft) There are several interesting-looking wooden buildings near the platform.
    Crossing the River Kiya, the train traverses a great wide plain, grazing land for cattle that you may see being rounded up on horseback.

Km6496: Pryiskovaya   Junction with the line to **Nerchinsk**, which lies 10km north of here. It was here that the Treaty of Nerchinsk was signed with the Chinese in 1689, depriving the Russians of the Amur region. Nerchinsk was the centre of a rich silver, lead and gold mining district in Tsarist times. The mines were known to the Buryats long before the arrival of the Russians in the seventeenth century. In 1700, a Greek mining engineer founded the Nerchinski Zavod (Works) and the first convict gangs arrived in 1722. George Kennan visited the mine in 1887 and was shown around by one of the convict labourers. Not all the mines were the property of the Tsar and some owners became immensely wealthy. In one mansion he visited in Nerchinsk, Kennan could hardly believe that such opulence and luxury (tapestries, chandeliers, Oriental rugs, silk curtains and a vast ball-room) were to be found in one of the wildest parts of Siberia.

Kms6511-2(S):   Standing just across the river is a large deserted church with another building beside it. In the middle of nowhere and with a thick forest of conifers rising behind them, these two lonely-looking buildings make an eminently photogenic scene.

Km6532: Kuenga Junction for the line to **Sretensk**, which was the eastern end of the Transbaikal Railway. Sretensk was a thriving river-port in the nineteenth and early twentieth centuries (considerably larger than Chita) before the Amur Railway was opened in 1916. Passengers transferred here from the train to the ships of the Amur Steamship and Trade Company. Most of the forty steamers that plied between Sretensk and Khabarovsk were made either in Belgium or the Glasgow yards of Armstrong and Co. Waiting here with her mother in 1900, Annette Meakin caught sight of some Chinese men with their traditional pig-tails. She was not impressed and wrote 'To me their appearance was quite girlish.'

Kuenga was the western starting point for the **Amur Railway**. The line leaves the Shilka River here, turns north, crosses the plain and climbs towards the eastern end of the Yablonovyy range.

Km6593: Chernishevsk (●●) After this stop the train ascends into the foothills of the Yablonovyy mountain range towards Zilovo.

Km6670: Zilovo (●) (Aksenovo Zilovskoye) South of this town were the gold mines of the Kara region, also visited by Kennan, who found 2500 convicts working under the most appalling conditions. These mines were the property of the Tsar and from them and the other Imperial mines in Eastern Siberia, he could expect an average of 3600 pounds (1630kg) of pure gold each year.

Km6789: Ksyenevskaya The line continues across the forested southern slopes of the Eastern Yablonovy Range for the next 200km. There are occasional good views over the trees.

Km6906: Mogocha (●) The town of **Olekminsk** on the River Lena lies about .1s1 700km due north of here (this being no more

MAP 13

MAP 14

Ульякан
ULYAKAN
Урюм
URYUM

CHITINSKAYA OBLAST

Сьега
SBEGA

Ксеньевская
KSENEVSKAYA

Кислый Ключ
KISLYY KLUG

313

Артеушка
ARTEUSHKA

Раздольное
RAZDOLNOYE

Могоча
MOGOCHA
Таптугары
TAPTUGARI
Семиозерный
SEMIOZERNYY

Амазар
AMAZAR

Жанна
ZHANNA

Ерофеи Павлович
YEROFEY PAVLOVICH

AMURSKAYA OBLAST

Уруша
URUSHA

192

Тахтамыгда
TAKHTAMIGDA
Бам
BAM
В.А.М.
Сковородино
SKOVORODINO.

than a short hike to a Siberian for, as Intourist guides love to tell you, 'In Siberia a thousand kilometres is nothing to travel, a hundred roubles is nothing to spend and a litre of vodka is nothing to drink', although with hyperinflation whittling away the buying power of the rouble they're going to have to rework this favourite saying). As well as holding the world record for greatest temperature range - from -60°C (-87°F) to 45°C (113°F) - Olekminsk was the place of exile in the eighteenth century for a bizarre Christian sect whose followers were known as the Skoptsy. They saw their salvation in sexual abstinence and castrated themselves to be sure of a place in heaven. They lived in mixed communities, which they referred to as 'ships', each having a 'helmsman' and 'crew'. They avoided drink and tobacco and were excellent farmers. Since Olekminsk is experiencing something of a baby-boom at present it must be assumed that the more unconventional practices of the Skoptsy have been abandoned.

Km7010: Amazar (●●) There is a large strategic reserve of steam engines here. About 100km south of here the Shilka flows into the Amur River ('Heiling Chu' to the Chinese). The Amur rises in Mongolia and flows 2,800km along the frontier with China into the Pacific Ocean at the Sea of Okhotsk. The river is exceptionally rich in fish and navigable for six months of the year. After initial explorations along the Amur by the Russians in the seventeenth century, following the Treaty of Nerchinsk with the Chinese in 1689, they were kept out of the region for the next 150 years. Colonisation began in the mid-nineteenth century and the Cossacks established garrisons along the river. By 1860 there were 60 villages with a population of 11,000 in the Amur Basin. The Amur is still a vital communications link in the area.

Km7075: The **administrative frontier** between Chitinskaya and Amurskaya oblasts also marks the border between Siberia and the Far Eastern Territories. **Amurskaya** covers 360,000 square kilometres in the middle part of the Amur basin and extends to the Stanovoy Range in the north. The southern region of the oblast is a fertile plain where wheat, soya-beans, flax and sun-flowers are grown Most of the area in the north is under thick forest.

Km7119: Yerofei Pavlovich (●●) Named in honour of the Russian fur trader Yerofei Pavlovich Khabarov who explored the Amur region in the 1650s, and gave his surname to the capital of the Far Eastern Territories (see p187). Having set out from the military outpost of Yakutsk (1,000km north of Skovorodino) in 1649, he plundered and raped his way through the villages of the Yakut and other local tribes, who appealed to the Manchus for protection. They sent large armies which put the Russians to flight and the Treaty of Nerchinsk ensured that they stayed out of the region until the mid-nineteenth century.

At the east end of the station (N) is a **preserved locomotive** (Em726 88) on a plinth.

Km7211: Urusha (●●) For the next 100kms the train passes through an area of taiga interspersed with uncultivated plains, most of it locked in permafrost.

Km7266: Takhtamigda A small settlement with a view (N) across the river valley. The good views to the north continue for the next 150kms. About half a kilometre east of the village, also (N), stands what looks like a prison, surrounded with barbed wire and patrolled by guards in blue uniforms.

Km7273: Bam (Bamovskaya) Junction with the line which runs north to join the Baikal-Amur Mainline (see p111). East of the junction there are good views (S) between km7295 and km7300.

Km7306: Skovorodino (●●) A ten-minute stop at this station where local women sell berries from the *taiga*. About 20 kilometres east of Skovorodino, the train passes through the town of Great Never (Bolshoi Never). A highway leads from here a thousand miles north over the Stanovoy Range to Yakutsk (see p178), the capital of the **Yakutsk Republic**. This must be one of the least pleasant parts of the world to live in, for the region, which is about thirteen times the size of Britain, is entirely covered with permafrost. Even in mid-summer, the soil in Yakutsk is frozen solid to a depth of over 100 metres. As you leave the station, travelling east, there's a **steam**

MAP 15

locomotive (P36-0091) (S). To the east the scenery becomes more interesting. Views at kms7318-25(N) and around km7335(N). After the tunnel (kms7343-5) there is a long view (S) down the valley towards China. More views (S) at km7387 and kms7426-28.

Km7501: Magdagachi (●●) The train continues to descend gently, through Magdagachi, out of the taiga and onto a wide plain. There may be a short stop at **Tigda (●)**, about 60kms after Magdagachi.

Km7602: Ushumun The border with China is no more than forty kilometres south-west of here. The train continues south-east across flat lands with small clumps of trees.

Km7723: Shimanovskaya (●) South of here the land becomes more fertile and parts of the wide plain are under cultivation.

The Yakuts

These people, who number about 300,000, form the largest ethnic group in the Far Eastern Territories. They were originally semi-nomadic herders who roamed around the lands beside the Lena River. What seems to have struck nineteenth-century travellers most about the Yakuts was their rather squalid lifestyle. They never washed or changed their clothes, they shared their huts with their reindeer and preferred their meat and fish once it had begun to rot. They drank a form of koumiss (fermented mare's milk) which they froze, sometimes into huge boulders.

To give the Yakuts their due, they were considerably more advanced than many other Siberian tribes. Although they were ignorant of the wheel (hardly much use in such a cold climate), they used iron for weapons and tools. Most Yakut clans possessed a blacksmith who was usually also a shaman, since metal-working was considered a gift from the gods. The Yakuts were unique among Siberian tribes in that they made pottery.

Russian colonists treated the Yakuts badly and demanded fur tributes for the Tsar. They have now almost completely adopted the Russian culture and although some are still involved in reindeer-herding, most Yakuts work in mining and the timber industry.

Km7815: Svobodny (●)   Founded in 1912 during the building of the Amur railway, this town was originally named Alekseyevsk, in honour of the Tsar's haemophiliac son, Alexis. It stands beside the Zeya River, which is a navigable tributary of the Amur. In 1924 the town's name was changed to Svobodny. It is now an important transport centre, with railway repair shops, a large river-port and a highway-link north to Fevralsk on the BAM Railway. Heading east from this city, the train crosses the Zeya River.

Km7873: Belogorsk (●●●)   Some of the older folk who make up the 70,000 inhabitants of this agricultural centre must find it difficult to remember the current name of their city, so many times has it changed. It was founded in 1860 with the original name of Aleksandrovka. This stuck until 1935 when the local council decided it should be changed in favour of the rather more impressive Kuybyshevkavostochnaya. Just when everyone had got used to this exotic mouthful, it changed again, to boring Belogorsk.

The Amur Railway (kms6532-8531)

The building of this line was proposed in the early 1890s but surveys showed that it would prove expensive, on account of the difficult terrain. More than one hundred bridges would be needed and many kilometres of embankments. Furthermore much of the region was locked in permafrost. In 1894, when the government signed the treaty with China allowing Russian rails to be laid across Manchuria, from Chita to Vladivostok, the Amur project was abandoned in favour of this considerably shorter route. This change of plan proved to be something of a false economy, for the East Chinese line, despite the considerable saving in distance, was ultimately to cost more than the whole of the rest of the Trans-Siberian Railway.

After Russia's embarrassing defeat by Japan in the 1904-5 War, the government realised the vulnerability of their East Chinese line. Japan was as keen as Russia to gain control of the rich lands of Manchuria and if they did decide to invade, the Russian naval base of Vladivostok would be deprived of a rail link with European Russia. A line within Russian lands was needed. The Amur project was reconsidered and, in 1907, approved.

Construction began in 1908 at Kuenga and for most of the 2,000kms the line would follow a route about 100km north of the Amur River, out of range of Manchuria on the southern bank of the river. Winters are particularly harsh in this region and consequently track-laying could only take place over the four warmer months and even in mid-summer considerable amounts of dynamite were needed to blast through the permafrost. There were the usual problems with insects and disease but now that the rest of the railway was operating it was comparatively easy to transport workers in from west of the Urals. By 1916 the long bridge over the Amur at Khabarovsk had been completed and the railway was opened. The Japanese were now Russia's allies and in 1918 (as allies to the White Russians) took over the running of the Amur Railway during the Civil War.

Belogorsk is the junction for the line to **Blagoveshchensk**, the administrative capital of Amurskaya oblast and a large industrial centre of 190,000 people, on the left bank of the Amur River. The name means 'Good News', for it was here in 1858 that Count Muravyev-Amurski announced the success of the treaty with China that granted Russia the Amur region. The city became a centre of colonisation and grew fast in the second half of the nineteenth century. The locals called it the New York of Siberia because its streets were laid out on a grid pattern, American-style. It became the major port on the voyage between Sretensk and Khabarovsk in the days before the completion of the Amur Railway.

In July 1900, Blagoveshchensk was the scene of the cold-blooded massacre of the entire Chinese population of the town (several thousand people) by the Cossack forces. This was in retaliation for the murders of Europeans in China during the Boxer Rebellion. Annette Meakin wrote: 'The Cossacks, who were little better than savages, threw themselves on the helpless Chinese.....and drove them down to the water's edge. Those who could not get across on rafts were either brutally massacred on the banks or pushed into the water and drowned. The scene which followed was horrible beyond description, and the river was black with dead bodies for weeks afterwards. I have this from no less than five eye-witnesses.'

Good relations between the people of Blagoveshchensk and their Chinese neighbours across the river in Heihe have been cemented over the last few years with the development of a major trade route here. Siberian lumber and machinery is ferried across the Amur to be exchanged for Chinese consumer goods.

Km8037: Bureya (●) On the river of the same name, this town was once the centre of a large gold-mining region. The area was once inhabited by several different tribes most of whom were Shamanists. The **Manegres** were a nomadic people whose sartorial trade-mark was to keep their heads shaven, except for one long pigtail. The **Birars** lived in hive-shaped huts beside the Bureya and grew vegetables and fruit. North of here lived **Tungus** (Evenki), who were hunters and the **Orochen** who herded reindeer.

To the east were the **Goldi**, described thus in the *Guide to the Great Siberian Railway*: 'They are below average stature, and have a broad and flat face with a snub nose, thick lips, eyes shaped after the Mongolian fashion and prominent cheek-bones.....The women adorn themselves with earrings and pendants. Some of them, as a mark of particular elegance, introduce one or several small rings into the partition of the nose. The people of this tribe are characterised by great honesty, frankness and good will ...Their costume is very various and of all colours; they may at different times be seen wearing a Russian overcoat, a fish-skin suit or the Chinese dress.'

Km8088: Arkhara (●●●) A long stop at the station here is usual, with women selling snacks and fruit on the platform.

Km8170: This is the **administrative frontier** between Amurskaya oblast and Khabarovskiy kray. **Khabarovskiy** is, like much of Russia east of the Urals, almost entirely composed of swampy taiga. In the far south, however, there is an area of deciduous trees. The kray is extremely rich in minerals but the economy is currently based on wood-processing, fishing and the petroleum industry.

Km8171-9441: Time zone MT + 7
Local time is now Moscow Time + 7hrs.

East of this frontier you enter an autonomous oblast within Khabarovsky kray. Between Obluchye and Pryamuskaya, some of the stations have their names written up in Yiddish as well as in Russian, for this is part of the **Yevreyskaya (Jewish) Autonomous Oblast**, otherwise known as **Birobidzhan**, after its capital. This remote region was thoughtfully set aside for Jewish emigration in 1928 (the oblast being formed in 1934) but it never proved very popular. The Jewish population today stands at less than 5% (some say less than 1%) of the total number of inhabitants of this 36,000 square kilometre territory.

A glossy coffee-table book about Birobidzhan (written in Russian, Yiddish and English) used to be sold in the bookshops of Khabarovsk. After pages of smiling cement-factory workers, beaming miners and happy-looking milk-maids, the book ended with the following statement: 'The flourishing of the economy

MAP 16

Серышево
SERUSHEVO
Белогорск
BELOGORSK
Возжаевка
VOZHAYEVKA
БЛАГОВЕЩЕНСК
BLAGOVESHCHENSK
Поздеевка
POZDEEVKA
Екатеринославка
YEKATERINOSLAVKA
Завитая
ZAVITAYA
Бурея
BUREYA
Домикан
DOMIKAN
Архара
ARKHARA
Рачи
RACHI
Кундур-Хабаровский
KUNDUR-KHABAROVSKIY
Облучье
OBLUCHE
Кимкан
KIMKAN
Известковая
IZVESTKOVAYA
Биракан
BIRAKAN
Теплое Озеро
TEPLOYE OZERO
Лондоко
LONDOKO
Бира
BIRA
БИРОБИДЖАН
BIROBIDZHAN

AMURSKAYA OBLAST
KHABAROVSKIY KRAY
Y.A. OBLAST
116

and culture of the Jewish Autonomous Region, the happiness of the people of labour of various nationalities inhabiting the Region, their equality, friendship and co-operation lay bare the hypocricy (sic) of the propaganda campaign launched by the ringleaders of Israel and international Zionism, about the "disastrous situation" of Jews in the Soviet Union, about the "oppression and persecution" they are supposedly being subjected to. The working people of Jewish nationality wrathfully condemn the predatory policy of the ruling circles of Israel and give a resolute rebuff to the Zionist provocateurs.'

Km8234: Izvyestkovaya The name of this town means 'limestone'. There are large quarries in the area.

Km8306: Bira (●●) Near the river of the same name. The obelisk on the platform commemorates the good works of local philanthropist Nikolai Trofemovich and his wife.

Km8351: Birobidzhan (●) The capital of the 'Jewish' region was founded in 1928 on the Bira River and was originally known as Tikhonkaya. It is especially famous for its bright red, self-propelled, rice-and-silage chain-track combine-harvesters, made at the Dalselmash factory and exported to Cuba, Mexico, Iraq and now China. Other industries include mining, fish-farming, wood-processing and the manufacture of hosiery, shoes, knitwear and other clothes.

The Ussuri Railway (kms8531-9441)

The first plans for the building of the Ussuri line, as this section between Khabarovsk and Vladivostok was called, were made in 1875 and the foundation stone for the whole of the Trans-Siberian Railway was laid in Vladivostok by the Tsarevich Nicholas in 1891. Priority was given to the Ussuri line as it was seen as vital to ensure that the strategic port of Vladivostok was not cut off by the Chinese.

This was difficult territory for railway building. There was a severe shortage of labour. The local Goldi tribe who at the time were happily existing in the Stone Age were no help. They were unable to grasp the concept of paid labour and couldn't understand the point of the work, never having seen a train. Prisoners recruited from the jails of Sakhalin Island were not as co-operative as convicts used on other sections of the Trans-Siberian, preferring an evening of robbery and murder in Vladivostok to the railway camps. Like their fellow-workers on other sections of the line, the men here were plagued not only by vicious mosquitoes but also by the man-eating tigers which roamed the thick forests beside the line. Siberian anthrax decimated the already small population of pack animals, and rails and equipment had to be shipped from Europe, taking up to two months to reach Vladivostok.

In spite of these difficulties, the line was opened in 1897, 43 million roubles having been spent on its construction. It was double tracked in the 1930s and the branch line to Nakhodka was built after the Second World War.

Crossing the Jewish oblast, the train passes through **Dezhnevka** (km8493), leaving the oblast about 20km after this. Just east of km8511, you reach the **bridge over the Amur**. This 2½km single-track bridge is the longest on the Trans-Siberian Railway and was completed in 1916. Khabarovsk stretches along the eastern bank of the river and the beaches here are packed with sunbathers at weekends in the summer.

Km8521: Khabarovsk (●●●) (Habarovsk) (96m/315ft). See p187 for more information.

From Khabarovsk the line runs south to Vladivostok following the Ussuri River and the border with China. This region is a mixture of hilly country interspersed with wide flat valleys. Two hundred miles east of the line lies the Sikhote Alin Range of mountains, in which most of the rivers you will cross have their source. In the south the firs and pines give way to a wide range of deciduous trees. Good views across the plains to China.

Km8561: Korfovskaya The town was founded by Cossacks in 1858.

Km8597 The longest bridge on the Ussuri Railway. It crosses the River Khor, one of the widest tributaries of the Ussuri, whose turbulent waters made the construction of the bridge extremely difficult in 1897.

Km8642: Viazemskaya Established as the centre of building operations for this northern part of the Ussuri line. There is often a good selection of things to buy from the old women on the platform - hot potatoes, berries and other fruit in season. From about 20 kms south of here the countryside changes dramatically with forests of maple, alder, willow, elm, cork-oak, acacia and walnut as well as the usual cedar, larch and birch. There are also wild vines, roses and jasmine.

MAP 17

MAP 18

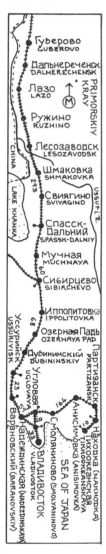

Km8756: Bikin A large town on the banks of the Bikin River. According to the *1900 Guide to the Great Siberian Railway*, the line crosses the river here and follows it south for 30kms. It states that 'this is one of the most picturesque parts of the line offering an alpine scenery. The cuttings made in basalt rocks seem to be protected by columns of cyclopean construction. Wide expanses lying amidst the cliffs are covered with a most various vegetation, shading numerous Chinese huts. The river is enlivened by the small boats of the Golds and other natives, moving swiftly on the water's surface.' Unfortunately the line does not follow exactly the same route now, traversing rolling hills and marshy land strewn with telegraph poles keeling over at drunken angles.

Between Bikin and Zvenevoi is the **administrative border** between Khabarovsky kray and **Primorsky** kray. The kray has a population of over half a million people, many of whom live in the capital, Vladivostok.

Km9050: Spassk Dalnyi (●●) About thirty kilometres west of here lies Lake Khanka which is drained by the Ussuri River. Although a mere drop of water compared to Lake Baikal, it covers 4,400 square kms.

Km9109: Sibirchevo A branch line runs from here through dairy-farming countryside to Lake Khanka. From Sibirchevo south, the line winds down to Ussuriysk.

Km9177: Ussuriyisk (●●) Originally called Nikolskoe, in honour of the Tsar, this was the largest station on the line. The area has been inhabited for over a thousand years, first as the legendary kingdom of Bokhai and then by the Manchus. In the mid-nineteenth century European emigrants began to settle on this fertile land and Nikolskoe increased in importance with the building of the railway.

The town stands at the junction of the Ussuri and the Chinese Eastern Railways. When the Tsarevich Nicholas visited it in 1891, there were three wooden churches, a half-built stone cathedral and a population of 8,000 people, many of whom were Chinese. This has risen to 140,000 and Ussuriysk is a now an agricultural and engineering centre. The border with China is about 100km to the west.

The scenery in this area is very different from the Siberian taiga. The train winds through the hills in misty forests of deciduous trees (oak, elm, alder, and maple) and across European-looking meadows filled with Friesian cows and willow trees.

Km9199: Baranovsk About 25km south of here, the branch line to Nakhodka begins. Since most passenger ships now leave from Vladivostok there's very little reason for visiting Nakhodka. If you do need to leave from this port it's 164km to **Nakhodka** and another 11km to **Tikhookeanskaya Port Station**.

Km9246: If you're heading east keep a look out on the right (S) for your first glimpse of the Pacific Ocean.

Km9255: Ugolnaya There's usually a brief stop by the waterfront here. The beaches are crowded at the weekends with day-trippers from Vladivostok.

Km9269: Sanatornaya The hotels that currently rate as Vladivostok's best are located here; but only local trains will make a stop.

Km9289: Vladivostok See p195 for more information.

Decline of the Amur Tiger

Once the scourge of the railway construction worker (see p93), the largest member of the cat family is now just another animal world statistic dwindling towards extinction. The tigers' habitat used to stretch as far west as Lake Baikal and to Beijing in the south but now only 250-350 remain in an area from Vladivostok north into the Sikhote Alin range.

Large scale forest clearance for timber sold to Japan and Korea forces tigers out of their territory. A male tiger can weigh up to 380kg (840lbs), almost twice the size of a lion, and requires about 400 square km of hunting ground. A decline in their food source (deer and wild boar) has also reduced the population and forced remaining tigers to roam even larger areas for prey. In 1987, a train just outside Nakhodka was held up by a tiger that had strayed onto the tracks. An Amur tiger can be worth as much as US$10,000 in China, Korea and Taiwan for the medicinal value that parts of its body are believed to have, and for its skin. Poachers now slip across Russian borders that are no longer tightly patrolled.

The animals are found in and around several nature reserves in this area: Kedrovaya Pad (near Vladivostok), Lazo and Sikhote-Alin but your chances of seeing a live Amur tiger here are close to zero. There are, in fact, about twice as many of the subspecies in zoos around the world as in the wild.

MAP 19

Trans-Mongolian Route

The branch line to Mongolia and China leaves the main Trans-Siberian route at Zaudinskiy, 8km east of Ulan Ude. From here it takes five and a half hours to cover the 250km to the Russian-Mongolian border. Between Ulan Ude and the southern border, the train travels through the heart of Buryatia, the Buryat Republic (see p254).

Note that the line now swings due south from its east-west route. However, in order not to confuse readers I shall continue to use (N) and (S) to show which side of the train points of interest are located, rather than changing to the more correct compass bearings. Thus (N) means left side of the train if you're coming from Moscow.

The Trans-Mongolian Line

This route to China is an ancient one, followed for centuries by the tea-caravans between Peking and Moscow. Travelling non-stop, foreigners and imperial messengers could manage the journey in forty days - forty days of acute discomfort. This was the route of the 1907 Peking to Paris Rally, the great motor race that was won by the Italian Prince Borghese and journalist Luigi Barzini in their 40 h.p. Itala. Until the middle of the present century, the rough track over the steppe-lands of northern Mongolia and the Gobi Desert in the south was the only route across this desolate country.

In 1940, a branch-line was built between Ulan Ude and Naushki on the border with Mongolia. After the Second World War, work started on the line from Naushki south, and in 1949 the track reached the Mongolian capital, Ulan Bator. The line between here and Beijing was begun in 1953 with a mixed work-force of Russians, Mongolians and Chinese. By the beginning of 1956 the work was completed and a regular rail service begun between Ulan Ude and Beijing.

The suburbs of Ulan Ude extend for several kilometres and there are good views back to the city at km5659(S) as the train climbs high above the east bank of the Selenga. The line follows the valley of the Selenga River all the way to the border with Mongolia. The scenery changes remarkably quickly to rolling green hills which are excellent pastures for the many cows in the area. Passing through the little station of Sayatun (km5677) the line crosses to the west bank of the river at km5689-90 and continues to climb through Ubukun (km5732), stopping briefly at Zagustay.

Km5769: Zagustay In the ugly shadow of a factory belching out thick smoke.

Kms5771-99 Goose Lake Between the stations of Zagustay and Gusinoye Ozero the line passes along the western shore of Lake Gusinoye (Goose Lake). Until the Revolution, the most important lamasery north of Urga (Ulan Bator) was at **Selenginsk**, 20km south east of Gusinoye Ozero and overlooking the lake. In 1887 George Kennan, who was researching his book on Siberian prisons, arrived in Selenginsk and visited the famous datsan (lamasery). 'We were tired of prisons and the exile system and had had enough misery,' he wrote. Nevertheless he found Selenginsk 'a wretched little Buriat town'. At the Lamasery of Goose Lake, Kennan and his companions were entertained by the Khamba Lama, the chief lama, who claimed through the interpreter that they were the first foreigners ever to visit his lamasery. They were treated to a dinner and a special dance display. The Khamba Lama had never heard of America, Kennan's native land, and was confused when Kennan explained that 'it lies nearly under our feet; and if we could go directly through the earth, this would be the shortest way to reach it'. The Lama was completely unaware that the earth was anything other than flat.

Km5780: Gusinoye Ozero The line leaves the lake after this station and continues to climb from one valley to another, passing though Selenduma (Km5827) and still following the river.

Km5852(S): Dzhida There appears to be a small air-base here with hangars dug into hummocks in the ground.

As the line climbs the next 40km to the border you often see border patrols in grey cruisers on the river in this area. The border post for the railway is at the modern town of Naushki. However the old border for the tea-caravans was near the large town of **Kyakhta**, 20kms east of Naushki. In the 18th and 19th centuries this town together with **Maimachen** (now named Altan Bulak, the Chinese town beside it on the Mongolian side of the border) formed one of the most important trading centres in the world, based almost entirely on the tea trade. Great caravans of camels would transport the precious beverage from Peking across the Gobi Desert to Maimachen and Kyakhta. Kyakhta was a bustling town of wealthy traders and tea-barons but once the Trans-Siberian was built the tea was shipped via Vladivostok to European Russia.

On 24 June 1907 Prince Borghese and his team roared into town in their Itala and were entertained royally by local dignitaries. The morale of the tea-merchants that had sunk with the recent decline in trade was greatly boosted by the arrival of the car and they began making plans for their own motor-caravans. An earlier visitor to these border towns was George Kennan who attended a banquet in Maimachen, where he was served dog-meat dumplings, cocks' heads in vinegar and fried lichen from birch trees, washed down by several bottles of French champagne. He was sick for the next two weeks.

Km5895·0: Naushki (●●● + +) At this Russian border post the train stops for at least two hours, usually for considerably longer if there are many traders on the train. Customs officials collect passports, visas and currency declaration forms, returning them (often to the carriage attendant) after about half an hour. It would be unwise to get off the train before you've got your passport back since guards may not let you on the train without it. The station tends to be crowded with black marketeers and some may get on the train and start selling roubles to travellers heading west; don't buy too many as the rate is unlikely to be in your favour. There's a bank on the platform where you can check the rate. Note that the bank is signposted in English but it's a long way down the platform (towards Mongolia). Eastbound travellers should exchange any unspent roubles here as it's very difficult to exchange them outside Russia.

Note that the loos on the train remain locked until you leave the border. The station lavatories would not win any awards but are located in the building to the left of the station building.

The **border** is marked by a menacing-looking electrified fence, about five kilometres beyond the Russian border post. The train may stop here while guards search for stowaways.

Most trains are timetabled to cross this border at night, which is unfortunate since the landscape is attractive. To the south is the

---

(Opposite) From late May to October ferries connect Vladivostok (the eastern terminus of the Trans-Siberian) with Japan (see p289). This five storey pagoda, constructed in 1407, is on Miyajima Island, near Hiroshima.

impressive Selenga River, prone to flooding in the late summer; hills reach up above the track to the north.

Have your insect repellent to hand as the air can be thick with mosquitoes in summer.

MONGOLIA

(Distances given here follow the Mongolian kilometre markers. For cumulative distances from/to Moscow/Beijing, see timetables: p299).

Km21: Sukhe Bator/Sukhbaatar (● ● ● + +) At this Mongolian border town the immigration process used to be a fairly nerve-racking affair. Whole compartments would be rigorously searched, magazines confiscated and film ripped out of cameras. It's all rather tame now for foreigners, although the baggage of local travellers is thoroughly inspected. During immigration and customs procedures a diesel engine is attached. The Mongolian dining-car, however, is not put on until Ulan Bator.

In the past some travellers have managed to get Mongolian visas here but the situation is subject to change; being turned back is not worth the hassle so don't rely on being able to get one here.

The station building is an excellent example of whimsical Mongolian railway architecture. It's an incredible mélange of architectural styles: mock Gothic, Moghul and Modern topped with crenellations and painted what looks like lime green in the artificial light. Strawberry pink is the other popular colour for station buildings in this country.

Situated at the confluence of the Selenga and Orhon Rivers, **Sukhe Bator** was founded in 1940 and named after the Mongolian revolutionary leader Damdiny Sukhe Bator. It grew quickly, superseding the border-town on the caravan route, Maimachen (now named Altan Bulak). Sukhe Bator is now the third largest industrial centre in the country (although in a country as sparsely populated and industrially primitive as Mongolia this is not a particularly impressive fact). Matches, liquor and flour are produced here by some of the 18,000 inhabitants.

Km123: Darhan (● ● ●) It takes about eight hours to cover the 380km between Sukhe Bator and Ulan Bator. The train passes through the town of **Darhan** (capital of Selenga *aimak*) which was

(Opposite) Top: The Trans-Mongolian route passes under the Great Wall in at Badaling (km73) in China (see p280). **Bottom:** Tiananmen Gate, Beijing, the main entrance gate to the Forbidden City.

founded in 1961 and is now the second most important industrial centre in Mongolia, after Ulan Bator. Darhan is a show town of planned urbanisation and its population increased from 1,500 in 1961 to over 80,000 in 1991. Main sources of employment are open-cast mining, food production, construction and the production of leather and sheepskin coats. The town is an important communications junction with a branch-line running west from here to the big mining complex at **Erdenet**, and the port serves many villages along the Selenga and Orkhon Rivers.

About 120km west of Darhan, in the foothills of Mt Burenkhan is **Amarbayasgalant Monastery**. This vast eighteenth century temple complex, which once housed 10,000 monks and drew pilgrims from many parts of Asia, was desecrated during the anti-religious movement in the 1930s but is now being restored with grants from the Mongolian government and UNESCO.

Mongolia

This is one of those countries, like Guyana or Chad, that rarely makes headline news, except when there's a dramatic change of leadership or policy. This was indeed the case with Mongolia in 1989-90 with the pro-democracy movement in the run up to the first free elections in July 1990.

Mongolia is a sparsely populated place with only 2¼ million people (50 per cent of whom are under the age of 25) in an area the size of Western Europe. It contains a surprising variety of terrain: the vast undulating plain in the east, the Gobi desert to the south, and in the west snow-capped mountains and extensive forests. Most of the eastern plain is at an altitude of 1,500m and in this area the sun shines for around 250 days each year.

For many centuries the deserts and grasslands of Mongolia have been inhabited by nomadic herders living in felt tents (*yurts* or *ghers*). At certain times in the course of world history they have been bound together under a leader, the most famous being Genghis and Kublai Khan in the thirteenth century. Kublai Khan introduced Tibetan Buddhism to the country but it was not until the early seventeenth century that the majority of the population was converted and Buddhism gained a strong grip on the country.

By the end of the seventeenth century, control of Mongolia and its trade routes was in the hands of the Manchus. In 1911 the country became an independent monarchy, in effect a theocratic state since power lay with the 'Living Buddha' (the chief representative of Buddhism in Mongolia) at Urga (now Ulan Bator). In 1921 the communist government that rules today took power and the struggle to modernise the country that was technologically in the Dark Ages began, with considerable help coming from the Soviet Union. Elections were held for the first time in 1990 and won by the People's Revolutionary Party (Communist Party), who pledged the introduction of a market-style economy. Their position was reaffirmed when they won the next elections, in June 1992.

The country is divided into 18 *aimaks* (districts) and the railway-line passes through three of these (Selenga, Tov and Dornogov).

Km381: Crossing wide open grasslands, with only the occasional *yurt* to break the monotony, the line begins to descend into the valley where Ulan Bator is situated. Looking south you catch the first sight (at km386) of the ugly factories on the outskirts of the city (km396).

Km404: Ulan Bator (●●● +) (1350m/4430ft) (See p203)
The train spends half an hour at the Mongolian capital, a good chance to stretch your legs. There is a whole (open-air) museum collection of old and new steam and diesel engines standing outside the locomotive shed on the east side of the line (N). The display includes a 2-6-2 S-116, T31-011 and T32-508 diesels, a 750mm gauge 0-8-0 469, and a 2-10-0 Ye-0266. They are beside the public road but quite accessible even though there is a fence in front of them. In the station building postcards (and weird Mongolian stamps which leave little room for a message on a card) can be purchased at the bar. Black Marketeers may approach you on the platform to change money but you should remember that Mongolian currency is of no use on the train. US$ only, for food and souvenirs in the dining-car (which is attached here if you're en route to Beijing but is usually detached if you're travelling in the other direction).

Km409: The city extends as far west as here. At around km425 the line starts to climb and for the next 50km, to km470, snakes round giving good opportunities for photos along the train. Good views over the rolling hills both sides of the train.

Km507: Bagakangai Airfield (S) with camouflaged bunkers.

Km521: Manit (●) The pink station with its tower and weathervane looks rather like a church.

Km560: Camels are occasionally to be seen roaming across the wide rolling plain.

Advice to nineteenth century travellers

If you'd been doing this part of the journey in the not too distant time before the railway was built, you would now be swaying back and forth in the saddle of a camel, one of many in the caravan you would have joined in Kyakhta.

In the 1865 edition of his *Handbook for Russia, Poland and Finland* , Murray gives the following advice: 'It is customary for caravans to travel sixteen hours a day and they come to a halt for cooking, eating and sleeping.....The Mongols are most trustworthy in their transactions, and the traveller may feel in perfect safety throughout the journey.' He also gives the following useful tips concerning local currency: 'The use of money is as yet almost unknown in this part of the country, brick-tea cut up into slices being the token of value most recognised; but small brass buttons are highly prized.'

Km649: Choyr (●●●)   Just behind this beautiful pink and white wedding-cake of a station is a statue of Mongolian cosmonaut, VVT Ertvuntz.

Km733-4(S): The pond here often attracts groups of camels and antelope.

Km751: Airag   The train doesn't usually stop at this small station, in the middle of nowhere and surrounded by scrap metal.

Genghis Khan
For many decades the name of this famous Mongolian conqueror has been taboo in his home country. The Soviets saw Genghis Khan as brutal invader to be erased from the history books but with their influence rapidly fading there has been a sudden rise in Mongolian nationalism. Genghis Khan, the founder of the thirteenth century Mongolian Empire, is a hero once more, lending his name to the newest (and most luxurious) hotel in town and also to a brand of vodka. The prestigious Mongolian pop group with the wonderful name of 'Honk' recently produced a record in his honour.

Along with his rehabilitation has come a number of interesting characters each claiming to be his legitimate descendant. One of the best publicised was Ganjuurijin Dschero Khan, who claimed to have been smuggled out of the country to escape the Communists when he was four years old. Mongolians were intrigued to meet him, although they didn't quite know what to make of his appearance. He arrived in a military tunic, decked out with medals inscribed 'Bazooka', 'Carbine', 'Paratroopers' and 'Special Forces', which he claimed to have won in Korea and Vietnam. Support for him waned after it became apparent that he didn't speak Mongolian.

The Gobi Desert
This vast wilderness extends for 1,000km north to south and 2,400km west to east. Most of the part crossed by the railway is not desert of the sandy Saharan type but rolling grassy steppes. It is impressive for its emptiness: very few towns and just the occasional collection of *yurts*, herds of stocky Mongolian horses and small groups of camels or gazelles.

Environmental threats   The Gobi is, in fact, rich in wildlife although numbers of some species are rapidly dwindling. This is mainly the result of poaching and the destruction of habitat and there are fears that the situation may worsen with the country's move towards a market economy. All political parties, including the ruling communists have pledged to open up the country to the West. It has large reserves of coal, copper, molybdenum, gold, uranium and other valuable exports. It's estimated that up to 10 billion tons of coal exist beneath the Gobi, and Japanese and Western companies are negotiating with Mongolia to extract it using strip mining techniques, which could seriously affect the delicate environmental balance. An American conservation group, Wildlife Conservation International, is helping the Mongolian Association for Conservation of Nature and Environment (MACNE) to monitor species at risk in the area. Among these are the 500 remaining wild Bactrian camels, the Gobi bear, the *kulan* (Asian wild ass) and Przewalski's wild horse (the last recorded sighting was in 1962).

Km875(N) There's a collection of old **steam locos** on display just to the west of Sayn Shand station.

Km876: Sayn Shand (●●●) (Sajnsand) This is the largest town between the capital and Dzamin Ude on the southern border. Main industries here include food-processing and coal-mining.

Km1113: Dzamyn Ude (●●●+) Mongolian border town with a station building that looks like a supermarket at Christmas with all its festive lights. There's a bank and a restaurant, both usually closed in the evening. Customs declaration forms and immigration forms are collected. Customs officers inspect the luggage of Chinese and Mongolian travellers but don't seem too interested in others.

Smokers roast in hell!

If you're a smoker having difficulty in coping with being allowed to pursue your habit only in the chilly areas at the end of each carriage, be thankful you weren't around at the time of the Third Mongolian Damba Lama Khutukhta, at the end of the eighteenth century. 'Smoking tobacco', he wrote, 'undermines virtue....The soul of the smoker can't avoid one of these three sad fates: the fires of hell, rebirth into the world as a *pret* (evil spirit tormented with eternal hunger) or as an animal. Oh you who have gone astray with tobacco! You will eternally wander in hell.'

THE PEOPLE'S REPUBLIC OF CHINA

(Kilometres below show distance to Beijing.)

Km842: Erlyan (Erenhot) (●●●++) The Chinese station master is obviously trying to outdo the show his Mongolian counterpart puts on in the evening over the border, with a full-blown son-et-lumière. There's the Vienna Waltz blaring out of the speakers to welcome the train and the building's decked out in red neon and fairy lights.

Chinese customs officials come on board here. If you're travelling to Beijing you'll be required to fill in a health declaration form and baggage/currency declaration form. Passports are collected.

Bogie-changing The train spends about 20mins at the platform and is then shunted off to the bogie-changing shed. It may be possible to stay on the train until it gets to the shed, get off before they lock the doors (for safety reasons while raising the carriages), and watch some of the bogie-changing operations. The Chinese railway system operates on Standard Gauge (as do Europe and North America) and this is 3½ inches narrower than Five Foot Gauge used in the CIS and Mongolia. Giant hydraulic lifts raise the carriages and the bogies are rolled out and replaced. Photography is now permitted but take care not to get in the way or the authorities may restore the ban on photography which was in force for many years. You can walk back to the station building but you should take care at night as the path is not well-lit.

Back in the station you can change money at the bank (passport not necessary but you do need to know your passport number), or visit the Friendship Store (Chinese vodka Y6, Chinese champagne Y20, beer, tea, Ritz crackers, and other snacks) and bar/restaurant (if open). Upstairs is a foreigners' waiting room where fictitious literature (eg *Human Rights in China*) is provided free of charge. The platform is crowded with traders and food and drinks are also sold here.

The Age of the Steam Train has not yet passed in China (more than half of its trains are steam-powered) and it is likely that the train will be shunted out of the bogie-changing shed and back to the platform by a puffing Class 2-10-2 locomotive built in Datong (see below). Passports are returned and you depart shortly thereafter, the whole operation taking between 2 and 3 hours.

Chinese trains ride on the left side of double tracks (unlike the CIS which is right-hand drive). Km markers come in a variety of sizes (usually like little grave-stones down by the track) and there seems to be some disagreement between them and the official kilometre location (on timetables etc) for many places. I've followed the markers where possible but for the last 70km of the journey they are not reliable, altering by 25km at one point!

Passing through towns with weird Mongolian names like Sonid Youqi and Qahar Youyi Houqi, you reach Jining in about five hours.

Km498: Jining (●) The bulky white station building here is topped by a line of red flags. Beside it is an extensive goods yard full of working steam engines.

Travelling due south from Jining the train leaves the province of Inner Mongolia and enters Shanxi Province. This mountainous area was a great cultural and political centre over a thousand years ago.

There are hills running parallel to the west and wide fields either side of the line. The train follows the course of a river which leads it into a valley and more rugged countryside after Fenezhen.

Km415: Fenezhen Between this drab town and Datong you pass through the line of the **Great Wall** for the first time. Occasional glimpses are all you will get until the spectacular crossing at Km82.

Km371: Datong (●●) This large city, founded as a military outpost by Han armies, has a population of more than half a million and stands in the centre of the coal-rich Datong Basin. Its major tourist attraction is the group of Buddhist cave temples known as the **Yungang Grottoes** in the foothills of Wuzhou Mountain (16km west of the city). These caves, dating back to 460AD, are richly decorated and renowned as one of China's three most impressive Buddhist complexes, the others being at Luoyang and Dunhuang.

If you're stopping off here, a visit to the **Datong Locomotive Works** is an interesting and educational experience. Until recently, this was one of the last places in the world where steam trains were made. In the 1980s they were turning them out at the rate of 240 locos per year. The manufacture of the Class QJ 8WT/12WT 2-10-2 engine (133 tonnes; max speed 80kph) ceased in 1986 and the Class JS 2-8-2 (104 tonnes; max speed 85kph) in 1989. Both classes are used for freight haulage and shunting work. The factory now produces parts for steam and diesel locomotives and has customers in many parts of the world. Tours are conducted twice a week and must be arranged through CITS.

At Datong the line turns east and follows the Great Wall, running about 20km south of it as far as Zhangjiakou. One hundred kilometres

MAP 20

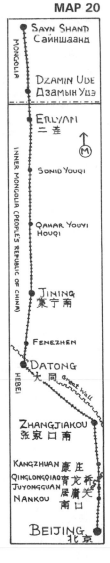

west of Zhangjiakou you leave Shanxi and enter Hebei province. Between Kms295-272(N) the Great Wall can be seen parallel to the line, on the hillside to the east. Best view is at km284(N).

Km193: Zhangjiakou (●●) Founded 2000 years ago, this city used to be known by its Mongolian name, Kalgan (meaning gate or frontier). It stands at the point where the old caravan route between Peking and Russia crossed the Great Wall. Luigi Barzini described it as being like one of those 'cities one sees pictured upon Fu-kien tapestries: varied and picturesque, spreading over the bank of a wide snowy river'. He would not recognise it now; it has grown into an industrial city of over one million people. Yet he might recognise the smell he noticed as he drove into town on 14 June 1907, for tanning and leather-work are still major industries here. About 15km south of the city a large factory pollutes the air with orange smoke.

From around km175 the scenery becomes hilly and more interesting as the line rises over the mountains north of Beijing. There are small valleys of sunflowers, groves of poplars and even some apple orchards. At km99 you cross San Gan River above which (N) can be seen a small isolated section of the Wall.

Km82: Kanzhuang (●) The train stops for a banking engine to be attached before the steep ascent up through the Great Wall.

Km73: Badaling The first of the stations for the **Great Wall**. To the east is a 2km tunnel beneath the Wall. Look up (N) to the east as you come out for a good view and be ready to get off for the short stop at Qinglongqiao ½km further on.

Km70: Qinglongqiao (●●) There are good views of the Great Wall high above this attractive station. After the stop the train reverses downhill through a spectacular series of tunnels alongside the road. Progress is very slow because of the tortuous bends and the need for heavy braking, which gives some people time to jump off the train and gather the wild marijuana plants which flourish near the tracks in this area. You pass the Tourist Reception Centre at km68.

Km63: Juyongguan (●) Continuous application of the brake blocks makes them very hot necessitating a stop here.

Km53: Nankou (●●) The name means 'Southern Pass'. After a short stop to detach the rear engine the train speeds off across the fertile plain to Beijing. Something strange has happened to the km markers in this area, with 30km suddenly added around km35.

Km0: Beijing Turn to p213 for more information.

MAP 21

Trans-Manchurian route

Km6293: Karymskaya (●) The branch line to Beijing via Manchuria leaves the main Trans-Siberian route at Tarskaya (formerly Kaidalovo), 12kms east of Karymskaya (see p258). Leaving Tarskaya, you cross the Ingoda River and head through open steppeland. Twenty kilometres south of here you enter the Buryat Republic (Buryatia).

Km6444: Olovyannaya (●●) Leaving this picturesque town you cross the Onon River, which flows north of the main Trans-Siberian line to join the Ingoda to form the Shilka. Genghis Khan was born on the banks of the muddy River Onon in 1162. Between Olovyannaya and Borzya you cross the Adun Chelon mountain ridge, passing through Yasnaya (km6464) and Birka (km6477).

Km6486: Mirnaya At the western end of the station there are two small tanks whose guns appear to be aimed at the train.

Km6509: Khadabulak Small village below a large telecommunications tower on the hill. Long views across the plains to the hills in the north around this area.

Km6543: Borzya (●●) Junction with the line to Solovyevsk on the border with Mongolia, 85km south-west of here. Black marketeers come aboard (if you're coming from Beijing) to tempt you with army uniforms, military watches (from the camp here?) and rabbit fur hats. Watch your valuables.

There are several opportunities for photographs along the train as it snakes around the curves between kms6554-70, and especially km6564-5(S). The line passes through

Kharanor (km6583) where there may be a short stop and **Dauriya** (km6609), a small village surrounded by a marsh of red weeds.

Km6661: Zabaikalsk - The Border (● ● ● + +) A small station on the Russian side of the border with China. The bogies are changed, the carriages being raised on hydraulic lifts while passengers go to the station building to have breakfast or lunch and visit the bank. Photography of the bogie-changing operation is now tolerated. It used to be forbidden and I once saw a disobedient tourist having the film ripped out of his camera by an irate border guard. Get off quickly and beat the queue for the **restaurant** (boiled eggs, fish, soup, beefsteak and rice). If you've just arrived in Russia, don't change too much money in the **bank** as there's little to spend it on in the train and anyway you will soon be approached by black marketeers. If you need smaller denomination US$ bills (for the black market) the bank seems happy to help you out. There is a **Beriozka shop**, in the building opposite the station building and across the line, where vodka, champagne and palekh boxes are sold. There's a small department store next door.

Customs formalities take place on the train and, if you are leaving Russia, you may still be required to produce your currency declaration form. Any remaining roubles are confiscated so don't admit to having them if you want some as souvenirs. If you're coming into the country and not going to change money on the black market, declare everything on the form.

THE PEOPLE'S REPUBLIC OF CHINA

(Note that the km markers along this route do not show the distance to Beijing until you reach Harbin. From the border to Harbin they show the distance to Harbin.)

Km935 (Bei:2323): Manzhouli (● ● ● +) (2135ft/651m) At this Chinese border town (formerly known as Manchuria Station) you're required to show officials your baggage and currency declaration form if you're leaving the country, or fill out this form as well as a health declaration form if you're just arriving.

The train spends 1½-2½hrs here so you can visit the **bank** and the **Friendship Store** (tins of high quality peanuts, Chinese vodka and beer). Postcards and stamps are also available here. Puffing steam locomotives shunt carriages around the yard, a particularly impressive sight if you arrive here in the early hours of a freezing winter morning. Loos stink, less so in winter.

The East Chinese Railway 1897-1901

The original plans for the Great Siberian Railway had not included the laying of tracks across territories that were outside the Russian Empire. However, when surveyors returned from the Shilka and Amur valleys in 1894 with the news that the Sretensk to Khabarovsk section of the line would prove extremely costly, owing to the difficult terrain, the Siberian Railway Committee were obliged to consider an alternative route. Their greedy eyes turned to the rich Chinese territory of Manchuria and they also noted that a line straight across this province to Vladivostok would cut 513 *versts* (544km) off the journey to the port. Since the Chinese would obviously not be happy to have Russian railway lines extending into their territory, the Committee had to think up a scheme to win Peking over to the idea.

The Manchurian Deal

It did not take the wily Russian diplomats long to work out a deal the Chinese were forced to accept. After the 1894 Sino-Japanese war the victorious Japanese concocted a peace treaty that included the payment of a heavy indemnity by the Chinese. Knowing that China was unable to pay, the Russians offered them a generous loan in exchange for the right to build and operate a railway across Manchuria. They were granted an eighty-year lease on the thin strip of land 1,400km long and the project was to be disguised as a Chinese enterprise financed through the Russo-Chinese Bank. The rest of the world suspected Russia of flagrant imperialism and she proved them right in 1897 by annexing Port Arthur.

Work begins

Construction of the Chinese Eastern Railway began in 1897 but it soon became obvious that the project was facing greater problems than any that had arisen during the building of other sections of the railway. There were difficult conditions (the Greater Khingan Range had to be crossed); there were not enough labourers; interpreters were needed to translate the orders of the Russian foremen to the Chinese coolies and the area through which the route passed was thick with *hunghutzes* (bandits). It was necessary to bring in a force of 5,000 policemen to protect the workers. After the Boxer (anti-foreigner) riots began in the late 1890s it became necessary to protect the rails, too, for when they were not murdering missionaries the Boxers tore up the track and derailed trains.

Set-backs

After the annexation of Port Arthur another Manchurian line was begun - from Harbin south through Mukden (now Shenyang) to Dalni (now Dalian) and Port Arthur (now Lushun). Work was disrupted in 1899 by the outbreak of bubonic plague and a doctor was rushed from St Petersburg to inoculate the labourers. In spite of the Chinese refusing to co-operate with the quarantine procedures, only 1,400 died, out of the total work-force of 200,000. In May 1900 the Boxers destroyed 200km of track and besieged Harbin. The Russians sent in a peace-keeping force of 200,000 men but by the time the rebellion had been put down, one third of the railway had been destroyed.

Despite all these set-backs, the line was completed at the end of 1901 although not opened to regular traffic until 1903. It would have been far more economical to have built the Amur line from Sretensk to Khabarovsk, for in the end the East Chinese Railway had cost the government more than the total spent on the entire Trans-Siberian track on Russian soil.

Leaving the station you pass **Lake Dalai Nor** and roll across empty steppe-lands. You may see mounted herders from the train as did Michael Myres Shoemaker in 1902 when he was passing through this area, on his journey to Peking. Of the first Chinese person he saw, he wrote (in *The Great Siberian Railway from St Petersburg to Pekin*) 'these northern Celestials appear on the whole friendly, and are flying around in all directions swathed in furs, and mounted on shaggy horses.' European newspapers of the time had been filled with reports of the atrocities committed by the anti-foreigner Boxer sect in Manchuria, hence his surprise at the apparent friendliness of the local population.

Km749 (Bei:2137): Hailar (●●) (2030ft/619m) From here to Haiman the rolling steppes continue. If you'd been travelling here in 1914, you would have the latest edition of the Baedeker's *Russia with Teheran, Port Arthur and Peking* with you and would therefore be looking out for 'the fortified station buildings (sometimes adorned with apes, dragons and other Chinese ornaments), the Chinese carts with their two high wheels and the camels at pasture'. Modern Hailar is an unexotic city of 180,000 people, the economic centre of the region. Local architecture is a blend of Russian and Mongolian: log cabins, some with 'yurt-style' roofs. The average temperature in this area in January is a cool minus 27°C.

Km674 (Bei:2062): Haiman Also known as Yakoshih, this town stands near the foot of the Great Khingan Range which extends from the northern border with Russia south into Inner Mongolia. The line begins to rise into the foothills of the range.

Km634 (Bei:2022): Mianduhe (●) The train continues to climb the gently rising gradient.

Km574 (Bei:1962): Yilick Ede (●●) Note that the train does not stop here on the journey **from** Beijing.

Km564 (Bei:1952): Xinganling/Khingan (●) (3140ft/958m) This station stands at the highest point on the line. The long tunnel (3km) that was built here in 1901-2 was a considerable engineering achievement since most of the drilling was done during the winter, with shift workers labouring day and night.

Km539 (Bei:1927): Boketu (●●●) The line winds down through partly-wooded slopes to the town of Balin/Barim (km7135/1866) and continues over the plains leaving Inner Mongolia and crossing into Heilongjiang Province.

Km270 (Bei:1658): Angangxi (● ● ●)

MAP 22

Forty kilometres south of the ancient city of Qiqihar (Tsitsikar). By the time he reached this point Michael Myres Shoemaker had become bored with watching 'Celestials' from the windows of the train and was tired and hungry. He writes 'In Tsitsikar, at a wretched little mud hut, we find some hot soup and a chop, also some coffee, all of which, after our days in lunch baskets, taste very pleasant.' Over their lunch, they may have discussed the nearby **Field of Death** for which the city was notorious. In this open area on the edge of Tsitsikar public executions were regularly performed. Most of the criminals decapitated before the crowds here were *hunghutzes* (bandits). Since the Chinese believed that entry to Heaven was denied to mortals who were missing parts of their bodies, their heads had to be sewn back in place before a decent burial could take place. However, so as not to lower the moral tone of Paradise, the government ordered that the heads be sewn on the wrong way round, facing backwards.

Twenty kilometres east of Angangxi you pass through a large area of marshland, part of which has been designated a nature reserve. The marsh attracts a wide variety of waterfowl since it is on the migration route from the Arctic and Siberia down to southern Asia. The **Zhalong Nature Reserve**, 20 km north of here, is best known for its cranes. Several of those found here (including the Siberian Crane) are now listed as endangered species.

Km159 (Bei:1547): Daqing (●)

At the centre of one of the largest oilfields in China, Daqing is an industrial model town producing plastics and gas as well as oil. Higher wages attract model workers from all over the country. Apart from the thousands of oil wells in this swampy district there's very little to see

ZABAIKALSK (USSR)
MANZHOULI
满州里
(P.R. of CHINA)
Lake Dalai Nor
HARGANT
赫尔洪得
INNER MONGOLIA
↑
Ⓜ
HAILAR
海拉尔
HAIMAN
海满
MIANDUHE
免渡河
GREAT KHINGAN MTNS
YILICK EDE
伊列吉得
XINGANLING
兴安岭
BOKETU
博克图
BALIN
巴林
ZHALANTUN
扎兰屯
HEILONGJIANG
ANGANXI
昂昂溪
QIQIHAR

Km96 (Bei:1484): Song   A small station in an island of cultivation amongst the swamps.

Km0 (Bei:1388): Harbin (●●●)   (152m/500ft) Crossing the wide Sungari (Songhua) River (a 1,840km long tributary of the mighty Amur to the north) the line reaches Harbin, the industrial centre of Heilongjiang Province. It was a small fishing village until the mid 1890s when the Russians made it the headquarters of their railway building operations in Manchuria. After Michael Myres Shoemaker visited the town in 1902 he wrote: 'The state of society seems even worse at this military post of Harbin than in Irkutsk. There were seven throats cut last night, and now, as a member of the Russo-Chinese Bank expressed it, the town hopes for a quiet season.' The *Imperial Japanese Railways Guide to East Asia (1913)* recommended 'the excellent bread and butter, which are indeed the pride of Harbin' and warned travellers away from the numerous opium dens. After the Revolution, White Russian refugees poured into the town and the Russian influence on the place continued.

There are few onion-domes and spires to be seen today in what is otherwise just another Chinese city. The Russian population is now small. The main tourist attraction is the **Ice Lantern Festival**, which takes place from January to early February. Winters here are particularly cold and during the festival the parks are filled with ice-sculptures: life-size elephants, dragons and horses as well as small buildings and bridges. Electric lights are frozen into these sculptures and when they are illuminated at night, the effect is spectacular.

At the station, good views along the track of the numerous steam locos can be obtained from the bridges between the platforms.

Km1260: The line crosses a wide tributary of the Songhua River. There are numerous small lakes in the area.

Km1146: Changchun (●●)   (230m/760ft) Between Harbin and Changchun you cross an immense cultivated plain, leaving Heilongjiang and entering Jilin Province. Changchun is the provincial capital. The station is quite interesting with white concrete sculptures of 'The Graces' and lots to buy from the snack sellers on the platform.

Back in 1913 the *Imperial Japanese Government Railways Guide to East Asia* was reminding its readers (all of whom would have had to have changed at this large junction) about 'the need of adjusting their watches - the Russian railway-time being 23 minutes earlier than the Japanese'. From 1933 to 1945 Changchun was the centre of the Japanese puppet state of Manchukuo and it has now grown into an industrial metropolis of more than one million people. Local

Trans-Manchurian route 287

MAP 23

industries include the car factory (where Red
Flag limousines are assembled: guided tours
possible), the rail-carriage factory and the film
studios. If you happen to get off here the local
delicacies include Antler Broth, Hedgehog
Hydnum stewed with Orchid, and the north-
eastern speciality, *Qimian*, which is the nose
of a moose. However, Changchun is probably
more popular with rail enthusiasts than with
epicureans. RM Pacifics and QJ 2-10-2s are to
be seen here and on the Changchun-Jilin line.

Km1030: Siping Unattractive town but
lots of working steam locos in the station. Ten
kilometres south of here the train crosses the
provincial border into Liaoning Province.

Km841: Shenyang (●●●) (50m/160ft)
An industrial giant founded two thousand
years ago during the Western Han dynasty
(206BC - 24AD). At different times during
the course of its long history the city has been
controlled by the Manchus (who named it
Mukden), the Russians, the Japanese and the
Kuomintang until it was finally taken over by
the Chinese Communists in 1948.

Shenyang is now one of the largest industrial centres in the People's Republic but there
are several interesting places to visit between
the factories, including a smaller version of
the **Imperial Palace** in Beijing. There is also
a **railway museum** situated beside Sujiatun
shed. The station has a green dome and the
square outside it is dominated by a tank on a
high pedestal.

Km599: Jinzhou (●●) From here the line
runs down almost to the coast which it follows
south-west for the next 300km, crossing into
Hebei Province. Beijing is just under eight
hours from here.

Km415: Shanhaiguan (●●) As you
approach the town from the north, you pass

through the **Great Wall** - at its most eastern point. This end of the Wanlichangcheng (Ten Thousand Li Long Wall) has been partially done up for the tourists. Although the views here are not as spectacular as at Badaling (70km north of Beijing and the usual tourist spot on the Wall, see p280) the restoration at Shanhaiguan has been carried out more sympathetically - it is restoration rather than reconstruction. The large double-roofed tower houses an interesting museum.

Km262: Tangshan The epicentre of the earthquake which demolished this industrial town on 28 July 1976. The official death toll stands at 150,000 but it is probably as high as 750,000. Many of the factories have been rebuilt and the town is once again producing consumer goods. Locomotives are built here at the Tangshan Works: which until 1991 produced the SY class 2-8-2 steam engine.

Km133: Tianjin/Tientsin (●●) One of the largest ports in China, with a population of seven million. In the mid-nineteenth century the English and the French marched on the capital and 'negotiated' the Treaty of Peking which opened Tianjin to foreign trade. Concessions were granted to foreign powers as they were in Shanghai. England, France, Austria, Germany, Italy, Belgium, Russia, Japan and the United States each controlled different parts of the city, which accounts for the amazing variety of architectural styles to be found here. Chinese resentment at the foreign presence boiled over in 1870 when (during the incident that came to be known as the **Tientsin Massacre**) ten nuns, two priests and a French official were murdered. To save female babies from being killed by their parents (the Chinese have always considered it far more important to have sons than daughters) the nuns had been giving money for them. This had led the more gullible members of the Chinese population to believe that the nuns were either eating the children or grinding up their bones for patent medicines.

Km0: Beijing The beginning or the end? You are now 9001kms from Moscow. See p213 for practical information on the city.

PART 6: DESTINATIONS & DEPARTURES

This section contains basic information for those spending a few days in Japan, Hong Kong, Helsinki, Berlin, Budapest and Prague at the end (or beginning) of the trip. Details of how to arrange tickets in these cities for the rail journey across Siberia, are given in Part 1.

JAPAN

General information

● **Visas** Visas are not necessary for passport holders from Britain, other Western European countries, North America and most Commonwealth countries (except Australia).

● **Money/costs** The unit of currency is the yen (Y). Japan has become one of the most expensive countries in the world for foreign visitors. You will need to allow for a minimum of £20-25 per day for the most basic accommodation and the cheapest meals.

● **Climate** Japan has four clearly-defined seasons, winter being cold and snowy, summer hot and humid, spring and autumn warm.

● **Language** Since English is taught in schools and the people are very keen to make contact with foreigners, you will always be able to find someone to help you except in the more out-of-the-way places. If you're really stuck dial 3502 1461 (in Tokyo) for the Tourist Information Center (TIC).

● **Local transport** If you plan to spend some time touring the country you should purchase a Japan Rail Pass but to qualify for the full discount, it must be bought before you arrive, from the JNTO branch in your country. For getting around the cities the metro system is best although you'll need help with the ticket machines.

Tourist information

Before you leave home visit the branch of the Japan National Tourist Organisation in your country. A good selection of useful maps and tourist brochures is provided free of charge. Addresses:

● 167 Regent St, London W1 (071-734 9638)
● 630 Fifth Ave, New York, N.Y. 10111 (212-757 5640)
● 165 University Ave, Toronto, Ont. M5II 3B8 (416-366 7140)
● 115 Pitt St, Sydney NSW 2000 (232 4522)

The Tokyo Tourist Information Center (3502 1461) at 6-6, Yuraku-cho 1-chome, Chiyoda-Ku should be your first stop in Tokyo.

Arrival
● **Niigata Port**   The Niigata City Tourist Information Center is directly in front of the railway station, at 1-1 Hanazono (tel 025-241 7914). The Niigata International Friendship Center, at Miyoshi Mansion 3F, Kami-Okwamae 6 (tel 025-225 2777) also has tourist information. Note that the boat service between Niigata and Vladivostok does not operate in winter.

● **Niigata airport**   There are flights between Niigata and Khabarovsk or Vladivostok twice weekly and a weekly flight to Irkutsk. The flight to Tokyo costs £70/US$100.

● **Narita Airport (Tokyo)**   Transport to the city centre is expensive since the airport is located forty miles outside the capital. The cheapest way to get in is to take the Keisei Limited Express train from the airport to Keisei Ueno Station in Tokyo (£6/US$9).

Accommodation in Tokyo
This can be expensive; a bed in a youth hostel will set you back £7.50/US$11. Youth hostels are cheapest followed by *minshuku* (bed and breakfast) and then business hotels. *Ryokans* (Japanese style hotels) are pricey but often include meals and are an interesting experience for the foreigner. The best way to find somewhere to sleep is to visit the TIC and collect an accommodation list and a map. Then phone the hotel/youth hostel (phone calls are one of the few bargains to be had in Japan). Check prices and places and then get them to give you directions. Some numbers to try for cheap accommodation in Tokyo are:

● Tokyo International Youth Hostel (Iidabashi) 3235 1107
● Yoyogi Youth Hostel (Shibuya) 3467 9163
● Takao Youth Hostel (Hachioji) 0426-61 0437
● Asia Center of Japan (Akasaka) 3402 6111

Sightseeing
In Tokyo the chief sights are the Emperor's Palace in the heart of the city; Ginza, the fashionable shopping district and the Meiji Shrine (surrounded by beautiful gardens). If you're staying more than a few days you should visit Kyoto, an ancient city of temples that is particularly attractive in November when the maple trees blaze with autumn colours.

Moving on
Flights are expensive in Japan so try to ensure you have one arranged before you arrive. For details of ferry services to China and Russia (as well as information about arranging **Trans-Siberian** tickets in Japan) refer to Part 1.

HONG KONG

General information

● **Visas** For most visitors planning a stay of less than 30 days a visa is not necessary. British passport-holders get a six-month stay.

● **Money/costs** The unit of currency is the Hong Kong dollar (HK$), divided into 100 cents. The current exchange rate is HK$11.30 to £1; HK$7.80 to US$1. Most things are cheap but budget accommodation is not such good value for money as in other parts of Asia. For changing money, banks offer both the best and the worst rates - it all depends on the commission they're charging. Ask other travellers and check the notice-board in the Travellers' Hostel (see accommodation below) for what's currently the best place. Money-changers are useful when banks are closed but watch their commission charges, some of which are concealed in the rate displayed. Some sell roubles cheaply but check on the going rate from recently-returned travellers. Note that roubles are confiscated if discovered (unlikely) by Russian customs at the border.

● **Climate** Mild with fairly hot and humid summers, cool winters.

● **Language** Cantonese and English.

Tourist information

The Hong Kong Tourist Association (HKTA) has branches in many countries and can provide you with useful maps and brochures. Branches at the airport and the Star Ferry terminal (Kowloon).

Arrival

● **Kai Tak Airport** Tucked into Kowloon, beside the bay. Landing here is quite an experience as the tips of the wings seem almost to touch the high-rise blocks. Visit the HKTA office and if you have to visit the *bureau de change* do not change more than the price of a bus-fare. There is an airport bus that runs into Tsimshatsui District (where there is budget accommodation available) in Kowloon and also to Hong Kong Island.

● **By rail** There are several alternatives. You can take the direct express train which runs between Canton (Guangzhou) and Kowloon (Hung Hom Station). It is cheaper, however, to take local trains, from Canton to Shenzhen; there is also a bus service on this route. You walk across the border into Hong Kong and then take a local train from Lo Wu station to Hung Hom.

● **Ferry/hovercraft from Canton (Guangzhou)** The overnight ferry between Canton and Hong Kong arrives and departs from the Tai Kok Tsui Wharf in Kowloon. There is also a hovercraft service operating between here and Canton (journey time: 3 hours).

● **Boat to/from Shanghai** There is one departure a week on this 60hr run; prices HK$750-1400. The service is popular and heavily booked in the summer. Contact China Merchants' Steam Navigation Co (tel 815 1006), 315 Des Voeux Rd, Central.

Local transport
Most famous is the Star Ferry service which operates across the bay between Kowloon and Hong Kong Island. There is also a fast and efficient subway system and the old trams still operate on Hong Kong Island. Taxis are cheap but traffic slow-moving.

Accommodation
For a cheap place to sleep, the name is **Chungking Mansions**. In this large block in Kowloon, near the bay and a stone's throw from the famous **Peninsula Hotel**, there are a large number of small hotels with tiny rooms but low prices. Have a look at a few before you settle for the first you see as the rooms vary in size, cleanliness and price. The **Travellers' Hostel** (16f Block A) is a popular meeting place for backpackers and has cheap dormitory accommodation, a restaurant and a travel agency that can organise visas for China. There's also the refurbished **YMCA** (next door to the Peninsula Hotel).

Food
An incredible variety including some of the best Chinese (Cantonese-style) food available anywhere. Try the floating restaurants of Aberdeen in the evening, have *dim sum* for lunch or if it's real junk food you want all the big names are here.

Sightseeing
The main attraction in Hong Kong is really the city itself and its location - thousands of buildings packed around the bay in the shadow of the Peak on Hong Kong Island. Take the Peak tram (rack railway) up to the top of the Peak for a magnificent view over the bay. A trip to the nearby Portuguese colony of Macau and its casinos is recommended (three hours by ferry).

Moving on
For cheap flights or **Trans-Siberian** tickets see p33. Visas for China are easy to get in Hong Kong. Either use a travel agent or DIY for HK$100 (Counter No 7, Visa Section of PRC, 5th floor, China Resources Building, Harbour Drive. Take the Star Ferry to Wanchai). Visas are issued the following day. For the same-day service, you pay HK$150.

FINLAND: HELSINKI

General information
- **Visas** Visas are not necessary for most nationalities.
- **Money/costs** The unit of currency is the marka (FIM) divided into 100 pennia. As in most Scandinavian countries prices are higher here than in many European countries. Basic youth hostel accommodation is available for under £7.00 per night.
- **Climate** Helsinki is pleasantly warm in summer but winters are long and severe.
- **Language** There are two official languages - Finnish and Swedish (the Swedish name for Helsinki being Helsingfors). Most people also speak English.

Tourist information
There are Finnish Tourist Offices in many capitals of the world. In Helsinki your first stop should be the Helsinki City Tourist Office at Pohjoisesplanadi 19, on the Esplanadia (the park next to the waterside market square). They provide good maps, an accommodation list and are particularly helpful and friendly.

Arrival
- **By sea** If you're arriving from Stockholm on a Viking Line ship, or from Travemunde (Germany) on Finnjet, both companies dock on the east side of the bay. If you're arriving from Poland (Gdansk) or on the Silja line (from Stockholm), boats dock on the west side of the bay, also a 15-20 minute walk from the city centre.
- **By air** The airport is situated 19km north of the city centre, at Vantaa. There is a regular bus service (bus No 615 to railway station). The journey takes about half an hour.
- **By rail** The railway station is six blocks west of the harbour and two blocks north.

Accommodation
A full list for all budgets (including youth hostels) is available from the Helsinki City Tourist Office. For cheap accommodation try:
- Stadionin maja (tel 496 071), Pohjoinen Stadiontie 3B
- Eurohostel (tel 664 452), Linnankatu 9

Moving on
There are ferries to Germany, Poland and Sweden (which is the usual rail route to the rest of Europe). Discounted flights are available to under 26s or student card holders. A recommended budget travel agent is Travela at Mannerheimintie 5 C, 00100 Helsinki 10. For information about booking the **Trans-Siberian** see Part 1.

GERMANY: BERLIN

General information
- **Visas** Not necessary for most nationalities.
- **Money/costs** The Deutsche mark (DM) is the unit of currency, divided into 100 pfennigs. Living and travelling costs can be high.
- **Language** It's useful to be able to speak a little German. Most Berliners study English at school and many speak it fluently.

Tourist information
The Berlin Tourist Office (tel 262 6031) is in the Europa Center (the building with the Mercedes star on the top of it) along Kurfursten-damm and a ten-minute walk from Zoo Bahnhof. Maps and an accommodation list are available. Open daily 08.00-22.30hrs.

Arrival in Berlin
Zoo Bahnhof (Zoo Station) is the station for international trains. There are left-luggage lockers and a *bureau de change*. The Berlin Tourist Office is a ten-minute walk away (see above).

Accommodation
The cheapest places are the **Youth Hostels** which are luxurious by YH standards but comparatively expensive (from 25-35DM). Ask the tourist office if the summer youth camp near Tegel is operating this year. In 1993 they charged only 8DM for a bed in a large tent.
- Ernst Reuter Jugendherberge (tel 404 1610), Hermsdorfer Damm 48, (Hermsdorf)
- Berlin Jugendhergastehaus (tel 261 1097), Kluckstrasse 3, (Tiergarten)
- Wannsee Jugendhergastehaus (tel 803 2034), Kronprinzessinnen-weg 27, Ecke Badeweg (Wannsee)

Around Zoo Station, which is where your train will arrive, try:
- Jugendhergastehaus am Zoo (tel 312 94 10), Hardenbergstrasse 9a Under 27s only; accommodation from 35DM.

The tourist office will give you a list of cheap accommodation including rooms in private houses.

Moving on
For cheap flights buy a copy of the weekly magazine *Zitty*, which has several pages of travel deals. The daily rail service to London (via Ostend) departs at 20.49; you reach London Victoria at 11.47.

A system of car-sharing can be arranged through *mitfahrzentrale* agencies; you pay the agency a fee to find you a ride in a private car to other European cities.

To make a booking on the **Trans-Siberian** in Berlin see Part 1.

HUNGARY: BUDAPEST

General information

● **Visas** North Americans and most European citizens do not need a visa.

● **Money/costs** The unit of currency is the Forint (Ft), divided into 100 fillers (f). Prices for hotels and restaurants are low.

● **Language** *Magyar* is one of the world's more difficult languages to learn. Most people connected with tourism speak a little English though knowledge of German is more widespread.

Tourist information

There are a number of tourist organisations that can help both with maps and information as well as with finding accommodation (see also below). The main organisations are **Tourinform**, Suto utca 2, (near Deak ter metro station; tel 117-9800; open 08.00-20.00 daily) and **IBUSZ**, V.Petofi ter 3, (money-changing facilities; tel 118-3925; open 24hrs daily). IBUSZ has several other branches.

Arrival

● **By rail** Trains from Vienna come into the East Station (**Keleti Palyaudvar**), and there is a tourist office here, where you can book accommodation. The West Station (**Nyugati Palyaudvar**) is used for trains to and from Prague. Both have metro stations nearby.

● **By air** The international airport is 10 miles from the city centre. There is a tourist office and there are shuttle buses to the city.

Accommodation

Budapest has a wide range of accommodation. At the top end there is the **Hilton** which blends well with the ancient walls of the castle tower it incorporates and stands on the hill above the city. For budget travellers the city's **colleges** offer their rooms during the summer holidays. Many local people let **rooms** in their houses and you can be put in contact with them by visiting one of the tourist offices listed below:

IBUSZ Hotel Service, V Petofi ter 3 (tel 118-3925; open 24hrs). IBUSZ also has branches at Keleti and Nyugati railway stations.
Volantourist, V Belgrad rakpart 6 (tel 118-2133)
Budapest Tourist, V Roosevelt ter 5 (tel 117-3555)

Moving on

Taking the train back to London requires a change at Vienna (3½hrs from Budapest) where there are daily departures at 18.44 for Ostend; you reach London at 15.17 the following day. For **Trans-Siberian** bookings see Part 1.

CZECH REPUBLIC: PRAGUE

General information
- **Visas** Most European citizens do not need a visa; but they are required for North Americans, Australians and New Zealanders.
- **Money/costs** The unit of currency is the krown. German DM accepted in some places. Prices for hotels and restaurants are low.
- **Language** Many Czech people involved in tourism now speak English. German and Russian are the two other foreign languages spoken here.

Tourist information
A good place for tourist information is **Prague Information Service**, 20 Na Prikope. **CKM Student Travel Centre**, 28 Jindrisska, also has tourist and accommodation information. The **International Students' Union**, 25 Parizska, sells student cards that allow discounts on international rail travel and on entry to some sights in the city.

Arrival
- **By rail** There are four railway stations: **Praha Holesovice** to the north, **Praha Hlavni** and **Praha Stred** near the centre, or **Praha Smichov** to the south (mainly local trains).
- **By air** The international airport is 10 miles from the city centre. There are two bus departures every hour between the airport and the airline office (Vltava Terminal, 25 Revolucni).

Accommodation
There's a good range of accommodation but everything gets very crowded in the summer, so start looking for a place to stay early in the day. **Pragotur**, U Obecniho Domu 2, has a booking service for private accommodation. There are also several camp sites around the city, some of which have chalets and dormitories. Full details are available from the tourist information agencies listed above.

Moving on
The cheapest way to get to Britain on public transport is by bus, US$75 on Kingscourt Express, which takes 24hrs and there are twice-weekly departures. Telephone 499 456 or 499 256 for details.

Rail tickets are sold at **Cedok**, 18 Na Prikope, where the queues are often very long. The rail journey to London requires a change at Cologne (Koln) for the Ostend train. Leaving Prague (Praha Hlavni) at 20.50 you reach Cologne at 08.01 next day, arriving in London (Victoria) at 16.47. See Part 1 for information on **Trans-Siberian** bookings.

Timetables for the Trans-Siberian, Trans-Mongolian, Trans-Manchurian routes are given below, plus the Beijing - Hong-Kong route. Unless otherwise indicated **departure times are shown**; for arrival times simply subtract the number of minutes shown as the stopping time. Since the timetables are subject to changes from year to year, you should consult the table posted on the wall of the carriage corridor to ensure times are correct. Another useful source of information is the Thomas Cook Overseas Timetable (available from Thomas Cook travel agents or by post from PO Box 227, Peterborough PE3 6SB, UK).

Table 1 Moscow-Vladivostok (Train Nos 1 & 2: *Rossiya*)

Departures are currently on every other day. from Moscow on odd dates; from Vladivostok on even dates. Note that the daily departure may be reinstated.

Station name		Km from Moscow	Stop (mins)	Departure time			
				Eastbound		Westbound	
				MT*	LT*	MT*	LT*
				▼ *Day 1* ▼			
Moscow	Москва		dep/arr:	14.00	14.00	06.45	06.45
Yaroslavl	Ярославль	284	5	18.30	18.30	02.10	02.10
Danilov	Данилов	357	15	20.05	21.05	00.50	01.50
Buy	Буй	448	2	21.27	22.27	23.13	00.13
				▼ *Day 2* ▼		▲ *Day 7* ▲	
Kirov	Киров	957	15	04.58	05.58	16.08	17.08
Perm	Пермь	1433	15	12.18	14.18	08.44	10.44
Ekaterinburg	Екатеринвург	1813	20	19.00	21.00	02.14	04.14
				▼ *Day 3* ▼		▲ *Day 6* ▲	
Tyumen	Тюмен	2140	10	23.39	01.39	21.29	23.29
Ishim	Ишим	2431	8	03.13	05.13	17.37	19.37
Omsk	Омск	2712	15	07.03	10.03	13.25	16.25
Tatarskaya	Татарская	2880	5	09.17	12.17	10.54	13.54
Novosibirsk	Новосивирск	3335	15	16.45	19.45	04.32	07.32
				▼ *Day 4* ▼		▲	▲
Taiga	Таига	3565	10	20.57	00.57	00.33	04.33
				▼	▼	▲ *Day 5* ▲	
Achinsk	Ачинск	3917	2	02.37	06.37	18.03	22.03
Krasnoyarsk	Красноярск	4098	15	06.23	10.23	14.34	18.34
Tayshet	Таишет	4516	2	13.44	18.44	06.34	11.34
				▼ *Day 5* ▼		▲ *Day 4* ▲	
Irkutsk	Иркутск	5185	20	01.38	06.38	19.01	00.01
Slyudyanka	Слюдянка	5312	15	04.33	09.33	16.24	21.24
Ulan Ude	Улан-Удэ	5642	15	10.10	16.10	11.02	17.02
Petrovskiy Zd	Петровский З.	5784	12	12.42	18.42	08.41	14.41
Khilok	Хилок	5932	5	15.03	21.03	06.15	12.15
				▼ *Day 6* ▼		▲	▲
Chita	Чита	6199	13	19.47	01.47	01.51	07.51

*(MT = Moscow time; LT = local time)

Station name		Km from Moscow	Stop (mins)	Departure time			
				Eastbound		Westbound	
				MT*	LT*	MT*	LT*
Karymskaya	Карымская	6293	12	21.56	03.56	23.44	05.44
				▼	▼	▲ Day 3 ▲	
Mogocha	Могоча	6906	8	09.13	15.13	11.58	17.58
Skovorodino	Сковородино	7306	10	17.03	23.03	04.07	10.07
				▼ Day 7 ▼		▲	▲
Belogorsk	Белогорск	7873	12	01.53	07.53	18.41	00.41
				▼	▼	▲ Day 2 ▲	
Khabarovsk	Хабаровск	8521	25	13.35	20.35	07.35	14.35
				▼ Day 8 ▼		▲	▲
Spassk-Dalny	Спасск-Д	9050	10	22.18	05.18	22.37	05.37
Ussuriyisk	Уссурииск	9177	10	00.43	07.43	20.21	03.21
Vladivostok	Владивосток	9289	--	02.45	09.45	18.05	01.05
						▲ Day 1 ▲	

Table 2 Moscow-Irkutsk (Train Nos 9 & 10: *Baikal*)

From late spring to early autumn departures are daily; for the rest of the year they are on every other day.

Station name		Km from Moscow	Stop (mins)	Departure time			
				Eastbound		Westbound	
				MT*	LT*	MT*	LT*
				▼ Day 1 ▼			
Moscow	Москва	dep/arr:		12.05	12.05	05.55	05.55
Yaroslavl	Ярославль	284	10	16.43	16.43	01.25	01.25
Danilov	Данилов	357	20	18.20	19.20	23.59	00.59
				▼	▼	▲ Day 5 ▲	
Shariya	Шарья	700	10	23.48	00.48	18.46	19.46
				▼ Day 2 ▼		▲	▲
Kirov	Киров	957	17	04.05	05.05	14.46	15.46
Perm	Пермь	1433	15	11.57	13.57	06.53	08.53
Ekaterinburg	Екатеринбург	1813	15	18.28	20.28	00.14	02.14
				▼ Day 3 ▼		▲ Day 4 ▲	
Tyumen	Тюмень	2140	15	23.10	01.10	19.21	21.21
Ishim	Ишим	2431	10	02.52	04.52	15.26	17.26
Omsk	Омск	2712	15	06.47	09.47	10.55	13.55
Novosibirsk	Новосибирск	3335	22	16.22	19.22	01.15	04.15
				▼ Day 4 ▼		▲	▲
Taiga	Таига	3565	8	20.39	00.39	21.13	01.13
				▼		▲ Day 3 ▲	
Achinsk	Ачинск	3917	2	02.28	06.28	14.49	18.49
Krasnoyarsk	Красноярск	4098	20	06.06	10.06	11.21	15.21
Nizhneudinsk	Нижнеудинск	4680	15	16.28	21.28	00.25	05.25
				▼ Day 5 ▼		▲ Day 2 ▲	
Zima	Зима	4940	20	20.39	01.39	20.16	01.16
Irkutsk	Иркутск	5185	-	01.30	06.30	15.10	20.10
						▲ Day 1 ▲	

*(MT=Moscow time; LT=local time)
Times shown are departure times - subtract stop for arrival time

Table 3 Moscow-Beijing via Mongolia (Train Nos 3 & 4)

Station name		Km from Moscow	Stop (mins)	Departure time			
				Eastbound		Westbound	
				MT*	LT*	MT*	LT*
				▼ *Tue* ▼			
Moscow	Москва	dep/arr at:		19.50	19.50	19.00	19.00
				▼ *Wed* ▼		▲	▲
Yaroslavl	Ярославль	284	5	00.15	00.15	14.25	14.25
Danilov	Данилов	357	15	01.50	02.50	13.01	14.01
Buy	Буй	448	5	03.06	04.06	11.23	12.23
Kirov	Киров	957	15	10.42	11.42	04.20	05.20
				▼	▼	▲ *Mon* ▲	
Perm	Пермь	1433	15	17.50	19.50	20.50	22.50
				▼ *Thur* ▼		▲	▲
Ekaterinburg	Екатеринбург	1813	15	00.04	02.04	14.30	16.30
Tyumen	Тюмень	2140	10	04.23	06.23	10.14	12.14
Ishim	Ишим	2431	8	07.57	09.57	06.32	08.32
Omsk	Омск	2712	15	11.42	14.42	02.18	05.18
				▼	▼	▲ *Sun* ▲	
Novosibirsk	Новосибирск	3335	15	20.24	00.24	17.28	21.28
				▼ *Fri* ▼		▲	▲
Taiga	Тайга	3565	10	00.20	04.20	13.43	17.43
Achinsk	Ачинск	3917	2	05.54	09.54	07.26	11.26
Krasnoyarsk	Красноярск	4098	15	09.34	13.34	04.09	08.09
				▼	▼	▲ *Sat* ▲	
Kansk	Канск	4343	1	13.35	17.35	23.28	03.28
Tayshet	Тайшет	4516	2	16.44	21.44	20.22	00.22
				▼ *Sat* ▼		▲	▲
Irkutsk	Иркутск	5185	15	03.49	08.49	09.19	14.19
Slyudyanka	Слюдянка	5312	15	06.20	11.20	06.49	11.49
Mysovaya	Мысовая	5477	2	09.03	14.03	03.53	08.53
Ulan Ude	Улан-Удэ	5642	20	11.49	17.49	01.23	07.23
				▼	▼	▲ *Fri* ▲	
Gusinoye Ozero	Гусиное Озеро	5780	2	14.42	20.42	22.15	04.15
Naushki	Наушки	5897	1hr§	18.20	00.20	20.25	02.25
				▼ MONGOLIA ▼		▲ RUSSIA ▲	
Sukhe Bator	Сухэ Баатор	5925	1hr§		01.20		22.05
				▼ *Sun* ▼		▲	▲
Darhan	Дархаан	6023	10		03.11		19.00
Ulan Bator	Улаан Баатор	6304	30		09.30		13.50
Choyr	Чойр	6551	15		14.06		09.02
Sayn Shand	Сайн Шаанд	6778	15		17.52		05.00
				▼	▼	▲ *Thur* ▲	
Dzamyn Ude	Дзамын-Удэ	7013	1hr§		22.33		00.40
				▼ CHINA ▼		▲ MONGOLIA ▲	

Times shown are departure times - subtract stop for arrival time
*(MT=Moscow time; LT=local time)
§(minimum stopping time - often considerably longer)

Station name		Km from Moscow	Stop (mins)	Departure time			
				Eastbound		Westbound	
				MT*	LT*	MT*	LT*
		▼ CHINA ▼				▲MONGOLIA ▲	
Erlyan	二在	7023	2hrs §		01.51		23.15
				▼ Mon ▼		▲	▲
Jining	集宁南	7356	10		06.28		16.29
Datong	大同	7483	13		08.34		14.25
Zhangjiakou	张家口南	7661	10		11.00		11.47
Kangzhuang	康庄	7771	8		12.34		10.01
Qinglongqiao	青龙桥	7783	10		13.19		09.38
Nankou	南口	7801	14		14.31		08.54
Beijing	北京	7865			15.33		07.40
							▲ Wed ▲

Table 4 Moscow-Beijing via Manchuria (Train Nos 19 & 20)

Station name		Km from Moscow	Stop (mins)	Departure time			
				Eastbound		Westbound	
				MT*	LT*	MT*	LT*
				▼ Fri** ▼			
Moscow	Москва	dep/arr at:		21.25	21.25	20.50	20.50
				▼ Sat ▼			
Yaroslavl	Ярославль	284	7	01.40	01.40	16.05	16.05
Danilov	Данилов	357	15	03.15	04.15	14.45	15.45
Kirov	Киров	957	15	12.03	13.03	06.18	07.18
				▼	▼	▲ Fri ▲	
Perm	Пермь	1433	15	19.31	21.31	22.56	00.56
				▼ Sun ▼		▲	▲
Ekaterinburg	Екатеринбург	1813	15	01.45	03.45	16.42	18.42
Tyumen	Тюмень	2140	8	06.07	08.07	12.26	14.26
Ishim	Ишим	2431	10	09.36	11.36	08.44	10.44
Omsk	Омск	2712	15	13.28	16.28	04.27	07.27
				▼	▼	▲ Thur ▲	
Novosibirsk	Новосибирск	3335	15	22.11	02.11	19.44	23.44
				▼ Mon ▼		▲	▲
Taiga	Тайга	3565	10	02.01	06.01	15.45	19.45
Achinsk	Ачинск	3917	2	07.31	11.31	09.27	13.27
Krasnoyarsk	Красноярск	4098	18	11.06	15.06	06.02	10.02
						▲ Wed ▲	
Tayshet	Тайшет	4516	2	18.18	23.18	22.26	03.26
				▼ Tue ▼		▲	▲
Irkutsk	Иркутск	5185	20	05.36	10.36	11.19	16.19
Slyudyanka	Слюдянка	5312	15	08.09	13.09	08.44	13.44
Mysovaya	Мысовая	5477	2	10.52	15.52	05.58	10.58
Ulan Ude	Улан-Удэ	5642	15	13.33	19.33	03.23	09.23
Petrovskiy Zd	ПетровскийЗ	5784	12	15.55	21.55	01.02	07.02

*(MT=Moscow time; LT=local time)
§(minimum stopping time - often considerably longer)
Times shown are departure times - subtract stop for arrival time
** From May to Sep there's a second service, leaving Moscow on Sat at 21.25,
leaving Beijing on Fri at 20.32. This may become a year-round service.

Station name		Km from Moscow	Stop (mins)	Departure time			
				Eastbound		Westbound	
				MT*	LT*	MT*	LT*
				▼ Wed ▼		▲ Tue ▲	
Khilok	Хилок	5932	5	18.16	00.16	22.36	04.36
Chita	Чита	6199	15	23.02	05.02	18.11	00.11
Karymskaya	Карымская	6293	5	01.07	07.07	16.08	22.08
Zabaikalsk	Забаикальск	6661	1hr§	14.06	20.06	06.47	12.47
			▼ CHINA ▼			▲RUSSIA▲	
Manzhouli	满洲里	6678	1hr§		22.07		07.01
				▼ Thur ▼		▲	▲
Hailar	海拉尔	6864	10		00.42		02.31
Mianduhe	免渡河	6979	6		02.23		01.16
Xinganling	兴安岭	7049	10		03.35		00.12
				▼	▼	▲ Mon ▲	
Boketu	博克图	7074	20		04.22		23.08
Angangxi	昂昂溪	7343	12		08.25		18.56
Daqing	大庆	7454	10		10.01		17.10
Harbin	哈尔滨	7613	15		12.08		14.53
Changchun	长春	7855	12		15.52		11.30
Shenyang	沈阳	8160	15		19.42		07.20
Jinzhou	锦州	8402	12		22.59		04.12
Shanhaiguan	山海关	8586	12		01.24		01.53
				▼ Fri ▼		▲ Sun ▲	
Tianjin	大津	8868	10		05.00		22.19
Beijing	北京	9001	--		06.32		20.32
						▲ Sat** ▲	

Table 5 Irkutsk-Ulan Bator (Train Nos 263 & 264)

Station name		Km from Ulan Bator	Stop (mins)	Departure time			
				Eastbound		Westbound	
				MT*	LT*	MT*	LT*
				▼ Day 1 ▼			
Irkutsk	Иркутск	dep/arr daily at:		14.10	19.10	03.50	08.50
				▼ Day 2 ▼		▲ Day 3 ▲	
Ulan Ude	Улан-Удэ	457	15	01.25	07.25	17.10	23.10
Gusinoye Ozero	Гусиное Озеро	595	2	05.35	11.35	13.15	19.15
Naushki	Наушки	712	1hr§	12.50	18.50	10.15	16.15
				▼ MONGOLIA ▼		▲RUSSIA▲	
Sukhe Bator	Сухэ Баатор	740	1hr§		21.10		08.45
Darhan	Дархаан	838	15		23.25		03.20
				▼ Day 3 ▼		▲ Day 2 ▲	
Ulan Bator	Улан Баатор	1119	--		06.40		21.00
						▲ Day 1 ▲	

** (see note on opposite page)
*(MT=Moscow time; LT=local time)
§(minimum stopping time - often considerably longer)
Times shown are departure times - subtract stop for arrival time

Table 6: Beijing - Guangzhou

Station name	Km from Beijing	Departure time			
	Train nos:	47	15	16	48
		▼	▼	▲	▲
Beijing	0	19.26	00.30	04.30	08.49
Baoding	152	21.22	----	----	06.55
Shijiazhuang	283	23.06	03.57	01.14	05.18
Anyang	508	02.05	----	----	02.18
Zhengzhou	695	04.36	08.56	20.10	23.48
Xinyang	997	08.33	12.53	16.10	19.48
Wuhan (Hankou)	1209	11.44	----	----	16.30
Wuhan (Wuchang)	1229	12.19	16.21	12.29	15.51
Yueyang	1447	15.31	19.33	09.19	12.41
Changsha	1587	17.39	21.41	07.15	10.37
Zhuzhou	1638	18.42	----	----	09.31
Hengyang	1772	20.46	00.35	04.19	07.22
Shaoguan	2093	01.51	05.36	23.21	02.28
Guangzhou	2313	04.59	08.45	20.00	23.06

(Change trains for Hong Kong)
(frequent departures)

BEIJING TO HONG KONG

The following information on the rail journey from Beijing to Guangzhou (Canton) and on to Hong Kong was supplied by Colin Baker (UK):

Trains
There are two trains a day from Beijing to Guangzhou. Both leave in the evening and arrive in Guangzhou in the morning of the second day.

I was travelling soft class which was in four-berth compartments. Our carriage was air-conditioned and attended by an ever-smiling conductor who supplied us each with a China Railways tea mug for our use on the journey and, of course, the usual thermos of hot water. As I was heading for Hong Kong I thought there would be other Westerners doing the same trip. However, apart from the three Poles sharing my compartment, the other passengers were all Chinese, some of them from Hong Kong.

The dining car served Cantonese style cuisine and lots of seafood. There was also an ecologically unsound trolley service offering chicken and rice in white polystyrene boxes. The boxes are thrown out onto the track and in some places along the line there are piles of them.

The line is double tracked from Beijing to Guangzhou and as Chinese trains run on the left, views to the left are not obscured by passing trains. Our train was diesel-hauled throughout the route although parts of the line were being prepared for electrification. Steam locos can be seen at several stations along the route, particularly at Xinyang (km980 from Beijing).

The scenery along the route is pleasant rather than dramatic - rolling hills and open fields. There's plenty of opportunity to observe rural Chinese life as you pass by.

Wuhan (km1190-1210 from Beijing)

This is one of the largest cities in China, with a population of three million, and lies on both sides of the massive Yangtse River. As we approached the city from the north we passed many small houses built within inches of the busy railway line. People were sitting outside and had their washing spread over the adjacent (hopefully little-used) track which bordered their front doors. The first of Wuhan's stations is Hankou after which the line crosses the River Hanshui, which is wide but not nearly as wide as the Yangtse which you cross a few minutes later. The bridge is over 1km long, also carries a road and is guarded by sentries at both ends. Before 1957 when it was constructed, the crossing would have been made by ferry. Best views are to the left (when heading south). A stop is made at Wuchang station just over the bridge.

Guangzhou to Hong Kong

This journey takes just under 2½ hours with a brief pause at Shenzen on the Chinese side of the border where the Chinese guards leave the train. Customs formalities take place in the termini at Guangzhou and Kowloon. Chinese yuan and HK$ can be exchanged in Guangzhou station. Note that in this station the entrance to the platform used by international trains is separate from the main entrance. The gates were opened 45mins before the departure and after customs and immigration we were herded into a large waiting-room with a duty-free shop.

Leaving Guangzhou the train travels through the Pearl River delta (crossing the main river at km69) to the border, past rich agricultural land with hills on the horizon. The train is hauled by a Chinese diesel all the way to the Kowloon terminus.

The city of Shenzhen which borders Hong Kong is reached after about 2 hours. Part of the Special Economic Zone, it seems very Westernised with large concrete office and apartment blocks, and advertising hoardings. There is a short stop and railway officials check that no one tries to climb aboard as you leave the station. A few minutes later you cross the river that forms the border and continue through the first Hong Kong station, Lo Wu to Hung Hom.

The line between Lo Wu and Kowloon is electrified with overhead cables. The signalling, trackside and station signs all resemble those used in Britain. The journey takes about 20mins through the New Territories to the Kowloon terminus. This used to be on the waterfront at Tsim Sha Tsui where the Star Ferries dock but only the old clocktower remains. The new terminus was built in 1975 further up the line at Hung Hom.

APPENDIX B: LIST OF SIBERIAN FAUNA

There are extensive displays of local animals in the natural history museums of Novosibirsk, Irkutsk and Khabarovsk but the labelling is in Russian and Latin. The following translation is given for non-Russian speaking readers whose Latin is rusty or non-existent.

In the list below the letters given beside the animal's English name indicate its natural habitat. NS = Northern Siberia/Arctic Circle; SP = Siberian Plain; AS = Altai-Sayan Plateau/Mongolia; BI = Lake Baikal/Transbaikal region; FE = Far Eastern Territories. Where a Latin name is similar to the English (e.g. Vipera = Viper) these names have been omitted.

Accipiter gentilis	goshawk (AS/SP/NS/BI/FE)
Aegoceras montanus	mountain ram (AS)
Aegoceras sibiricus	siberian goat (BI)
Aegolius funereus	boreal/Tengmalm's owl (BI/FE)
Aegypius monachus	black vulture (AS)
Aethia cristatella	crested auklet (NS/FE)
Alces alces	elk/moose (SP/BI/FE)
Allactaga jaculus	five-toed jerboa (SP/BI)
Alopex lagopus	arctic fox (NS)
Anas acuta	pintail (BI)
Anas clypeata	shoveler (SP/BI/FE)
Anas crecca	teal (BI/SP/FE)
Anas falcata	falcated teal (SP/BI/FE)
Anas formosa	baikal teal (BI)
Anas platyrhynchos	mallard (AS/SP/BI/FE)
Anas poecilorhyncha	spotbill duck (AS/BI)
Anser anser	greylag goose (SP/BI)
Anser erythropus	white-fronted goose (AS/SP/BI/FE)
Antelope gutturosa/crispa	antelope (FE)
Arctomis bobac	marmot (AS/SP)
Ardea cinerea	grey heron (AS/SP/BI)
Aquila clanga	greater spotted eagle (SP)
Botaurus stellaris	bittern (SP/BI/FE)
Bubo bubo	eagle owl (BI/FE)
Buteo lagopus	rough legged buzzard (NS/SP/FE)
Butorides striatus	striated/green heron (FE)
Canis alpinus	mountain wolf (AS/FE)
Canis corsac	korsac/steppe fox (BI/FE)
Canis lagopus	arctic fox (NS)
Canis lupus	wolf (SP/BI/FE)
Canis procyonoides	Amur racoon (FE)
Capra sibirica	Siberian mountain goat/ibex (AS/BI)
Capreolus capreolus	roe deer (SP/BI/FE)
Castor fiber	beaver (SP/BI/FE)
Certhia familiaris	common treecreeper (AS/BI/FE)
Cervus alces	elk (AS/BI/FE)
Cervus capreolus	roe-buck (BI/FE)
Cervus elephas	maral deer (AS/BI/FE)

Cervus nippon	sika/Japanese deer (FE)
Cervus tarandus	reindeer (NS/FE)
Circus aeruginosus	marsh harrier (SP/BI)
Citellus undulatus	arctic ground squirrel/ Siberian souslik (NS/BI/FE)
Cricetus cricetus	common hamster (AS/SP/BI/FE)
Cygnus cygnus	whooper swan (SP/BI)
Dicrostonyx torquatus	arctic lemming (NS)
Dryocopus martius	black woodpecker (SP/BI/FE)
Enhyra lutris	Kamchatka beaver (FE)
Equus hemionus	kulan/Asian wild ass (FE)
Eumentopias Stelleri	sea lion (NS/FE)
Eutamias sibiricus	Siberian chipmunk (AS/SP/BI/FE)
Falco columbarius	merlin (NS/SP/BI/FE)
Falco peregrinus	peregrine (NS/SP/BI/FE)
Falco tinnunculus	kestrel (SP)
Falco vesperinus	hawk (SP)
Felis irbis	irbis/panther (FE)
Felis lynx	lynx (SP/BI/FE)
Felis manul	wild cat (AS/BI/FE)
Felis tigris altaica	Amur tiger (FE)
Foetorius altaicus	ermine (SP/BI)
Foetorius altaicus sibiricus	polecat (SP/BI)
Foetorius vulgaris	weasel (SP/BI)
Fulica atra	coot (SP/BI/FE)
Gallinago gallinago	common snipe (SP/BI/FE)
Gavia arctica	black-throated diver/loon (BI)
Gavia stellata	red-throated diver/loon (SP/BI)
Gazella subgutturosa	goitred gazelle (AS)
Grus cinerea	grey crane (SP)
Grus grus	common crane (SP/BI/FE)
Grus leucogeranus	Siberian white crane (NS/SP/FE)
Gulo gulo	wolverine/glutton (SP/BI/FE)
Gypaetus barbatus L.	lammergeyer (AS)
Haematopus ostralegus	oystercatcher (SP/BI/FE)
Lagomis alpinus	rat hare (FE)
Lagopus lagopus	willow grouse/ptarmigan (NS/SP/FE)
Larus argentatus	herring gull (BI/FE)
Larus canus	common gull (BI/FE)
Larus ridibundus	black-headed gull (BI/FE)
Lemmus obensis	Siberian lemming (NS/SP)
Lepus timidus	arctic hare (NS/BI/FE)
Lepus variabilis	polar hare (NS)
Lutra vulgaris	otter (BI/FE)
Marmota camtschatica	Kamchatka marmot (FE)
Marmota sibirica	Siberian marmot (AS/SP/BI)
Martes zibellina	sable (SP/BI/FE)
Melanitta deglandi	American black scoter (BI)
Melanocorypha mongolica	Mongolian lark (BI/FE)
Meles meles	Eurasian badger (AS/BI/FE)
Microtus hyperboreus	sub-arctic vole (NS/SP/FE)
Moschus moschiferus	musk deer (AS/BI/FE)
Mustela erminea	ermine (NS/AS/SP/BI/FE)

Mustela eversmanni	steppe polecat (AS/SP/BI/FE)
Mustela nivalis	common weasel (NS/SP/BI/FE)
Mustela sibirica	kolonok (FE)
Myodes torquatus/obensis	Ob lemming (NS)
Nucifraga caryocatactes	nutcracker (AS/SP/BI/FE)
Nyctea scandiaca	snowy owl (NS)
Ochotona alpina	Altai pika (AS)
Oenanthe isabellina	Isabelline wheatear (AS/SP/BI)_
Omul baikalensis	omul (BI)
Otaria ursina	sea bear (NS/FE)
Otis tarda	bustard (SP/BI)
Ovis ammon	argalis (sheep) (AS)
Ovis Argali	arkhar (AS)
Ovis nivicola	Siberian bighorn/snow sheep (FE)
Panthera pardus orientalis	Amur leopard (FE)
Panthera tigris altaica	Siberian/Amur tiger (FE)
Panthera uncia	snow leopard (AS)
Perdix perdix	grey partridge (AS/SP/BI/FE)
Perisoreus infaustus	Siberian jay (BI/FE)
Phalacrocorax carbo	great cormorant (BI/FE)
Phoca barbata groenlandica	seal (NS/FE)
Phoca baicalensis	Baikal seal (BI)
Phocaena orca	dolphin (NS/FE)
Picoides tridactylus	three-toed woodpecker (SP/BI/FE)
Plectophenax nivalis	snow bunting (NS)
Podiceps auritus	Slavonian/horned grebe (AS/BI)
Podiceps cristatus	great crested grebe (AS/SP/BI)
Procapra gutturosa	Mongolian gazelle (FE)
Pteromys volans	Siberian flying squirrel (SP/BI/FE)
Rangifer tarandus	reindeer/caribou (NS/BI/FE)
Ranodon sibiricus	five-toed triton (AS/SP)
Rufibrenta ruficollis	red-breasted goose (NS)
Salpingotus crassicauda	pygmy jerboa (SP/AS)
Sciurus vulgaris	red squirrel (SP/BI/AS/FE)
Spermophilus eversmanni	Siberian marmot (BI)
Spermophilus undulatus	arctic ground squirrel (FE)
Sterna hirundo	common tern (BI/FE)
Strix nebulosa	great grey owl (SP/BI/FE)
Surnia ulula	hawk owl (SP/BI/FE)
Sus scrofa	wild boar (AS/BI/FE)
Tadorna ferruginea	ruddy shelduck (SP/BI/FE)
Tamias striatus	striped squirrel (BI)
Tetrao urogallus	capercaillie (SP/BI/FE)
Tetrao parvirostris	black-billed capercaillie (BI/FE)
Tetraogallus himalayanensis	Himalayan snowcock (AS)
Tetraogallus altaicus	Altai snowcock (AS)
Tetrastes bonasia	hazel grouse (SP/BI/FE)
Turdus sibiricus	Siberian thrush (SP/BI/FE)
Uria aalge	guillemot (NS/FE)
Ursus arctus	bear (SP/FE)
Ursus maritimus	polar bear (NS)
Ursus tibetanus	Tibet bear (FE)
Vulpes vulpes	red fox (AS/SP/BI/FE)

APPENDIX C: PHRASE LISTS

English-speaking travellers are unforgivably lazy when it comes to learning other people's languages. As with virtually every country in the world, it's possible to just about get by in Russia, Mongolia and China on a combination of English and sign language. English is spoken by tourist guides and some hotel staff but most of the local people you meet on the train will be eager to communicate with you and unable to speak English. Unless you enjoy charades it's well worth learning a few basic phrases in advance. Not only will this make communication easier but it'll also earn you the respect of local people. You might even consider evening classes before you go, or teaching yourself with books and cassettes from your local library.

The sections here highlight only a few useful words. It's well worth also taking along phrasebooks: Lonely Planet's pocket-size *language survival kits* in Russian and Chinese are recommended.

Russian

CYRILLIC ALPHABET AND PRONUNCIATION GUIDE

It is vital to spend the few hours it takes to master the Cyrillic alphabet before you go, otherwise you'll have trouble deciphering the names of streets, metro stations and, most important, the names of stations along the Trans-Siberian and Trans-Mongolian routes. (Mongolian also uses Cyrillic script).

The Cyrillic alphabet is derived from the Greek. It was introduced in Russia in the tenth century, through a translation of the Bible made by the two Greek bishops, Cyril (who gave his name to the new alphabet) and Methodius.

Cyrillic letters		Roman letter	Pronunciation*	Cyrillic letters		Roman letter	Pronunciation*
А	а	a	(f<u>a</u>r)	П	п	p	(<u>P</u>eter)
Б	б	b	(<u>b</u>et)	Р	р	r	(<u>R</u>ussia)
В	в	v	(<u>v</u>odka)	С	с	s	(<u>S</u>iberia)
Г	г	g	(<u>g</u>et)	Т	т	t	(<u>t</u>rain)
Д	д	d	(<u>d</u>og)	У	у	u/oo	(r<u>u</u>le)
Е	е	e	(y<u>e</u>t)	Ф	ф	f/ph	(<u>f</u>rost)
Ё	ё	yo	(<u>yo</u>ghurt)	Х	х	kh	(lo<u>ch</u>)
Ж	ж	zh	(trea<u>s</u>ure)	Ц	ц	ts	(lo<u>ts</u>)
З	з	z	(<u>z</u>ebra)	Ч	ч	ch	(<u>ch</u>ill)
И	и	ee	(s<u>ee</u>k)	Ш	ш	sh	(fi<u>sh</u>)
Й	й	y	(read<u>y</u>)	Щ	щ	shch	(fre<u>sh ch</u>icken)
К	к	k	(<u>K</u>iev)	Ы	ы	i	(d<u>i</u>d)
Л	л	l	(<u>L</u>enin)	Э	э	e/ih	(t<u>e</u>nt)
М	м	m	(<u>M</u>oscow)	Ю	ю	yu	(<u>u</u>nion)
Н	н	n	(<u>n</u>ever)	Я	я	ya	(<u>ya</u>k)
О	о	o	(<u>o</u>ver)	Ь	ь		softens preceding letter

* pronunciation shown by underlined letter/s

KEY PHRASES

The following phrases in Cyrillic script may be useful to point to if you're having problems communicating:

Please write it down for me   **Запишите это для меня, пожалуйста**

Help me, please   **Помогите мне, пожалуйста**

I need an interpreter   **Мне нужен переводчик с английского**

CONVERSATIONAL RUSSIAN

Run the hyphenated syllables together as you speak and roll your 'R's:

General

Hello	*Zdrah-stvoo-iteh*
Good morning	*Dob-royeh-ootro*
Good afternoon/evening	*Dobree den/vecher*
Please	*Po-zhalsta*
Do you speak English?	*Gavar-iteh lee vy pa anglee-skee?*
No/Yes	*nyet/da*
thank you	*spasee-ba*
excuse me (sorry)	*izveen-iteh*
good/bad	*haroshaw/plahoy*
cheap/expensive	*deshoveey/daragoy*
Wait a minute!	*Adnoo meenoo-too!*
Please call a doctor	*Vi'zaveete, po-zhalsta, vracha*
Goodbye	*Das-vedahneya*

Directions

map	*karta/schema*
Where is ...?	*G'dyeh ...?*
hotel	*gastee-neetsoo*
airport	*aeroport/aerodrom*
bus-station	*stantsia afto-boosa*
metro/taxi	*metro/taksee*
tram/trolley-bus	*tramvai/trolleybus*
restaurant/cafe	*restarahn/kafay*
museum/shop	*moo-zyey/maga-zyeen*
bakery/grocer's	*boolach-naya/gastra-nohm*
box office (theatre)	*teatrahl-naya kassa*
lavatory (ladies/gents)	*too-alet (zhen-ski/moozh-skoy)*
open/closed	*at-krita/za-krita*
left/right	*na-prahva/na-leva*

Numerals/time

1 *adeen*; 2 *dvah*; 3 *tree*; 4 *chetir*; 5 *p'aht*; 6 *shest*; 7 *s'em*; 8 *vosem*; 9 *d'evat*; 10 *d'e'sat*; 11 *adeen-natsat*; 12 *dve-natsat*; 13 *tree-natsat*; 14 *chetir-natsat*; 15 *pyat-natsat*; 16 *shes-natsat*; 17 *sem-natsat*; 18 *va'sem-natsat*; 19 *d'evat-natsat*; 20 *dvatsat*; 30 *tree-tsat*; 40 *so'rok*; 50 *p'ad-desaht*; 60 *shez-desaht*; 70 *sem-desaht*; 80 *vosem-desaht*; 90 *d'even-osta*; 100 *sto*; 200 *dve-stee*; 300 *tree-sta*; 400 *chetir-esta*, 500 *p'at-sot*, 600 *shes-sot*, 700 *sem-sot*, 800 *vosem-sot*, 900 *devet-sot*; 1000 *tees-acha*.

How much/many?	*Skolka?*
rouble/roubles	*rooble/rooblah/roobley**
Please write down	*Nap'eesheet'eh, pazhalsta,*
the price	*tse-noo*
ticket	*beel-yet*
1st/2nd/3rd Class	*perviy/ftoroy/treteey class*
express	*express*
What time is it?	*Kato'riy chuhs?*
hours/minutes	*chasof/meenoot*
today	*sevodna*
yesterday/tomorrow	*fcherah/zahftra*
Monday/Tuesday	*pani-dell-nik/ftor nik*
Wednesday/Thursday	*sri-da/chit-virk*
Friday	*pyat-nit-sah*
Saturday	*sue-boat-ah*
Sunday	*vraski-sen-yah*

*1st word is for 1 unit, 2nd word for 2-4 units, 3rd word for 5 or more.

Food and drink

menu	*menoo*
mineral water	*meenerahl-noi vady*
fruit juice	*sokee*
vodka/whisky	*vodka/veeskee*
beer	*peeva*
wine/cognac	*veenah/kanya-koo*
champagne	*sham-pahn-skoya*
Cheers!	*Zah vasheh zdaro-vyeh!*
caviare	*eek-ry*
salmon/sturgeon	*lasa-seeny/aset-reeny*
chicken/duck	*tsy-plonka/oot-koo*
steak/roast beef	*beef-shteks/rost-beef*
pork	*svee-nooyoo*
veal	*atbeef-nooyoo telyah-choo*
ham/sausage	*vechina/kalba-soo*
bread/potatoes	*khlee-ep/kar-toshka*
butter/cheese	*mah-sla/sir*
eggs/omelette	*yait-sa/amlet*
salt/pepper	*sol/perets*
tea/coffee	*chai/koh-fee*
milk/sugar	*mala-ko/sahk-har*
bill	*shchot*

Questions and answers

What's your name?	*Kak vahs zavoot?*
My name is …	*Menyah zavoot*
I'm from Britain/USA	*Yah preeyeh-khal eez Anglee-ee/S-Sh-Ah*
Canada/Australia	*Kanadah/Avstralee*
New Zealand/Japan	*Novee Zeelandee/Yaponee*
Sweden/Finland	*Shvetsee/Finlandee*
Norway/Denmark	*Norveggee/Danee*
Germany/Austria	*Germanee/Avstree*
France/Netherlands	*Frantsee/Gollandee*

Where are you going?	Kudah vhee idyotyeh?
I'm going to ...	Yah idoo ...
Are you married?	Vee zhyehnaht/zamoozhyem?*
Have you any children?	Yest ly oo vas dety?
boy/girl	mahl-cheek/de-vooshka
How old are you?	Skolka vahm l'et?
What do you do?	Shto vhee delayetyeh?
student/teacher	stoo-dent/oochee-tel (-neetsa)*
doctor/nurse	vrach/myeh-sestra
actor/artist	aktor/khoo-dozh-neek
engineer/lawyer	een-zheneer/advokaht
office worker	sloo-zhash-chey
Where do you live?	G'dyeh vhee zhivyotyeh?

*(feminine form)

Mongolian

Westerners tend to have difficulty mastering the tricky pronunciation of the national language of Mongolia. Mongolian is written in the same script as Russian (see p307), with two additional characters Ө (pronounced 'o') and Y ('u'). When Mongolian is transliterated into Roman script note that stress is indicated by doubling vowels. You may see Ulan Bator written as 'Ulaan Baatar' to show that the first 'a' in each word is stressed.

Hello	*Sayn bayna uu*
Thank you	*Bayar-lalaar*
Yes/No	*Teem/Ugu-i*
Sorry	*Ooch-laarai*
I don't understand	*Bi oilgokh-gu-i bayna*
What's your name?	*Tani ner khen beh?*
Where do you live?	*Ta khaana ami-dardag beh?*
Goodbye	*Bayar-tai*
Where is ...?	*.....khaana bayna veh?*
hotel/airport	*zochid buudal/nisyeh ongotsni buudal*
railway station/bus station	*galt teregniy buudal/avtobusni zogsool*
temple/museum	*sum/moosei*
lavatory	*zhorlon*
left/right	*zuun/baruun*
soup/egg/mutton	*shol/ondog/honini makh*
rice/noodles/bread	*budaar/goimon/talh*
cheese/potato/tomato	*byaslag/toms/ulaan lool*
tea/coffee	*tsai/kofee*
beer/fermented mare's milk	*peevo/airag*
How much?	*Khed?*
cheap/expensive	*khyamd/kheterhiy unetiy yum*

1 *neg*; 2 *khoyor*; 3 *gurav*; 4 *dorov*; 5 *tav*; 6 *zurgaar*; 7 *doloo*; 8 *naym*; 9 *ee-us*; 10 *arav*; 11 *arvan neg*; 12 *arvan khoyor*; 13 *arvan gurav*; 14 *arvan dorov*; 15 *arvan tav*; 20 *khori*; 21 *khori neg*; 30 *guchin*; 31 *guchin neg*; 40 *doch*; 50 *tavi*; 60 *zhar*; 70 *dal*; 80 *naya*; 90 *er*; 100 *zuu*; 200 *khoyor zuu*; 1000 *neg myanga*

Chinese

Particularly tricky. The problem with Chinese is one of pronunciation – so much depends on your tone and emphasis that if you do not get the sound exactly right you will not be understood at all. The best way to learn in advance is either to take lessons, or to buy a cassette course (simple ones are under £10/US$15 and come with a useful phrasebook).

The country's main dialect is Mandarin, spoken by about three-quarters of the population. Mandarin has four tones: high tone (–), rising (ʹ) where the voice starts low and rises to the same level as the high tone; falling-rising (ˇ) where the voice starts with a middle tone, falls and then rises to just below a high tone; and falling (ˋ) which starts at the high tone and falls to a low one.

READING PINYIN CHINESE

Pinyin is the system of transliterating Chinese into the Roman alphabet. Pronunciation is indicated by the underlined letters below:

Vowels

a	as in f<u>a</u>r	e	as in w<u>e</u>re
i	as in tr<u>ee</u>	o	as in <u>or</u>
	or as in w<u>e</u>re	u	as in P<u>oo</u>h
	after c, r, s, z, ch, sh, zh	ü	as in c<u>ue</u>

Consonants

c	as in ea<u>ts</u>	h	as in lo<u>ch</u> or the kh in an
q	as in <u>ch</u>eap		Arabic word, with the sound
r	as in t<u>r</u>ill		from the back of the throat.
x	as in <u>sh</u>eep	z	as in piou<u>s</u>
zh	as in <u>j</u>aw		

KEY PHRASES

The following phrases in Chinese characters may be useful to point to if you're having problems communicating:

Please write it down for me　请写下

Help me, please　请帮我

Please call a doctor　请你叫医生

USEFUL WORDS AND PHRASES

General

Hello	*Nǐ hǎo*
Please	*Qǐng*
Do you speak English?	*Nǐ huì shuō yīng yǔ ma?*
Yes/No	*Dùi/Bū dùi* (literally correct/ incorrect)
Thank you	*Xiè xie*

Excuse me (sorry)	*Duì bù qǐ*
Excuse me (may I have your attention?)	*Qǐng wèn*
good/bad	*hǎo/bu hǎo*
Wait	*Děng*
Goodbye	*Zài jiàn*
UK/USA	*Yīng guó/Měi guó*
Canada/Australia	*Jīa ná dà/Ào dà lia*
France/The Netherlands/Germany	*Fǎ guó/Hé lán/Dé guó*
I understand/do not understand	*Wǒ dǒng le/Wǒ bù dǒng*
Translator	*Fān yì*

Directions

Where is…?	*Zài nǎr…?*
toilet (ladies/gents)	*cè sǔo (nü/nan)*
airport	*jī chǎng*
bus station	*chē zhàn*
railway station	*hǔo chē zhàn*
taxi	*chū zū qì chē*
museum	*bó wù guǎn*
hotel/restaurant	*lǔ guǎn/fàn guǎn*
post office	*yóu*
PSB/CAAC office	*Gōng ān jú/Zhōng háng gǒngsi*
What time will we arrive at…?	*Liè chē shénme shí jiān dào…?*
What station is this?	*Zhè shì nà yí zhàn?*

Numerals/time

1 *yī*, 2 *èr*, 3 *sān*, 4 *sì*, 5 *wǔ*, 6 *liù*, 7 *qī*, 8 *bā*, 9 *jiǔ*, 10 *shí*, 11 *shí yī*, 12 *shí èr*, 13 *shí sān*, 14 *shí sì*, 15 *shí wǔ*, 16 *shí liù*, 17 *shí qī*, 18 *shí bā*, 19 *shí jiǔ*, 20 *èr shí*, 21 *èr shí yī*, 30 *sān shí*, 40 *sì shí*, 50 *wǔ shí*, 100 *yì bǎi*, 101 *yì bǎi líng yī*, 110 *yì bǎi yī shí*, 150 *yì bǎi wǔ shí*, 200 *èr bǎi*, 500 *wǔ bǎi*, 1000 *yì qiān*, 10,000 *yí wàn*, 100,000 *shí wàn*, 1 million *yì bǎi wàn*,

Monday/Tuesday/Wednesday	*Xīng qī…yī/èr/sān*
Thursday/Friday/Saturday/Sunday	*Xīng qī…sì/wǔ/liù/rì*
How much?	*Duō shao?*
That's too expensive	*Tài guì le*
yesterday/tomorrow/today	*zuó tiān/míng tiān/jīn tiān*

Transport

ticket	*piào*
Hard Seat/Soft Seat	*Yìng Zuò/Luǎn Zuò*
Hard Sleeper/Soft Sleeper	*Yìng Wò/Luǎn Wò*
Please may I upgrade this ticket to….	*Qǐng nǐ huan gao yī ji de piào*

Food and drink

menu	*cài dān*
mineral water/tea/beer	*kuàng quán shuǐ/chá/pí jiǔ*
noodles/noodle soup	*miàn/tāng miàn*
(fried) rice	*(chǎo) fàn*
bread/egg	*miàn bāo/jī diàn*
pork/beef/lamb	*zhū ròu/niú ròu/yáng ròu*
chicken/duck/fish	*jī/yā/yú*
vegetables	*shū cài*
Do you have any vegetarian dishes?	*Nǐ zhèr yǒu sù-cài ma?*

APPENDIX D: BIBLIOGRAPHY

Baedeker, Karl *Russia with Teheran, Port Arthur and Peking* (Leipzig 1914)

Barzini, Luigi *Peking to Paris. A Journey across Two Continents* (London 1907)

Byron, Robert *First Russia Then Tibet* (London 1933)

Collins, Perry McDonough *A Voyage down the Amoor* (New York 1860)

De Windt, Harry *Siberia as it is* (London 1892)

Des Cars J. and Caracalla, J.P. *Le Transsiberien* (1986)

Dmitriev-Mamonov, A.I. and Zdziarski, A.F. *Guide to the Great Siberian Railway 1900* (St Petersburg 1900)

Fleming, H.M. and Price J.H. *Russian Steam Locomotives* (London 1960)

Gowing, L.F. *Five Thousand Miles in a Sledge* (London 1889)

Hill, S.S. *Travels in Siberia* (London 1854)

Hollingsworth, J.B. *The Atlas of Train Travel* (London 1980)

Imperial Japanese Government Railways *An Official Guide to Eastern Asia Vol 1: Manchuria & Chosen* (Tokyo 1913)

Jefferson, R.L. *Awheel to Moscow and Back* (London 1895)

Jefferson, R.L. *Roughing it in Siberia* (London 1897)

Jefferson, R.L. *A New Ride to Khiva* (London 1899)

Johnson, Henry *The Life of Kate Marsden* (London 1895)

Kennan, George *Siberia and the Exile System* (London 1891)

Lansdell, Henry *Through Siberia* (London 1883)

Levin, M.G. and Potapov, L.P. *The Peoples of Siberia* (Chicago 1964)

Manley, Deborah *The Trans-Siberian Railway* (London 1988)

Marsden, Kate *On Sledge and Horseback to Outcast Siberian Lepers* (London 1895)

Meakin, Annette *A Ribbon of Iron* (London 1901)

Massie, R.K. *Nicholas and Alexandra* (London 1967)

Murray *Handbook for Russia, Poland and Finland* (London 1865)

Newby, Eric *The Big Red Train Ride* (London 1978)

Pifferi, Enzo *Le Transsiberien*

Poulsen, J. and Kuranow, W. *Die Transsibirische Eisenbahn* (Malmo 1986)

St George, George *Siberia: the New Frontier* (London 1969)

Shoemaker, Michael Myres *The Great Siberian Railway from St Petersburg to Pekin* (London 1903)

Theroux, Paul *The Great Railway Bazaar* (London 1975)

Tupper, Harmon *To the Great Ocean. Siberia and the Trans-Siberian Railway* (London 1965)

Other guides from Trailblazer Publications

Silk Route by Rail (Dominic Streatfeild-James)
Traversing some of the most inaccessible lands on earth, the Silk Route stretched
some 5000 miles west from the ancient Chinese capital, Chang'an (Xi'an), all
the way to the Roman Empire. Countless travellers, including Marco Polo,
experienced its dangers. Many never returned.

Travel on this route is no longer dangerous but it is no less of an adventure.
In 1992 a passenger service was inaugurated on the recently-built rail link
between Alma Ata (Almati) in Kazakhstan and Urumqi in north-west China. It
is, therefore, now possible to travel by rail between Moscow and Beijing on a
new route stopping off in Samarkand, Bukhara and many other cities on the Silk
Route. This guide shows you how to arrange your trip independently or with a
group.
ISBN 1-873756-03-8 320pp (+16pp in colour)   £9.95

Trekking in the Everest Region (Jamie McGuinness)
The first title in the Nepal Trekking Guides series covers the most famous trekking route in the country. It is, however, through a very fragile environment and
this guide shows how to tread lightly and minimise your impact on the trek to
Gorak Shep and Everest Base Camp.

Written by an experienced trek leader and climber, the book includes detailed
background information on preparing for your trek, getting to Nepal, hotels and
restaurants in Kathmandu and protecting your health. There's a fully comprehensive route guide based on 30 detailed maps with inset plans of major villages and
information about where to sleep and eat along the way.
ISBN 1-873756-02-X 240pp (+16pp in colour)   £6.95

Trekking in the Annapurna Region (Bryn Thomas)
This second title in the Nepal Trekking Guides series covers the classic treks in
the region north of Pokhara, including the Annapurna Circuit, Pokhara to
Jomsom, and the Annapurna Sanctuary. The guide provides comprehensive
background information on preparing for a trek, getting to Nepal, hotels and
restaurants in Kathmandu, safeguarding your health and protecting the environment. There are highly detailed route guides giving information on where to
sleep and eat along the trails.

Includes 40 maps with inset plans of the larger villages.
ISBN 1-873756-01-1 256pp (+16pp in colour)   £6.95

These guides are available in any bookshop with a good travel section or through
the distributors listed on p2. You can also order direct from the publisher (see p2
for address). Cheques should be drawn on a UK bank and made payable to
Trailblazer Publications. Add 10% for UK postage and packing, 30% for airmail
overseas.

Route guides for the adventurous traveller

INDEX

Abbreviations: (M) Moscow (SP) St Petersburg

Abakan 177-8
accommodation
  Beijing 217-18
  Berlin 294
  Bratsk 177
  Budapest 295
  Ekaterinburg 149
  Helsinki 293
  Hong Kong 292
  hotels (general) 10-11, 13, 55-6
  Irkutsk 163-4
  Khabarovsk 189
  Lake Baikal 173-4
  Moscow 134-5
  Novosibirsk 155-6
  Prague 296
  St Petersburg 118-19
  Tokyo 290
  train 11-12, 103-10
  Ulan Bator 205-6
  Ulan Ude 182
  Vladivostok 198
  Yakutsk 178
Achinsk 242-3
air and rail services
  Abakan 178
  Beijing 221
  Berlin 294
  Budapest 295
  Bratsk 177
  Helsinki 293
  Hong Kong 291-2
  internal flights 59
  Japan 290
  Moscow 131, 145
  Prague 296
  St Petersburg 117, 123, 128
  UK 23
  Ulan Bator 211
  Ulan Ude 181
  Yakutsk 178
Akademgorodok 159-60
Alcksandrov 225
Alexander Nevsky Monastery
  (SP) 125
Altan Bulak (Maimachen) 271, 272
Amarbayasgalant Monastery
  (Mongolia) 274
Amazar 260

Amur Railway 96, 259, 263
Amur River 187
Amur tigers 190, 269
Angangxi (China) 285
Angara, steamship 169
Angara River 250
Angarsk 250
Arkhara 265
Australia, bookings from 28-9
Austria, bookings from 24

Bada aerodrome 255
Badaling (China) 219, 280
Bagakangai (Mongolia) 275
Baikal, Lake 171-6, 250
ballet 65
Balyezino 228
Bam 261
BAM Railway 111-12, 246
banks 60, 205, 217, 282
Barabinsk 238
Baranovsk 269
Barzini, Luigi 39, 280
Beijing 31-2, 213-21, 280, 288
Belgium, bookings from 24
Belogorsk 263
Beriozka shops 68, 123, 282
Berlin 25, 294
Bikin 268
Bira 266
Birobidzhan 194, 265, 266
Black Market 69
Blanch, Lesley 39
Blagoveshchensk 264
boat trips 59, 137, 179
Bogdanovich 232
Bogdo Khan Palace (Ulan Bator) 207
bogie-changing 278, 282
Bogotol 242
Boketu (China) 284
Bolshoi (M) 144
Bolshoi Koti 175
bookings (Trans-Siberian) 15-33
Borghese, Scipione, *Prince* 39
Borzya 281
Bratsk 176-7
bridges 100-1, 239-40, 267
Budapest 25, 295
Buddhism 53, 181, 183

Buret 249
Bureya 264
Buryatia 251
Buryats 254
buses 58-9, 172
Buy 226

Canada, bookings from 28
car hire 59, 137
cathedrals and churches
    Irkutsk 164-6, 167-8
    Moscow 137, 139-40
    Novosibirsk 158
    Omsk 236-7
    Sergiyev Posad (Zagorsk) 224-5
    St Petersburg 123, 124, 126
    Ulan Ude 185, 186
caviare 62, 69
Changchun (China) 286
Chany, Lake 238
Cheptsa 228
Cheremkhovo 248
Chernishevsk 259
Chernovskaya 256
China 277-80, 282-8
    Beijing 31-2, 213-21, 280, 288
    bookings and visas 18, 19, 31
    embassies 23, 28, 31-2, 133-4
Chinese language 311-12
Chita 257
Choyr (Mongolia) 276
Chulimskaya 239
church car 99
cinema 66
Circumbaikal line 96, 253
climate 14, 43
clothing 34, 69
coal 241
costs and budgeting 9-13
crime 70
currency see money
customs procedures 54-5, 282
Czech Republic 24, 296

Danilov 226
Daqing (China) 285
Darasun 257
Darhan (Mongolia) 273
Datong (China) 279
Datsan (Ulan Ude) 183-4
Dauriya 282
Decembrists 80, 123, 168, 255, 257
Denmark, bookings from 24

Dering Yuryakh 179, 249
Dezhnevka 267
dinosaurs 208
Dmitriev-Mamanov, A.I. *Guide
    to the Great Siberian Railway* 39
Dostoyevsky, F.M. 40, 236
drinking water 42
drinks 63-4, 69
duty free 55
Dzamyn Ude (Mongolia) 277
Dzhida 271

East Chinese Railway 93, 283
Ekaterinburg 147-53, 231
electricity 59
embassies in
    Beijing 32, 215
    London 23
    Moscow 133
    Ulan Bator 205
    Vladivostok 198
Erdene-dzu (Mongolia) 212
Erdenet (Mongolia) 274
Erlyan (China) 277
Europe/Asia obelisk 231
Evenkis 246
exile system 75-81

Fenezhen (China) 279
festivals 61
Finland 24, 293
flora and fauna 44-5, 304-6
food 36-7, 61-3, 69
France, bookings from 24
furs and fur trapping 169

Galich 226
Ganden Monastery (Ulan Bator) 207
geographical background 43-4
Germany 25, 294
gifts 36
Glazov 228
Gobi Desert 276-7
Goose (Gusinoye) Lake 271
Gostiny Dvor (SP) 125
Great Siberian Post Road 82-6
Great Wall of China 219, 280, 288
guide books 40
GUM Department Store (M) 67, 139
Gusinoye Ozero 271

Hailar (China) 284
Haiman (China) 284

handicrafts 68
Harbin (China) 285
health precautions 41-2
Hermitage Museum (SP) 122-3
Hill, S.S. (traveller) 86
historical background 45-50
  Siberia 70-81
  Beijing 213-4
  Ekaterinburg 147-8
  Irkutsk 161-3
  Khabarovsk 187-8
  Mongolia 274
  Moscow 129-31
  Novosibirsk 154-5
  railway 89-102
  St Petersburg 115-16
  Ulan Bator 203-4
  Ulan Ude 181-2
  Vladivostok 195-7
Hong Kong 32-3, 291-2
hotels see accommodation
Humboldt, Baron von 75, 234-5
Hungary 25, 295
hydrofoil 59, 172, 177, 179

Ilanskaya 245
inoculations 41-2, 54
Intourist 10, 20, 24-8, 56-7
Irkutsk 161-70, 250
Irkutsk Sort 250
Irtysh River 236
Ishim 234
Itat 242
Ivan the Terrible Tsar 46
Ivolginsky Datsan (Ulan Ude) 183-4
Izvyestkovaya 266

Japan 17, 30, 289-90
Jefferson, R.L. (traveller) 88, 97-101
Jining (China) 278
Jinzhou (China) 287
Juyongguan (China) 280

Kadilnaya Pad 175
Kama River 229
Kamchatka 194
Kamyshet 246
Kansk 245
Kanzhuang (China) 280
Karakorum (Mongolia) 212
Karymskaya 258, 281
Kazan Cathedral (SP) 124
Kennan, George 76

Khabarov 73
Khabarovsk 187-93, 267
Khadabulak 281
Khangai, hot springs (Mongolia) 212
Kharanor 282
Khilok 256
Khingan (China) 284
Khungur 230
Khurzhirt (Mongolia) 212
kilometre posts 222
Kirghiz people 239
Kirov 227
Korfovskaya 267
Kotelnich 227
Krasnoyarsk 243-4
Kremlin (M) 139
Ksyenevskaya 259
Kuenga 259
Kultuk 250
Kuytun 248
Kuzino 230
Kyakhta 271, 272

Lena Pillars 179
Lena River 178, 179
Lenin's Mausoleum (M) 138
Limnological Institute and Museum
  (Baikal) 174
Listvyanka 173-4
Lomonosov Palace 126
luggage 34-5

Magadan 194
Magdagachi 262
Maina 177
Malta 248
Manchuria 281-2
Manit (Mongolia) 275
Manzhouli (China) 282
Mariinsk 242
Marsden, Kate (nurse) 87-8
Meakin, Annette (traveller) 39,
  97-101
medical services 42
medical supplies 35
Meget 250
metro 58, 120-1, 136
Mianduhe (China) 284
Mid-Siberian Railway 93, 243
Minusinsk 177
Mirnaya 281
Mogocha 259
Mogzon 256

money 37, 59-60, 70, 133, 205, 217
Mongolia 273-7
  bookings and visas 18, 19
  embassies 23, 28, 32, 134, 163, 215
  Ulan Bator 203-11, 275
Mongolian language 310
Moscow 129-45, 224
museums and galleries
  Abakan 177
  Akademgorodok 160
  Baikal, Lake 172-3, 174
  Beijing 219
  Bratsk 177
  Ekaterinburg 152, 153
  Irkutsk 166, 168, 169
  Khabarovsk 190, 192
  Moscow 141-2
  Novosibirsk 158
  Shenyang 287
  St Petersburg 122-3, 124, 126
  Sushenskoye 177
  Ulan Bator 207, 208, 209, 275
  Ulan Ude 184, 185
  Vladivostok 199-200
  Yakutsk 178, 179
Mutianyu (China) 219
Mysovaya 252

Nakhodka 194, 269
Nankou (China) 280
national holidays 61
Naushki 271-2
Nazevayevskaya 236
Nerchinsk 258
Netherlands, bookings from 25
Nevsky Prospekt (SP) 123-5
New Zealand, bookings from 29
newspapers 61
Nicholas II, Tsar 47
nightlife 128, 144, 193
Nizhneudinsk 247
Norway, bookings from 26
Novaya 257
Novodevichy Convent (M) 141-2
Novokuznetsk 241
Novosibirsk 154-60, 240

Ob Dam 160
Ob river and bridge 239-40
Ob station 239
Olekminsk 259
Olkhon Island 176
Olovyannaya 281

Om River 236
Omsk 236-7
Omskaya 235
Onokhoy 254
Onon 258
opening hours (shops) 68
opera 66
Orkhon Falls (Mongolia) 212
Ostankino Palace (M) 142
Oyash 240

Pacific Fleet 199, 200
Paris Exhibition 97
passports 54
Pavlovsk 126
Peking to Paris Rally 39, 229
Perelk 194
Perm 229
permafrost 44, 178
Permafrost Institute (Yakutsk) 178
Pervoralsk 230
Peter and Paul Fortress (SP) 126
Peter the Great, Tsar 46, 74, 115, 126
Petrodvorets (Peterhof) 126
Petrovskiy Zavod 255
photography 38
population 52
Port Baikal 175
Posolskaya 252
postal services 60-1
Powers, Gary 148, 150, 232
Prague 24, 296
provisions 36
Pryiskovaya 258
Pushkin 126
Pushkin Museum of Fine Arts (M)
  141
Pyongyang (North Korea)

Qinglongqiao (China) 280
Qiqihar (China) 285

rail enthusiasts' tours 22
rail services see air and rail
  services
railway
  construction of 89-96
  early travellers on 96-101
  in twentieth century 101-2
  see also trains, steam locomotives
Razgon 246
Red Square (M) 137
religions 53

Repin, Ilya 127, 141
Reshoti 246
restaurants 64-5
  Beijing 220-1
  Ekaterinburg 153
  Irkutsk 170
  Khabarovsk 192-3
  Moscow 142-4
  Novosibirsk 158-9
  St Petersburg 127
  Ulan Bator 210
  Ulan Ude 186
  Vladivostok 201
Romanovs, 147-8, 150-1
routes of trains 9, 17
Russia
  bookings from 26
  embassies 23, 24, 27, 30, 32, 215
  visas 18-19
Russian Museum (SP) 124
Russian language 307-10
Russian Revolution 47

Sakhalin Island 194
Sakhalin Railway 113
Sanatornaya 269
Sayan Range 247
Sayano-Sushenskoye Dam 177
Sayatun 271
Sayn Shand 277
sea crossings
  Finland 293
  Shanghai 292
  Vladivostok-Japan 17, 195, 290
Selenginsk 252, 271
Sergiyev Posad (Zagorsk) 142, 224-5
Shalya 230
Shaman Rock 175
Shamanism 167
Shanhaiguan (China) 287
Shariya 226
Shenyang (China) 287
Shilka Pass 258
Shimanovskaya 262
Shoemaker, M.M. (traveller) 97-100
shops and shopping 66-9
  Beijing 221
  Irkutsk 170
  Khabarovsk 193
  Moscow 141, 144-5
 -Novosibirsk 159
  St Petersburg 123-5, 128
  Ulan Bator 211

shops and shopping contd
  Ulan Ude 186
  Vladivostok 201
Sibirchevo 268
Silk Route (railway) 113
Siping (China) 287
Skovorodino 261
Slyudyanka 251
Sokhondo 256
Song (China) 285
South Africa, bookings from 29
South Gobi 212
Spassk Dalnyi 268
speculation 69
speed calculations 223
Sputnik 57
Sretensk 259
St Basil's Cathedral (M) 137-8
St Innocent Monastery 250
St Isaac's Cathedral (SP) 123
St Peter & St Paul Cathedral (SP) 126
St Petersburg 115-28
steam locomotives 110-11, 181, 185,
  225, 226, 228, 229, 234, 237, 240,
  242, 245, 250, 252, 254, 255, 256,
  261, 262, 275, 277, 279, 287, 288
stops 223
Sukhe Bator (Mongolia) 273
Summer Palace (Beijing) 220
Sushenskoye 177
Sverdlovsk see Ekaterinburg
Svetcha 227
Svobodny 263
Sweden. bookings from 26
Switzerland, bookings from 26

taiga 44
Taiga 240-1
Takhtamigda 261
Tangshan (China) 288
tarantass 82, 83
Tarskaya 258
Tatarskaya 238
taxis 57-8
Tayshet 246
tea trade 271-2
telephones 60
Temple of Heaven (Beijing) 220
Terelj (Mongolia) 212
theatre 66
Tiananmen Square (Beijing) 219
Tianjin/Tientsin (China) 288
Tiazhin 242

Tikhookeanskaya Port 269
time 59
timetables, railway 297-303
tipping 60
Tobolsk 235
Tokyo 30, 289-90
Tomsk 241
tour groups 15
tour operators and travel agents 15,
    20-33
tourist information
  Beijing 215-7
  Ekaterinburg 149
  Irkutsk 163
  Khabarovsk 188
  Moscow 133
  Novosibirsk 155
  St Petersburg 118
  Ulan Bator 204
  Ulan Ude 182
  Vladivostok 198
tourist season 14
tours *see* transport and tours
trains
  accommodation on 11-12, 103-10
  early travellers, reports of 97-101
  restaurant car 106
  see also steam locomotives
Trans-Manchurian route 281-8
Trans-Mongolian route 270-80
Transbaikal Railway 93, 255
transport 57-9
transport and tours
  Beijing 218-19
  Ekaterinburg 150
  Irkutsk 164
  Khabarovsk 189-90
  Moscow 136-7
  Novosibirsk 156-7
  St Petersburg 120-1
  Ulan Bator 206
  Ulan Ude 182-3
  Vladivostok 199
Tretyakov Art Gallery (M) 141
Tulun 248
tundra 44
Tunguska Event 247
Tyumen 233-4

UK, bookings from 20-3
USA, bookings from 27-8
Ubukun 271
Ugolnaya 269

Ulan Bator (Mongolia) 203-11, 275
Ulan Ude 181-6, 252, 270, 271
Ural Mountains 229, 230, 231
Urusha 261
Ushumun 262
Ussuri Railway 93, 266
Ussuriyisk 268
Uyar 245

vaccinations 41-2, 54
Vereshagino 228
Viazemskaya 267
visas 16, 18-19, 54, 118, 133
Vladimir, *Tsar* 45
Vladivostok 17, 195-201, 269
Volga River 226

War Memorial (M) 139
West Siberian Railway 93, 237
wildlife 44-5, 304-6
Winter Palace (SP) 122

Xinganling (China) 284

Yablonovy Range 254
Yakutia Railway 112-13
Yakuts 178, 262
Yakutsk 178, 194, 261
Yar 228
Yaroslavl 225-6
Yaroslavskii Station (M) 224
Yenisei River 244
Yermak 73, 235
Yerofei Pavlovich 261
Yilick Ede (China) 284
Yungang Grottoes (China) 279
Yurga 240

Zabaikalsk 282
Zagorsk *see* Sergiyev Posad
Zagustay 271
Zaudinskiy 270
Zeya River 263
Zhalong Nature Reserve 285
Zhangjiakou (China) 280
Zhuulchin 18, 23, 25
Zilovo 259
Zima 248